ARKANSAS MAMMALS

ARKANSAS MAMMALS

Their Natural History,
Classification, and Distribution

REVISED AND ENLARGED EDITION

John A. Sealander
and
Gary A. Heidt

THE UNIVERSITY OF ARKANSAS PRESS
FAYETTEVILLE   LONDON   1990

The publication of this book
was made possible in part
by a grant from
The Arkansas Game and Fish Commission.

94   93   92   91   90   5   4   3   2   1

DESIGNER: B. J. Zodrow
TYPEFACE: Linotron Bodoni Book
TYPESETTER: G&S Typesetters, Inc.
PRINTER: Dong-A Publishing & Printing Co., Ltd.
BINDER: Dong-A Publishing & Printing Co., Ltd.

The paper used in this publication meets the minimum requirements of
the American National Standard for Permanence of Paper for Printed
Library Materials
Z39.48-1984. ∞

Library of Congress Cataloging-in-Publication Data

Sealander, John A., 1917–
   Arkansas mammals: their natural history, classification, and
distribution / John A. Sealander and Gary A. Heidt.
     p. cm.
  Bibliography: p.
  Includes index.
   ISBN 1-55728-102-5 (alk. paper).—ISBN 1-55728-103-3 (pbk.: alk.
paper
   1. Mammals—Arkansas. I. Heidt, Gary A., 1942– . II. Title.
QL719.A8S43 1989
599.09767—dc19   89-4795
                                                         CIP

To Sherman A. Hoslett who first aroused my interest in mammals and later Burton T. Ostenson who guided my early research on mammals, my students who contributed to our knowledge of Arkansas mammals, and lastly my wife, Lucile, for her patience and many hours taken from family life.

J. A. S.

To Rollin H. Baker who taught me about the fundamentals and enjoyment of mammalogy, and without whose support and guidance I never would have completed my studies, to my students who have made this profession worthwhile, and to my wife, Marcia, who always provides patience and support during the long hours of commitment to teaching and research.

G. A. H.

CONTENTS

PREFACE

It has been ten years since the publication of the first edition of this book. Since then there have been some changes in nomenclature, and much additional information concerning mammal distributions in the state has accumulated.

We have written this book with a mixed audience in mind—lay persons with no formal background or training in zoology, high school and college students engaged in serious studies of mammals, and professional mammalogists and wildlife biologists. Therefore, an attempt has been made to keep descriptive terms used in the text as nontechnical as possible, but since use of such terms was, at times, unavoidable, we have included a glossary. Also, in connection with the species accounts, the meaning or derivation of scientific names applied to each described species is given.

No attempt has been made to deal extensively with geographic variation at the subspecific level. Mammal subspecies (or races) occurring in the state are mentioned in the text, and where more than one race of a species is present, the approximate range boundaries in the state are mentioned. The average observer may often note differences in color, size, and behavior of different individuals of a species which may relate to differences between races. Such variations are chiefly of interest to specialists in mammalogy. In some cases (e.g., the red fox) several color variations may occur in the same litter and are not to be classified as distinct races.

Mammal distributions undergo temporal changes due to a variety of factors including alterations in climate, changes in land use patterns, and introductions of nonnative species, or reintroductions of game species that have become extinct or nearly extinct in the state. The distributions described or depicted on the maps are the best approximations of actual ranges of different Arkansas mammals at the time this book went to press. In the future, additional locality records within the state or evidence of disappearance due to loss of suitable habitat will help clarify the status of species considered to be threatened or endangered.

We hope that this revised edition will stimulate greater interest in the mammal fauna of Arkansas among individuals of various callings and lead to better measures for conserving this resource. The responsibility for preserving a sufficient amount of suitable habitat throughout the state is in the hands of the present generation which can thereby insure that this invaluable portion of the state's wildlife heritage is passed on to future generations.

We are indebted to many people who have provided aid and encouragement in this undertaking. It is not practical to single out more than a few persons individually; nonetheless, we wish to express our sincere appreciation to all those individuals who have contributed in any way.

First and foremost, however, we want to thank the many students with whom we have had contact over the years. These students have helped collect many of the specimens upon which this work is based. In addition, their tireless labor, quick minds, and probing questions have provided us with the incentives necessary to undertake and complete this work.

The late James H. Quinn, professor emeritus of geology at the University of Arkansas at Fayetteville, contributed a great deal to the section on prehistoric mammals and provided valuable critiques of the sections dealing with the paleozoic background and physiographic features of Arkansas. Renn Tumlison has provided the figures of the various skulls and key characteristics. Rebecca Hudson provided the figures for the tracks. Finally, Diana Garland is due special thanks for her efforts as research assistant for this edition.

Much information concerning the distribution and abundance of game and furbearing animals and the more easily recognized species of smaller mammals has been contributed by wildlife officers, wildlife biologists, and other personnel of the Arkansas Game and Fish Commission, the Arkansas Heritage Commission, the U.S. Forest Service, the U.S. Soil Conservation Service, and by fur buyers throughout the state. We are especially grateful to Joe Clark, Sammy Barclay, Bill Shepherd, Ken Smith, David A. Saugey, and Parker Dozhier.

Many individuals have generously provided photographs of mammal species found in Arkansas. We are especially indebted to Phil A. Dotson (a former Arkansas resident) of Great Basin Film Productions, Ogden, Utah, for the many superb photographs he has contributed. Many splendid photographs were also provided by David A. Saugey of the U.S. Forest Service.

In addition to the collections at the University of Arkansas Museum at Fayetteville and the Department of Biology at the University of Arkansas at Little Rock, there are several other mammal collections housed at various educational institutions in Arkansas. These include Arkansas Tech University, the University of Arkansas at Monticello, the Little Rock Museum of Science and History, and the state's most extensive collection, under the direction of V. R. McDaniel, at Arkansas State University.

Also, a number of out-of-state institutions have at various times provided information on Arkansas mammals in their collections. These include the following: American Museum of Natural History, Memphis State University, the University of Oklahoma, Oklahoma State University, the University of New Mexico, Texas Tech University, Texas A & M University, Louisiana State University, Louisiana State University at Shreveport, Louisiana Tech University, Northwestern Louisiana State University, Northeastern Louisiana State University, Tulane University, Centenary College, the University of Kansas, and Southwestern Missouri State University.

We are also grateful to the personnel of the University of Arkansas Press for their encouragement and help in the preparation of this book. In particular we would like to thank Miller Williams, Jim Scott, and Scot Danforth.

Finally, without the material support provided by a grant from the Arkansas Game and Fish Commission and the Arkansas Game and Fish Foundation, this undertaking would not have been possible. Our sincere appreciation is extended to Steve Wilson (Director), the Arkansas Game and Fish Commissioners, and George Purvis.

ARKANSAS MAMMALS

• INTRODUCTION •

Paleoclimatic Background

To understand the composition and distributions of the present mammalian fauna of the state, it is necessary to have some knowledge of geological history and climatic conditions of this region during past ages. The region's geological history is based upon evidence contained within rocks, whereas its climatic history can be pieced together from geological, paleontological, and botanical evidence, such as pollen profiles from sediments in bogs, lakes, and ponds. There is no general agreement regarding conditions in past ages, but various, largely inferential, reconstructions of past history and events show many similarities (see Table 1, geological timetable).

The Precambrian erosional surface of this area was carved into granite mountains which today are buried beneath more than 4,500 m (13,720 ft) of more recent deposits. In the Cambrian time of the early Paleozoic Era, the valley area and what is now part of the Ouachita Mountains were inundated by the sea. The highest part of the mountain region, in what is now southeastern Missouri, was a low-lying island called Ozarkia. A hypothetical island called Llanoria was supposedly located to the south, and the sea between, which supposedly received sedimentary deposits from Ozarkia and Llanoria, has been called the Ouachita Seaway. This sea island lasted for about 105 million years into the Late Mississippian, with only brief episodes of diastrophism to form land in the Ordovician and Devonian Periods.

During Mississippian time, there was rapid subsidence of the Ouachita Seaway, forming a deep oceanic trough with attendant fracturing of rocks bordering Llanoria. Volcanic activity accompanied these geological events and produced ash beds which hardened into rock now included in ridges in the central Ouachita Mountains. In late Mississippian and early Pennsylvanian time, vigorous folding and uplifting movements occurred that resulted in the formation of high mountains. Rock waste washed from the mountains filled the northern part of the seaway by the late Pennsylvanian, and a broad delta was built by southward flowing streams from Ozarkia. The massive Atoka formation, Bloyd shale, and Kessler limestone, now exposed as surface rocks, resulted from debris laid down under sea water. Contrary to earlier views, there is no evidence that these mountains were worn down to flat plains by stream erosion in the Permian, Triassic, and Jurassic Periods, but that the Ouachita-Ozark Highlands remained above sea level. Much of the ancient flat land surrounding the uplands was covered by the sea during the Cretaceous and early Tertiary (periods when violent volcanic activity occurred and fold-mountain building began). During mid-Tertiary time (late Miocene-Pliocene), the upland appeared as a high dome-like area. During Pleistocene time, stream formation and drainage to the sea occurred at the present site of Little Rock. The Arkansas River was formed and cut the old mountain roots to form the present-day Ozarks and Ouachitas (Quinn 1958a, 40–41).

The climate of Arkansas, based on various botanical, zoological, and geological evidence, has undergone various changes during relatively recent geological history related mainly to Pleistocene climates. As compared to the present, Arkansas's climate has fluctuated between being warmer and more humid, cooler and drier, and cooler and more humid, but not necessarily in that order. A tropical or mild semitropical climate probably prevailed during the Cretaceous and into the Eocene Epoch, as indicated by fossil remains of pleurodiran turtles and crocodiles (Dowling 1956). Fossil turtles from Nebraska and South Dakota indicated that the climate in the Miocene and early Pliocene epochs was apparently warm and mild at times. A long arid period, alternating with humid times, began in mid-Miocene and lasted until near the end of the Pliocene and was broken by pluvial conditions accompanied by advances of glaciers of the Pleistocene Epoch (Dowling 1956; Quinn 1957, 1958b). During the later Pleistocene, southward advancing Kansan and Illinoian glaciers extended to the edge of the Ozark Plateau in Missouri. The climate at this time (about 11,000 years ago) was probably cool and moist (Antevs 1955). Also at this time, the Ozarks must have been a re-

TABLE 1
Geologic Timetable

ERA	PERIOD	EPOCH	MILLIONS OF YEARS AGO
Cenozoic	Quaternary	Recent	0–.01
		Pleistocene	.01–1
	Tertiary	Pliocene	1–13
		Miocene	13–25
		Oligocene	25–36
		Eocene	36–58
		Paleocene	58–63
Mesozoic	Cretaceous		63–135
	Jurassic		135–181
	Triassic		181–230
Paleozoic	Permian		230–280
	Pennsylvanian		280–310
	Mississippian		310–345
	Devonian		345–405
	Silurian		405–425
	Ordovician		425–500
	Cambrian		500–600
Precambrian			600–5000

fugium for northern mammals forced southward by advancing glaciers. After the last glacial advance, the climate became progressively warmer and more arid until about 7,000 years ago when a cooling trend led to cold, dry desert conditions in the Ozarks by about 6,000 years ago (Anon. 1974). The climate continued to cool until about 4,500 years ago when it apparently began to become more temperate, leading to present conditions. However, bones found in Peccary Cave, Newton County, dated to 3,000 B.P. (before the present), indicate that the climate was cold and dry at that time. Indian artifacts recovered near prairie mounds close to Fayetteville also suggest a desert vegetation as recent as 3,000 B.P. (Quinn 1961, 1972).

Physical and Biotic Features of Arkansas

PHYSIOGRAPHY

Arkansas is broadly divided into two major physiographic regions—uplands and lowlands—based on topography, soils, and to a lesser degree, climate (Branner 1942; Croneis 1930; Foti 1974; Reinhold 1969). The uplands lie west and north of a dividing line which extends diagonally across the state from southwest to northeast. To the east and south of this line are the lowlands. The uplands are referred to as the Interior Highlands or Paleozoic Upland, and the lowlands collectively as the Gulf Coastal Plain (fig. 1).

The geological formations which make up the Interior Highlands were deposited during the Pennsylvanian Period and earlier; during this time, the formations were deformed by compressive forces accompanied by vigorous uplifting, folding, and faulting. The folding developed from south to north with the greatest intensity in the Ouachita Mountains of central and western Arkansas. The Ozark uplift area was little disturbed but was probably further elevated. The Arkansas River Valley is in a deep structural trough which lies between the two structural elements and was filled with early and mid-Pennsylvanian sediments. The Arkansas River carved its valley here, and now the river meanders through this area. The Ozarks and the Ouachitas are the only mountainous areas between the Black Hills of South Dakota and the Cumberlands of Tennessee.

The Ozark Mountains were first formed as a dome-shaped uplift which was subsequently eroded and uplifted again. There are currently three plateaus (Springfield Plateau, Salem Plateau, and Boston Mountains) which have been eroded by numerous swift-flowing streams. The entire area is characterized by horizontal bedrock strata which have resulted in a drainage pattern radiating in all directions.

The Springfield Plateau is rather narrow, except in northwestern Arkansas. It is mostly gently rolling land with elevations ranging from 380 to 520 m (1,250–1,700 ft), giving it a flat profile. The surface rocks are mostly limestone and dolomite. On the slopes, soils are thin with numerous rocks, making agricultural practices difficult.

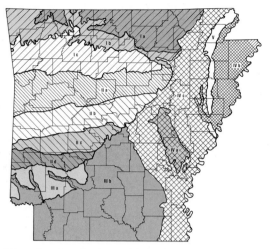

Map of major physiographic regions.

INTERIOR HIGHLANDS	GULF COASTAL PLAIN

I. OZARK MOUNTAINS (OZARKS) (division)
  a. Salem Plateau (subdivision)
  b. Springfield Plateau (subdivision)
  c. Boston Mountains (subdivision)
II. OUACHITA MOUNTAINS (OUACHITAS) (division)
  a. Arkansas River Valley (subdivision)
  b. Fourche Mountains (subdivision)
  c. Central Ouachita Mountains (subdivision)
  d. Athens Piedmont Plateau (subdivision)
	III. WEST GULF COASTAL PLAIN (COASTAL PLAIN) (division)
	  a. Southwestern Arkansas (subdivision)
	  b. South-central Arkansas (subdivision)
	IV. MISSISSIPPI ALLUVIAL PLAIN (DELTA) (division)
	  a. Grand Prairie (subdivision)
	  b. Northeastern Arkansas (subdivision)
	  c. Eastern Alluvial Plain (subdivision)
	V. CROWLEY'S RIDGE (division)

The Boston Mountains have the highest elevations in the Ozarks. They are about 1,295 sq km (500 sq mi) above 600 m (1,970 ft). The massive Atoka sandstone, which is more than 460 m (1,500 ft) thick, forms the bluffs at the summits of the Boston Mountains. Soils are well-drained clay and sandy loams of medium texture which tend to be relatively thin. Geo-

logically, the Boston Mountains are the youngest portion of the Ozarks as well as the smallest of the plateaus.

The Salem Plateau, which lies north and east of the Springfield Plateau, has rough to rolling contours with elevations averaging about 380 m (1,250 ft). It has a few large sandstone outcrops, but surface rocks are mostly limestone and dolomite. It represents the oldest portion of the Ozarks.

The Ouachita Mountains comprise a series of narrow east-west ridges separated by narrow valleys with some of the ridges attaining elevations of 760 m (2,500 ft) or more. Geologically, the Ouachita Mountains are a part of the Appalachian trend. Due to the east-west pattern of ridges, drainage patterns are very regular and major streams flow mostly west to east between the ridges. Furthermore, the pattern seen in the ridges results in different microclimates between the north- and south-facing slopes. The Ouachitas are extensively folded and faulted and exhibit only minor uplifting. They are further subdivided into the Arkansas River Valley, the Fourche Mountains, the Central Ouachita Mountains, and the Athens Piedmont Plateau.

Structurally, the folded and faulted ridges of the Arkansas River Valley resemble the Ouachita Mountains and separate them from the Ozarks. Petit Jean Mountain and Magazine Mountain are prominent features of this subdivision. The highest point in the state is Mount Magazine with an elevation of 860 m (2,820 ft) above sea level. Sandstone and shale are the primary surface rocks, with a thin layer of alluvium along the Arkansas River.

The Fourche Mountain subdivision is a narrow east-west belt about 40 km (25 mi) wide (north to south). Sandstone is prominent in the ridges and shale is very widespread. The Central Ouachita Mountain subdivision is a somewhat narrower east-west belt lying south of the Fourche Mountains which is formed of Ordovician and Silurian sandstones and shale. It is bounded almost entirely by novaculite ("whetstone") outcrops. South of the Central Ouachita Mountain subdivision is the Athens Piedmont Plateau formed of sandstones and shales and with elevations ranging from 120 to 300 m (400–985 ft). The southern boundary which separates the Ouachitas from the Gulf Coastal Plain often has precipitous slopes that give it the name "fall line."

The Gulf Coastal Plain is a belt of relatively flat land lying east and south of the Interior Highlands. It is subdivided into a southwestern portion, the West Gulf Coastal Plain (the Coastal Plain), and an eastern and northeastern portion, the Mississippi Alluvial Plain (the Delta).

The West Gulf Coastal Plain is bounded along its northeastern edge by the Ouachita Mountains. Its terrain is rolling and hilly and eroded by south and southeastwardly flowing streams. Elevations range from 60 to 230 m (200–755 ft). Underlying this plain are Cretaceous and early Tertiary deposits which separate the Coastal Plain from the Paleozoic formations of the mountains. Most of it is covered with more recent Pleistocene and Recent age deposits. Soils consist of well drained, deep sandy, or silty clay loams with recent alluvium along the southerly flowing streams and rivers.

The Mississippi Alluvial Plain is a fairly level south- and southeast-sloping plain covered with recent alluvium and terrace deposits, and with elevations ranging from 30–90 m (98–295 ft) above sea level. A prominent feature of this lowland is Crowley's Ridge, an isolated remnant of an old plain running in a general southwesterly and southerly direction. This ridge, which is heavily mantled with loess, varies from about 0.8 to 19 km (0.5–12 mi) in width and has a maximum elevation of 168 m (551 ft) above sea level (Sealander et al. 1975). It is considered a fifth major natural physiographic division of Arkansas (Foti 1974). Another prominent feature of this lowland is a large natural grassland, the Grand Prairie, located in Lonoke, Prairie, Arkansas, and Monroe counties. It is a flat, wide, poorly drained plain with a probable origin in the late Pleistocene Period from glacial materials deposited as a delta by the Arkansas and Mississippi rivers (Sealander et al. 1975). The Grand Prairie has been an almost treeless expanse as far back as recorded history of the area.

CLIMATE

The climate of Arkansas is characterized by short winters with brief cold periods and long, warm summers. Mean temperatures range from about 11–23°C (52–74°F) during the year. Maximum temperatures may exceed 38°C (100°F) in summer, and in northern Arkansas, temperatures as low as −20 to −26°C (−3 to −12°F) have been recorded for some years. Most precipitation in the state falls as rain. Rainfall is greatest in southeastern Arkansas where it generally averages 110–130 cm (43.5–52 in) more than in other parts of the state. Average annual precipitation for the state is about 120 cm (47.3 in). Winter and spring are the wettest seasons. The wettest period in northern Arkansas is March through May and in southern counties it is during December and January. Autumn is the driest time of the year with monthly precipitation averaging 5–8 cm (2–3.15 in).

Western and northern sections of the state generally are somewhat cooler and have greater extremes of temperature and humidity than the rest of the state. In northern Arkansas snowfall averages about 30 cm (11.8 in) in winter months, and in some areas of the Ozarks and Ouachitas yearly precipitation may average 130–140 cm (51.1–55.1 in).

Severe climatic extremes are not characteristic of southern Arkansas. The mean annual temperature is about 18°C (64.4°F) as compared to about 16°C (60.8°F) in northern Arkansas, and yearly precipitation averages about 130 cm (51.1 in). Rainfall is somewhat heavier in the Delta where it averages 125–140 cm (49.2–55.1 in) annually. Dry, sunny weather prevails during early fall.

Arkansas has a long growing season that averages about 200 days (April through September) in northern parts of the state and at higher elevations. It averages well over 230 days (February or March through October and into November) in southern sections.

VEGETATION

Arkansas lies entirely in the Eastern Deciduous Forest Biome; however, glades, prairies, and other nonforest communities are represented. Vegetation in the state is quite diverse: there are more than 2,500 species (Smith 1988) ranging from swamp and bottomland hardwoods to oak-hickory forests of the uplands to prairies and glades (fig. 2).

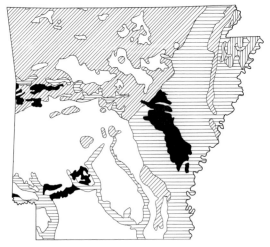

Natural vegetation zones of Arkansas. *Shepherd 1984*

⊟ CYPRESS-TUPELO & HYDROPHYTIC OAK
    COVER CLASSES
☑ OAK-HICKORY COVER CLASS
☐ OAK-PINE COVER CLASS
■ PRAIRIE
⊞ NON-TYPED WETLANDS

Except for valley lands and flatter tops of plateaus, large areas of the Interior Highlands are heavily forested with hardwoods and pines. The Ozarks are mainly covered with an upland oak-hickory forest, although shortleaf pine (*Pinus echinata*) occurs on cherty escarpments of the northern Ozarks and on drier south slopes near the southern boundary of this division. Typical climax type hardwoods are red oak, white oak, and shagbark hickory. Red cedar glades are found on xeric exposures, and upland prairies are scattered through the Springfield and Salem plateaus in areas with claypans or shallow, rocky soils, especially in the western Ozarks. Upland prairie is especially prominent in the extreme northwestern corner of the Springfield Plateau. Beech-maple cove forests occur in cool, moist north-facing ravines. This is a relict forest type persisting under conditions somewhat similar to those which existed during Pleistocene glaciation when this type of forest was much more widespread. The warmer climate prevailing today confines this type of forest to such isolated ravines.

A mixed shortleaf pine-upland hardwood forest occurs in the Ouachitas. The east-west orientation of the principal ridges in the Ouachitas results in greatly varying temperature and humidity conditions on the mountain slopes. The cooler, moister north-facing slopes support typically mesic upland oak-hickory forests, while the warmer, drier south-facing slopes are covered with more xeric forests in which shortleaf pine predominates. Hardwoods include a mixture of various oak species, such as red, white, black, and post oak, and other species such as shagbark hickory, black hickory, and elm. Cedars occur on bluffs, hills, bald knobs, and in rocky glades. Beech-maple cove forests are found, as in the Ozarks, in the coolest and moistest north-facing ravines.

Bottomland forests, which formerly covered much of the Delta, are composed of a variety of hardwoods adapted to wet, poorly drained soils. It is probable that only about one-half million ha (1.4 million acres) of woodlands now remain in the entire Delta region (Holder 1970). Red oak, white oak, and swamp white oak, sweetgum, elm, pecan, and water oak occur on the lighter soils and better drained areas, while on low-lying clay flats the forest is composed largely of honey locust, bitter pecan, overcup oak, water oak, and hackberry along with other species such as persimmon, willow, cottonwood, green ash, and elm (Allred and Mitchell 1955). Bald cypress and swamp tupelo are found in poorly drained, swampy areas which lie under water for prolonged periods.

The general vegetation type found on the West Gulf Coastal Plain is loblolly pine-hardwood. Bottomland hardwoods occur along the major river drainages. Hardwoods include sweetgum, white oak, southern red oak, blackjack oak, post oak, and hickory. Upland hardwood forest, cedar glades, and blackland prairie occur in the western portion of the coastal plain. Blackland prairies which occurred on Cretaceous formations in pioneer days have now nearly disappeared.

The major vegetation type on Crowley's Ridge is upland hardwood forest which appears most similar to the tulip tree-oak forest of the Tennessee Hills to the east. Shortleaf pine also occurs on this ridge.

The Grand Prairie is a lowland prairie dominated by big and little bluestem (*Andropogon gerardi* and *A. scoparius*), Indian grass (*Sorghastrum nutans*), and switch grass (*Panicum virgatum*). Most of the Grand Prairie has been converted to rice growing, and only a few small relict stands of the original prairie vegetation remain today. Scattered through the Grand Prairie are isolated groves or thickets of ash, persimmon, locust, overcup oak, and pin oak.

PRESENT LAND USE PATTERNS

In 1819 Arkansas was separated from Missouri and acquired new political boundaries. Within these boundaries lie about 13.8 million ha (34.1 million acres), or more than 83,684 sq km (52,000 sq mi). In 1819, Thomas Nuttall described Arkansas as "one vast trackless wilderness of trees." This statement was, in fact, relatively accurate because over 13 million ha (32 million acres) of forest land covered Arkansas around the turn of the nineteenth century; the remainder was primarily made up of prairies. Farming operations slowly claimed the forest in the fertile valleys of the uplands and the flatlands of the Delta and Grand Prairie, and by 1935 forest lands were reduced by around 4 million ha (10 million acres). With advancing agricultural technology after World War II,

land was cleared at an alarming rate, especially in the Delta region of eastern Arkansas. In pioneer days, this region was covered by a huge bottomland hardwood forest intermingled with streams, lakes, bayous, and cypress brakes (Holder 1970; Kaffka 1969). Holder (1970) states that approximately 0.6 million ha (1.5 million acres) of such forests were cleared in the period from 1960 to 1970 alone. Drainage and clearing of forests in the Delta have resulted in the conversion of much of this region to a largely treeless expanse devoted to cultivation of row crops. Clearing of upland areas for pasturelands has also accelerated greatly in recent years. At present about one-half of the state's forest land has been cleared.

It was reported in 1984 (Shepherd 1984) that currently 53.4% of Arkansas remains forested, 39.3% lies in agricultural crops and ranges, 2.2% is urban, and 5.1% is composed of water bodies and wetlands. Furthermore, the federal government owns approximately 9.4% of the land, while the state owns 1.6%, and the remaining 89.0% is in private ownership.

TABLE 2
Lands Devoted to Wildlife Preservation and/or Management

AREA	TOTAL ACREAGE
Arkansas Game and Fish Wildlife Management Areas	313,607
Arkansas Natural Heritage Commission State Natural Areas	7,913
Arkansas Parks and Tourism State Parks	44,078
Federal Wilderness Areas	64,000
U.S. Forest Service National Forests	2,483,217
U.S. Fish and Wildlife Service Wildlife Refuges	315,083
Total	3,227,898

Arkansas's native flora and fauna are accorded differing degrees of protection and/or management. At one extreme are private landowners who may or may not take wildlife into account when dealing with their land. In this regard, however, the Arkansas Game and Fish Commission's Acres for Wildlife program attempts to encourage landowners to take an active role in preserving habitat for the state's wildlife resource. At the other extreme are state natural areas and federally designated wilderness areas which are protected by law. Table 2 lists lands which benefit from some protection and management. From this list it can be seen that approximately 9.5% of the state's area is under some form of protection.

· MAMMALOGY IN ARKANSAS ·

Mammal Characteristics and Success

Mammals, as a group, attract a great deal of attention and are considered by many people to be the most interesting and important animals. This is due, in part, to the fact that humans are also mammals. Mammals serve as an important natural resource in terms of their fur and meat; they support many businesses related to hunting, trapping, ranching, and aesthetics; and they play an essential role in our environment.

Mammals belong to the phylum Chordata, which includes those animals with a dorsal structural support (the notochord) in their bodies, pharyngeal gill pouches (at least during their embryonic development), a dorsal hollow nerve cord, and a postanal tail. Within this phylum they are placed in the subphylum Vertebrata, which includes those forms in which the notochord is replaced by either bone or cartilage to form vertebrae. Other vertebrates include fish, amphibians, reptiles, and birds. Mammals are further placed in the class Mammalia. The term mammalia is derived from the Latin word *mammae*, meaning breast, a major characteristic of all mammals. There are 18 orders and more than 4,000 species of mammals in the world, of which eight orders and 72 naturally occurring species currently are found in Arkansas.

Mammals range in size from a small shrew weighing but a few grams to the blue whale, which is the largest animal ever to live on earth and may weigh over 113 tons. In Arkansas the smallest mammal is the southeastern shrew, which weighs 2–4 g (0.07–0.14 oz), and the largest is the elk, which may weigh more than 300 kg (660 lbs). Mammals owe their success among other animals to a number of unique and/or superior characteristics. In general, these features further intelligence and sensory ability, increase reproductive efficiency, add to the ability for obtaining and processing food, and help maintain endothermy or "warm bloodedness." Some of these characteristics include:

MAMMARY GLANDS   All mammals nourish their newborn young from specialized glands that secrete milk. With the exception of the monotremes (e.g., the duckbilled platypus and spiny echidna), the milk moves from the glands through a series of ducts to a prominence, the nipple or teat. In monotremes, milk is released onto the hair from pores in the skin.

The production of milk, or lactation, for the feeding of very young mammals provides several important adaptive advantages. First, the mother only has to find food for herself. In times of food scarcity this may allow both mother and young to survive. Furthermore, by not having to search for food for her young, the female is less exposed to predators. Although milk composition varies between species, it is very rich and provides a food source which is nutritionally well balanced, allowing for rapid growth of the young. This association between the mother and her young forms close social bonds, which provide, for many mammals, a period of training and of preparing the young for survival.

HAIR   At some point in their lives, all mammals possess hair. However, for some, such as whales and dolphins, hair may be lacking in the adult or limited to a few bristles about the nostrils. Hair is derived from the epidermis of the skin and consists of dead epithelial cells containing keratin (a tough proteinaceous material found in the skin of vertebrates). The hair grows from a hair follicle found in the dermis of the skin. Each hair is composed of an outer layer of cells arranged in a distinct scalelike pattern (the cuticle), a central core which may contain air spaces (the medulla), and a middle layer of highly packed cells (the cortex). Hair color is determined by the pattern of pigment found in the medulla and cortex.

Hair is collectively called the pelage and usually consists of thick, soft underhairs—fur lying next to the skin—and longer coarse guard hairs which lie over the underhairs. The soft white hairs of a newborn are referred to as velli. Most mammals also have specialized sensory hairs with tactile sensory properties.

Since hair is nonliving, it is subject to much weathering and abrasion. In addition, as the seasons change different amounts of hair are needed for insulation. Therefore, hair is regularly replaced, or molted, in a systematic fashion, usually in the spring and autumn. During these molts, not only may the thickness and density of hair change, but color patterns may also be different (as in the case of the arctic hare or fox turning white in the winter). When a winter coat is in place the fur is said to be prime.

Hair serves several important functions. As a body covering, it protects the underlying skin and provides an insulating barrier. In this latter role, hair permits the mammal to maintain a high and relatively constant body temperature (homeothermy). This quality, in turn, allows the mammal to function efficiently regardless of outside temperatures. Color patterns provided by hair also serve several functions. For most mammals, color patterns are protective, either concealing the animal (somber colors of a mouse) or confusing predators (stripes of a zebra). Color patterns of other mammals may provide warnings to conspecifics (white tail of deer) or to other species (bold black and white color of skunks).

TEETH AND JAWS   The lower jaw of mammals is unique among vertebrates in that it consists only of a single pair of dentary bones. These bones articulate directly with the squamosal bones of the skull and allow for more efficient chewing and greater stability.

Among the vertebrates, mammalian dentition alone is differentiated into specific teeth as well as having specializations within the types of teeth. These advances have allowed mammals to procure food and to process more efficiently foods which might otherwise be unavailable (for example, large bones and dry grass). In fact, dentition and its associated musculature and skull adaptations allow one to tell a great deal about the habits of a mammal from the skull alone.

Mammal dentition is heterodont, that is, the teeth are differentiated into specific types: incisors, canines, premolars, and molars. The incisors and canines are used primarily to gather and/or kill food, and the premolars and molars (cheek teeth) grind or slice food in preparation for swallowing. The numbers and types of these teeth may vary depending on the needs of the mammal. Most mammals have two sets of teeth. The milk teeth or deciduous set develop early and consist of incisors, canines, and premolars. The permanent teeth replace the milk teeth and consist of incisors, canines, premolars, and molars.

Typically, the mammalian tooth consists of an inner layer of dentine covered by a layer of very hard enamel. Within the dentine is a central pulp cavity that contains nerves and blood vessels. The tooth is located in a socket or alveolus, and that portion is termed the root, while the crown projects above the gum line. Usually there are thin layers of cementum covering the root and adhering to the jaw. In some herbivorous mammals cementum may be found covering portions of the crown. Vegetation may be extremely abrasive, and this additional cementum may help prevent the wearing down of the teeth. As an added adaptation against tooth erosion, some mammals have evergrowing teeth (e.g., incisors of rodents, rabbits, and hares). Often, the types of teeth, tooth wear, and layers of cementum are used by biologists to age mammals.

The number and types of teeth are expressed as the dental formula. This is written as the number of each type of tooth in one half of the upper jaw over the same in the lower jaw. Teeth are designated by an "I" for incisor, "C" for canine, "P" for premolar, and "M" for molar. Since the dental formula only lists the teeth for one half of the mouth, the total number of teeth would be derived by adding the number of teeth shown in the formula and doubling the result. The maximum number of teeth for a placental mammal would be:

$$I\ 3/3,\ C\ 1/1,\ P\ 4/4,\ M\ 3/3 = 44$$

REPRODUCTION   With the exception of the oviparous monotremes, which lay eggs, mammals are viviparous (they give birth to live young). The young of marsupials, such as the opossum, are born in a very immature condition and complete their development in a pouch or marsupium. The remaining species are referred to as placental mammals, and when born, the young are either altricial (born naked, blind, and helpless, such as mice and rats) or precocial (born with hair, sighted, and able to move shortly after birth, such as deer).

Most mammals reproduce during a specific breeding season. During this time both sexes will become sexually active, and while males may breed at any time, females undergo one or more estrous cycles during which males will be accepted for only a short period. During the nonbreeding season, the reproductive organs of the female usually become smaller and quiescent, and the testes of males may regress and withdraw into the body cavity. Some mammals, such as carnivores, primates, and ungulates, have permanently descended testes; in others, the testes are permanently abdominal (e.g., shrews, pachyderms, and sea mammals).

In the vast majority of species, the normal sequence of events in reproduction involves specific mating behavior patterns followed by copulation. Fertilization of the egg takes place in the oviducts, and the embryo moves to the uterus where it implants. Development takes place in the uterus, and the growing fetus receives nourishment from the mother through the placenta. After a specific gestation period, the young are born, passing out through the vagina; this process is known as parturition.

One major deviation from the normal pattern is referred to as delayed implantation. In some species (long-tailed weasel, otter, mink, badger, armadillo, and black bear in Arkansas) the egg is fertilized, but upon reaching the uterus the embryo ceases development for a period of time before it implants in the uterine wall. Once it implants, development continues as in other species. The delay varies from species to species; for example, in the armadillo it is 3.5–4.5 months, while in the black bear it is 6 months.

A second major deviation from the normal pattern occurs when many species of bats mate during the autumn and winter and the sperm are stored in the female reproductive tract. In the spring, when the female ovulates, the stored sperm fertilize the eggs. This pattern is referred to as delayed fertilization.

BRAIN AND SENSE ORGANS   The mammalian brain has developed proportionally larger than brains of other vertebrates. This increase in size has been due primarily to an increase in the size of the cerebral hemispheres (the neopallium). In addition, cross-connections, the corpus callosum, are found between the two sides of the cerebrum. This provides for better communication within the brain.

The unique and varied behavior patterns seen in mammals are largely due to the neopallium. The neopallium functions as a control center that dominates the original, more primitive brain centers. In addition, sensory input is relayed to the neopallium. Thus, present actions are greatly influenced by previous experiences, and learning becomes much more prominent.

Concomitant with the advanced development of the brain, sensory structures in mammals have become much more refined and efficient. It must be remembered that sensory development is not the same for all mammals. For example, bobcats rely primarily on sight for hunting; therefore, their vision is acute and their sense of smell is not well developed. Dogs, on the other hand, have a very acute sense of smell since they hunt primarily by smell. Overall, however, the combination of highly developed senses together with the increased development of the brain has allowed mammals to more fully exploit and react to their environment.

Other anatomical characteristics which distinguish mammals from other vertebrates include:

- A double occipital condyle, providing articulation for the skull with the first cervical vertebra.
- A four-chambered heart with a left aortic arch. Birds have a right aortic arch and amphibians and reptiles have two arches.
- A muscular diaphragm which separates the lungs from the abdominal cavity.
- Nonnucleated, biconcave red blood cells, which allow a greater capacity for carrying oxygen to the cells.
- Seven cervical vertebrae. Exceptions include the manatee and two-toed sloth with six, the anteater with eight, and the three-toed sloth with nine. These differences result from shifts in the attachment of the pectoral girdle to the vertebral column.
- Three ear ossicles in the middle ear, which allow for greater acuity in hearing.
- The number of bones (phalanges) in the toes and fingers number 2−3−3−3−3.

Geographic Affinities of Arkansas Mammals

Due to their geographic location in the south central United States, the native mammal fauna of Arkansas is made up of at least four main elements with respect to late Pleistocene and recent geographic origins in North America. The principal elements are Northern-Northwestern, Southern-Southwestern, Eastern-Southeastern, and Western-Southwestern. These groupings indicate the general directions from which each major faunal unit reached Arkansas but do not always reflect their original centers of dispersal. The geographic origins of a fifth rather widespread faunal element are somewhat obscure and cannot be included in any of the above categories.

Some northern-northwestern species, such as the southern bog lemming (*Synaptomys cooperi*) and the prairie vole (*Microtus ochrogaster*), reach or near the southern limits of their ranges in Arkansas, while some southern-southwestern species, such as the ringtail (*Bassariscus astutus*) and the fulvous harvest mouse (*Reithrodontomys fulvescens*), reach or near the northern and eastern limits of their ranges in the state. Some eastern-southeastern species which reach or near their northern and/or western range limits in Arkansas are the southeastern shrew (*Sorex longirostris*), the eastern big-eared bat (*Plecotus rafinesquii*), and the cotton mouse (*Peromyscus gossypinus*). Western-southwestern species which reach or near their eastern and/or northern range limits in the state are the desert shrew (*Notiosorex crawfordi*), the Texas mouse (*Peromyscus attwateri*), and the badger (*Taxidea taxus*).

EASTERN-SOUTHEASTERN SPECIES

The species which apparently invaded Arkansas from the east and southeast comprise the largest segment of the mammal fauna of the state. These are mostly species associated with the eastern deciduous forest which once covered most of Arkansas, with the exception of prairie peninsulas on the western edge of the state and the Grand Prairie in the Gulf Coastal Plain. Included in this assemblage are the following species:

Sorex longirostris
Blarina carolinensis
Cryptotis parva
Scalopus aquaticus
Myotis keenii
Myotis sodalis
Pipistrellus subflavus
Lasiurus borealis
Nycticeius humeralis
Plecotus rafinesquii
Sylvilagus floridanus
Sylvilagus aquaticus
Lasiurus seminolus
Tamias striatus
Marmota monax
Sciurus carolinensis
Sciurus niger
Glaucomys volans
Reithrodontomys humulis
Peromyscus leucopus
Neotoma floridana
Microtus pinetorum
Urocyon cinereoargenteus

SOUTHERN-SOUTHWESTERN SPECIES

A fairly large component of the state's mammal fauna consists of species with southern and southwestern affinities. Some of these, like the ringtail (*Bassariscus astutus*) and the armadillo (*Dasypus novemcinctus*), are relatively recent invaders, while others, like the opossum (*Didelphis virginiana*) and the hispid cotton rat (*Sigmodon hispidus*), with Neotropical affinities, apparently expanded their ranges into the Southwest from South and Central America and from there into Arkansas over long periods. The genus *Didelphis* was probably in Middle America prior to the Pliocene closing of the Panamanian Seaway (Gardner 1973). The gray myotis (*Myotis grisescens*), which now has a restricted range in the south central United States, apparently has southern affinities. Although well adapted to relatively cold caves,

this species has been unable to extend its range beyond 39° north latitude despite an abundance of available caves (Tuttle 1975).

Included in the southern-southwestern assemblage of species are the following:

Didelphis virginiana
Myotis austroriparius
Myotis grisescens
Tadarida brasiliensis
Dasypus novemcinctus
Oryzomys palustris
Reithrodontomys fulvescens
Peromyscus gossypinus
Ochrotomys nuttalli
Sigmodon hispidus
Bassariscus astutus
Canis rufus

WESTERN-SOUTHWESTERN SPECIES

Arkansas lies adjacent to the Great Plains in Oklahoma and farther west, and at one time, extensive prairie peninsulas extended into Arkansas on its western edge. Some remnant prairie areas still remain in extreme western Arkansas, but in recent history most of the original prairie areas in the state and their biotas have undergone ecological succession toward the deciduous forest vegetation type.

A relatively small group of species comprise the western-southwestern mammal element in Arkansas. Some typically western species, such as the desert shrew (*Notiosorex crawfordi*), which occurs on the extreme western edge of the state, may be relict from a formerly cooler and drier climate which was present in this part of Arkansas several thousand years ago. Others, such as the black-tailed jackrabbit (*Lepus californicus*), may have invaded Arkansas from the west relatively recently with the clearing of land for agricultural pursuits. Or, as in the case of the coyote (*Canis latrans*), not only the clearing of land for farming and ranching, but also the removal of a major competitor, the red wolf, helped in the introduction of the coyote into Arkansas from the west.

Mammals comprising the western-south-western assemblage are:

Notiosorex crawfordi
Myotis leibii
Plecotus townsendii
Lepus californicus
Geomys breviceps
Reithrodontomys montanus
Reithrodontomys megalotis
Peromyscus attwateri
Canis latrans
Taxidea taxus
Spilogale putorius

NORTHERN-NORTHWESTERN SPECIES

During Pleistocene glaciations many northern mammal species were displaced southward and found a refugium in the highlands of Arkansas and Missouri. With the retreat of the glaciers, many of these species dispersed northward again. Species such as the southern bog lemming (Synaptomys cooperi) and the prairie vole (Microtus ochrogaster) have invaded Arkansas from the west and northwest. Others show northern or boreal affinities.

Included in this faunal element are the following:

Blarina hylophoga
Myotis lucifugus
Lasionycteris noctivagans
Castor canadensis
Microtus ochrogaster
Synaptomys cooperi

WIDESPREAD SPECIES

A fairly large assemblage of species which have widespread distributions in North America are included in this category. Many of them may have reached Arkansas from the north or east in glacial times. The probable dispersal routes into the state of other species in this category are somewhat obscure due to their present wide-spread distribution.

Species included in this assemblage are:

Eptesicus fuscus
Lasiurus cinereus
Peromyscus maniculatus
Ondatra zibethicus
Vulpes vulpes
Ursus americanus
Procyon lotor
Mustela frenata
Mustela vison
Mephitis mephitis
Lutra canadensis
Felis concolor
Felis rufus
Odocoileus virginianus

Prehistoric Mammals of Arkansas

A much larger assemblage of mammals lived in what is now Arkansas during the Pleistocene and Sub-Recent than is present today. Many species were northern forms forced southward by advancing ice sheets. Some of these forms are extant today but have a more northern distribution. Other species apparently flourished when the climate was much warmer and drier or warmer and more humid than today, and these species have since become extinct.

Maximum shrinkage of the ice sheet lying north of Arkansas occurred during the comparatively warm Hypsithermal interval which dated from about 9,000 to 2,500 B.P. (Flint 1971). A period of cooler, drier climate, sometimes referred to as the "little ice age," probably lasted from about 6,000 to 3,000 B.P. in the Ozarks, although there is not complete agreement on this. A climatic period referred to as the Altithermal (Antevs 1955; Beckman 1969), or the "long drought," was a time of extremely arid and cool to cold climate apparently related to decreased precipitation. During this time, a surface feature called "prairie mounds," prominent near Fayetteville, formed around scattered

desert vegetation sometime between 4,000 and 3,000 B.P. (Quinn 1961). Following the Altithermal, precipitation increased and was accompanied by a transition to a more mesic type of vegetation.

The prehistoric mammal fauna of Arkansas is best documented by two major bone deposits and one minor deposit located in northwestern Arkansas. In addition to these major and minor deposits, there have been several isolated discoveries of fossil mammals in various parts of the state.

One of the major deposits of prehistoric mammal fauna was described by Barnum Brown (1908) from the Conard Fissure, located on a hill about a mile north of the Buffalo River south of Harrison in Newton County. This deposit lies about 240 km (149 mi) directly south of the southern extension of Pleistocene glaciation and is supposed to have accumulated sometime about the middle of the Pleistocene (Brown 1908; Hay 1924). The Conard Fissure contained remains of 48 mammal species (not counting subspecies), including 24 extinct forms which made up about one-half of the total. Three extinct peccaries, genus *Mylohyus*, described as separate species, are probably all referable to *M. nasutus*, which would reduce the total to 46. Larger species of mammals apparently underwent extinction to a greater degree than smaller ones and are probably not as well represented in the collection, so the estimated proportion of extinct species possibly is too low. Barnum Brown speculated that the physiography at the time the fossil deposit was entombed consisted of semi-open glades and forest-covered hills. More recent evidence (Hallberg et al. 1974) indicates that the vegetation type was an open coniferous parkland (taiga) at the fringe of the boreal forest. Numerous temperate species found in the Conard Fissure deposit, many of which live in Arkansas today, suggest higher winter temperatures and a more deciduous type of vegetation. The assemblage of mammals comprising the deposit was probably driven southward by glacial advances in the early Pleistocene and lived in Arkansas at about the time of the final wasting of the great ice sheet. This period evidently marked a time of redistribution of some mammal species and extinction of others.

The second major fossil bone deposit was discovered in 1965 in Peccary Cave located near the mouth of Ben's Branch, a tributary to Cave Creek which joins the Buffalo River in Newton County (Davis 1969; Quinn 1972). This deposit accumulated at a very late date and is unique among Arkansas caverns in that it contains bones of extinct taxa. Remains of recent and extinct mammals and human artifacts in the cave were carbon-14 dated from charcoal associated with the remains as 2,230 ± 120, 2,980 ± 180, and 4,290 ± 110 B.P., in order of depth from the surface. Bone collagen from a peccary in the top 15 cm (5.9 in) of matrix was dated 16,700 ± 250 B.P. Although Graham and Semken (1976) consider the Conard Fissure material to be of Kansan age (early Pleistocene), the presence of an extinct horse (*Equus caballus*) and Indian dog (*Canis familiaris*) indicates a much later age. The absence of the sloth (*Megalonyx*), which was present in Arkansas more than 30,000 years ago and in south-eastern Missouri as recently as 10–12,000 years ago, as well as the general correspondence of Conard Fissure and Peccary Cave faunal assemblages, suggest that the material is less than 10,000 years old. Remains of at least 58 mammal species (not counting subspecies) were recovered from Peccary Cave. Nine extinct species were included in the assemblage, and a larger number of still extant, largely boreal species were present, as compared with the Conard Fissure material. As in the Conard Fissure deposit, remains of a considerable number of mammal species still extant in Arkansas or neighboring states were recovered. Sixteen human teeth, representing several individuals, were also recovered from four different levels in the cave, along with clam shell beads and a leaf-shaped green chert scraper. There was no indication of ashes, fireplaces, or smoked surfaces in the cave, but some fire-burned rocks and one large fragment of green chert were recovered which came from downstream and must have been deposited by humans. At the time of deposition, the summers were probably cooler than at present, and temperature and moisture ratios were similar to present conditions in southern Minnesota.

The Ten Mile Rock site was a very limited strip at the foot of a limestone cliff near Fayetteville on Highway 71 South. Most of the fossils were contained in a 15–25 cm (5.9–9.8 in) clay deposit. The small mammals were taken out of the clay. This deposit contained remains of more than 40 mammal species, including five extinct forms, and human remains. Several extant species not now living in Arkansas were present in the assemblage.

Mammal remains from the three bone deposits may be grouped into three general categories: 1) extinct species or subspecies; 2) extant recent, mostly boreal species which now live much farther north; and 3) extant recent species now living in or near Arkansas. Scientific names of the species determined by Brown and others have been changed to conform to present taxonomic usage in the groups below. The abbreviations CF, PC, and TMR, which follow after each species name, designate the occurrence in the Conard Fissure, Peccary Cave, and Ten Mile Rock bone deposits.

1. Extinct Species and Subspecies
    ORDER INSECTIVORA
        Sorex cinereus fossidens, Masked Shrew—CF
        Microsorex minutus, Pygmy Shrew—CF
        Blarina ozarkensis, Short-tailed Shrew—CF

    ORDER CHIROPTERA
        Eptesicus fuscus grandis, Big Brown Bat—CF

    ORDER EDENTATA
        Dasypus bellus, Giant Armadillo—PC, TMR

    ORDER LAGOMORPHA
        Lepus giganteus, Hare—CF

    ORDER RODENTIA
        Tamias nasutus, Chipmunk—CF
        Geomys parvidens, Pocket Gopher—CF
        Reithrodontomys simplicidens, Harvest Mouse—CF
        Neotoma ozarkensis, Woodrat—CF
        Ondatra annectans, Muskrat—CF

    ORDER CARNIVORA
        Canis dirus, Dire Wolf—PC, TMR
        Mustela erminea angustidens, Ermine—CF
        Mustela gracilis, Weasel—CF
        Mephitis newtonensis, Skunk—CF
        Brachyprotoma pristina, Skunk—CF
        Brachyprotoma spelaea, Skunk—CF
        *Felis longicrus**, Mountain Lion—CF
        Lynx compressus, Lynx—CF
        Smilodontopsis troglodytes, Sabre Tooth Tiger—CF
        Smilodontopsis conardi, Sabre Tooth Tiger—CF

    ORDER PROBOSCIDEA
        Mammut sp., Mastodon (tooth fragment)—PC, TMR
        Mammuthus sp., Mammoth (tooth fragment)—PC

    ORDER PERISSODACTYLA
        Equus caballus (=*E. scotti*), Horse—CF, PC, TMR

    ORDER ARTIODACTYLA
        Mylohyus nasutus (=*M. browni*), Peccary—CF
        Platygonus compressus, Giant Peccary—PC, TMR
        Cervalces roosevelti, Elk—PC
        Sangamona fugitiva, Deer—PC
        Symbos australis, Musk Ox—CF, PC
    **Felis cougar* = *F. concolor* included on Brown's original list is considered by Simpson (1941) to be referable to *F. longicrus*.

2. Extant Recent Mostly Boreal Species
    ORDER INSECTIVORA
        Sorex cinereus, Masked Shrew—CF, PC
        Sorex vagrans, Vagrant Shrew—CF
        Sorex palustris, Water Shrew—PC
        Sorex fumeus, Smoky Shrew—CF
        Sorex arcticus, Arctic Shrew—PC
        Microsorex hoyi, Pygmy Shrew—PC
        Blarina brevicauda, Short-tailed Shrew—TMR
        Blarina b. brevicauda, Short-tailed Shrew—PC
        Blarina b. kirtlandi, Short-tailed Shrew—PC
        Condylura cristata, Star-nosed Mole—PC, TMR

    ORDER LAGOMORPHA
        Lepus americanus, Snowshoe Rabbit—CF

    ORDER RODENTIA
        Tamiasciurus hudsonicus, Red Squirrel—PC, TMR
        Glaucomys sabrinus, Northern Flying Squirrel—PC
        Clethrionomys gapperi, Gapper's Red-backed Vole—PC, TMR
        Phenacomys intermedius, Heather Vole—PC, TMR
        Microtus pennsylvanicus, Meadow Vole—PC, TMR
        Microtus xanthognathus, Yellow-cheeked Vole—PC
        Synaptomys borealis, Northern Bog Lemming—PC

ORDER CARNIVORA
  Canis lupus, Gray Wolf—CF
  Martes pennanti, Fisher—CF, PC

ORDER PERISSODACTYLA
  Tapirus terrestris, Andean Tapir (extinct in North America)—PC, TMR

ORDER ARTIODACTYLA
  *Sus scrofa***, Pig (reintroduced in North America)—PC, TMR
  Odocoileus hemionus, Mule Deer (western North America)—PC, TMR

**Quinn (1970a, 1970b) on the basis of C^{14} dating believes that the pig was present in North America prior to its introduction by Spaniards in 1492 or later. An incisor recovered from clay at the Ten Mile Rock site is very difficult to refute.

3. Extant Recent Species Presently in or Near Arkansas

ORDER MARSUPIALIA
  Didelphis virginiana, Virginia Opossum—PC, TMR

ORDER INSECTIVORA
  Blarina carolinensis, Southern Short-Tailed Shrew—PC (may be referable to *B. hylophaga*, Elliot's Short-tailed Shrew)
  Cryptotis parva, Least Shrew—PC
  Scalopus aquaticus, Eastern Mole—CF, PC, TMR

ORDER CHIROPTERA
  Myotis leibii, Small-footed Myotis—CF
  Unidentified Bats—TMR

ORDER LAGOMORPHA
  Sylvilagus floridanus, Eastern Cottontail—CF
  Unidentified rabbits—TMR

ORDER RODENTIA
  Tamias striatus, Eastern Chipmunk—PC, TMR
  Marmota monax, Woodchuck—CF, PC, TMR
  Spermophilus tridecemlineatus, Thirteen-lined Ground Squirrel—CF, PC, TMR
  Sciurus niger, Fox Squirrel—PC
  Sciurus sp., Tree Squirrel—TMR (probably *S. niger* or *S. carolinensis*)

Geomys bursarius, Plains Pocket Gopher—PC, TMR
Castor canadensis, Beaver—CF, PC, TMR
Peromyscus maniculatus, Deer Mouse—PC
Peromyscus leucopus, White-footed Mouse—PC
Peromyscus sp. indet., Deer Mouse—CF, PC, TMR
Neotoma floridana, Eastern Woodrat—PC, TMR
Microtus ochrogaster, Prairie Vole—CF, PC, TMR
Microtus pinetorum, Woodland Vole—PC
Ondatra zibethicus, Muskrat—PC, TMR
Synaptomys cooperi, Southern Bog Lemming—PC, TMR
Zapus hudsonius, Meadow Jumping Mouse—PC (near Arkansas)
Erethizon dorsatum, Porcupine—PC, TMR (near Arkansas)

ORDER CARNIVORA
  Canis latrans, Coyote—PC, TMR
  Canis familiaris, Indian Dog—CF, PC
  Vulpes vulpes, Red Fox—CF, PC, TMR
  Urocyon cinereoargenteus, Gray Fox—CF, PC, TMR
  Ursus americanus, Black Bear—CF, PC, TMR
  Procyon lotor, Raccoon—CF, PC, TMR
  Mustela frenata, Long-tailed Weasel—PC
  Mustela vison, Mink—PC, TMR
  Taxidea taxus, Badger—PC, TMR
  Spilogale putorius, Eastern Spotted Skunk—CF
  Lutra canadensis, River Otter—PC, TMR
  Felis rufus, Bobcat—CF, PC, TMR

ORDER ARTIODACTYLA
  Cervus elaphus, Elk—CF
  Odocoileus virginianus, White-tailed Deer—CF, PC, TMR

In addition to the major bone deposits discussed above, there have been several isolated discoveries of fossil mammals in Arkansas. A mastodon (*Mammut* sp.) possibly of Pleistocene occurrence was found on the south bank of the Red River near Garland in Miller County (Fay 1959). Hay (1924) reported a tooth and dorsal vertebra of the American mastodon (*Mammut americanus*) from near Trumann, Poinsett County, and also reported other mastodon records from gravel dredged from the Mississippi River, Chicot County (an upper second molar tooth), bones from Helena, Phillips County, could have been those of mastodon or possibly mammoth. Mammoth (*Mammuthus columbi*) remains were recovered from near Hazen, Prairie County, in 1865 (Puckette 1975a). This species was widely distributed in southeastern North America in the Sangamon-Wisconsin stages of the late Pleistocene. Puckette (1975b) reported remains of a mountain lion (*Felis concolor*), which he estimated to be late Pleistocene or Sub-Recent, from Svendsen Cave, Marion County. Skeletal remains of the pipistrelle bat (*Pipistrellus* sp.) were also found with the cat remains. Remains of the giant beaver (*Castoroides ohioensis*), which was about as large as a bear, have been found on Crowley's Ridge, and remains of the huge ground sloth (*Megalonyx jeffersoni*), which was about the size of an ox, have also been reported from Arkansas.

Mammal remains of more recent origin have been reported from a number of bluff shelters in northwestern Arkansas. A bluff shelter on the White River near Springdale in Washington County with about a 4,000 B.P. C^{14} date yielded the remains of 25 species of native mammals, including the red wolf, which became extinct quite recently (Morrison 1970). Other species of wild mammals identified from the archaeological site are still extant in Arkansas. Additionally, the Indian dog (*C. familiaris*), pig (*S. scrofa*), and sheep (*Ovis aries*) were recovered from the site. The location of the sheep horn indicated that it probably did not belong with the older assemblage. Excavations of several other bluff shelters in northwestern Arkansas have yielded remains of 21 species of native mammals, all of which are extant today with the exception of the bison and the red wolf (Cleland 1965). Most of the mammal species were those that are predominantly associated with a deciduous forest habitat. It is probable that the area was lightly forested at the time, with frequent openings and small prairies. Pig and dog remains were also found in several of the shelter sites.

Early Recorded Chronology
of Mammals in Arkansas

Much of the information in this brief chronology has been drawn from "A Survey of Arkansas Game" (Holder 1951), and the reader is referred to this publication for more details.

Our knowledge of mammals during Indian occupancy and early European explorations in Arkansas is very limited. Journals of the De Soto expedition which entered Arkansas territory in 1541 and 1542 described buffaloes, wildcats, panthers, and bears and mentioned great stores of tanned hides and pelts of deer, bear, wildcat, and panther in Indian towns of the Delta region (Irving 1857). An intensive period of French exploration in Arkansas began with Père Marquette's arrival at the mouth of the Arkansas River in 1673. Arkansas Post was established by Henry de Tonti in 1686 and served as a center for trade in hides, furs, and bear oil with Indians until after the Louisiana Purchase. The French established other trading posts in Louisiana from which commercial hunters employing Indians went up the Ouachita, Red, and other rivers and streams in the West Gulf Coastal Plain to kill deer and furbearers. Trade was chiefly in skins of deer, bear, otter, mink, and beaver.

Buffalo hides were shipped from Arkansas Post, but apparently most of them were obtained in what is now Oklahoma. The major buffalo herds in Arkansas were found in prairies, canebrakes, and open woods in the Gulf Coastal Plain along major rivers such as the Red, Saline, Arkansas, and St. Francis through the 1700s. By the early 1800s, they were found mainly in southern and eastern Arkansas. Buffaloes were hunted commercially in Arkansas until the last large herd of about 150 animals was killed in the Saline River bottoms in 1808. Buffaloes were present in open woods and prairies of the Ozarks but apparently did not occur in large numbers. An early naturalist, Henry Schoolcraft, who traveled in the White River country in 1818 and 1819, apparently saw no large herds, although dried buffalo meat was evidently common pioneer fare in the region. A few buffaloes were still present in the Bayou DeView and Cache River bottoms as late as 1837 (Gerstaecker 1856).

There are few historical records of elk in Arkansas. They were evidently present in the bottoms near the big St. Francis Swamp in the early 1800s, and their presence in the Ozarks can be inferred from Schoolcraft's observations in 1818 and 1819 (Schoolcraft 1821). The last native elk was apparently killed in the vicinity of Elkhorn Tavern in Benton County in the 1830s. Gerstaecker (1856) saw no elk in Arkansas in 1837.

Red wolves were present in large numbers throughout the state in early days. They decreased in numbers as the state was settled but did not become scarce in some areas until after 1900. Gerstaecker (1856) mentions an encounter with an immense black wolf with a white star on its breast along the Fourche le Fave River near Little Rock in 1837, and in further accounts of Gerstaecker's hunting exploits in Arkansas, Hartley (1859) mentions other encounters with wolves. Featherstonhaugh (1844) also gives an account of seven wolves (four black and three gray) in the vicinity of Brown's Creek near the Little River, between Hempstead and Little River counties. One wolf, an extremely large black one, was killed.

The black bear has been closely identified with the history of Arkansas. Until 1923, Arkansas was unofficially known as "The Bear State" and was still referred to by that name in the *World Almanac* as late as 1929. Bears were hunted by Indians and early pioneers for meat, hides, and bear oil, which was used for cooking fat and for hair dressing. Thousands of bears were killed every year by commercial hunters during the Spanish and French occupations of Arkansas. Gerstaecker (1856) mentioned several exciting encounters with bears when he visited the state in 1837. In one instance in which he entered a cave along the Mulberry River after a bear, he mentioned seeing immense numbers of bats. There were still many bears in the state until about the turn of the nineteenth century. It was recorded around this time that single hunting parties near Elaine in Phillips County would kill as many as 30–40 bears. The black bear was nearly exterminated in the Ouachita Mountains by 1910, but a small population survived in the area of the White River National Wildlife Refuge in eastern Arkansas and began to increase about 1935. It

was estimated that 40–50 bears remained in the state around 1950.

Mountain lions were common in Arkansas during its early history and were greatly feared by pioneers. Gerstaecker recalled several panther hunts while in Arkansas. In one encounter, he and a hunting companion chased a wounded mountain lion into a cave during late January. Gerstaecker wounded it again and then knifed the lion when it attacked him, but he received two deep gashes in his shoulder. The two hunters were able to leave the cave and later returned to find the panther dead. A mountain lion was killed on Easter morning near Harrisburg, Poinsett County, in 1919. This was apparently the last record for the state until another mountain lion was killed near Mount Ida, Montgomery County, in 1949.

Early travelers in Arkansas tell of killing bobcats, which were usually called wildcats, but the wildcats were evidently not considered important enough to mention often in their journals. Beaver were also plentiful in Arkansas's early days and received similar treatment. Early accounts make scant mention of other mammal species. Gerstaecker in his book tells of shooting a raccoon and wounding a fox, and he also mentions cooking an opossum. The ocelot was present in southwestern Arkansas in its early days. The type locality was given as Arkansas when it was described in 1855. It is possible that some early reports supposedly about wildcats were really reports about ocelots.

With the exception of the armadillo, the nutria, and possibly the ringtail, the mammal fauna of Arkansas over the last several hundred years was probably very similar to the fauna at present. The armadillo is a relatively recent invader that was not recorded in the United States before 1849 (Audubon and Bachman 1854). The ringtail is a species that has been expanding its range in a northward and eastward direction in recent years (Hoffman and Jones 1970), and it was probably not present in Arkansas before 1900. Destruction of habitat, uncontrolled hunting, trapping, and other factors have resulted in the extermination of the buffalo, elk, ocelot, red wolf, and possibly other species in the state during recorded history. Habitat alteration may provide the opportunity for the invasion of other species in future years that are not present in the state today.

Species introduced by man, such as the house mouse, Norway rat, and nutria, have become firmly established and now are important members of the state's mammal fauna. What the future holds in store is conjectural.

Extirpated Recent Mammals of Arkansas

Several species of native mammals have been exterminated in Arkansas during recent history. Some species, such as the buffalo, are now held in captivity by private owners or in zoos. The mountain lion, which was once believed to be extinct in the state, has made a modest comeback with an increase in the state's deer population. In addition, otter, beaver, black bear, and deer have been, at one time or another, dangerously close to extermination, but all have now recovered and are doing well.

One of the first native mammals to become extinct in Arkansas was the ocelot (*Felis pardalis*), which was once found near the Red River in the southwestern corner of the state. The type locality for the race *albescens* of this species is Arkansas (Hall 1981) although no exact locality in southwestern Arkansas is given. The race *F. p. albescens* was described in 1855, and it is probable that it was exterminated well before the turn of the century since no mention is made of it in early accounts.

Hornaday (1889) listed the buffalo (*Bison bison*) as extinct in Arkansas by 1820, although a few still existed in the Bayou DeView and Cache River bottoms as late as 1837 (Gerstaecker 1856). The buffalo had a statewide distribution about 1800, and Roe (1951, 352) quotes Dr. Josiah Gregg in accounts of his western travels as saying that buffaloes were still abundant over much of Arkansas about 1810. However, their numbers must have dwindled rapidly shortly thereafter. Seton (1929) indicated that the range in Arkansas had contracted to the western half of the Interior Highlands by 1829.

The elk (*Cervus elaphus*) was once abundant over much of the state (see Species Account) but presumably was exterminated about 1840. A small herd of elk was reintroduced in western Arkansas by the Forest Service in 1933 and grew to about 200 head by the mid-1950s before illegal hunting and other factors brought about the herd's extinction in the late 1950s and early 1960s. A second reintroduction occurred in the early 1980s, when about 100 animals were released in the area of Newton County. The Arkansas Game and Fish Commission reports that reproduction has occurred and the herd is currently stable. The Commission found, however, five mortalities due to the meningeal worm (*Parelaphostrongylus tenuis*) during the summer of 1988. Thus, investigators believe that the prognosis for the success of elk is guarded.

One of the last native mammals to become extinct in Arkansas was the red wolf, *Canis niger* (see Species Account). A few specimens of hybrid origin which show red wolf characteristics may still occur in isolated sections of the state, but these are rapidly disappearing. The red wolf was a victim of changing agricultural practices which placed it at a competitive disadvantage to the invading coyote and of uncontrolled hunting and trapping (Sealander and Gipson 1974).

Endangered and Threatened Species
of Arkansas Mammals

Several native mammal species in Arkansas have been placed on the endangered list of the U.S. Fish and Wildlife Service. The Endangered Species Act of 1973 imposes severe penalties for taking or wantonly destroying any species on the list without specific authorization. Endangered species on the list are: The gray bat (*Myotis grisescens*), the Indiana bat (*Myotis sodalis*), the Ozark big-eared bat (*Plecotus townsendii ingens*), the Florida panther or mountain lion (*Felis concolor coryi*), and the red wolf (*Canis rufus*), which is already extinct in Arkansas. The status of each of these species is discussed in the Species Accounts.

Insectivorous bats play a very important role in the total ecosystem, and it is important that all species of bats receive protection as well as endangered species of bats. Survival of endangered species of bats is dependent upon a minimum amount of disturbance in caves where they hibernate. When awakened too often, hibernating bats will metabolize energy too rapidly so that energy reserves, consisting of stored fat, are exhausted long before the available food supply is adequate and weather conditions outside caves are tolerable. When forced emergence from hibernation occurs too early due to exhaustion of energy reserves, many bats die from starvation. Gating or otherwise restricting access by the public to caves used by endangered species may be necessary to insure their survival for the benefit of future generations.

The continued existence of panthers in Arkansas is dependent upon a suitable amount of near wilderness habitat and an adequate food supply. The deer herd in Arkansas is now more than adequate to support a small mountain lion population without affecting the deer population significantly. Education of the public concerning the protection afforded mountain lions by their endangered status, together with habitat preservation, may insure their survival in the state.

The endangered red wolf has already passed the point of no return as a viable biological species in Arkansas and in its remaining range in Texas and Louisiana. The only hope for the continued existence of this species now rests with captive breeding programs of the U.S. Fish and Wildlife Service and possible future re-establishment of specimens to suitable areas of its historic range.

The small-footed bat (*Myotis leibii*) is one of the rarest bats in the eastern United States. It is known only from a few records in the state and is considered rare. Six other species of Arkansas mammals are probably uncommon and certainly should be considered mammals of special concern. In each case, the species is approaching the geographic limits of its range and there are relatively few records of its occurrence. These species include: the desert shrew (*Notiosorex crawfordi*), the southeastern shrew (*Sorex longirostris*), the eastern harvest mouse (*Reithrodontomys humulis*), the plains harvest mouse (*Reithrodontomys montanus*), the badger (*Taxidea taxus*), and the ringtail (*Bassariscus astutus*).

Observing and Studying Mammals

Since most mammals are shy, wary, and nocturnal, attempts to observe them and their behavior are often time-consuming as well as frustrating. Nevertheless, for those individuals armed with a camera or binoculars, a notebook or tape recorder, and a little patience, the results can be very satisfying. Even if a mammal is not seen, a great deal can be learned concerning the natural history and ecology of it through careful observation of its habitat and mammal signs. Such signs include tracks, runways or trails, scats or droppings, home sites, food caches, tooth marks, and other evidence of feeding activity.

Tracks are most easily observed in fresh snow, dry sand, or mud. The species can often be identified from the size and shape of its track, along with such identifying characteristics as the presence or absence of claws or tail marks. Careful comparison with drawings of tracks in various publications on mammals will enable the observer to become familiar enough with the tracks of many species to recognize them on sight. Tracks of some common species of mammals found in Arkansas (together with their scats) are illustrated in Appendix B.

Some species, such as the otter, leave their scat on rocks or logs in streams; others defecate along their runways or trails. Some species are quite sanitary and defecate in special chambers in their burrow systems. The size, shape, color, and contents of scats are all useful in identifying mammals to the species level. For example, the droppings of the bog lemming, deposited in their runways, have a characteristic bright green color while those of the otter often have a glistening or grayish appearance caused by the presence of fish scales. For readers who may wish to pursue this subject further, the book *A Field Guide to Animal Tracks* by Murie (1974) can be very helpful.

Home sites of several common species of mammals, such as the beaver, muskrat, and tree squirrels, are easily recognized by the average observer. Beaver and muskrat in Arkansas do not often build lodges in marshy places, as they do farther north, but they often construct burrows in stream banks. The entrances of these burrows are often concealed below the water surface. A burrow with a nearby mudslide may be that of an otter. Leaf and twig nests in the outer branches of tall trees are usually the homes of gray and fox squirrels, although old, abandoned ones are sometimes taken over by flying squirrels. Woodrats living in rock crevices will often betray their presence by leaving piles of bark-stripped twigs near the entrance. In lowland areas they build large stick houses against the base of a tree or the end of a log. Well-worn trails leading from such houses are good evidence of occupancy. The habit of the woodrat or pack rat of transporting stones, bones, broken glass, and other objects to its nest is further proof of the identity of the nest builder. Large burrows with remains of birds, rabbits, and other mammals near the entrance often belong to foxes. Smaller burrows (30.5–40.6 cm [12–16 in] in diameter) located in woods, along fencerows, or in fields probably belong to an armadillo, opossum, or skunk. The observer should not be misled by the number of burrows and possible population of the inhabitants; armadillos may construct and use 4–5 burrows. If the burrow has a musky odor its occupant may be a skunk.

Hollow trees or logs are often the home sites of opossums, raccoons, flying squirrels, mice, and certain species of bats. The gray fox often makes its nest in a large hollow tree. Careful watching will sometimes reveal the occupant of such tree cavities. Other mammal species have their homes in underground tunnels. The size and location of the tunnel will often provide clues to the identity of the occupant. Humped up subsurface runs associated at intervals with steep, conical earth mounds are the work of moles. Pocket gophers also bring dirt to the surface to form earth mounds, but these are not associated with visible subsurface runs. Moles and pocket gophers seldom emerge on the surface for more than short intervals, but occasionally a patient observer will be rewarded with a brief glimpse.

Other evidences of mammal activity are food caches and tooth marks on the bark of trees or shrubs made by beaver, rabbit, muskrat, and other rodents. Tooth marks which range from 3 to 6 mm (0.01–0.24 in) in width generally are those of beaver. Neatly clipped shoots of trees or shrubs near a stream, often associated with well-defined trails, also indicate the presence of beaver. Careful measurements and comparisons with known tooth marks are needed to identify feeding activities of other species. Squirrels and various species of mice often accumulate large food caches during fall and early winter. Underground caches of seeds, bulbs, tubers, etc., are usually those of mice or, in some cases, moles or pocket gophers. Stores of nuts in tree cavities generally denote the presence of squirrels. Knowledge of the feeding habits of various species will often provide clues concerning the presence of certain kinds of mammals based on food fragments that accumulate near their feeding and resting places.

Most mammals are much like humans in that they prefer to travel along paths of least resistance. Therefore, man-made roads and highways are favorite areas for movement. In addition, careful observation in a woods or along a fencerow will often reveal paths which may be used by a variety of different species. Close observation of a path through a fence may reveal bits of hair which may be used to identify a species which regularly uses that trail. Voles and cotton rats construct an intricate system of small (5–7.6 cm [2–3 in] wide) runways in the grass. These runways are easily identified and are used by a variety of animals including shrews, other mice, and snakes. In the woods, mammals such as shrews and mice have runways beneath the forest litter and under fallen logs.

Large mammals such as deer and bear can also be "observed" through their signs. In addition to tracks, scat, resting spots, and feeding areas, both species may leave signs indicating reproductive and territorial activities. In marking territories, bears often establish trees on which they indicate their presence by claw marks and scrapes. During the autumn, when deer are in rut, males will rub the velvet from their antlers on trees and small shrubs. In addition, they may mark their presence by establishing scrapes in which they urinate.

In order to study many aspects of mammalian biology, however, the animal must be collected. Mammals are usually collected with a variety of sizes and kinds of traps, snares, nets, and guns. Special types of traps are often designed with only one species in mind. It must be remembered that mammals in Arkansas are protected by law. Before any specimens are collected, therefore, appropriate permits and/or licenses must be obtained through the Arkansas Game and Fish Commission.

For the reader who may be interested in techniques of collecting mammals and preparing museum specimens, the following references in the bibliography are worth consulting: Anderson (1948); Booth (1982); DeBlase and Martin (1974); Hall (1962); Novak et al. (1987).

• SPECIES ACCOUNTS •

Explanation of Species Accounts

HOW TO USE THE KEYS

Keys consist of pairs of contrasting statements called key couplets. Each couplet is preceded by a number. To use a key, start at the beginning and decide which of the two statements best fits the specimen you are "keying down." At the end of the statement selected you will find a number that directs you to the next step. Follow down the key to that number and repeat the selection process. By proceeding through a series of numbered couplets, you will come to a statement with the name of an order, family, or species.

If you are not certain of the order in which your specimen belongs, begin with the "Key to Orders." You will then find the group in which your specimen belongs. In some orders it will be necessary to again key the specimen down to its family. Using a key to families in the order selected, you will then be able to determine in which family your specimen belongs. Using the proper family key, you will then be able to key the specimen down to genus and species. In some instances an order or family is repre-

sented by only one species, and it will not be necessary to use a key to species.

In general, persons who are not professionally trained biologists will find the keys to whole animals most useful. These keys are less technical than the skull keys, and in most instances, identification can be made with a whole animal key without resorting to a skull key. However, in some cases in which the identification of the specimen is still in doubt, it may be necessary to use the skull key to supplement the whole animal key. Skull keys necessarily include more technical terms, which are defined in the glossary or explained by figures that accompany the keys. A diagram of a typical mammalian skull, with parts labeled, is included in Appendix A. Bare skulls are sometimes found in the field, and these can, in most cases, be identified to species using the skull keys.

Once you have made an identification in the key, you may check your identification by comparing your specimen with the description given in its species account. If there is still doubt as to the identity of the specimen, it should be compared with specimens in a reference collection in a museum or educational institution, or sent to a professional mammalogist for identification.

SPECIES ACCOUNTS

The vernacular or common name precedes the account of each species discussed in the guide. Vernacular names follow Jones et al. (1986). Scientific names, in which the first word is the name of the genus to which the species belongs and the second is the species name, are given below the vernacular name. The complete scientific name is given in the checklist that precedes the Species Accounts. The genus and species names are followed by the name of the describer or describers. If the describer's name is enclosed in parentheses, the species is not included in a genus to which it was originally assigned. The sequence of orders, families, and species also follows Jones et al. (1986), with the exception of the family Cricetidae in the order Rodentia, which is included in the family Muridae (see family Muridae for a more detailed explanation).

Each species account consists of the following: Explanation of Scientific Name; Identification and Description; Measurements; Arkansas Distributions; Life History; Importance and/or Management; and Selected References.

Identifications summarize diagnostic characteristics of the species such as size, prominent external features, or color, and provide a means of verifying the results obtained by use of keys.

All measurements are expressed in metric units (followed by English units in parentheses). All linear measurements are in millimeters (inches) and weights are in grams or kilograms (ounces or pounds). The standard body measurements used are: total length, measured from tip of the nose to tip of the last tail vertebrae; tail length, measured from the base when at a right angle to the body axis to the tip of the last vertebra; hind foot, measured from the back of the heel to the tip of the longest claw; and ear, measured from the notch to the tip of the pinna. Measurements are given first over the species range. Where the range is very extensive in the United States of North America, and where there are large variations in different races of species, measurements pertain mainly to Arkan. as and surrounding states. Dental formulae are in the same format as described in the section above, Mammalian Characteristics and Success.

Arkansas distributions are based on information that is currently available. Mammalogical research in Arkansas is quite active and, no doubt, distributional limits and county records will be modified in the future. Range limits, especially for some of the small mammals, are imprecisely known, and subspecies boundaries are based largely on inferences drawn from the literature. Geographic variations in species characteristics of Arkansas mammals, especially size variation, have not been studied in any great detail until quite recently. Characteristics used to define races of a species are largely morphological and depend heavily upon skull measurements. Size measurements within a species may be somewhat transitory and subject to change with time. Depending upon the species, such changes, which are part of the selection process in evolution, may occur at different rates.

Life history accounts are abbreviated and primarily concerned with habitat, feeding habits, and reproductive biology. Since the biology of some species is better known than others, some accounts are more extensive. Much of the life history information concerning the various mammal species dealt with in this book represents a body of common knowledge shared by mammalogists and has been drawn from a variety of sources. As far as possible, generalizations are avoided and information is as pertinent to Arkansas species as possible.

Economic importance and/or management needs follow the section on life history. For species which have important economic impact on the Arkansas economy (e.g., furbearers and game mammals) some statistics are provided. Also discussed are chronologies of reintroductions and comments on rare, threatened, or endangered species. The subspecies found in

Arkansas are listed at the end of this section.

A few selected references are included after each species account to enable the interested reader to consult more detailed accounts of specific aspects of the life history. These references usually are to more recent literature or to accounts that are considered to be the most authoritative. It is impossible to include all of the available sources; therefore, we apologize to authors whose works have been omitted.

DISTRIBUTION MAPS

United States and Arkansas maps are included for all species. Counties in Arkansas where specimens have been collected are indicated with a solid circle. Reliable reports from professional mammalogists, wildlife biologists, and reputable observers are indicated by solid stars. The presence of specimens or observations within a county are only indicated once, however. No county records are indicated for those species which are numerous and have been recorded throughout the state. The two main physiographic regions of the state, the Interior Highlands and the Gulf Coastal Plain, are also indicated on the distribution maps.

Distributional limits of many of the larger species of mammals, especially game and fur-bearing mammals, are fairly well known. For many of the smaller species, however, distributional records are spotty, and the range limits within the state are poorly defined. Much additional collecting will be required to accurately delineate range limits of some species. Until this is accomplished, determination of the factors that limit distributions of certain species within the state cannot be dealt with effectively.

A few species of mammals occurring in the state are either rare over their range or approach their range limits in the state and hence

County map of Arkansas showing two major physiographic regions.

are rarely encountered. In some cases, one is fortunate to obtain reliable records at 15- to 20-year intervals. Species which fall in this category include the southeastern shrew, the desert shrew, the plains harvest mouse, and the eastern harvest mouse.

LITERATURE CITATIONS

Literature citations in the bibliography include some general background reference material that may not be cited directly in the text. The method of citing publications is in accordance with the style manual prepared by the Council of Biology Editors.

GLOSSARY

Technical terms which may be unfamiliar to the reader are defined in the glossary at the end of the book. Diagrams of typical carnivore (bobcat) and rodent (woodrat) skulls, with labeled parts, are included in Appendix A.

Checklist of Present Native and Naturalized Wild Mammals of Arkansas

ORDER MARSUPIALIA Marsupials
Family Didelphidae   New World Opossums
 Didelphus virginiana Kerr   Virginia Opossum

ORDER INSECTIVORA Insectivores
Family Soricidae   Shrews
 Sorex longirostris Bachman   Southeastern Shrew
 Blarina carolinensis (Say)   Southern Short-tailed Shrew
 Blarina hylophaga Elliot   Elliot's Short-tailed Shrew
 Cryptotis parva (Say)   Least Shrew
 Notiosorex crawfordi (Coues)   Desert Shrew
Family Talpidae   Moles
 Scalopus aquaticus (Linnaeus)   Eastern Mole

ORDER CHIROPTERA Bats
Family Vespertilionidae   Vespertilionid Bats
 Myotis lucifugus (Le Conte)   Little Brown Myotis
 Myotis austroriparius (Rhoads)   Southeastern Myotis
 Myotis grisescens A. H. Howell   Gray Myotis
 Myotis keenii (Merriam)   Keen's Myotis
 Myotis sodalis Miller and Allen   Indiana Myotis
 Myotis leibii (Audubon and Bachman)   Small-footed Myotis

Lasioncyteris noctivagans (Le Conte)	Silver-haired Bat
Pipistrellus subflavus (F. Cuvier)	Eastern Pipistrelle
Eptesicus fuscus (Palisot de Beauvois)	Big Brown Bat
Lasiurus borealis (Müller)	Red Bat
Lasiurus seminolus (Rhoads)	Seminole Bat
Lasiurus cinereus (Palisot de Beauvois)	Hoary Bat
Nycticeius humeralis Rafinesque	Evening Bat
Plecotus townsendii Cooper	Townsend's Big-eared Bat
Plecotus rafinesquii Lesson	Rafinesque's Big-eared Bat
Family Molossidae Molossid Bats	
Tadarida brasiliensis (I. Geoffroy St.-Hilaire)	Brazilian Free-tailed Bat

ORDER EDENTATA Edentates
Family Dasypodidae

Dasypus novemcinctus Linnaeus	Nine-banded Armadillo

ORDER LAGOMORPHA Lagomorphs
Family Leporidae   Hares and Rabbits

Sylvilagus floridanus (J. A. Allen)	Eastern Cottontail
Sylvilagus aquaticus (Bachman)	Swamp Rabbit
Lepus californicus Gray	Black-tailed Jackrabbit

ORDER RODENTIA Rodents
Family Sciuridae   Squirrels

Tamias striatus (Linnaeus)	Eastern Chipmunk
Marmota monax (Linnaeus)	Woodchuck
Sciurus carolinensis Gmelin	Gray Squirrel
Sciurus niger Linnaeus	Fox Squirrel
Glaucomys volans (Linnaeus)	Southern Flying Squirrel
Family Geomyidae Pocket Gophers	
Geomys breviceps Baird	Baird's Pocket Gopher
Family Castoridae Beavers	
Castor canadensis Kuhl	Beaver
Family Muridae Rats, Mice, and Voles	
Oryzomys palustris (Harlan)	Marsh Rice Rat
Reithrodontomys montanus (Baird)	Plains Harvest Mouse
Reithrodontomys humulis (Audubon and Bachman)	Eastern Harvest Mouse
Reithrodontomys megalotis (Baird)	Western Harvest Mouse
Reithrodontomys fulvescens J. A. Allen	Fulvous Harvest Mouse
Peromyscus maniculatus (Wagner)	Deer Mouse

Peromyscus leucopus (Rafinesque)	White-footed Mouse
Peromyscus gossypinus (Le Conte)	Cotton Mouse
Peromyscus attwateri J. A. Allen	Texas Mouse
Ochrotomys nuttalli (Harlan)	Golden Mouse
Sigmodon hispidus (Say and Ord)	Hispid Cotton Rat
Neotoma floridana (Ord)	Eastern Woodrat
Microtus ochrogaster (Wagner)	Prairie Vole
Microtus pinetorum (Le Conte)	Woodland Vole
Ondatra zibethicus (Linnaeus)	Muskrat
Synaptomys cooperi Baird	Southern Bog Lemming
Rattus rattus (Linnaeus)*	Black Rat
Rattus norvegicus (Berkenhout)*	Norway Rat
Mus musculus Linnaeus*	House Mouse

Family Capromyidae Capromyids

Myocastor coypus (Molina)*	Nutria

ORDER CARNIVORA Carnivores

Family Canidae Canids

Canis latrans Say	Coyote
Canis rufus Audubon and Bachman**	Red Wolf
Canis familiaris (Linnaeus)*	Feral Dog
Vulpes vulpes (Linnaeus)	Red Fox
Urocyon cinereoargenteus (Schreber)	Gray Fox

Family Ursidae Bears

Ursus americanus Pallas	Black Bear

Family Procyonidae Procyonids

Bassariscus astutus (Lichtenstein)	Ringtail
Procyon lotor (Linnaeus)	Raccoon

Family Mustelidae Mustelids

Mustela frenata Lichtenstein	Long-tailed Weasel
Mustela vison Schreber	Mink
Taxidea taxus (Schreber)	Badger
Spilogale putorius (Linnaeus)	Eastern Spotted Skunk
Mephitis mephitis (Schreber)	Striped Skunk
Lutra canadensis Schreber	River Otter

Family Felidae Cats

Felis concolor Linnaeus	Mountain Lion
Felis catus Linnaeus*	Feral House Cat
Felis rufus Schreber	Bobcat

ORDER ARTIODACTYLA Even-toed Ungulates

Family Suidae Pigs

    Sus scrofa Linnaeus*   Feral Pig

Family Cervidae Cervids

    Cervus elaphus Linnaeus*   Wapiti or Elk

    Odocoileus virginianus (Zimmerman)   White-tailed Deer

Family Bovidae Bovids

    Bison bison (Linnaeus)**   Bison or Buffalo

* Introduced

** Extinct (occurs only in captivity or under domestication)

Key to Orders *(Including Domestic Mammals)*

WHOLE ANIMALS

1. Forelimbs in form of wings .... Order CHIROPTERA (bats), page 61

   Forelimbs in form of legs 2

2. Feet with 1 or more large, hard hoofs 3

   Feet with 4 or 5 clawed toes 4

3. Each foot with only 1 hoof .... Order PERISSODACTYLA (horse), page 241

   Each foot with 2 or 4 hoofs .... Order ARTIODACTYLA (deer, pigs, cattle, etc.), page 242

4. Innermost toe of each hind foot thumblike, opposable and without claw; tail long, nearly naked
   and capable of grasping; female with pouch on
   belly .... Order MARSUPIALIA (opossum), page 42

   Innermost toe of each hind foot not thumblike
   and with claw; tail either short or long, haired
   or naked, not grasping; female without pouch on
   belly 5

5. Upper part of body and tail completely covered
   with a hard, bone-like shield .... Order EDENTATA (armadillo) page 104

   Body and tail not covered with a bone-like shield 6

6. Tail a cotton-like tuft; ear much longer than tail . . . . Order LAGOMORPHA (rabbits), page 108

Tail not a cotton-like tuft; ear much longer than
tail 7

7. Snout long and pointed, highly flexible and protruding conspicuously beyond the mouth; eyes
very small, often hidden in the fur . . . . Order INSECTIVORA (shrews and moles), page 46

Snout normal, not protruding conspicuously be-
yond mouth; eyes normal 8

8. A conspicuous gap (diastema) between front teeth
(incisors) and cheek teeth (molars) in both upper
and lower jaw; coat without well-developed guard
hairs . . . . Order RODENTIA (rodents), page 117

No conspicuous gap between incisor and molar
teeth in upper and lower jaw; prominent, sharp-
pointed teeth (canines) behind incisor teeth in
both upper and lower jaw which project beyond
the incisor and molar teeth; coat with well-
developed guard hairs . . . . Order CARNIVORA (flesh eaters), page 190

SKULLS

1. Teeth peg-like and shaped alike (homodont);
narrow, tubular rostrum (nose) . . . . Order EDENTATA (armadillo), page 104

Teeth not peg-like and shaped differently
(heterodont) 2

2. Upper jaw without front (incisor) and fang (ca-
nine) teeth . . . . Order ARTIODACTYLA; in part (cattle, deer, etc.), page 242

Upper jaw with incisor and canine teeth 3

3. Total number of teeth 50, 26 above and 24 below; each posterior angle of lower jaw with
inward-curving process; braincase smaller than
rostrum and with a high, median ridge; roof of
mouth (palate) perforated posteriorly . . . . Order MARSUPIALIA (opossum), page 42

Total number of teeth less than 50; posterior
angle of lower jaw without inward-curving pro-
cess; braincase larger than rostrum 4

4. Eye socket (orbit) enclosed by a solid bony ring;
no opening (foramen) with canal in skull above
eye socket; canine teeth usually absent, but if
present not prominent and smaller than incisors;
molar teeth squarish or rectangular in cross-
section . . . . Order PERISSODACTYLA (horse), page 241

Eye socket not enclosed by solid bony ring 5

5. A wide gap (diastema) between front and cheek teeth; canine teeth absent 6

No wide gap between front and cheek teeth; canine teeth present 7

6. Four upper incisors, the second pair small and peg-like, directly behind the first pair; jawbone in front of eye socket with bony lattice work .... Order LAGOMORPHA (rabbits), page 108

Only two upper incisors; jawbone in front of eye socket without bony lattice work .... Order RODENTIA (rodents), page 117

7. Tusks (canines) in upper and lower jaw triangular in cross-section, curved outward; molar teeth rounded or oval in cross-section; opening with canal in skull above eye socket; skull elongated, sloping from back to front .... Order ARTIODACTYLA; in part (pig), page 242

Canines not triangular in cross-section and not curving outward 8

8. Canine teeth small, almost same size as other teeth; bony arch (zygomatic arch), which forms the outside of each eye socket, weak or absent .... Order INSECTIVORA (shrews and moles), page 46

Canine teeth (fangs) distinctly larger than other teeth; zygomatic arch well developed 9

9. Anterior end of skull broad and blunt, with a distinct U-shaped notch; one or two incisors on each side of upper jaw; length less than 25 mm (0.98 in) .... Order CHIROPTERA (bats), page 61

Anterior end of skull without U-shaped notch; three incisors in each side of upper jaw; length more than 25 mm (0.98 in) .... Order CARNIVORA (flesh eaters), page 190

Order Marsupialia *Marsupials*

Marsupials are characterized by the presence of a marsupium or pouch on the abdomen of females. Gestation in most species is brief, and the young are small and incompletely developed at birth. After birth, they attach to mammary glands in the pouch where they complete their development until they are able to move about independently. The order Marsupialia is a very primitive one, and the greatest species diversity is found in Australia and adjacent islands. Several species occur in South America, but only one species, the Virginia opossum, occurs in the United States and Canada.

FAMILY DIDELPHIDAE

NEW WORLD OPOSSUM

Members of this family are in the oldest known family in the order. They originated in North America, but are presently found primarily in tropical and subtropical areas. The general characteristics of this family are as follows: Long, nearly naked, grasping tail; long nose; five toes on front and hind feet, inner toe on hind foot opposable and without a nail; very pronounced crests on midline and back of skull; 50 teeth.

VIRGINIA OPOSSUM

Didelphus virginiana

NAME   From the Greek word *didelphis*, meaning double womb. The specific name, *virginiana*, means "of Virginia." Opossum is derived from the Algonquin Indian name, *apasum*.

IDENTIFICATION AND DESCRIPTION   The opossum is about the size of a large domestic cat. It has a long, scaly, flesh-colored, scantily haired, grasping tail. The muzzle is long and slender. The ears are thin and naked. The legs are short and the feet have five toes with the inner toe on each hind foot thumb-like, without a nail, and opposable. Females have a fur-lined pouch on the abdomen. The fur is long and coarse, and is usually grizzled gray in color but ranges from nearly white to cinnamon or black. Males are larger than females.

Didelphus virginiana, Opossum. *Phil A. Dotson*

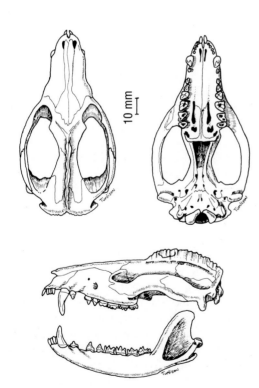

Skull of *Didelphus virginiana*

MEASUREMENTS AND DENTAL FORMULA

Total Length:	600–850 mm (24–33.5 in)
Tail Length:	250–350 mm (9.8–13.8 in)
Hind Foot:	50–75 mm (2–3 in)
Ear:	45–60 mm (1.8–2.5 in)
Skull Length:	90–125 mm (3.5–5 in)
Weight:	3–6 kg (6.6–13 lb)
Dental	I 5/4, C 1/1, P 3/3,
Formula:	M 4/4 = 50

ARKANSAS DISTRIBUTION AND ABUNDANCE
The opossum is common statewide, particularly in heavily timbered bottomlands and mountainous regions of state.

LIFE HISTORY   The opossum is generally an inhabitant of deciduous woodland. It prefers bottomland forests along streams and is found less frequently in dry upland woods. Opossums nest or make dens in sheltered spots such as hollow logs, brush piles, rockpiles, under exposed roots of uprooted trees or partially undermined trees along streams, or under buildings. The opossum is an excellent climber but is most often observed on the ground. On the ground, opossums generally move with a slow, ambling gait and as a result are one of the most

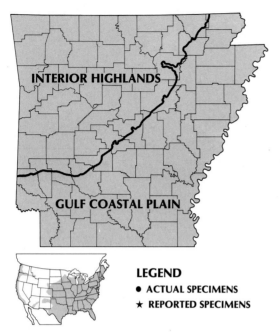

LEGEND
- ● ACTUAL SPECIMENS
- ★ REPORTED SPECIMENS

Distribution of the opossum, *Didelphus virginiana*

frequent "road kills" observed along highways in the state. When surprised, the opossum exhibits a characteristic death-feigning behavior pattern (commonly called "playing possum"). If picked up while in this state it offers no resistance, but if it is left alone it soon recovers and makes its escape (Fitch and Sandidge 1953).

Opossums are slow-witted, non-aggressive, largely nocturnal mammals. Usually they are silent but may give low growls, snarls, or hisses if disturbed. They are omnivorous and will eat almost any kind of available food. Persimmon is a favorite fruit, but the seeds are rarely eaten. Scats with large numbers of persimmon seeds are more likely to be from raccoons or coyotes. Corn and fruits constitute a substantial portion of its diet in fall and early winter. Contrary to popular belief, the opossum seldom molests poultry.

In northern Arkansas the opossum breeding season begins during the first week in February, but it may begin in mid-January in southern Arkansas. A second breeding period occurs from early April to mid-June. Females may produce two litters per year, and both males and females reach sexual maturity during the first year after birth. Females are characterized by having two vaginas opening into the urogenital sinus. In order to facilitate breeding, males have a forked penis, which may give rise to the myth that opossums breed through the nose.

Litters may be produced in all months except October and November. As many as 20–25 young may be born at one time, but the number of milk-producing nipples in the pouch usually does not exceed 13, which sets an upper limit on the number of young that can be accommodated in the pouch. The average litter size varies from about seven to nine young, but the number of surviving young in a litter may be considerably less. The young are very tiny at birth, about the size of a honeybee, and embryolike in appearance. Young opossums remain firmly attached to the nipples until they are about 60 days old when they reach the size of a house mouse. When 70–80 days old, they are rat-sized and may leave the pouch for short periods. After leaving the pouch, the young may climb about the mother's body and make short trips to the ground, but they return to the pouch to nurse. They leave the mother when they are about 3 months old. Usually they move less than one-quarter mile from their place of birth (Hartman 1952).

Ticks, lice, fleas, flukes, roundworms, and tapeworms are known to parasitize opossums. In addition, opossums may contract or serve as reservoirs for many protozoan, fungal, viral, and bacterial diseases. Rarely, however, do they contract rabies. Major predators of opossums include dogs, foxes, bobcats, coyotes, great horned owls, and humans.

IMPORTANCE AND/OR MANAGEMENT   Opossums are sometimes used for food, especially in the South. They have traditionally been major furbearers, although their fur has a low monetary value and is most commonly used to trim inexpensive coats. In terms of total harvest in Arkansas, between 1942 and 1984 the opossum ranked first, accounting for 36% of the total fur harvest. In pelt value, however, it ranked twelfth of thirteen furbearers. Regionally, the Ozark Mountains (35%) produced the greatest number of pelts, followed by the Mississippi Delta (32%), the Gulf Coastal Plain (15%), and the Ouachita Mountains (13%); an additional 5% were unassignable (Clark et al. 1985; Peck et al. 1985).

Despite its low order of intelligence, the opossum has an extraordinary vitality which, coupled with its high reproductive rate, favorable habitat, and omnivorous feeding habits, has enabled it to maintain and increase its numbers and extend its range as far north as southern Canada.

The subspecies found in Arkansas is *D. v. virginiana* (Gardner 1973; McManus 1974).

SELECTED REFERENCES
Fitch and Sandidge (1953); Gardner (1973, 1982); Hartman (1952); McManus (1974); Clark et al. (1985); Peck et al. (1985).

Order Insectivora *Insectivores*

The name Insectivora (insect eater) refers to the predominant kind of food eaten by members of this order, but the insectivores are by no means exclusively insect eaters. Shrews and moles feed upon many kinds of small animals, such as earthworms, snails, sowbugs, centipedes, and millipedes. Some species, such as the short-tailed shrew, are large enough to capture and feed upon mice, salamanders, and animals of a similar size. A significant amount of vegetable matter is included in the diet of other species of insectivores.

Members of this order occur in all parts of the world, with the exception of Australia, extreme southern South America, and the polar regions. Representatives included are shrews, moles, hedgehogs, and tenrecs. This order is extremely ancient and includes the earliest placental mammals.

Two families of Insectivora occur in Arkansas: Talpidae (moles) and Soricidae (shrews). Members of the order in Arkansas are small mammals with long, flexible, pointed snouts and very small eyes and ears. Their fur is soft and dense, and most species have prominent scent glands.

WHOLE ANIMALS

1. Front feet more than twice as wide as hind feet, paddlelike; external ear absent; eyes nonfunctional; total length more than 150 mm (5.9 in) (Family Talpidae, moles) .... *Scalopus aquaticus*, Eastern Mole

   Front feet longer than broad, approximately same width as hind feet; external ear present; eyes small but functional; mouselike in appearance; total length less than 150 mm (5.9 in) (Family Soricidae, shrews) 2

2. Ear protrudes conspicuously beyond fur; tail about equal to or more than one-half length of head and body 3

   Ear does not protrude conspicuously beyond fur; tail much less than one-half length of head and body 4

3. Fur reddish brown, underparts paler; tail indistinctly bicolored .... *Sorex longirostris*, Southeastern Shrew

   Fur brownish gray to dark gray (juvenile pelage silvery gray), underparts whitish; tail bicolored .... *Notiosorex crawfordi*, Desert Shrew

4. Fur slate-gray to brownish gray; tail indistinctly bicolored; total length of adult usually more than 88 mm (3.46 in) 5

   Fur olive-brown to gray-brown; tail bicolored; total length of adult less than 88 mm (3.46 in) .... *Cryptotis parva*, Least Shrew

5. Total length more than 100 mm (3.94 in); weight about 15 g (0.5 oz); occurring in northwest Arkansas .... *Blarina hylophaga*, Elliot's Short-tailed Shrew

   Total length less than 100 mm (3.94 in); weight about 9 g (0.32 oz); occurring in southeastern two-thirds of Arkansas .... *Blarina carolinensis*, Southern Short-tailed Shrew

SKULLS

1. Number of teeth 36, unpigmented; upper front (incisor) teeth not visible from top (dorsal) view of skull, slightly recurved; weak zygomatic arches present (Family Talpidae, moles) .... *Scalopus aquaticus*, Eastern Mole

   Number of teeth fewer than 36, tipped with orange, red or brown; upper incisors protrude forward, visible from dorsal view of skull and with an accessory cusp (fig. 1a); zygomatic arches absent (Family Soricidae, shrews) 2

2. Number of teeth in upper jaw 16 or 18; three unicuspid (single cusp) teeth visible from side 3

Number of teeth in upper jaw 20; four or five unicuspid teeth visible from side 4

3. Incisors, unicuspids and first molar (grinding tooth) tipped with orange, remaining molars pure white; three unicuspids on each half of upper jaw, visible from side (fig. 1e); total number of teeth 28; length 17–18 mm (0.67–0.71 in); width less than 9 mm (0.35 in) .... *Notiosorex crawfordi*, Desert Shrew

Teeth tipped with brown; four unicuspids on each half of upper jaw, fourth unicuspid very tiny and not visible from side, often difficult to locate (fig. 1d); total number of teeth 30; length about 16.5 mm (0.65 in); width less than 11 mm (0.43 in) .... *Cryptotis parva*, Least Shrew

4. Four unicuspids visible from side in upper jaw, first two unicuspids of same size, third and fourth of actual size (smaller than the first pair), fifth unicuspid present but very small and not visible from side (fig. 1b); total number of teeth 32, tipped with dark brown; skull robust and strong with a distinct median crest in adults 5

Five unicuspids visible from side in upper jaw, third unicuspid smaller than fourth (fig. 1c); total number of teeth 32, tipped with brown; skull delicate with no median crest; length less than 20 mm (0.8 in); width less than 11 mm (0.43 in) .... *Sorex longirostris*, Southeastern Shrew

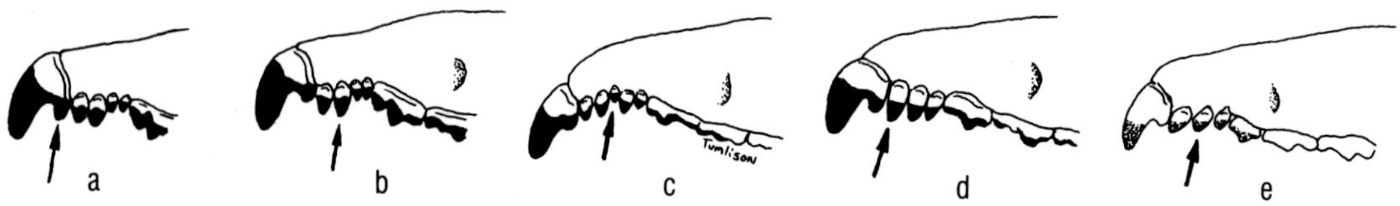

FIGURE 1. Lateral view of upper jaws of shrews: a) accessory cusp on upper incisor of members of family Soricidae; b) *Blarina*; c) *Sorex longirostris*; d) *Cryptotis parva*; e) *Notiosorex crawfordi*.

5. Condylobasal length usually more than 20 mm (0.79 in); occurring in northwest Arkansas .... *Blarina hylophaga*, Elliot's Short-tailed Shrew

Condylobasal length usually less than 20 mm (0.79 in); occurring in southeastern two-thirds of Arkansas .... *Blarina carolinensis*, Southern Short-tailed Shrew

FAMILY SORICIDAE

SHREWS

Members of this family are very small and mouse-like in general appearance. They are mostly inhabitants of moist, shady woodland areas. General characteristics of the family are: Long, pointed nose extending well beyond supporting skull; long, narrow skull lacking zygomatic arches and auditory bullae; first upper incisor in each jaw hook-shaped with a second cusp near its base; three to five simple teeth (unicuspids) behind larger front teeth; upper cheek teeth W-shaped; tibia and fibula usually united; no cecum; fur plush.

From an ecological standpoint, shrews are valuable components of an ecosystem. Their burrowing and foraging activities help work and enrich the soil, and they consume a great many insects and other small invertebrates. In turn, they serve as prey sources for larger animals.

The family is represented in Arkansas by five species.

Sorex longirostris, Southeastern Shrew. *Tom French*

MEASUREMENTS AND DENTAL FORMULA

Total Length:	72–108 mm (2.8–4.25 in)
Tail Length:	25–40 mm (1–1.5 in)
Hind Foot:	9–13 mm (0.4–0.5 in)
Ear:	4.5–6 mm (0.2–0.24 in)
Skull Length:	14–17 mm (0.5–0.7 in)
Weight:	2.1–3.0 g (0.07–0.1 oz)
Dental Formula:	I 3/1, C 1/1, P 3/1, M 3/3 = 32

SOUTHEASTERN SHREW

Sorex longirostris

NAME Sorex is the Latin word for "shrew." The specific name, *longirostris*, is from two Latin words, *longus* and *rostrum*, meaning "long snout."

IDENTIFICATION AND DESCRIPTION The most distinguishing characteristic of this shrew is the long (one-third of total length), indistinctly bicolored tail. As with all shrews, the eyes are tiny and the snout elongated. The pelage is reddish brown or brownish above and ashy gray washed with pale drab brown below. There are 32 teeth tipped with brown, and the third unicuspid is smaller than or the same size as the fourth.

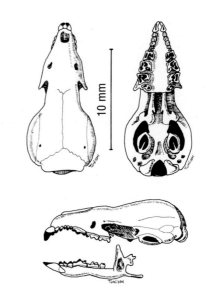

Skull of *Sorex longirostris*

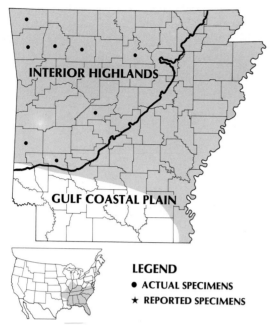

LEGEND
• ACTUAL SPECIMENS
★ REPORTED SPECIMENS

Distribution of the southeastern shrew (*Sorex longirostris*)

ARKANSAS DISTRIBUTION AND ABUNDANCE
This species is presently known from relatively few records. However, because of recent records in eastern Oklahoma (Taylor and Wilkinson 1988) and existing records in southwestern Missouri (Schwartz and Schwartz 1981), it would appear that its distribution covers at least all but the extreme southwestern part of Arkansas. Extensive "pit-trapping" (Garland and Heidt 1989) indicates that the southeastern shrew is uncommon.

LIFE HISTORY   Very little is known about the life history of the southeastern shrew. A number of specimens have been taken in dry upland woods and fields (Brown 1961; Dusi 1959; Tuttle 1964), but most captures have been from marshy or swampy areas and damp woods which may be the preferred habitat types (Jackson 1928).

The reproductive biology of this shrew is poorly known. The young are born in April or May, and there are four to five young per litter. Like other species in the genus, the diet of the southeastern shrew probably consists largely of spiders, insects, earthworms, and other small invertebrates.

The apparent scarcity of this shrew may relate to its behavior and seasonal activity patterns. Evidently it seldom ventures above ground during dry weather and is caught in snap and live traps only infrequently. More often it is captured by hand when stones or logs are overturned, or in "pit" traps set to collect ground-dwelling beetles, other invertebrates, or small vertebrates. Like other shrews, it uses well-worn runways of other small mammals, such as voles and cotton rats, and traps placed in such runways have yielded more captures than randomly placed ones.

IMPORTANCE AND/OR MANAGEMENT   Since this shrew is apparently uncommon in Arkansas, it should be considered a "Species of Special Concern." Its habitat is rather widespread and no special management plans are necessary.

The subspecies which occurs in Arkansas is *S. l. longirostris*.

SELECTED REFERENCES
Brown (1961); Dusi (1959); Garland and Heidt (1989); Graham (1976); Jackson (1928); Schwartz and Schwartz (1981); Sealander (1960, 1977, 1981); Taylor and Wilkinson (1988); Tuttle (1964).

SOUTHERN SHORT-TAILED SHREW
Blarina carolinensis

NAME   *Blarina* is a coined name given by J. E. Gray in 1938. The specific name, *carolinensis*, is a Latinized word meaning "of Carolina."

IDENTIFICATION AND DESCRIPTION   The southern short-tailed shrew has a stocky body with a very short tail (less than one-third of its total length). It has a long, pointed snout, tiny eyes, and very small external ears concealed by fur. Its pelage is velvety, slate-gray to brownish gray above and paler below. The teeth are tipped with dark chestnut brown.

Blarina carolinensis, Southern Short-tailed Shrew.
Charles R. Preston

MEASUREMENTS AND DENTAL FORMULA

Total Length: 75–100 mm (2.9–3.9 in)
Tail Length: 15–22 mm (0.6–0.9 in)
Hind Foot: 9–15 mm (0.4–0.6 in)
Ear: 2–4 mm (0.07–0.25 in)
Skull Length: 16–21 mm (0.6–0.8 in)
Weight: 5–11 g (0.2–0.4 oz)
Dental   I 3/1, C 1/1, P 3/1, M 3/3
   Formula: = 32

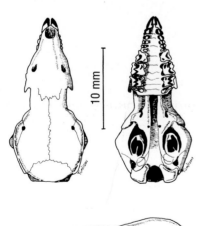

10 mm

Skull of *Blarina carolinensis*

ARKANSAS DISTRIBUTION AND ABUNDANCE
The southern short-tailed shrew is common in the southeastern two-thirds of Arkansas. The exact geographic boundary between *B. carolinensis* and *B. hylophaga* is unknown, and further research is needed to delineate this area.

LIFE HISTORY   The short-tailed shrew is most often found in moist deciduous woods or brushy areas; it is less common in meadows, old fields, or swamplands. This shrew makes runways under leaves or surface litter and in loose soil, but it also uses burrows of rodents and moles. It makes nests of shredded grass, dry leaves, and vegetable fibers. Small nests used for resting are located in the shrew's shallow runway system; larger nests, 15–20 cm (5.9–7.9 in) in diameter, used for breeding, are found under decaying logs, under stumps, or in a deeper burrow system a foot or more beneath the surface.

This shrew is usually solitary, but several individuals sometimes use the same burrow system. Contrary to statements in earlier literature, fighting seldom occurs among shrews if they have enough room (Rood 1958). The short-tailed shrew is almost completely nocturnal and has a poor sense of smell and very poor eyesight. It relies mostly upon its acute hearing and highly developed sense of touch to locate prey, avoid enemies, and find its way through its burrow system.

Blarina is very active and has a voracious appetite. Although many accounts state that it must consume more than its own weight in food per day to survive, recent evidence indicates that *Blarina* usually eats less than one-half its weight in food per day (Buckner 1964; Martinsen 1969). Its food in the wild consists of insects, snails, earthworms, various small invertebrates, and considerable plant material such as nuts and berries. Live snails often are collected and stored in its burrow system for winter use. Short-tailed shrews will attack and kill adult mice in captivity, but there is little documented evidence that they are able to capture many adult mice in the wild. When vole populations are high, this shrew may prey heavily on the young mice. It is aided in subduing

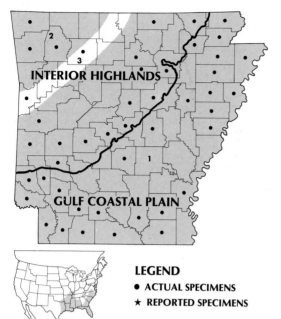

LEGEND
● ACTUAL SPECIMENS
★ REPORTED SPECIMENS

Probable distribution of: 1. southern short-tailed shrew (*Blarina carolinensis*); 2. Elliott's short-tailed shrew (B. hylophaga); and 3. possible contact zone between the two species (modified from George et al. 1982).

large prey by a potent poison secreted by its submaxillary glands. In turn, predators such as weasels, foxes, bobcats, and house cats frequently prey upon short-tailed shrews even though they are reputed to be highly distasteful to most mammalian predators.

The breeding season extends from February through October. Adult females may produce two to three litters per year. The litter size may vary from three to ten young with an average of five to seven per litter. The gestation period is 21–22 days. At birth the young weigh slightly more than 1 gram and double their birth weight in the first week. At the end of 1 month, they leave the nest. Short-tailed shrews are essentially mature at the age of 3 months.

There is some evidence that *Blarina* may undergo marked changes in abundance over a period of years. The amount of moisture in the habitat seems to be quite limiting, and populations may be sharply reduced in number during severe droughts.

IMPORTANCE AND/OR MANAGEMENT   No management or control measures are needed.

Two races apparently occur in Arkansas. The nominate race, *carolinensis*, occurs in the western part of its range, and the race *minima* occurs along the eastern edge of the state (Easterla 1968b). A zone of intergradation may be present in the east central portion of Arkansas (see map). Research is needed to solve the systematic problems of this species.

SELECTED REFERENCES
Blair (1941); Buckner (1964); Easterla (1968b); Garland and Heidt (1989); Genoways and Choate (1972); George et al. (1981, 1982); Graham and Semken (1976); Hamilton (1931); Jones and Glass (1960); Martinsen (1969); Rood (1958).

ELLIOT'S SHORT-TAILED SHREW
Blarina hylophaga

NAME   *Blarina* is a coined name given by J. E. Gray in 1838. The specific name, *hylophaga*, is derived from two Greek words, *hylo*, meaning "woods," and *phag*, meaning "to eat." This indicates the habitat of the shrew is primarily in forested areas.

IDENTIFICATION AND DESCRIPTION   Elliot's short-tailed shrew is larger than the southern short-tailed shrew, but in other respects they are similar.

MEASUREMENTS AND DENTAL FORMULA
Total Length: 103–120 mm (4.0–4.75 in)
Tail Length: 19–25 mm (0.35–1.0 in)
Hind Foot: 12–16 mm (0.5–0.6 in)
Ear: 2–4 mm (0.07–0.25 in)
Skull Length: 20–23 mm (0.78–0.9 in)
Weight: 13–17 g (0.45–0.60 oz)
Dental   I 3/1, C 1/1, P 3/1, M 3/3
  Formula: = 32

ARKANSAS DISTRIBUTION AND ABUNDANCE
Elliot's short-tailed shrew apparently is found in the northwestern one-third of Arkansas. As discussed under *B. carolinensis*, the geo-

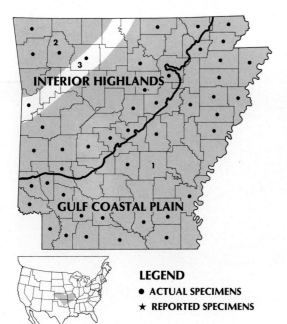

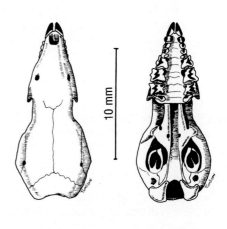

The tail is short, measuring about one-fourth of the total length. It has a long, pointed snout and tiny eyes, and its external ears are concealed by fur and are very small; the ear opening, however, is large. The pelage is nearly uniform brown or grayish brown above and ashy gray below. Teeth are tipped with dark chestnut brown. The least shrew has 30 teeth, which distinguishes it from the other species of shrews in Arkansas.

MEASUREMENTS AND DENTAL FORMULA
Total Length: 60–85 mm (2.4–3.3 in)
Tail Length: 12–20 mm (0.5–0.75 in)
Hind Foot: 9–12 mm (0.35–0.5 in)
Ear: 0.5–2 mm (0.009–0.07 in)
Skull Length: 12–15 mm (0.5–0.6 in)
Weight: 3.3–7.5 g (0.1–0.26 oz)
Dental I 3/1, C 1/1, P 2/1, M 3/3
  Formula: = 30

LEGEND
● ACTUAL SPECIMENS
★ REPORTED SPECIMENS

Probable distribution in Arkansas of: 1. southern short-tailed shrew, (*Blarina carolinensis*); 2. Elliot's short-tailed shrew (*B. hylophaga*); and 3. possible contact zone between the two species (modified from George et al. 1982).

graphic boundary between these two species is not clearly known.

LIFE HISTORY See discussion under *B. carolinensis*.

IMPORTANCE AND/OR MANAGEMENT No management or control measures are needed.

SELECTED REFERENCES
George et al. (1981, 1982)

Skull of *Cryptotis parva*

Least Shrew

Cryptotis parva

NAME *Cryptotis* is from the Greek words *kryptos*, meaning "hidden," and *otos*, meaning "ear." The specific name, *parva*, is Latin for "small," emphasizing the small size of the shrew.

IDENTIFICATION AND DESCRIPTION The least shrew is similar to *Blarina* but much smaller.

ARKANSAS DISTRIBUTION AND ABUNDANCE
The least shrew is common statewide. It is most often found in grasslands and brushy areas.

Cryptotis parva, Least Shrew. *Phil A. Dotson*

LIFE HISTORY Least shrews occur in grass-lands or old fields and along overgrown fence-rows. They also may be found in brushy or marshy areas but seldom, if ever, inhabit mature forests. These shrews sometimes make their own runways but usually use those of cotton rats, voles, or other rodents. The least shrew makes a globular nest about 75–125 mm (2.95–4.9 in) in diameter, consisting mainly of dried grass and leaves and lined with partially shredded grass and leaves. The nest is located somewhere in its tunnel system, usually under a rock, log, or stump. Special places are used for defecation, and the nest is never fouled with feces.

In captivity, *Cryptotis* is quite gregarious, and in the wild they apparently sleep together and cooperate to some degree in constructing tunnels and capturing food. McCarley (1959) reported an unusual instance of 31 adult or nearly adult *Cryptotis* sharing a single nest. A large accumulation of feces near the nest indi-cated that it had been occupied for some time. Others have reported as many as 12 shrews in one nest. Such aggregations usually have been associated with cold weather, suggesting that they may serve as a form of social temperature regulation which has been noted in several spe-cies of rodents.

The least shrew is active at all hours but is most active at night. *Cryptotis* has poor eye-sight and relies chiefly upon smell and well-developed senses of touch and hearing for lo-cating prey, avoiding enemies, and guiding itself through its burrow system.

The feeding habits of *Cryptotis* probably differ little from those of *Blarina* except that smaller prey items are selected. Such items as small in-sects, spiders, sow bugs, and snails are eaten along with some vegetable matter. It is a pro-digious eater, and the food intake of this shrew per unit body weight is very high. Barrett (1969) observed that a captive *Cryptotis* regularly ate

Distribution of the least shrew (*Cryptotis parva*)

shrews with conventional snap or live traps usually is poor, and pit traps may provide a better index of their true abundance. Some studies have suggested that irruptive population increases may occur in some years.

Like other shrews, the least shrew has a very strong odor, which has been described as resembling decaying garlic. This odor may provide some protection from mammalian predators, but it is evidently not offensive to owls, other avian predators, and possibly snakes as well.

Evidence that this shrew secretes a poison in its saliva is inconclusive, but earthworms and other prey have been reported to have been paralyzed by its bite.

IMPORTANCE AND/OR MANAGEMENT   No management or control measures are necessary.

The subspecies in Arkansas is *C. p. parva*.

SELECTED REFERENCES
Barrett (1969); Conaway (1958); Garland and Heidt (1989); Hamilton (1944); McCarley (1959); Mock (1982); Moore (1944); Walker et al. (1968); Whitaker (1974).

more than its own weight per day throughout a three week period.

The breeding season extends from February until November at this latitude. Usually there are four to six young in a litter, but the number may range from two to nine. Walker et al. (1968) present evidence that the gestation period is 15 days or less, whereas Conaway (1958) and Mock (1982) found it to be from 21 to 23 days. The shorter gestation period may be accounted for by post-partum rather than post-lactation pregnancy. At birth, the young weigh about 0.3 g (0.01 oz) and double their birth weight in 3 or 4 days. They continue to grow rapidly and are weaned at about three weeks of age when they resemble adults except for their size and sleeker juvenile pelage. Adult size is reached when they are about 30 to 40 days of age. Mock (1982) found that the maximum survival time of least shrews in captivity was 889 days.

Little is known about the population dynamics of this shrew. In some years they are very numerous, as indicated by a high frequency of skeletal remains in barn owl pellets or, more frequently, in traps. Success in trapping least

Desert Shrew

Notiosorex crawfordi

NAME   *Notiosorex* is derived from the Greek word *notio*, meaning "southern," and the Latin word *sorex*, meaning "shrew." The specific name, *crawfordi*, was coined by E. Coues in 1877.

IDENTIFICATION AND DESCRIPTION   The desert shrew is small with a slender body, protruding ears, tiny eyes, and a long, pointed snout. Its tail is short (less than one-third of total length), indistinctly bicolored, and well haired with a slightly penciled tip. The pelage is silver-gray to brownish gray above and paler gray washed

Notiosorex crawfordi, Desert Shrew.
Laurence M. Hardy

Dental   I 3/1, C 1/1, P 1/1, M 3/3
Formula: = 28

ARKANSAS DISTRIBUTION AND ABUNDANCE
The desert shrew is probably quite rare in Arkansas. It has been recorded only from Natural Dam in Crawford County, from 8.05 km (5 mi) south of West Fork in Washington County, and, more recently, Steward et al. (1988) found two skulls of these shrews in barn owl pellets collected from Hempstead County. The most northwesterly limits of the species range is in Arkansas (Preston and Sealander 1969, Sealander 1952).

with buff below. It has 28 teeth; the incisors, unicuspids, and first molar tooth on each side of the jaw are lightly tipped with orange. The conspicuous ears and 28 teeth distinguish this species from the other shrews in Arkansas.

MEASUREMENTS AND DENTAL FORMULA
Total Length: 77–95 mm (3.0–3.7 in)
Tail Length: 24–32 mm (0.9–1.25 in)
Hind Foot: 9–12 mm (0.35–0.5 in)
Ear: 7–9 mm (0.3–0.35 in)
Weight: 3–6 g (0.1–0.2 oz)

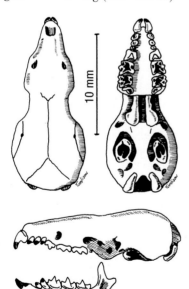

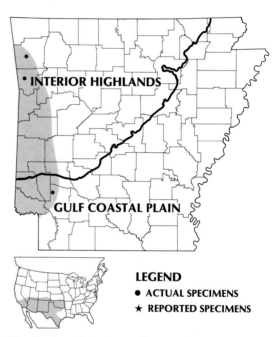

LEGEND
● ACTUAL SPECIMENS
★ REPORTED SPECIMENS

Distribution of the desert shrew (Notiosorex crawfordi)

Skull of Notiosorex crawfordi

LIFE HISTORY Hoffmeister and Goodpaster (1962) have made the most detailed observations on captive Notiosorex, and Armstrong and Jones (1972) compiled an extensive literature survey of all aspects of biology of this shrew. Most of the life history information on the desert shrew that follows is based on these accounts.

Over their range, desert shrews are found in

a variety of dry habitats such as desert sagebrush, mesquite-cactus, yucca-cactus, agave-grassland, and the lower edge of pinon-juniper. Although the macroclimate in which this shrew occurs is usually very arid, the microclimate which it occupies is generally mesic.

Desert shrews live in woodrat nests, in various kinds of litter, beneath agave plants, and even inside beehives. Because they occasionally build nests in beehives and feed on the larvae, both *Notiosorex* and *Cryptotis* have been referred to as bee shrews. The nest of *Notiosorex* is made of fine-textured plant fibers, fine grass, tightly packed leaves, the hairlike inner bark of cottonwood trees, and other materials. Like *Cryptotis*, it is scrupulously clean, and deposits of feces generally are found several feet away from the nest.

Field and laboratory observations indicate that these shrews are quite sociable and less aggressive than other species of shrews. Most observations seem to indicate that *Notiosorex* normally does not burrow like other shrews. Apparently desert shrews see and hear quite well but rely mainly on smell and touch in searching for food. In captivity they accept a wide variety of foods, but in the field they probably subsist largely on larval and adult insects, sow bugs, and other small invertebrates. Individuals have been maintained in captivity for well over a year on a diet of mealworms and crickets.

Desert shrews are most active at night and spend much of the day sleeping. If hungry they will actively forage for food during the day. There is some indication that they may enter into a state of torpor during daytime sleep, which may enable them to conserve energy. Periods of food deprivation ranging from 24 to 36 hours are survived without ill effects.

The breeding season apparently extends from mid-April to mid-November over its range; peak reproduction evidently occurs in early and late summer. The gestation period is not definitely known. Usually there are from three to five young in a litter. The young are blind and hairless at birth, but development is rapid. They are almost fully furred by day 11; at 40 days of age, they are about 90% grown, and they reach adult size at an estimated 50–90 days.

IMPORTANCE AND/OR MANAGEMENT   The exact status of this shrew is unknown. From the locality records and the extreme limits of its geographical range, we would suspect that it is quite rare in Arkansas. On the other hand, it may very well live in woodrat nests located in deep crevices at the base of overhanging limestone escarpments. If this is the case, the desert shrew may be much more common than suspected. Whichever is the case, because of its habits and extensive potential habitat, little has to be done for its management or protection.

SELECTED REFERENCES
Armstrong and Jones (1972); Clark (1953); Coulombe and Banta (1964); Garland and Heidt (1989); Hibbard and Taylor (1960); Hoffmeister and Goodpaster (1962); Merriam (1895); Preston and Sealander (1969); Sealander (1952); Steward et al. (1988).

FAMILY TALPIDAE

MOLES

Members of this family are small, heavy-bodied mammals adapted for living underground. General characteristics of the family are: Neck very short; eyes minute, often concealed by fur; external ears absent; nostrils positioned on the upperside or laterally (sometimes terminal) on snout; front feet greatly enlarged with palm held facing outward and not downward; front legs shortened; enlarged shoulder girdle; tibia and fibula united; long, slender skull with complete zygomatic arches; dense, velvety fur.

The family is represented in Arkansas by one species.

Eastern Mole

Scalopus aquaticus

NAME *Scalopus* is derived by combining the two Greek words *skalops*, meaning "to dig," and *pous*, meaning "foot." The specific name, *aquaticus*, is from the same Latin word, meaning "water dweller." This derivation is misleading, but it probably refers to the mole's webbed feet.

IDENTIFICATION AND DESCRIPTION The eastern mole has a thick body with a short, nearly naked tail. It has a long, pointed snout with nostrils opening upward, no external ears, and tiny eyes covered with a thin membrane (eyelids are fused). The front feet are as broad as they are long, with long, stout claws. The pelage is velvety and silvery-gray to brownish gray or clove brown above; the underparts are usually of the same color as the upperparts, but sometimes are faintly washed with orange or with occasional white or orange patches. The

eastern mole undergoes spring and autumn molts.

MEASUREMENTS AND DENTAL FORMULA
Total Length: 130–185 mm (5.1–7.25 in)
Tail Length: 20–35 mm (0.75–1.4 in)
Hind Foot: 18–23 mm (0.7–0.9 in)
Skull Length: 28–38 mm (1.1–1.5 in)
Weight: 50–75 g (1.75–2.6 oz)
Dental Formula: I 3/2, C 1/0, P 3/3, M 3/3 = 36

ARKANSAS DISTRIBUTION AND ABUNDANCE
The eastern mole is found statewide. It is most common in moist, pliable soils.

LIFE HISTORY The eastern mole occurs in pastures, cultivated fields, gardens, lawns, and thin woods. It prefers moist sandy or light loamy soils and tends to avoid dry sands, rocky soils, and heavy clays. Most of the mole's life is spent underground, and it seldom ventures above

Scalopus aquaticus, Eastern Mole. *Charles R. Preston*

ground. The mole digs two types of burrows: shallow surface runs and deep runs. The surface runs, marked by ridges of earth, are temporary and associated with foraging activities; they are seldom used more than a few times. Surface runs are dug at a rate of 3 to 6 m (10–20 ft) per hour. The deep runs, dug 15–50 cm (5.9–19.7 in) below the surface, are permanent burrows used for protection and rearing of young and for foraging in dry or cold weather.

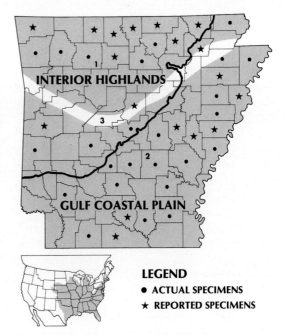

Distribution of the eastern mole (*Scalopus aquaticus*)

Probable distribution in Arkansas of: 1. *S.a. machrinoides*; 2. *S.a. aereus*; and 3. intergradation zone between *machrinoides* and *aereus*.

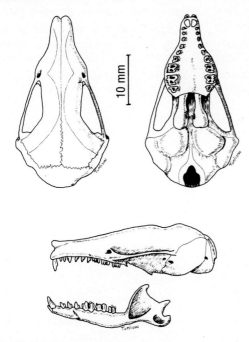

Skull of *Scalopus aquaticus*

The nest made of dry grass, rootlets, and leaves is located in the burrow system about 30 cm (11.8 in) below the surface. It is built in a chamber about 12–20 cm (4.7–7.9 in) in diameter and is usually placed beneath a log, stump, or rock, or near the base of a tree trunk, often at the end of a deep run. A single nest site is used in winter, but moles may use more than one nest in summer. Special places for sanitation are found in the deeper tunnels.

The eastern mole feeds mainly on small invertebrates such as insects and their larvae, earthworms, snails, slugs, sow bugs, centipedes, and millipedes. A small amount of plant material also is included in its diet.

Moles are comparatively long-lived (3–4 years) and relatively free from disease, parasites, and predation. Little information is available concerning population dynamics of moles; two to three moles per acre is sometimes considered to be a relatively high population. The home range varies from about 0.2 to 1.8 ha (0.5–4.5 acres); males generally range over a much larger area than females.

The breeding season extends from February through April and into early May. In Arkansas, the peak of the breeding season is in mid-February. *Scalopus* breeds at the age of one year and produces only one litter of two to five young per year. The average litter size is four. The gestation period generally is considered to be 42–45 days, although Conaway (1959) suggests that it may be about four weeks or less. The young are naked and blind at birth and resemble adults in all but size. They have a covering of fine, velvety fur by 10–11 days of age and are more than half grown at five weeks of age. Young moles leave the nest and are able to care for themselves when about one month old; they become full grown in about three months.

Moles are active during all hours of the day or night and in all seasons of the year. Activity peaks usually occur before sunrise and after sunset. *Scalopus* tends to be solitary except during the breeding season, but several individuals sometimes share the same burrow system. During the breeding season, they often travel overland in search of mates. Individuals captured by owls, hawks, and cats, which do not dig for their prey, provide evidence for such surface activity.

IMPORTANCE AND/OR MANAGEMENT Moles are frequently nuisances in gardens and lawns. They sometimes do considerable damage to golf greens also, but as far as net economic worth is concerned, they are one of our most valuable mammals. The good they do in destroying insects and insect larvae in the soil and in opening up soil for penetration of air and moisture far outweighs the small amount of damage they do. Control measures include placing traps in their runs. Sometimes when the mole is working a surface run, it can be dug up with a spade.

Two races of moles are recognized in Arkansas. The race *machrinoides* occurs in the northern tier of counties and apparently intergrades with the race *aereus*, which is distributed over nearly two-thirds of the southern portion of the state. The race *aereus* is somewhat smaller but differs very little in general coloration from *machrinoides* (Hall 1981).

SELECTED REFERENCES
Arlton (1936); Conaway (1959); Hall (1981); Jackson (1915); Yates and Schmidly (1975); Yates and Pedersen (1982).

Order Chiroptera   *Bats*

Bats (from the Middle English word *bakke*, meaning "to flutter") are the only mammals capable of true flight. The arm bones, particularly the fingers, are greatly elongated to support a double-layered extension of skin, which forms the flight membrane, or plagiopatagium. The wing also connects with the uropatagium (interfemoral membrane), which connects the hind legs and tail. The thumb of the front foot is short and has a claw. The remaining fingers on the forearm lack claws. The hind limbs are small with backward directed knees, and the toes are clawed. The eyes of bats are very small but are functional; in fact, many bats have good eyesight. Most species of bats have very prominent ears and a highly developed sense of hearing. Bats emit high frequency sounds and, by receiving the echoes, are able to locate and capture prey and navigate in dark caves or at night.

Most types of bats are active mainly at twilight, during the night, or in early morning before sunrise. Often it is possible for an experienced observer to identify certain species by their characteristic flight patterns and the height at which they usually fly.

Bats are often misunderstood. This may be, in part, because they have long been associated with superstitions and folklore, such as the Dracula legends. In fact, however, bats do a great deal of good, because they consume large numbers of insects annually. For example, a colony of gray bats that live near Batesville in Independence County are estimated to consume over 35,560 kg (35 tons) of insects yearly (Harvey 1986). Bat droppings, or guano, has long been used as fertilizer, is used in cosmetics, and was used during the Civil War in the making of gunpowder. Furthermore, bats are one of the few mammals that people can actually observe: their foraging activities can be witnessed around lights and over water.

Bats, like all mammals, may carry rabies. In Arkansas, bat rabies was not reported until 1961. During the 1980s, there have been an average of 16 reported cases each year (Heidt et al. 1987). Thus, while the reported incidence of rabies is low, persons should not handle bats that may appear docile or sick.

On occasion bats may inhabit houses and

become a nuisance. One may discourage bats from roosting by sprinkling moth crystals (naphthalene) around the roosting site. If openings to a roost are found, they can be closed after the bats have exited for the evening. The use of poisons and insecticides should be discouraged because other animals may be affected.

Many species of vespertilionid bats are very similar in appearance and difficult to identify.

When in doubt, consult an authority for proper identification, especially when it seems probable that the bat may be one of the endangered species.

The species accounts included under this order of mammals rely heavily upon the excellent publication *Bats of America* (Barbour and Davis 1969). There are 16 species of bats found in Arkansas.

KEY TO BATS

WHOLE ANIMALS

1. Tail (about one-half) extending beyond the tail (interfemoral) membrane, (Family Molossidae, molossid bats) . . . . *Tadarida brasiliensis*, Brazilian Free-tailed Bat.

    Tail extending only slightly or not at all beyond the interfemoral membrane (Family Vespertilionidae, vespertilionid bats) 2

2. Ears very large, more than 25 mm (1 in) long, and leaf-like (curled like a ram's horn when resting or torpid); a prominent lump on each side of muzzle; fur dark at base; dorsal color gray to brown or blackish 3

    Ears shorter, usually less than 20 mm (0.8 in) long; no lumps on muzzle 4

3. Belly fur white; long hairs on foot extend well beyond toes; gray or dark brown above; fur distinctly bicolored, blackish basally, contrasting sharply with tips. . . . . *Plecotus rafinesquii*, Rafinesque's Big-eared Bat

    Belly fur tan to brown; hairs on foot not extending beyond toes; pale brown to nearly black above; fur not distinctly bicolored, basal part of hair not contrasting sharply with tip. . . . . *Plecotus townsendii*, Townsend's Big-eared Bat

4. Upper surface of interfemoral membrane well furred to tip of tail, naked below; underside of wing furred to wrist 5

    Upper surface of interfemoral membrane naked except for scattered hairs, or furred only on extreme base or on basal one-third or one-fourth 8

5. Ears conspicuously black-edged, with patches
   of yellowish hair scattered inside them; general
   coloration yellowish gray to grizzled brown,
   strongly frosted with white, throat yellow; total
   length more than 120 mm (4.7 in) .... *Lasiurus cinereus*, Hoary Bat

   Ears not conspicuously black-edged, bare, or
   at most scant-haired inside 6

6. Color red-orange or yellowish brown, hairs
   tipped with white.. *Lasiurus borealis*, Red Bat

   Color rich mahogany-brown, not red-orange 7

7. Color rich mahogany-brown, not yellowish
   except about face, only slightly frosted white.................. *Lasiurus seminolus*, Seminole Bat

   Color pale yellowish-brown to red .... *Lasiurus borealis*, Red Bat

8. Color black, sometimes dark reddish brown,
   with conspicuously silver-tipped fur................. *Lasionycteris noctivagans*, Silver-haired Bat

   Color not black; fur not silver-tipped.. 9

9. Size large, total length usually more than
   100 mm (3.93 in); forearm usually more than
   45 mm (1.8 in) long; color tan to dark brown .... *Eptesicus fuscus*, Big Brown Bat

   Size medium to small, total length usually less
   than 100 mm (3.93 in); forearm usually less
   than 45 mm (1.8 in) long 10

10. Fur on back uniform in color from base to tips;
    color dull brown to mouse gray; wing mem-
    brane attached to foot at ankle; forearm usually
    more than 40 mm (1.6 in) long................................. *Myotis grisescens*, Gray Bat

    Fur on back with hairs darkened at bases;
    wing not attached at ankle; forearm usually
    less than 40 mm (1.6 in) long 11

11. Fur on back distinctly tricolored, dark at base
    and tip but lighter in the middle; back grizzled
    yellow, underneath yellowish brown; interfem-
    oral membrane sparsely furred on anterior one-
    fourth or one-third of upper surface; wing
    membranes black, reddish brown around
    joints .... *Pipistrellus subflavus*, Eastern Pipistrelle

    Fur on back not distinctly tricolored; inter-
    femoral membrane naked or furred at extreme
    base only 12

12. Tragus rounded, blunt, and curved inward,
    less than 4 mm (0.16 in) long (fig. 2a); ears
    thick and leathery, almost naked, rounded at
    tips; black ears and wing membranes; color
    dark brown above, yellowish brown below; fur
    blackish at base.. *Nycticeius humeralis*, Evening Bat

FIGURE 2.   Ear with short, blunt tragus (a) and long, pointed tragus (b).

Tragus slender, straight and pointed, more
than 4 mm (0.16 in) long (fig. 2b); ears not
thick and leathery, pointed or rounded at tips. 13

13. Ear when gently laid forward extends about
4 mm (0.16 in) beyond tip of muzzle; ear 17–19
mm (6.7–7.5 in) long. . . . . *Myotis keenii*, Keen's Myotis

Ear when gently laid forward extends less than
2 mm (0.08 in) beyond tip of muzzle; ear less
than 16 mm (6.3 in) long 14

14. Calcar with a small but usually definite keel
(fig. 3a); free edge of interfemoral membrane
without fringe of stiff hairs. 15

FIGURE 3.   Calcar with keel (a) and without keel (b).

Calcar long, not keeled (fig. 3b); free edge of
interfemoral membrane with fringe of stiff
hairs, especially on border near tail 16

15. Color dark gray, sometimes brownish; dorsal
fur dull, not glossy, fur sometimes appears tricolored but not obviously so; wing membranes
dark brown, attached at base of toes; foot about
9 mm (0.35 in) long. . . . . *Myotis sodalis*, Indiana Myotis

Color usually brown, varying from light tan to
dark brown; dorsal fur glossy; black ears and
black facial mask; membranes dark brown, al-
most black; foot about 8 mm (0.31 in) long . . . . *Myotis leibii*, Small-footed Myotis

16. Ear with pointed tips; fur on back with a conspicuous sheen; upperparts pale tan through
reddish brown to dark brown; hairs on belly
buff-tipped; foot about 10 mm (0.39 in) long . . . . *Myotis lucifugus*, Little Brown Myotis

Ears with blunt or rounded tips; fur on back dense, woolly, dull, not glossy; upperparts yellowish brown to gray; hairs on belly white-tipped; foot about 10–11 mm (0.39–0.43 in) long .... *Myotis austroriparius*, Southeastern Myotis

SKULLS

1. Lower incisors bifid (fig. 4a); anterior border of palate with narrow posteriorly widening notch, upper incisors pointing in (fig. 5a) (Family Molossidae, molossid bats)...................... *Tadarida brasiliensis*, Brazilian Free-tailed Bat

    Lower incisors trifid (fig. 4b); anterior border of palate with square or round indentation, not long and narrow, upper incisors not pointing inward (fig. 5b) 2

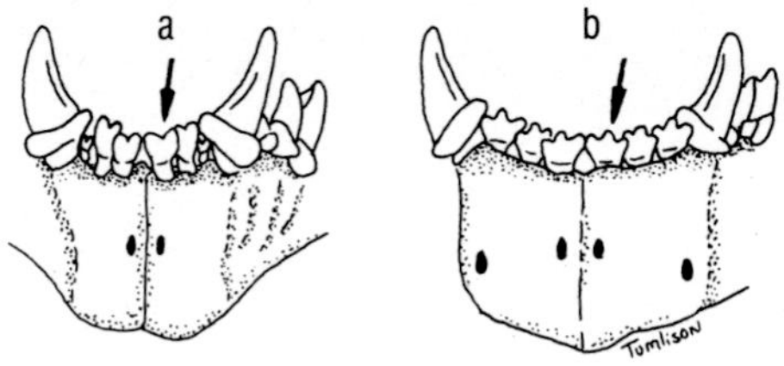

FIGURE 4.   Bifid lower incisor (a) and trifid lower incisor (b).

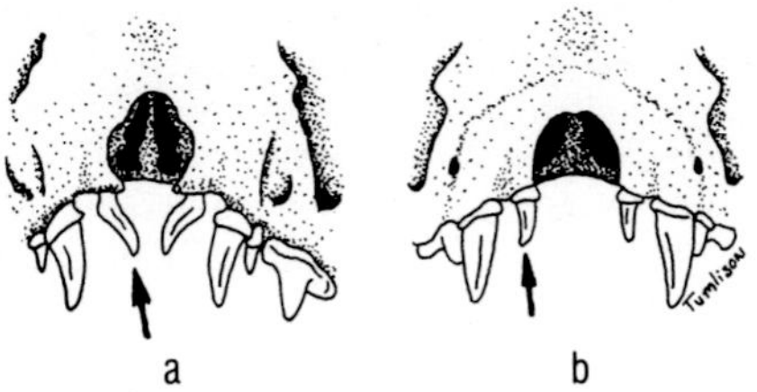

FIGURE 5.   Upper incisors pointing inward (a) and not pointing inward (b).

2. One front tooth (incisor) in each side of upper jaw... 3

    Two incisors in each side of upper jaw 6

3. One premolar in each side of upper jaw, not tiny; total number of teeth 30; length about 14.5 mm (0.57 in)..................................... *Nycticeius humeralis*, Evening Bat

    Two premolars in each side of upper jaw, first premolar tiny and located at base of inner surface of canine; total number of teeth 32 4

4. Length more than 15.5 mm (0.61 in); breadth of braincase more than 8.5 mm (0.34 in)........................ *Lasiurus cinereus*, Hoary Bat

    Length less than 15.5 mm (0.61 in); breadth of braincase less than 8.5 mm (0.34 in) 5

5. A prominent lacrimal shelf present in the area of the first molars (fig. 6a) .... *Lasiurus borealis*, Red Bat

    Shelf on lacrimal not prominent (fig. 6b) .... *Lasiurus seminolus*, Seminole Bat

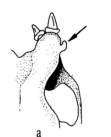

FIGURE 6.   Prominent lacrimal shelf of *Lasiurus borealis* (a) and absence of lacrimal shelf of *L. seminolus* (b).

6. One premolar in each side of upper jaw; length
    19–20 mm (0.74–0.79 in); total number of
    teeth 32 . . . . *Eptesicus fuscus*, Big Brown Bat

    Two or three premolars in each side of upper
    jaw; length less than 17 mm (0.67 in); total
    number of teeth more than 32 7

7. Cheek teeth fewer than six on each side of
    upper and lower jaw; two or three premolars on
    each side of lower jaw; total number of teeth
    36 or less 8

    Cheek teeth six on each side of upper and
    lower jaw; three premolars on each side of
    lower jaw; total number of teeth 38 11

8. Two premolars on each side of lower jaw; total
    number of teeth 34; length less than 15 mm
    (0.59 in), usually about 12 mm (0.47 in) . . . . *Pipistrellus subflavus*, Eastern Pipistrelle

    Three premolars in each side of lower jaw;
    total number of teeth 36. 9

9. Rostrum (snout) broad and distinctly concave
    on each side dorsally (fig. 7) . . . . *Lasionycteris noctivagans*, Silver-haired Bat

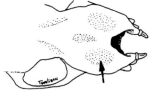

FIGURE 7.   Dorsal view of skull of *Lasionycteris noctivagans* showing
concave areas of rostrum.

    Rostrum narrow and convex on each side 10

10. First upper incisor bifid (fig. 8b); median post-
    palatal process triangular (fig. 9a) . . . . *Plecotus rafinesquii*, Rafinesque's Big-eared Bat

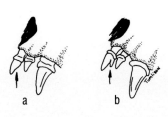

FIGURE 8. Unicuspid upper incisor of *Plecotus townsendii* (a) and bifid upper incisor of *P. rafinesquii* (b).

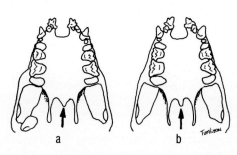

FIGURE 9. Triangular median postpalatal process of *P. rafinesquii* (a) and more rounded styliform process of *P. townsendii* (b).

First upper incisor unicuspid (fig. 8a); median postpalatal process more rounded and styliform (fig. 9b) . . . . *Plecotus townsendii*, Townsend's Big-eared Bat

11. Least width of interorbital constriction less than 4 mm (0.16 in); median (sagittal) crest absent or not clearly defined 12

Least width of interorbital constriction 4 mm (0.16 in) or more; median crest present or absent 13

12. Skull very flat in profile; braincase squarish; interorbital width 3.3 mm (0.13 in) or less; width of braincase 6.5 mm (0.26 in) or less; length of cheek tooth row 5.4 mm (0.21 in) or less. . . . . *Myotis leibii*, Small-footed Myotis

Skull not noticeably flat in profile, evident forehead sloping upward from rostrum; braincase more rounded; interorbital width more than 3.3 mm (0.13 in); width of braincase more than 6.5 mm (0.26 in); length of cheek tooth row more than 5.4 mm (0.21 in) . . . . *Myotis keenii*, Keen's Myotis

(Note: Skulls of the above two species are very difficult to distinguish from each other and from M. lucifugus *below; whenever possible, use features other than skull characters to insure positive identification.)*

13. Median crest absent; length 14–15 mm (0.55– 0.59 in). . . . . *Myotis lucifugus*, Little Brown Myotis

Median crest present and clearly defined 14

14. Length 15.5 mm (0.61 in) or more; median crest conspicuous . . . . *Myotis grisescens*, Gray Myotis

Length less than 15.5 mm (0.61 in); median crest present but not conspicuous 15

15. Skull with high profile, forehead rising abruptly
from rostrum; width of braincase more than 7.2
mm (0.28 in); braincase almost spherical when
viewed from side. . . . . *Myotis austroriparius*, Southeastern Myotis

Skull profile low, forehead rising gradually
from rostrum; width of braincase less than 7.2
mm (0.28 in); braincase not evidently spheri-
cal when viewed from side . . . . *Myotis sodalis*, Indiana Myotis

FAMILY VESPERTILIONIDAE

VESPERTILIONID BATS

All but one species of bat found in Arkansas belong to this family. General characteristics of the family are: Muzzle never with leaflike outgrowths; eyes very small; ears separate and with well-developed tragi; only two phalanges in third finger; interfemoral membrane wide and attached to tail nearly to its tip. This family is represented in Arkansas by 15 species.

LITTLE BROWN MYOTIS

Myotis lucifugus

NAME *Myotis* is from the Greek words, *mys*, meaning "mouse," and *ous*, meaning "ear," thus meaning "mouse ear." The specific name, *lucifugus*, is from the Latin words, *lux*, meaning "light" and *fugio*, meaning "to flee," which refers to the nocturnal habits of the bat.

IDENTIFICATION AND DESCRIPTION The little brown bat is medium-sized with a hairy face. Its ears are narrow and pointed with slender pointed tragi. When laid forward, the ears do not extend beyond the muzzle. The wings and tail membrane are dark brown, nearly black, and almost hairless. Hairs on the toes extend beyond the tips of the claws. Pelage is pale tan through olive-brown to dark brown above, grayish tinged with buff below; hairs on the back have dark bases and burnished tips, giving a metallic or bronzy sheen to the pelage. The little brown myotis is very similar to the south-

eastern myotis but has smooth, glossy fur rather than woolly fur.

MEASUREMENTS AND DENTAL FORMULA
Total Length:	75–105 mm (3–4.1 in)
Tail Length:	30–48 mm (1.2–1.9 in)
Hind Foot:	8–11 mm (0.3–0.4 in)
Ear:	13–16 mm (0.5–0.62 in)
Forearm:	34–41 mm (1.3–1.6 in)
Wingspread:	222–272 mm (8.75–10.7 in)
Skull Length:	15 mm (0.6 in)
Weight:	5–12 g (0.18–0.42 oz)
Dental Formula:	I 2/3, C 1/1, P 3/3, M 3/3 = 38

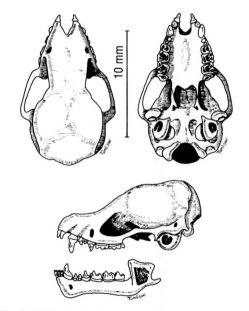

Skull of *Myotis lucifugus*

Myotis lucifugus, Little Brown Myotis. *Roger W. Barbour*

ARKANSAS DISTRIBUTION AND ABUNDANCE
This species is very common in northern states, but it is not common in Arkansas. It occurs mainly in the cave regions of the Interior Highlands from Sevier County northeastward to Randolph County. It may be scattered statewide during the summer months.

LIFE HISTORY   The little brown myotis hibernates in caves or abandoned mines during winter, and in summer it inhabits hot attics, church steeples, hollow trees, or other sheltered spots. In the eastern part of its range, where it has been studied more intensively, this bat follows regular migration routes or "flyways" from its more northern summer range to cave regions in eastern or southern states. These migration routes often cover distances from 80 to 320 km (50–200 mi). In the spring, after emergence from hibernation, these bats disperse along the same routes northward. Hibernation is entered

into in late September or early October. Males enter hibernation caves first, followed by older females and then by young born that year. Females entering hibernation are heavier than males due to greater fat storage. Males select colder regions of caves in which to hibernate and, by avoiding higher temperatures, tend to have a lower annual metabolism. The bats emerge from hibernation in the spring. Females disperse to maternity colonies first, in late April or early May, depending upon the latitude, followed by males a week or so later.

The bats emerge to feed upon a variety of insects shortly after sunset. Foraging usually occurs close to the surface of a body of water. If water is not nearby, feeding may take place at 3–6 m (10–20 ft) above ground among trees and over lawns and pastures. Their prey is located by echolocation and captured on the wing. Small insects may be eaten in flight, while larger insects are held in the mouth until

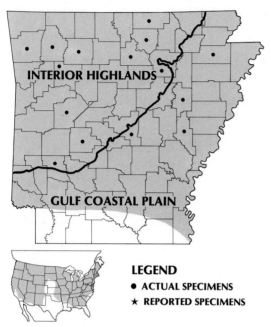

Distribution of the little brown myotis (*Myotis luci-fugus*)

the bat can alight and consume them. At dawn the bats return to roost.

Mating takes place in autumn. Sporadic mating also may take place during short periods of arousal from hibernation. Sperm are stored in the reproductive tract of the female, and delayed fertilization occurs in April and May when the females emerge from hibernation. Young are born from May to July depending upon the geographic location (later in the north) of the breeding colony. Maternity colonies are established in hot attics or other warm retreats where growth of the young is rapid. Until the young are weaned, very few males are present in the nursery colonies. In late summer males begin appearing in greater numbers. Breeding females produce only a single young per year although twins have occasionally been recorded. The young are able to fly at about 3 weeks of age, before they are weaned. At 1 month of age, when they have reached adult weight, they fly outdoors and learn to forage for themselves.

The young enter hibernation with less fat than the adults and remain outside the caves

longer before going into hibernation. Mortality is highest among individuals in this age group since their accumulated fat stores often may be insufficient to sustain them through the lengthy period of hibernation.

The homing ability of the little brown myotis is well established. Experimental data indicate that most bats return to the same cave to hibernate in successive winters, but this tendency is relatively weak with respect to summer colonies.

The life span of the little brown myotis is remarkably long for such a small mammal. One was recaptured 24 years after it was tagged (Griffin and Hitchcock 1965), and several individuals have been known to reach the age of 19–20 years. Survival to the age of 8–10 years is commonplace.

Predators of this bat include mink, raccoons, cats, and rat snakes. Humans are responsible for the extermination of many of these bats because the odor of a colony may become very obnoxious, and there is an understandable fear that rabies may be transmitted from the bats to the human occupants of the residences the bats are roosting in.

IMPORTANCE AND/OR MANAGEMENT   See introduction to the order.

The subspecies *M. l. lucifugus* occurs in Arkansas.

SELECTED REFERENCES
Griffin and Hitchcock (1965).

Southeastern Myotis

Myotis austroriparius

NAME   *Myotis* is from the Greek words, *mys*, meaning "mouse," and *ous*, meaning "ear," thus meaning "mouse ear." The specific name, *austroriparius*, is from two Latin words, *austro*, meaning "southern," and *riparius*, which means "frequenting the banks of streams."

IDENTIFICATION AND DESCRIPTION   The southeastern myotis is medium-sized with blunt-

Myotis austroriparius, Southeastern Myotis. *David Saugey*

tipped or rounded ears and slender, pointed tragi. Its wing and tail membranes are grayish black. Hairs on the toes extend well beyond the tips of the claws, and the calcar is not keeled. The nose of live individuals is flesh colored. The fur has a thick woolly appearance with little contrast between the base and tips of hairs on the dorsum. Pelage is dull yellowish or grayish brown above, tan to grayish white below, and the hairs on the belly are long and white-tipped. This species is most easily mistaken for the little brown myotis, but the fur of the southeastern myotis is dense and woolly rather than smooth and glossy.

MEASUREMENTS AND DENTAL FORMULA

Total Length:	80–100 mm (3.2–4 in)
Tail Length:	33–44 mm (1.3–1.7 in)
Hind Foot:	10–13 mm (0.4–0.5 in)
Ear:	11–16 mm (0.43–0.63 in)
Forearm:	33–42 mm (1.3–1.65 in)
Wingspread:	238–270 mm (9.4–10.6 in)
Skull Length:	14–15 mm (0.55–0.59 in)
Weight:	5–12 g (0.18–0.42 oz)
Dental Formula:	I 2/3, C 1/1, P 3/3, M 3/3 = 38

ARKANSAS DISTRIBUTION AND ABUNDANCE

This bat is relatively rare in Arkansas and is probably found mainly in the West Gulf Coastal Plain. It probably also occurs in the Mississippi Alluvial Plain (Baker and Ward 1967; Davis et al. 1955; LaVal 1970).

LIFE HISTORY   In Arkansas, this species resides mainly in old mine shafts, buildings, and hollow trees since its range lies predominantly outside of the cave regions of the state. It is usually associated with water and forages for insects just above the surfaces of ponds and streams. It is most easily captured with mist nets placed over water near the surface.

In the southern portion of its range, this species apparently remains active and feeds throughout the year. During cold spells, these bats may become torpid for short periods of time until a warming trend occurs when they again become active, but evidently there is no extended hibernating period as in the northern part of the species' range. Heath et al. (1986) reported finding 150 hibernating individuals (both red and gray color phases) in an abandoned mine in Pike County. The entrance shaft of this mine projected some 20 m (65.6 ft) into the mountain before it expanded to form a chamber some 7 m (23 ft) in diameter and 7 m in height.

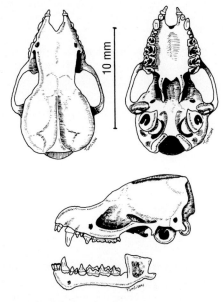

Skull of *Myotis austroriparius*

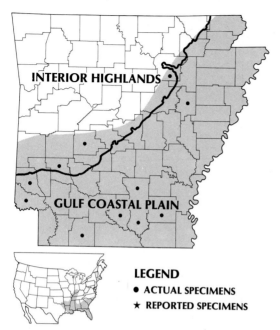

LEGEND
- **ACTUAL SPECIMENS**
- ★ **REPORTED SPECIMENS**

Distribution of the southeastern myotis (*Myotis austroriparius*)

Most of our recent knowledge about reproduction in this species is based upon the work of Rice (1957) with cave populations in Florida, where the bat is very abundant. Breeding takes place in both fall and spring, and most pregnant females produce twins; the remainder give birth to a single young. Both yearling males and females mate and produce young in the first year. Males are largely absent from nursery colonies while the young are being reared, but many join the colony after the young mature. The colonies disperse to winter quarters mainly in October, with the males tending to leave before the females. Whether small nursery colonies are formed in hollow trees or in buildings where caves are absent remains conjectural.

Rat snakes and corn snakes are important predators of this bat. Other predators include owls and various species of carnivorous mammals.

IMPORTANCE AND/OR MANAGEMENT   See introduction to order.

The subspecies *M. a. mumfordi* occurs in Arkansas.

SELECTED REFERENCES
Baker and Ward (1967); Davis et al. (1955); Heath et al. (1986); LaVal (1970); Rice (1957).

GRAY MYOTIS

Myotis grisescens

NAME   *Myotis* is from the Greek words, *mys*, meaning "mouse," and *ous*, meaning "ear," thus meaning "mouse ear." The specific name, *grisescens*, is from the Latin word *griseus*, meaning "becoming gray."

IDENTIFICATION AND DESCRIPTION   The gray bat is similar to the other myotis bats in Arkansas, but the wing and tail membranes are grayish, and the wing is attached to the foot at the ankle. The calcar is not keeled. Its foot is large, and the ears are pointed with slender tragi. Pelage is dull brown to mouse gray above with hairs uniform in color from base to tips, and paler below with hairs darker basally; hairs are somewhat woolly in texture.

MEASUREMENTS AND DENTAL FORMULA
Total Length: 80–105 mm (3.14–4.13 in)
Tail Length: 33–45 mm (1.29–1.77 in)
Hind Foot: 9–12 mm (0.35–0.47 in)
Ear: 14–16 mm (0.55–0.63 in)
Forearm: 40–46 mm (1.57–1.81 in)
Wingspread: 275–300 mm (10.8–11.8 in)
Skull Length: 15.5–16.5 mm (0.61–0.65 in)
Weight: 7–14 g (0.25–0.49 oz)
Dental Formula: I 2/3, C 1/1, P 3/3, M 3/3 = 38

ARKANSAS DISTRIBUTION AND ABUNDANCE
This endangered species is found in the cave region of the northern Arkansas Ozarks comprising the Salem and Springfield Plateaus. Maternity colonies are known from Benton, Madison, Stone, Boone, Newton, Searcy, Baxter, Sharp, Independence, and Washington counties. Large hibernating colonies are found in Baxter, Newton, and Independence coun-

Myotis grisescens, Gray Myotis. *John R. MacGregor*

ties. In addition, bachelor and transient colonies are scattered throughout the area.

One Arkansas hibernation cave (Baxter County) houses about 250,000 bats, over 15% of the total gray bat population. About 150,000 gray bats occupy Arkansas caves in the summer. Others migrate to summer caves in eastern Oklahoma, southwestern Missouri, and southeastern Kansas. Although their numbers are still relatively high in Arkansas, as well as in some other areas, their total population has decreased significantly (Harvey 1986).

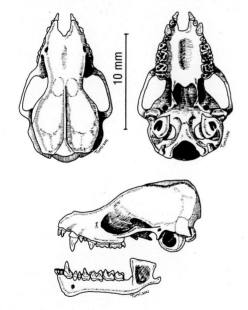

Skull of *Myotis grisescens*

LIFE HISTORY   The gray bat is almost exclusively a cave bat. A few have been found in the vicinity of Fayetteville, Arkansas, in drill holes in abandoned limestone quarry caves, but none have been found in other man-made structures. Maternity colonies are found in large caves containing streams; hibernating colonies usually are found in rather inaccessible caves with deep, vertical, pit-like entrances.

This bat emerges to feed at dusk, much like other species of *Myotis*. It most often forages over bodies of water as well as among trees and over land. It is a rapid and high flier. When foraging over water, it flies within about 3 m (10 ft) of the surface (Tuttle 1976); mayflies are its preferred food.

Males are sexually active in autumn and mating takes place in late fall. Delayed ovulation and fertilization occur in late March and early April when the females emerge from hibernation. In Arkansas, each pregnant female gives birth to a single young from late May until mid-June. During development the embryo is almost invariably implanted in the right horn of the uterus. The young mature rapidly, and the growth rate is more rapid in large nursery colonies due to energy saved from decreased heat dissipation by clustering behavior and the selection of roosts in heat-trapping domes or other places offering opportunity for microenvironmental alteration (Tuttle 1975). Females usually leave the young in the roost when they forage. First flights of young take place between 24 and 33 days after birth, and after they are weaned the nursery colonies disperse; many nursery caves are deserted in August or early September.

Migration to wintering caves takes place in September and October. Dispersal movements from summer colonies to hibernation colonies may cover distances from 80 to 160 km (50–100 mi). Nearly all summer colonies from widely scattered areas in a region tend to congregate in just a few large caves for hibernation. Each hibernating cave may harbor nearly all the bats from a single populational home range (Hall and Wilson 1966). Maximum fat deposition prior to hibernation takes place in September

A colony of gray myotis in Blanchard Springs Caverns. *John R. MacGregor*

and October (Krulin and Sealander 1972). Gray bats generally hibernate in deep vertical caves with large rooms that act as cold traps. Temperatures in the hibernaculum average 5.6–11.1° C (42.1–52.0° F). These bats hibernate in clusters of up to several thousand individuals.

IMPORTANCE AND/OR MANAGEMENT   Since a large portion of the gray bat population is concentrated in just a few caves during winter, the species is especially vulnerable to disruption by amateur spelunkers who are challenged by the particular characteristics of caves that are used for hibernation. A few unnatural arousals brought about by cave visitations during the hibernating period may result in the depletion of sufficient stored energy reserves, which may prevent many of the bats from surviving through the entire hibernating period. Maternity colonies are extremely intolerant of disturbance, especially when nonvolant young are present. Disturbances by spelunkers, as well as by scientists

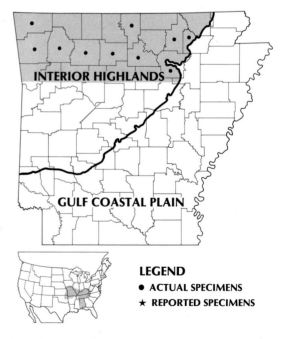

LEGEND
- ● **ACTUAL SPECIMENS**
- ★ **REPORTED SPECIMENS**

Distribution of the gray myotis (*Myotis grisescens*)

studying the species, have in some cases caused the dropping of young or abandonment of caves harboring maternity colonies (Harvey 1986). Commercialization of caves, flooding caused by newly created reservoirs, and vandalism also have contributed to a rapid decline in numbers of the bat. Caves known to house gray bats should be protected and/or gated.

SELECTED REFERENCES
Harvey (1976a, 1984, 1986); Hall and Wilson (1966); Krulin and Sealander (1972); Tuttle (1975, 1976).

KEEN'S MYOTIS

Myotis keenii

NAME   *Myotis* is from the Greek words, *mys*, meaning "mouse," and *ous*, meaning "ear," thus meaning "mouse ear." The specific name, *keenii*, is a patronym recognizing the Rev. John Keen, who collected the first specimen from which this species was described.

IDENTIFICATION AND DESCRIPTION   Keen's bat is similar to the other myotis bats in Arkansas. It can be identified by its long ears, which extend beyond the tip of the muzzle when laid forward. The tragus is narrow, long, and pointed (more than one-half the length of the ear). Its wing membranes are grayish and attach at the base of the toes, and the calcar is slightly keeled. The pelage is brownish olive or light reddish brown above, and buffy gray below; the fur is not glossy. This species is often confused with *M. lucifugus*, but it may be distinguished by its long ears which often extend forward beyond the tip of the muzzle.

MEASUREMENTS AND DENTAL FORMULA
Total Length: 80–98 mm (3.2–3.8 in)
Tail Length: 34–45 mm (1.34–1.77 in)
Hind Foot: 7–10 mm (0.28–0.39 in)
Ear: 14.5–19 mm (0.57–0.75 in)
Forearm: 32–39 mm (1.26–1.54 in)
Skull Length: 14.5–15.5 mm (0.57–0.61 in)
Weight: 4.5–10 g (0.16–0.35 oz)

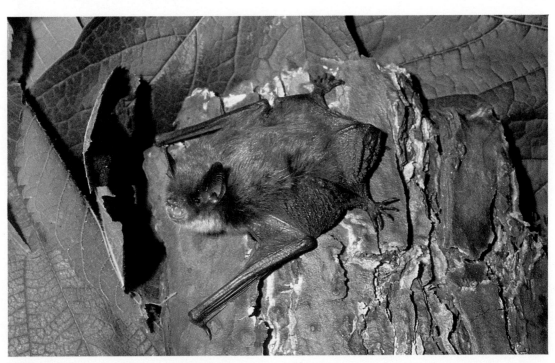

Myotis keenii, Keen's Myotis. *John R. MacGregor*

Dental   I 2/3, C 1/1, P 3/3, M 3/3
  Formula: = 38

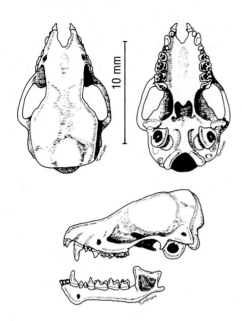

Skull of *Myotis keenii*

ARKANSAS DISTRIBUTION AND ABUNDANCE
Although Hall (1981) shows this species' range to include most of Arkansas, it appears to be restricted to the Interior Highlands where it is relatively uncommon; however, Harvey and McDaniel (1983) reported that mist-netting resulted in higher numbers than indicated by observation of hibernating bats in caves and mines. Aggregations of up to 350 hibernating individuals have been reported. On the other hand, Heath et al. (1986) reported a maximum of 12 (both males and females) from an abandoned mine in the Ouachita Mountains. They reported that the usual number of hibernating bats was one to three individuals. The largest aggregation found in an abandoned mine was 57 females in the spring of 1985.

LIFE HISTORY   In winter, Keen's bat hibernates in mines or caves, and in summer it may be found in caves, mine tunnels, beneath loose bark of trees, behind window shutters, under eaves of houses, or in similar kinds of shelter. Small maternity colonies form during the breed-

ing season, but otherwise this species is usually solitary in its habits.

Very little is known about reproduction in this bat. Hamilton (1943), from observations of large embryos in uteri of females in late June and early July, inferred that a single young is produced in July. It seems probable that parturition occurs at an earlier date in the southern portion of the species range since Easterla (1968a) captured a female with a newly born young in a mist net on 5 June 1965 in Missouri. A longevity of 18.5 years has been recorded for *M. keenii* (Hall et al. 1957).

Keen's myotis forages for insects late at night and seldom returns to roost until dawn. According to Kunz (1973), this bat shows a bimodal activity pattern with peaks in foraging activity at 1–2 and 7–8 hours after sunset. The primary activity period occurs within 5 hours after sunset, and a secondary foraging period occurs between 5 and 11 hours after sunset.

Swarming at hibernating caves has been observed in late August and early September. Apparently this bat begins hibernating during Sep-

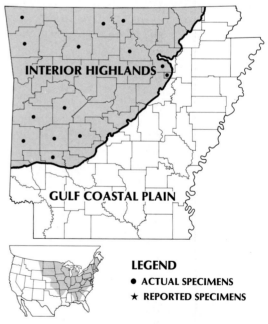

Distribution of the Keen's myotis (*Myotis keenii*)

tember or October, depending upon geographic location.

IMPORTANCE AND/OR MANAGEMENT   See section in the introduction to the order.

SELECTED REFERENCES
Easterla (1968a); Hall et al. (1957); Hamilton (1943); Harvey and McDaniel (1983); Heath et al. (1986); Kunz (1973).

INDIANA MYOTIS

Myotis sodalis

NAME   *Myotis* is from the Greek words, *mys*, meaning "mouse," and *ous*, meaning "ear," thus meaning "mouse ear." The specific name, *sodalis*, is the Latin word for "companion" and refers to this species' habit of hibernating in large numbers.

IDENTIFICATION AND DESCRIPTION   The Indiana bat is similar to the other myotis bats in Arkansas. It has small feet and the hairs on each foot do not extend beyond the toes. The calcar has a small but definite keel, which is not too evident in museum specimens. Its fur is loose textured, fine and fluffy, and not glossy. The pelage is dark gray to brownish or nearly black above, pinkish gray below; the hairs on the dorsum are tricolored.

MEASUREMENTS AND DENTAL FORMULA
  Total Length: 75–102 mm (2.95–4.02 in)
  Tail Length: 27–44 mm (1.06–1.73 in)
  Hind Foot: 7–11 mm (0.26–0.43 in)
  Ear: 11–16 mm (0.43–0.63 in)
  Forearm: 35–41 mm (1.38–1.61 in)
  Wingspread: 240–267 mm (9.45–10.5 in)
  Skull Length: 14.2–15 mm (0.56–0.59 in)
  Weight: 5–11 g (0.18–0.39 oz)
  Dental I 2/3, C 1/1, P 3/3, M 3/3
    Formula: = 38

ARKANSAS DISTRIBUTION AND ABUNDANCE
The Indiana bat is found in the Ozark Mountain division of the Interior Highlands. It is endangered in Arkansas and other parts of its range.

Myotis sodalis, Indiana Myotis. *John R. MacGregor*

Less than 3,000 Indiana bats hibernate in Arkansas caves located in Madison, Newton, Stone, and Independence counties. Only a few bats have been recorded from Arkansas during summer months (Harvey 1986).

LIFE HISTORY   Swarming at cave entrances begins in August, and by late November, the bulk of the population has returned from its summer range. During September and October, most of the bats remain active and make nightly excursions out of the caves to feed. At this time, rapid deposition of body fat occurs which supplies enough stored energy to sustain the bats through the hibernating period. The body weight may increase by 35 to 50% within a short time, mostly in the form of fat. The Indiana myotis is primarily associated with limestone caves during the winter hibernating period. They usually hibernate in dense clusters of up to several thousand individuals. Temperatures range between 3.3 and 6.1°C (37.9–42.9°F) and relative humidity of 66–95%. In

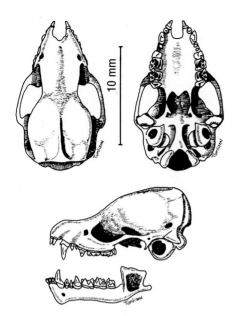

Skull of *Myotis sodalis*

males emerge from hibernation. Only one egg is ovulated at a time, and the pregnant females apparently give birth to a single young late in June. Young are born under the loose bark of dead trees in wooded stream habitats. The first known maternity colony of Indiana bats was discovered in 1974 and numbered about 50 individuals (Humphrey et al. 1977).

Apparently Indiana bats are selective opportunists with respect to their feeding habits. Brack and LaVal (1985) studied feces from an aggregation site for male bats in Missouri and found that Lepidopterans composed the greatest food item taken; greater, in fact, than their proportion of abundance. Insects from five other orders were also eaten, but they were eaten less frequently than the proportion of their availability might have allowed. Dietary intake of aquatic insects was low.

Arkansas, they have been found hibernating where temperatures are slightly warmer (Harvey 1986). Like other species of cave bats, *M. sodalis* arouses at intervals of 8–10 days or longer during the hibernating period, flies for short periods of time, and feeds upon insects present in the cave. Arousals take place more frequently and activity periods are longer at the beginning and at the end of the hibernating period.

Dispersal from caves to the summer range takes place from late March to late April. Females leave the caves first and migrate to their summer range, which is usually considerably north of the wintering range. In Kentucky, this species is primarily a winter resident and spends the summer in Ohio, Indiana, and Michigan. It seems probable that this bat is mainly a winter resident in Arkansas and spends the summer in Missouri and Illinois. Although most males accompany the females to the summer range, some wander about in small bands during the summer, frequenting the same caves in which they hibernated (Hall 1962).

Mating takes place in September or early October (Asdell 1964), and ovulation and fertilization probably occur shortly after the fe-

IMPORTANCE AND/OR MANAGEMENT Populations of the Indiana myotis have declined drastically in many parts of its range, and the species is considered endangered over its entire range. Adequate protection of populations in

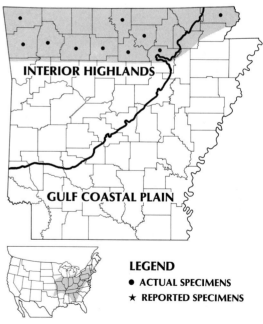

Distribution of the Indiana myotis (*Myotis sodalis*)

A hibernating cluster of the Indiana myotis.
John R. MacGregor

MEASUREMENTS AND DENTAL FORMULA
Total Length: 73–82 mm (2.87–3.23 in)
Tail Length: 30–40 mm (1.18–1.57 in)
Hind Foot: 7–8 mm (0.26–0.32 in)
Ear: 12–15 mm (0.47–0.59 in)
Forearm: 30–36 mm (1.18–1.42 in)
Wingspan: 212–248 mm (8.35–9.76 in)
Skull Length: 12.1–13.4 mm (0.48–0.53 in)
Weight: 4–6 g (0.14–0.21 oz)
Dental Formula: I 2/3, C 1/1, P 3/3, M 3/3 = 38

major hibernating caves must be provided if this species is to avoid extinction.

SELECTED REFERENCES
Asdell (1964); Brack and LaVal (1985); Hall (1962); Harvey (1986); Humphrey et al. (1977).

ARKANSAS DISTRIBUTION AND ABUNDANCE
Although this is a relatively common species in the western United States, it is considered one of the rarest species of bats in the eastern United States (Robbins et al. 1977). Sealander (1967) recorded this species from Stone and Searcy counties, and he speculated that it probably occurred in scattered localities through the western Ozark Highlands. McDaniel et al. (1982) further documented its occurrence in Stone and Independence counties and in Madison County in Missouri. It appears that, while uncommon, this species occupies a larger distribution than was previously thought.

SMALL-FOOTED MYOTIS

Myotis leibii

NAME *Myotis* is from the Greek words, *mys*, meaning "mouse," and *ous*, meaning "ear," thus meaning "mouse ear." The specific name, *leibii*, is a patronym recognizing Dr. George Leib, collector of the type specimen. This species was formerly known as *M. subulatus*.

IDENTIFICATION AND DESCRIPTION This species is small, has tiny feet, a black face, short black ears, and a relatively long tail. All other species of *Myotis* in Arkansas are larger and always have larger feet than the small-footed myotis. The calcar is strongly keeled. The pelage is blackish brown above, paler below with dark hairs basally.

Myotis leibii, Small-footed Myotis.
John R. MacGregor

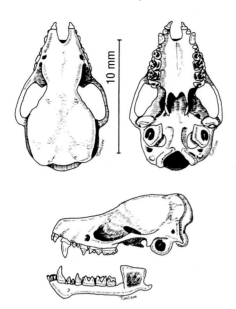

Skull of *Myotis leibii*

LIFE HISTORY
Little is known about the habitat of this bat. In winter, it hibernates in caves and mines, and often among rocks and in crevices on the floor; in summer, it has been found under loose bark of trees, beneath rocks, and in buildings. This bat has been described as one of the hardiest species of bats in the East. It does not move into caves until late November or early December, and it shows a definite preference for cooler caves. During the hibernating period, the bats are often very active, fly about frequently, and are easily aroused from sleep. Departure from caves in spring also is much earlier than that of most species and usually occurs in March.

The breeding and feeding habits of this bat are poorly known. It emerges at dusk to feed upon insects over bodies of water and on land; its flight is low, seldom higher than 6 m (20 ft), and slow. Apparently most pregnant females give birth to a single young in June or July, although Bailey (1926) and Tuttle and Heaney (1974) have observed the birth of twins in North and South Dakota. Tuttle and Heaney (1974) examined 12 occupied roosts of this bat between 21 and 29 July 1972 and found 11 juvenile bats among seven lactating females, two postlactating females, one nonreproductive female, and one adult male. The weight of the juveniles ranged from 1.6 to 3.9 g (0.06–0.14 oz); only one was able to fly, and then for no more than 100 m (328 ft). All but two juveniles were moderately to completely furred. Maternity roosts were of fairly uniform high temperature, ranging from 26–29°C (78.8–84.2°F), and averaging 5°C (9°F) lower than outside shade temperatures taken 1 m (3.28 ft) distant.

IMPORTANCE AND/OR MANAGEMENT
See commentary in introduction to the order.

The subspecies *M. l. leibii* occurs in Arkansas.

SELECTED REFERENCES
Bailey (1926); McDaniel et al. (1982); Robbins et al. (1977); Sealander (1967); Tuttle and Heaney (1974).

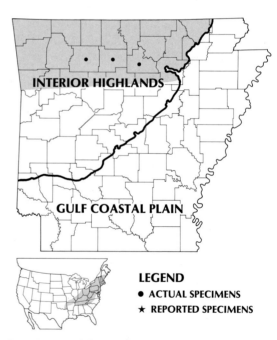

Distribution of the small-footed myotis (*Myotis leibii*)

LEGEND
- ● ACTUAL SPECIMENS
- ★ REPORTED SPECIMENS

SILVER-HAIRED BAT

Lasionycteris noctivagans

NAME   *Lasionycteris* is from two Greek words, *lasios*, meaning "hairy," and *nycteris*, meaning "bat," referring to the heavy fur on the upper surface of the uropatagium near the body. The specific name, *noctivagans*, is from two Latin words, *nox*, meaning "night," and *vagans*, meaning "wanderer," thus meaning "night wanderer."

IDENTIFICATION AND DESCRIPTION   The silver-haired bat is medium-sized; the ears, wings, and tail membranes are black, and the upper surface of the tail membrane is heavily furred near the body. The ears are short, rounded, and naked with a broad, blunt tragus (less than one-half the length of the ear). The pelage is black or blackish brown above with many of the hairs white-tipped, giving a frosted, silvery appear-ance. Coloration on the venter is similar but is less conspicuously frosted. A few individuals have dark brown, yellowish tipped fur. The silver-haired bat is distinguished from all other Arkansas bats by its coloration.

MEASUREMENTS AND DENTAL FORMULA
    Total Length: 92–112 mm (3.62–4.41 in)
    Tail Length: 35–48 mm (1.38–1.89 in)
    Hind Foot: 8–12 mm (0.32–0.47 in)
    Ear: 13–16 mm (0.51–0.63 in)
    Forearm: 37–44 mm (1.5–1.7 in)
    Wingspread: 270–310 mm (10.6–12.2 in)
    Skull Length: 16–16.9 mm (0.63–0.67 in)
    Weight: 7–15 g (0.25–0.53 oz)
    Dental   I 2/3, C 1/1, P 2/3, M 3/3
        Formula: = 36

ARKANSAS DISTRIBUTION AND ABUNDANCE
Although it is not collected in great numbers,

Lasionycteris noctivagans, Silver-haired Bat. *Phil A. Dotson*

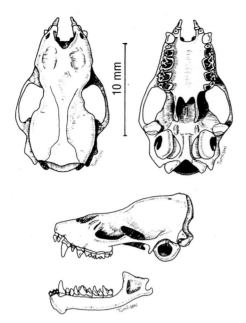

Skull of *Lasionycteris noctivagans*

records of this bat indicate that the species has a statewide distribution. Increasing use of mist nets for collecting may show that this species is not as scarce as the relatively few specimens seem to indicate.

LIFE HISTORY   This species is a forest dweller and roosts during the day in hollow trees, behind loose bark on trees, or in abandoned woodpecker holes. They are found in a wide variety of other shelters such as woodpiles, outbuildings, and open sheds during migration. Usually they roost singly or in small groups.

Silver-haired bats migrate from the northern parts of their range to long distances southward in autumn. Most of the migrants apparently winter in southern states, but some fly for long distances over the ocean. They have been reported from ships at sea, and some have been taken in Bermuda. This species also has strong homing instincts and will home from distances as great as 160 km (100 mi).

In winter, it hibernates in hollow trees or beneath loose bark. Sometimes it winters in buildings, but it seldom uses caves. Saugey et al. (1978) and Heath et al. (1986) documented the presence of this species in a cave and an aban-

doned mine in Arkansas. In southern Illinois, it frequently hibernates in silica mines, but it has rarely been found in limestone caves.

This bat forages for insects in and among trees, most often near ponds or woodland streams. They are low and slow fliers. Usually this species is most active 3−4 hours after sunset; a secondary activity period occurs 6−8 hours after sunset (Kunz 1973). The secondary activity period of juveniles is somewhat longer, stretching between 5 and 10 hours after sunset.

The breeding habits of *L. noctivagans* are poorly known. Females apparently segregate from males and form small maternity colonies in spring and summer. They usually produce two young in late June or early July.

IMPORTANCE AND/OR MANAGEMENT   No management or control measures are needed. However, the preservation of dead snags in clearcuts will provide roosting sites.

SELECTED REFERENCES
Baker and Ward (1967); Gardner and McDaniel

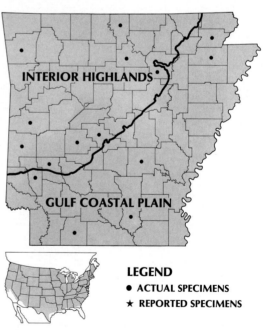

Distribution of the silver-haired bat (*Lasionycteris noctivagans*)

(1978); Heath et al. (1983, 1986); Kunz (1973); Saugey et al. (1978); Sealander (1960).

EASTERN PIPISTRELLE

Pipistrellus subflavus

NAME   *Pipistrellus* is the Latinized form of the Italian word, *pipistrello*, meaning "bat." The specific name, *subflavus*, is derived from two Latin words, *sub*, meaning "below" and *flavus*, meaning "yellowish," thus indicating the yellowish belly.

IDENTIFICATION AND DESCRIPTION   The eastern pipistrelle is a small bat with blackish wing membranes. The anterior third of the tail membrane is furred. The calcar is not keeled. Its ears are short and rounded with a blunt but straight, tapering tragus. The forearms are slightly red- dish in color. The pelage is yellowish brown or gray to reddish brown or drab-brown above and lighter below; hairs, especially on the back, are tricolored.

MEASUREMENTS AND DENTAL FORMULA

Total Length:	71–95 mm (2.8–3.7 in)
Tail Length:	30–46 mm (1.2–1.8 in)
Hind Foot:	7–11 mm (0.28–0.43 in)
Ear:	9–15 mm (0.35–0.59 in)
Forearm:	30–36 mm (1.2–1.4 in)
Wingspread:	208–258 mm (8.2–10.2 in)
Skull Length:	12–13.5 mm (0.47–0.53 in)
Weight:	3.5–8.3 g (0.12–0.29 oz)
Dental Formula:	I 2/3, C 1/1, P 2/2, M 3/3 = 34

ARKANSAS DISTRIBUTION AND ABUNDANCE   The eastern pipistrelle occurs statewide; it is very common. This is perhaps the most abundant species of bat in Arkansas.

Pipistrellus subflavus, Eastern Pipstrelle. *David A. Saugey*

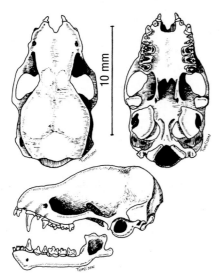

Skull of *Pipistrellus subflavus*

LIFE HISTORY The eastern pipistrelle hibernates in caves, mines, and rock crevices in winter, but relatively little is known about its summer habits. During summer, pipistrelles probably roost most often in trees, as indicated by their appearance near treetops early in the

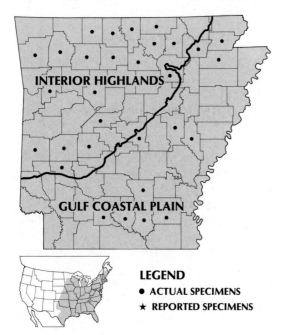

LEGEND
● ACTUAL SPECIMENS
★ REPORTED SPECIMENS

Distribution of the eastern pipstrelle (*Pipistrellus subflavus*)

evening; they also roost in crevices of cliffs, in caves and mines, or occasionally in buildings. In the South, this bat is rarely found in buildings, but there are a number of records from northern states of small nursery colonies in buildings.

Pipistrelles forage for insects early in the evening and often may be observed flitting about in the shade of trees before sundown. A secondary foraging flight may be made toward midnight or early in the morning. This bat has a small foraging area near treetop level at the forest edge and often hunts for its prey along watercourses or over ponds. It is a weak, erratic flier and small enough to be easily mistaken for a large moth. The diet of pipistrelles consists mainly of tiny flies, moths, and the smaller beetles and wasps.

Mating occurs from late August into November and again in spring. Fertilization is delayed until March or April in females impregnated in autumn. Females leave the hibernating caves and mines earlier than the males, and some males may still be found in caves and mines well into June. Small nursery colonies are established by females in hollow trees, buildings, and protected parts of cliffs in the same general vicinity as the wintering site. During the period of parturition and rearing of young, the females remain apart from males. Both sexes have been observed roosting together again as early as August. Usually two—rarely one or three—young are born from late May to mid-July, depending upon the latitude (Asdell 1964). During the first few days of development, the female carries the young with her when foraging in the evening. The young mature rapidly and fly at about 1 month of age. Saugey et al. (1988b) reported catching a 4 g (0.14 oz) juvenile in mid-July. Some young enter into hibernation before they are fully grown and may be recognized by their dark juvenile pelage and their finger bone development. Cockrum (1952) reported a longevity of more than 7 years for this species.

In northern Arkansas, pipistrelles usually begin hibernating from October to December. Entry into hibernation is delayed during mild winters. During hibernation, these bats are

An eastern pipstrelle in hibernation.
David A. Saugey

largely solitary or form clusters of only two or three individuals. In one abandoned mine in the Ouachita Mountains, Heath et al. (1986) reported 600–800 hibernating individuals. Once they have become torpid, they are less easily aroused than other species of cave bats and may remain in one spot for weeks. During this time, moisture condenses on the surface of the fur, giving the bat a white appearance when caught in the beam of a lantern. This species is very site tenacious and often returns to the same spot in a cave to hibernate in successive years. Although they roost in many parts of caves, they seem to prefer vertical walls and flat ceilings rather than holes and crevices. During hibernation, these bats most often roost in the warmer (11–13°C [51.8–55.4°F]), highly humid (80–100% r.h.), and relatively draft-free parts of caves. In May and June, small numbers of males may be found roosting in somewhat warmer regions near cave entrances.

IMPORTANCE AND/OR MANAGEMENT No management or control measures are needed.

The subspecies *P. s. subflavus* occurs in Arkansas.

SELECTED REFERENCES
Asdell (1964); Cockrum (1952); Heath et al. (1986); Saugey et al. (1988b, 1989).

BIG BROWN BAT

Eptesicus fuscus

NAME *Eptesicus* is obscure, but may be from the Latin or Greek words for "house flier." The specific name, *fuscus*, is Latin for "brown," referring to the bat's color.

IDENTIFICATION AND DESCRIPTION The big brown bat is easily distinguished from the other bats in Arkansas by its large size, long fur, and two-toned color, which is easily revealed when the fur is separated by blowing on it. The base of each hair is blackish, and the outer half is brown, often giving a dull chestnut to cinnamon or bronzy brown appearance above (slightly paler on the venter). The wings and interfemoral membrane are black and lack hair. The ears are black (slightly furred at the base), short, thick, and leathery, with broad rounded tragi. The calcar is keeled. Females are slightly larger than males.

Eptesicus fuscus, Big Brown Bat. *David A. Saugey*

MEASUREMENTS AND DENTAL FORMULA

Total Length: 100–134 mm (3.9–5.3 in)
Tail Length: 30–54 mm (1.2–2.1 in)
Hind Foot: 8–14 mm (0.31–0.55 in)
Ear: 14–20 mm (0.55–0.79 in)
Forearm: 42–51 mm (1.7–2.0 in)
Wingspread: 315–350 mm (12.4–13.8 in)
Skull Length: 17.5–20 mm (0.69–0.79 in)
Weight: 10–33 g (0.35–1.16 oz)
Dental   I 2/3, C 1/1, P 1/2, M 3/3
  Formula: = 32

Distribution of the big brown bat (*Eptesicus fuscus*)

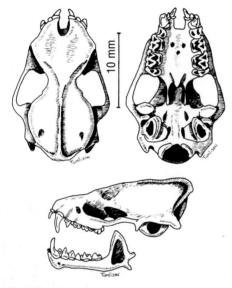

Skull of *Eptesicus fuscus*

ARKANSAS DISTRIBUTION AND ABUNDANCE
The big brown bat occurs statewide and is abundant.

LIFE HISTORY   This bat is commonly found in buildings and dwelling places where it roosts in attics, under eaves of roofs, behind shutters or awnings, in chimneys, in church towers, or in other types of shelter. Occasionally it is found in hollow trees, rock crevices, caves, or under the loose bark of dead trees. In winter, this bat hibernates in caves, mines, and buildings. It is a very hardy bat, and in warmer southern states, it may hibernate only for brief periods during the coldest part of winter.

The big brown bat begins to forage at dusk and is most active 1–3 hours after sunset. Juveniles have a secondary activity period which extends 3–10 hours after sunset (Kunz 1973). The flight pattern of this bat is relatively slow and direct at a height of 5–10 m (16.5–33 ft), and it follows the same route repeatedly during the course of an evening. Because of its large size, it is able to capture and eat some larger insects including June beetles, click beetles, large moths, houseflies, and parasitic wasps. Phillips (1966) found that beetles were their principal food. When foraging among trees, this bat prefers to fly among the treetops rather than under the canopy. After about an hour of feeding activity, it flies to a night roost, such as a breezeway, porch, or the shutters of a dwelling, to digest its meal; before dawn it seeks a cool, dark daytime roost.

E. fuscus mates in autumn and winter. Females ovulate in late March or early April and form maternity colonies from late April until mid-May. The gestation period is about two months, and the young are born from the last week in May until the second week in June (Kunz 1974). The litter size is usually two but may range from one to four. In the western part of its range, the usual number of young is one. The young weigh about 3 g (0.11 oz) at birth and grow rapidly; they are weaned at 3 weeks of age and most are flying by early July at the age of 4 weeks (Kunz 1974). Nursery colonies usually are located in hot attics, but this species is intolerant of temperatures above 35°C (95°F). During the period of parturition and lactation, males are usually absent from the nursery colonies, but an influx of males into such colonies takes place after the young mature and begin to fly. As is true of some species of cave bats, nearly all of the young in a given colony are born within about 48 hours of each other. This indicates that ovulation followed by delayed fertilization probably occurs nearly simultaneously in the females as the result of some favorable factor, such as an increase in the ambient temperature. *E. fuscus* is known to reach the age of 9–10 years.

Big brown bats are rather sedentary and proba-

A female big brown bat nursing young. *David A. Saugey*

A big brown bat maternity colony. *David A. Saugey*

bly seldom move more than 50 km (31 mi) from their summer and winter roosts. They have excellent homing instincts, however, and individuals transported for distances as great as 400–725 km (250–450 mi) have returned within four or five days.

This species may weigh as much as 30 g (1.06 oz) or more in late autumn, and as much as one-third of the body weight may be fat. They enter into hibernation late in November and December, and most have left the caves again by February or March. During mild winters in the South, this bat probably does not hibernate. When hibernating, big brown bats seem to prefer the drier and cooler parts of caves, often near the entrance (Rysgaard 1942).

IMPORTANCE AND/OR MANAGEMENT Sometimes this bat becomes a nuisance when it occupies houses, churches, or schools. Usually its return can be prevented when it leaves in the fall by closing all entrance holes to the colony. (See also control measures in introduction to the order.)

SELECTED REFERENCES
Kunz (1973, 1974); Phillips (1966); Rysgaard (1942); Saugey et al. (1989).

Lasiurus borealis, Red Bat. *David A. Saugey*

RED BAT
Lasiurus borealis

NAME *Lasiurus* is derived from two Greek words, *lasios*, meaning "hairy," and *oura*, meaning "tail," referring to the heavily furred interfemoral membrane. The specific name, *borealis*, is the Latin word for "northern."

IDENTIFICATION AND DESCRIPTION The red bat is medium-sized with short, broad, rounded, and partly furred ears. Its tragus is broad basally, tapering to a point. The tail membrane is densely furred on the upper surface. The pelage is bright rufous to yellowish red or brownish yellow above, with a yellowish white shoulder patch and a wing patch near the thumb; it is paler below. The hairs on the back and breast are white-tipped, giving a frosted appearance; males are usually more brightly colored than females.

This bat can be distinguished from all the bats in Arkansas, with the exception of the seminole bat, by its coloration and heavily furred tail. It can be distinguished from the seminole bat by the deep mahogany color of the seminole bat.

MEASUREMENTS AND DENTAL FORMULA

Total Length:	81–124 mm (3.2–4.9 in)
Tail Length:	40–60 mm (1.6–2.4 in)
Hind Foot:	6–11 mm (0.24–0.43 in)
Ear:	8–13 mm (0.32–0.51 in)
Forearm:	35–46 mm (1.4–1.8 in)
Wingspread:	232–290 mm (9.1–11.4 in)
Skull Length:	12–14 mm (0.47–0.55 in)
Weight:	7–16 g (0.25–0.56 oz)
Dental Formula:	I 1/3, C 1/1, P 2/2, M 3/3 = 32

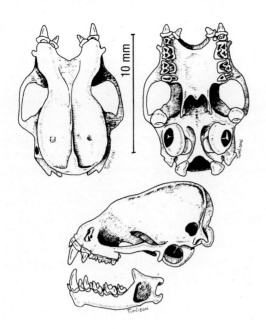

Skull of *Lasiurus borealis*

ARKANSAS DISTRIBUTION AND ABUNDANCE
The red bat occurs statewide and is abundant.

LIFE HISTORY   Red bats are tree dwellers and seldom enter buildings or caves. During the daytime, they roost in the foliage of trees and show a preference for the south or southwest side of trees. The roosting site usually is 1–6 m (3.3–19.7 ft) above ground, densely shaded above, and concealed from view from any direction except from below; there is no obstruction below the roost so that the bat can drop downward to begin its flight. Sometimes they roost on the edge of tree crowns, often fully exposed to sunlight (Mumford 1973). These bats hang by one foot from a leaf petiole or twig and bear a surprising resemblance to a dead leaf when at rest.

Red bats appear early in the evening, well before dark, flying very high. At this time, they display a slow, erratic flight pattern. At dusk, when other species of bats become active, red bats begin foraging close to the ground to near treetop level; their flight also becomes rapid and direct. The most active foraging period is within five hours of sunset, but reduced forag-

ing activity occurs until 10 hours after sunset (Kunz 1973). Red bats are easily captured in mist nets stretched across streams or ponds while they are swooping to drink or capture insects. The diet consists mainly of small flying insects such as moths, flies, bugs, and tiny beetles, but the presence of cricket remains in stomachs of red bats suggests that at least some of their food is obtained on the ground. Insects swarming about lights often attract these bats, and frequently they are captured in black light insect traps.

The daytime abode of this species in winter is not definitely known. Evidently it is very hardy since it is frequently observed flying on warm days during all months of winter in the late afternoon in northern Arkansas, Missouri, West Virginia, southern Illinois, and southern Indiana. In these regions, temperatures often drop below freezing for extended periods. Presumably red bats roost in trees during winter, possibly under loose bark or in hollow trunks. Apparently this bat does not winter to any extent in the more northern part of its range, although at least some individuals, chiefly males, winter

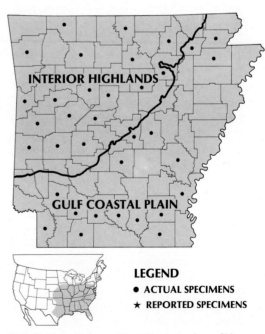

LEGEND
● ACTUAL SPECIMENS
★ REPORTED SPECIMENS

Distribution of the red bat (*Lasiurus borealis*)

at or above 40° north latitude; possibly these are migrants from Canada and more northern states. Members of the northern population migrate southward from September until November in small to fairly large sexually unmixed flocks. Groups of migrating red bats have been captured on ships 160 km (100 mi) or more distant from the coast, and some fly as far south as central Sonora, Mexico, and Bermuda. Flight characteristics of low wing loading and streamlining, similar to that of swifts or swallows, fit the red bat morphologically for making migratory movements. Although some observers have alluded to massive north-south migrations, it seems more likely that most red bat populations make relatively small seasonal movements, resulting in a net displacement of northern limits and denser population levels to the south in winter with a reversal of such movements and population levels in the spring. Segregation of sexes prior to migratory movements appears to take place in late summer. Evidence (Kunz 1971) seems to indicate that females depart from local areas before males.

L. borealis mates in August and September; copulation is initiated, and sometimes completed, in flight. Sperm are stored in the female's reproductive tract through the winter and delayed fertilization occurs in spring. After 80–90 days gestation, the young are born from late May until early July, depending upon the latitude. The usual litter size is two to three, but it ranges from one to four. Mortality of the young is fairly high, especially from blue jay predation. Young are left in the roost while the female forages for food, but females are sometimes captured with attached young, apparently while transferring them to a different roost. Young red bats grow rapidly, and it has been estimated that they fly at 3–4 weeks of age and are weaned at 5–6 weeks of age. Relatively little direct information on the growth rate of young red bats is available; inferences on growth rates have been made mainly from data on weights of young carried by females in relation to probable dates of parturition.

IMPORTANCE AND/OR MANAGEMENT Red bats, as well as other tree bats, are frequently infected with rabies, and any red bat behaving strangely should be approached with caution. Between 1982 and 1986, red bats accounted for 40% of bats submitted to the Arkansas Department of Health for rabies testing. Forty-four (72%) of the total bats that tested positive were red bats. Red bats that tested positive for rabies were reported from 24 counties (Heidt et al. 1987).

The subspecies *L. b. borealis* occurs in Arkansas.

SELECTED REFERENCES
Heidt et al. (1987); Kunz (1973); Mumford (1973); Saugey et al. (1989).

SEMINOLE BAT
Lasiurus seminolus

NAME *Lasiurus* is derived from two Greek words, *lasios*, meaning "hairy," and *oura*, meaning "tail," referring to the heavily furred interfemoral membrane. The specific name, *seminolus*, refers to the Seminole Indian region where the bat was first known.

IDENTIFICATION AND DESCRIPTION The seminole bat is medium-sized with general characteristics similar to *L. borealis* but differing in color, being a rich mahogany-brown above, slightly frosted with white, and slightly paler below. It also has whitish shoulder and wing patches.

MEASUREMENTS AND DENTAL FORMULA
Total Length: 89–114 mm (3.5–4.5 in)
Tail Length: 35–50 mm (1.4–2.0 in)
Hind Foot: 6–11 mm (0.24–0.43 in)
Ear: 7–14 mm (0.28–0.55 in)
Forearm: 35–45 mm (1.4–1.8 in)
Wingspread: about 300 mm (11.8 in)
Skull Length: 12–14 mm (0.47–0.55 in)
Weight: 8–15 g (0.47–0.55 oz)
Dental Formula: I 1/3, C 1/1, P 2/2, M 3/3 = 32

The seminole bat begins to fly early in the evening but does not fly when the temperature falls below 21°C (70°F). Usually it feeds at tree-top level but occasionally flies near the ground (Lowery 1974). *L. seminolus* flight is swift and direct and foraging takes place over water, pine barrens, and cleared land. It feeds on a variety of insects such as bugs, flies, beetles, and moths which it captures in and around the tree canopy.

This bat is active throughout the year over most of its range. Small seasonal movements southward may occur in autumn and winter from the northern limits of its breeding range. After the young are weaned, seminole bats may wander far north of the breeding range, as indicated by late season records from New York and Pennsylvania (Layne 1955).

Very little is known about reproduction in *L. seminolus*. Young are born from late May until mid-June, and the litter size ranges from one to four. Presumably other events in the reproductive cycle are similar to those in *L. borealis*.

IMPORTANCE AND/OR MANAGEMENT Aside from predation by birds, especially blue jays, it has been suggested that since seminole bats

Lasiurus seminolus, Seminole Bat.
Roger W. Barbour

ARKANSAS DISTRIBUTION AND ABUNDANCE
The seminole bat probably occurs over most of the lower two tiers of counties in southern Arkansas, but it is known only from relatively few records (see map) (Baker and Ward 1967; Heath et al. 1983; Saugey et al. 1989; Sealander and Hoiberg 1954).

LIFE HISTORY This species is a tree dweller and usually roosts in the interior of Spanish moss clumps at a height of 1–6 m (3.3–19.7 ft) above the ground. Occasionally it is found beneath loose bark or among clumps of foliage. The roost is generally located on the southwest side of a tree at the forest edge. The area below the roost is always free of obstructions, allowing the bat to drop downward when it begins its flight.

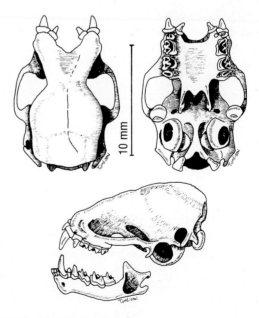

Skull of *Lasiurus seminolus*

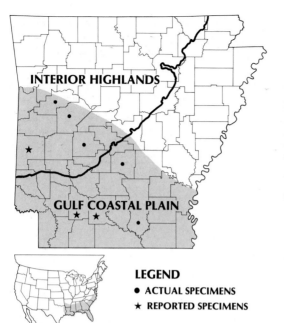

Distribution of the Seminole bat (*Lasiurus seminolus*)

often roost in Spanish moss, commercial moss collecting is a major mortality factor in this bat (Lowery 1974).

SELECTED REFERENCES
Baker and Ward (1967); Heath et al. (1983); Layne (1955); Lowery (1974); Saugey et al. 1989; Sealander and Hoiberg (1954).

Hoary Bat

Lasiurus cinereus

NAME *Lasiurus* is derived from two Greek words, *lasios*, meaning "hairy," and *oura*, meaning "tail," referring to the heavily furred interfemoral membrane. The specific name *cinereus* comes from the Latin word, *cinera*, for "ashen" or "gray."

IDENTIFICATION AND DESCRIPTION The hoary bat is the largest bat in Arkansas and is easily distinguished by its size and coloration. The pelage on the dorsum is a mixture of yellows, browns, and deep amber, with white tips of many hairs giving a decidedly frosted, hoary appearance; the venter is yellower. The throat and wing linings are yellowish or buffy, and the belly is more whitish than black. The ears are relatively short, rounded, furred almost to the tip, and rimmed with black or dark brown. Wing membranes are brownish black, and the tail membrane is densely furred on the upper surface.

MEASUREMENTS AND DENTAL FORMULA

Total Length:	130–150 mm (5.1–5.9 in)
Tail Length:	53–65 mm (2.1–2.6 in)
Hind Foot:	11–14 mm (0.43–0.55 in)
Ear:	16–20 mm (0.63–0.79 in)
Forearm:	46–58 mm (1.8–2.3 in)
Wingspread:	380–410 mm (14.9–16.1 in)
Skull Length:	15.5–17.5 mm (0.61–0.69 in)
Weight:	20–35 g (0.70–1.2 oz)
Dental Formula:	I 1/3, C 1/1, P 2/2, M 3/3 = 32

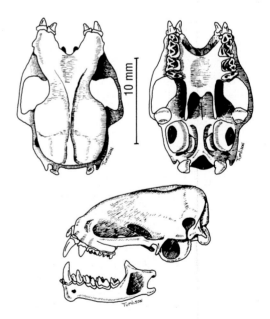

Skull of *Lasiurus cinereus*

Lasiurus cinereus, Hoary Bat. *David A. Saugey*

ARKANSAS DISTRIBUTION AND ABUNDANCE
The hoary bat probably occurs statewide. This bat probably is more abundant than the scarcity of specimens in collections indicates (see map). Mist-netting has shown that it is much more common in many areas than previously suspected. (Baker and Ward [1967] captured 14 in 12 nights of netting over ponds in southeastern Arkansas.)

LIFE HISTORY   The hoary bat is usually solitary, and in the summer it hangs in the foliage of trees near the forest edge. It roosts 3–5 m (9.8–16.4 ft) above ground in a roost site clear of obstruction below. In much of its range, it is closely associated with coniferous forests.

L. cinereus is a strong, rapid flier and usually begins to forage in late evening; the peak activity period is 3–6 hours after sunset (Kunz 1973). Occasionally, however, they emerge before sunset, especially during warm days in winter. Hoary bats capture a variety of insects on the wing, but very little detailed information is available about their feeding habits. It has been reported that this bat occasionally preys upon smaller species of bats.

The hoary bat is a migratory species. Females migrate northward before the males and occupy a summer breeding range in eastern and central North America, whereas males are found mainly in western North America during summer. With the onset of cold weather in August and September, hoary bats migrate in waves from the northern part of their range to their winter range in the southern United States, especially southern California, other southwestern states, and Mexico. There is some indication that at least part of the wintering range may be in the Caribbean.

The breeding habits of this bat are poorly known. Mating apparently occurs in late fall before migration or upon reaching the wintering range, since females migrating northward in spring are already pregnant and males play no

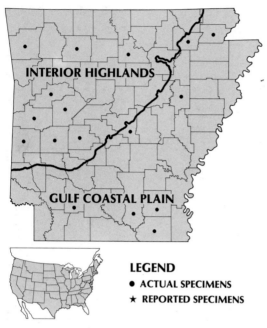

LEGEND
- ● ACTUAL SPECIMENS
- ★ REPORTED SPECIMENS

Distribution of the hoary bat (*Lasiurus cinereus*)

role in spring reproductive activities (Findley and Jones 1964). The young are born from late May to early July; usually there are two young in a litter, but females sometimes produce only one young (Bogan 1972). Kunz (1971) observed that young were flying by 22 July in central Iowa, and Bogan noted that young were capable of purposeful flight 33 days after parturition. Weaning was completed when the young were 34 days old, and the young were accomplished fliers 44 days after birth. The young are left hanging to a leaf or twig while the female forages; females captured with young usually are in the process of moving them to a new roost.

IMPORTANCE AND/OR MANAGEMENT   See general comments concerning bats.

The subspecies *L. c. cinereus* occurs in Arkansas.

SELECTED REFERENCES
Baker and Ward (1967); Bogan (1972); Findley and Jones (1964); Kunz (1971, 1973).

EVENING BAT
Nycticeius humeralis

NAME   *Nycticeius* is of Greek and Latin origin, from *nyx*, meaning "night," and *eius*, meaning "belonging to." The specific name, *humeralis*, is from the Latin *humerus*, meaning "humerus," and *alis*, meaning "pertaining to."

IDENTIFICATION AND DESCRIPTION   The evening bat is small- to medium-sized. Its ears are rounded, thick, and leathery, with a short tragus which is curved and rounded. The ears, wings, and tail membranes are naked and blackish. The pelage is dark chocolate or dull brown above and paler, buffy brown below. This bat looks like a small version of the big brown bat, but it can be distinguished by the fact that it has only two upper incisors whereas all other brown bats have four. The females are larger than the males.

MEASUREMENTS AND DENTAL FORMULA
Total Length: 80–105 mm (3.2–4.1 in)
Tail Length: 32–45 mm (1.3–1.8 in)
Hind Foot: 6–10 mm (0.24–0.39 in)
Ear: 8–14 mm (0.32–0.55 in)
Forearm: 33–39 mm (1.3–1.5 in)
Wingspread: 260–280 mm (10.2–11.0 in)
Skull Length: 13–14 mm (0.28–0.56 in)
Weight: 8–16 g (0.28–0.56 oz)
Dental   I 1/3, C 1/1, P 1/2, M 3/3
 Formula: = 30

ARKANSAS DISTRIBUTION AND ABUNDANCE The evening bat occurs statewide; it is common in southeastern Arkansas.

LIFE HISTORY   Female evening bats form large nursery colonies in attics of houses, walls of buildings, and cavities of trees; the males appear to be solitary. The free-tailed bat, *Tadarida brasiliensis*, is often found in the same attic roosts with *N. humeralis* in the southeastern states. Nursery colonies have been located in Crossett, Hope, Monticello, and Warren, Arkan-

Nycticeius humeralis, Evening Bat. *David A. Saugey*

sas. Data from an unpublished study of maternity colonies in Crossett, Arkansas (Sealander in collaboration with Mr. Harry E. Stephens during 1963 and 1964), indicates that the colonies are established early in March. In 1963, the first arrivals were noted on 9 March and the colonies were complete by 17 March. In 1964, the first bats arrived on 8 March and the colonies were complete by 15 March. The nursery colonies were abandoned after the young were reared. Colonies began thinning out in early July and by late September or October, nearly all bats had departed.

Although this bat migrates southward in winter from the northern part of its range, at least some individuals seem to winter in the South. One individual was shot on the wing in northwestern Arkansas on 15 February (Sealander 1960), and Baker and Ward (1967) collected ten on 22 December in southeastern Arkansas.

This bat begins foraging for insects shortly before or after sunset and has a slow, steady flight. It commonly hunts over ponds and streams or among trees. During early evening, they fly above the treetops but descend to a lower level when it becomes dark. Females from the nursery colonies in Crossett, Arkansas, foraged for about one hour after first leaving the roost. During this time they gained an average 2.5 g (0.09 oz) in weight. *N. humeralis* exhibits a bimodal activity pattern (Watkins 1971) with a peak in activity lasting for approximately one hour after first leaving the roost, little activity through the night, and a second peak activity period 9–10 hours after sunset which lasts about one hour before the bats re-enter the roost. With the onset of cool nighttime temperatures in the fall, the activity pattern tended to be compressed into a single, somewhat bimodal, period 1–5 hours after sunset.

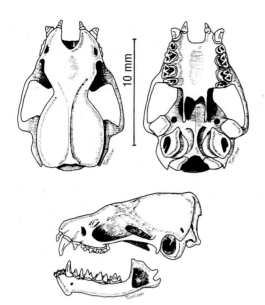

Skull of *Nycticeius humeralis*

IMPORTANCE AND/OR MANAGEMENT   See general comments concerning bats.

The subspecies *N. h. humeralis* occurs in Arkansas.

SELECTED REFERENCES
Baker and Ward (1967); Jones (1967); Saugey et al. (1988b); Sealander (1960); Watkins (1969, 1971, 1972).

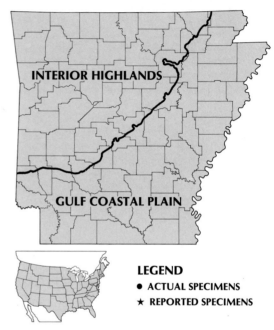

LEGEND
● ACTUAL SPECIMENS
★ REPORTED SPECIMENS

Distribution of the evening bat (*Nycticeius humeralis*)

The time and place of mating in this species are unknown. In the South, young are born from late May until mid-June, but the time of parturition may extend into early July in the northern part of the range (Watkins 1969, 1972). Growth and development of the young has been documented by Jones (1967). The young grow rapidly and are capable of flight at 18–21 days of age. In Crossett, Arkansas, young bats began to fly from nursery colonies in the last week of June and the first week in July.

During a study of bats in Hot Springs National Park, Garland County, Saugey et al. (1988b) reported that evening bats represented 44% of all bats netted. Pregnant females were netted in late May and early June. Juveniles weighing 5 and 6 g (0.17–0.21 oz) were netted in late June and early July, which indicates that young probably begin to fly within a month of birth.

Evening bats accumulate large fat deposits in autumn which evidently sustain them in migration and during the winter. However, there are relatively few observations documenting extensive southward movements (Watkins 1972).

TOWNSEND'S BIG-EARED BAT
Plecotus townsendii

NAME   *Plecotus* is from two Greek words, *pleko*, meaning "twisted," and *otus*, referring to the ear, hence meaning "twisted ear." The specific name, *townsendii*, is a patronym honoring Dr. John K. Townsend.

IDENTIFICATION AND DESCRIPTION   Townsend's big-eared bat is medium-sized, with very large ears that have narrow tips. The ears are curled like a ram's horn when at rest or torpid. The tragus is relatively broad and long. Prominent lumps are present on each side of the muzzle in front of the eyes. Hairs on the foot do not extend beyond the toes. The pelage is pale brown to nearly black above and pinkish buff or brownish below; the fur is not sharply bicolored. Females are larger than males. This bat is distinguished from its close relative, Rafinesque's big-eared bat, by the pinkish buff hairs on the belly, hairs not projecting beyond the toes, and the lack of bicolored hairs.

MEASUREMENTS AND DENTAL FORMULA

Total Length:	90–116 mm (3.5–4.6 in)
Tail Length:	35–54 mm (1.4–2.1 in)
Hind Foot:	8–14 mm (0.32–0.55 in)
Ear:	29–39 mm (1.1–1.5 in)
Forearm:	39–48 mm (1.5–1.9 in)
Wingspread:	297–325 mm (11.7–12.8 in)
Skull Length:	13–15 mm (0.51–0.59 in)
Weight:	7–12 g (0.25–0.42 oz)
Dental Formula:	I 2/3, C 1/1, P 2/3, M 3/3 = 36

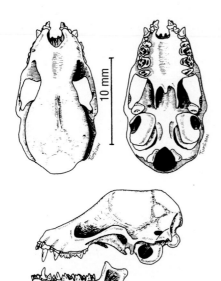

Skull of *Plecotus townsendii*

Plecotus townsendii, Townsend's Big-eared Bat. *John R. MacGregor*

ARKANSAS DISTRIBUTION AND ABUNDANCE

The race in Arkansas, the Ozark big-eared bat (*P. t. ingens*), is endangered. Its range includes only a few caves in northwestern and north central Arkansas, southwestern Missouri, and eastern Oklahoma. The total surviving population of this race is probably less than 500. Roughly 50% (250 individuals) are found in Arkansas. These are known from a hibernation cave and a maternity cave (Harvey 1976a, 1976b, 1978, 1986).

LIFE HISTORY   This bat is a true cave dweller in the eastern United States and often inhabits the same caves or mines during summer and winter. Unlike *P. rafinesquii*, it has not been known to roost in trees (Handley 1959); however, a few have been found in dwellings. It hibernates in caves, mines, or limestone fissures where the temperatures are about 12°C (54°F) or less but above freezing. Cave hibernation sites are often near entrances in well-ventilated areas. If temperatures near entrances become too extreme, the bats move to more thermally stable parts of the cave. During hibernation, *P. townsendii* may form tight clusters on the walls of caves or mines. This behavior apparently minimizes changes in body temperature of individuals in the cluster, thus probably serving to

FAMILY VESPERTILIONIDAE   97

reduce the overall energy expenditure and conserve fat reserves during hibernation. *P. townsendii* is very intolerant of human disturbance during hibernation, and it will desert caves that are subject to frequent human intrusion.

Relatively little is known about the behavior of this species. It is a late flier and usually begins to forage after dark. Before emerging from a cave, it exhibits a light sampling behavior consisting of flying to the entrance, then turning back into the cave and hanging up for a few minutes before sampling the light again (Handley 1959). They fly very high at first but may descend to within a few feet of the ground when it becomes dark. In Arkansas, most bats return to the roost before midnight, although some may leave or return throughout the night (Harvey 1986). Hamilton (1943) found only the remains of Lepidoptera in the stomachs of this species; little else is known about its feeding habits in the eastern United States, but it seems likely that it consumes other kinds of insects as well as moths.

The most detailed study of reproduction in *P. townsendii* was made by Pearson et al. (1952) in California. Most of their findings probably apply to the eastern races of the species as well as the western races, although there may be some differences in timing of events in the reproductive cycle. Mating occurs from October through February, and sexual segregation occurs in spring when the females form nursery colonies. Ovulation takes place from February to April, and the single offspring is born in late May or early June. The young grow rapidly and are able to fly when about 3 weeks old. At the age of 1 month they are nearly full grown. Maternity colonies disband in August after the young are weaned. Maximum record longevity for the species, based on banding records, is 16 years.

Ozark big-eared bat maternity colonies are found in warm parts of caves, and the only known maternity cave in Arkansas is in a small warm cave. Harvey (1986) reported the temperature under the roost to average 15.6°C (60°F) and the relative humidity to be 97%.

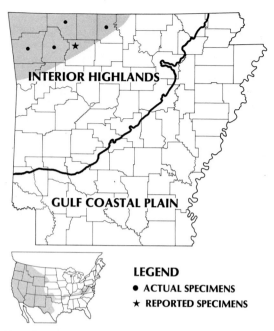

Distribution of Townsend's big-eared bat (*Plecotus townsendii*)

IMPORTANCE AND/OR MANAGEMENT   The Arkansas Nature Conservancy has recently purchased the Ozark big-eared bat hibernation cave and has entered into an agreement with the owner of the maternity cave to protect that site. Protection of this and possibly other sites may help ensure the survival of this bat.

SELECTED REFERENCES
Hamilton (1943); Handley (1959); Harvey (1976a, 1976b, 1978, 1986); Pearson et al. (1952); Sealander (1951a, 1956).

RAFINESQUE'S BIG-EARED BAT
Plecotus rafinesquii

NAME   *Plecotus* is from two Greek words, *pleko*, meaning "twisted," and *otus*, referring to the ear, hence meaning "twisted ear." The

Plecotus rafinesquii, Rafinesque's Big-eared Bat.
David A. Saugey

Skull Length: 13–15 mm (0.51–0.59 in)
Weight: 7–13.6 g (0.25–0.48 in)
Dental I 2/3, C 1/1, P 2/3, M 3/3
  Formula: = 36

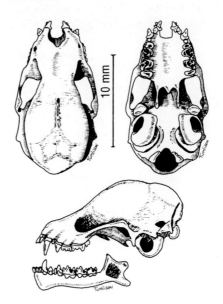

Skull of *Plecotus rafinesquii*

specific name, *rafinesquii*, is a patronym for Constantine S. Rafinesque, an early American naturalist.

IDENTIFICATION AND DESCRIPTION Rafinesque's big-eared bat is medium-sized, with very large ears having narrow tips joined at the base. The ears are curled like a ram's horn when at rest or torpid. The tragus is relatively broad and long. Prominent lumps are present on each side of the muzzle in front of the eyes. Hairs on the foot extend well beyond the toes. Its pelage is gray or grayish brown above and nearly white or silvery in appearance below; the fur is distinctly bicolored, black or blackish basally. This bat closely resembles Townsend's big-eared bat, but it can be distinguished by white-tipped hairs on the venter, bicolored hairs, and hairs extending beyond the toes.

MEASUREMENTS AND DENTAL FORMULA
  Total Length: 80–100 mm (3.2–3.9 in)
  Tail Length: 33–54 mm (1.3–2.1 in)
  Hind Foot: 8–13 mm (0.32–0.51 in)
  Ear: 27–37 mm (1.1–1.5 in)
  Forearm: 39–44 mm (1.5–1.7 in)
  Wingspread: 265–301 mm (10.4–11.9 in)

ARKANSAS DISTRIBUTION AND ABUNDANCE This species has been recorded from all the physiographic provinces except the Ozark Mountains.

LIFE HISTORY *P. rafinesquii* is one of the least known North American bats. This bat roosts in barn lofts, attics, and old buildings, but it is seldom found in caves. It prefers dimly lit rooms of badly dilapidated, abandoned buildings in rural areas. This is a hardy bat and is probably intermittently active throughout the cold months in Arkansas. In the northern part of its range, this species hibernates in the cool twilight zone of caves, often within 10–35 m (32.8–115 ft) of the entrance. In summer months it may become torpid (Jones 1977). This bat usually is solitary and seldom encountered in clusters, except in summer nursery colonies. Saugey et al. (1989), however, observed a colony of more than 100 individuals in an abandoned school in Little River County in autumn.

P. rafinesquii emerges only after dark and never forages in twilight. Presumably this bat is insectivorous like other vespertilionid bats, but there are no records of its feeding habits.

The time of mating and length of gestation is not definitely known; mating probably occurs in autumn and winter. Small nursery colonies consisting of 10–30 females form in spring. A single young is born in late May or June. The young are essentially full grown but by late June or July are somewhat smaller in weight than adults (Jones and Suttkus 1971).

IMPORTANCE AND/OR MANAGEMENT   See general comments concerning bats.

Two subspecies occur in Arkansas (Jones 1977). The race *P. r. macrotis* is found in the Delta, and the race *P. r. rafinesquii* occurs in the West Gulf Coastal Plain, the Ouachita Mountains, and the Arkansas River Valley.

SELECTED REFERENCES
Jones (1977); Jones and Suttkus (1971); Saugey et al. (1989).

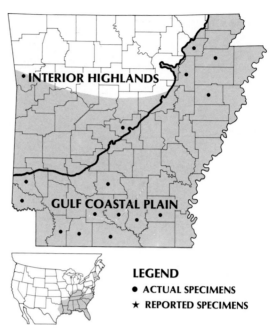

Distribution of Rafinesque's big-eared bat (*Plecotus rafinesquii*)

Rafinesque's big-eared bat female nursing young.
David A. Saugey

FAMILY MOLOSSIDAE
FREE-TAILED BATS

Members of this family are swift fliers and migrate southward in late fall and winter for long distances. General characteristics of the family are: Tail extends conspicuously beyond tail membrane; ears are broad, short, thick, and leathery, projecting forward over face; small blunt tragus; long and narrow wings.

Only one species occurs in Arkansas.

BRAZILIAN FREE-TAILED BAT
Tadarida brasiliensis

NAME   *Tadarida* was coined by Rafinesque, who gave no clue as to its etymology. The specific name, *brasiliensis*, is a combination of the country name, Brazil, and the Latin word, *enis*, meaning "belonging to."

Tadarida brasiliensis, Brazilian Free-tailed Bat. *David A. Saugey*

IDENTIFICATION AND DESCRIPTION The Brazilian free-tailed bat is medium-sized, and its tail extends conspicuously beyond the tail membrane. It has long, narrow wings. The ears are short, almost meeting at the midline, and project forward over the face. There are deep vertical grooves on the upper lip. Hairs as long as the foot protrude from the toes. The pelage is dark gray or brownish gray above and grayish brown below.

MEASUREMENTS AND DENTAL FORMULA
Total Length: 88–109 mm (3.5–4.3 in)
Tail Length: 29–48 mm (1.1–1.9 in)
Hind Foot: 7–14 mm (0.28–0.55 in)
Ear: 13–20 mm (0.51–0.79 in)
Forearm: 36–46 mm (1.4–1.8 in)
Skull Length: 15–19 mm (0.59–0.75 in)
Weight: 8–15 g (0.28–0.53 oz)
Dental I 1/2, C 1/1, P 2/2, M 3/3
 Formula: = 30 or
 I 1/3, C 1/1, P 2/2, M 3/3
 = 32

ARKANSAS DISTRIBUTION AND ABUNDANCE
This species has been reported in 14 counties in the Ouachita Mountains, the West Gulf Coastal Plain, and the Mississippi Alluvial Plain. Saugey et al. (1988a) speculate that it is even more widespread. Relatively mild winters, the protracted period of the year when plentiful insect prey are available, and the abundance of suitable roost and foraging habitats may contribute to its eventual statewide occurrence.

LIFE HISTORY The habitat of this bat varies in different regions of the United States. The race *cynocephala*, which occurs in Arkansas and other southeastern states, is, at least in part, nonmigratory, occupies buildings, and is never found in caves. The smaller race, *mexicana*, is primarily a cave bat in Texas, Oklahoma, and Arizona but occupies buildings on the West Coast; this subspecies migrates for great distances. In Arkansas, the free-tailed bat is commonly associated with *N. humeralis* and *E. fuscus*.

This bat leaves the roost to forage shortly after sunset, and its feeding grounds may be far from the roost. Individuals from large colonies may fly to feeding grounds as far as 65–80 km (40–

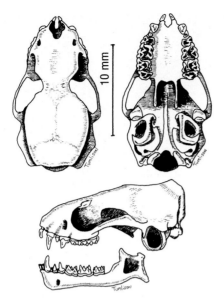

Skull of *Tadarida brasiliensis*

50 mi) from the roost. It is not known whether the less migratory race, *cynocephala*, performs such long evening flights. The bat's flight is rapid and erratic, and flight speeds up to 95 km/hr (60 mi/hr) have been clocked. A large part of the diet of *T. brasiliensis* apparently consists of small moths (Barbour and Davis 1969), although they also eat chironomid midges, winged ants, dytiscid beetles, and chalcids (Sherman 1939).

Mating takes place in late February through March (Sherman 1937; Pagels and Jones 1974) after which the sexes segregate. At least part of the resident population in the deep South may make only small seasonal movements. Mating is immediately followed by ovulation and fertilization (Cockrum 1955), and the gestation period lasts about 11 to 12 weeks (Asdell 1964). Yearling females bear young later than older females so that birth dates within a colony vary widely. Females usually give birth to a single young from very early June until early July (Pagels and Jones 1974), but twins and occasionally triplets are sometimes produced (DiSalvo et al. 1969). A few young may be born in late May or late July, but the majority are born during the first three weeks in June. The young grow quite rapidly and reach adult body

weights within 3–4 weeks, have adult body size at 2 months, and have black juvenile pelage at 45 days of age. Most young are capable of independent flight at the age of about 5 weeks, and at this time the pattern of sexual segregation begins to break down. Young females become sexually mature at the age of about 9 months. Saugey et al. (1983) reported the occurrence of maternity colonies in Faulkner, Pulaski, and Garland counties. These colonies numbered between a few hundred and a few thousand individuals. In addition, they were utilized throughout the year. Others have also reported that at least part of the population winters near some of the nursery colonies (LaVal 1973; Pagels 1975; Spenrath and LaVal 1974).

IMPORTANCE AND/OR MANAGEMENT   Western populations of this species have been heavily implicated in the transmission of rabies (Baer 1975). The role of the free-tailed bat in Arkansas rabies epidemiology is not known; however, between 1982 and 1986 only 1 of 94 bats tested was positive (Heidt et al. 1987).

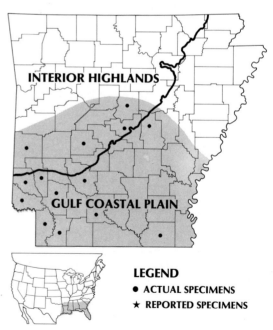

Distribution of the Brazilian free-tailed bat (*Tadarida brasiliensis*)

The subspecies *T. b. cynocephala* occurs in Arkansas.

SELECTED REFERENCES
Asdell (1964); Baer (1975); Barbour and Davis (1969); Cockrum (1955); Constantine (1967); DiSalvo et al. (1969); Heidt et al. (1987); LaVal (1973); Pagels (1975); Pagels and Jones (1974); Sealander and Price (1964); Saugey et al. (1983, 1988); Sherman (1937, 1939); Spenrath and LaVal (1974).

Order Edentata   *Edentates*

This order includes the sloths, anteaters, and armadillos. The order seems to have originated in North America and probably migrated to South America in the late Cretaceous Period. During the early Tertiary, members of the order disappeared in North America. When a land bridge was re-established between North and South America in the Pliocene, members of the order invaded North America. Ground sloths were present into the Recent Epoch in the southwestern United States, but have been extinct for several thousand years.

Living edentates are found in South and Central America and northward into the United States. The name Edentata refers to a tendency toward reduction or loss of teeth in members of the order. Incisor and canine teeth are absent, and cheek teeth, when present, are of simple cylindrical form without enamel, growing from persistent pulps.

The order is divided into three families. Only one family and one species occurs in the United States.

FAMILY DASYPODIDAE

ARMADILLOS

Members of this family are mostly small- to medium-sized mammals. The greatest species diversity is found in South America. General characteristics of the family are: The body is elongated, narrow, and covered with a jointed armor consisting of bony scutes covered by horny epidermis; a shell-like coat consisting of a head shield and a variable number of movable rings between a scapular (shoulder) shield and a pelvic (hip) shield; a long tail, tapering and encased in bony rings; legs covered with bony scutes; a long, narrow snout; long, egg-shaped, erect ears placed on back of head; front feet with four toes, hind feet with five, all specialized for digging with strong, curved, pointed claws; ball-and-socket joints converted into strongly keeled hinge joints; fused tibia and fibula; simple peg-like persistent teeth lacking enamel; one pair of inguinal and one pair of pectoral mammary glands.

Nine-banded Armadillo

Dasypus novemcinctus

NAME   *Dasypus* comes from a combination of two Greek words, *dasy*, meaning "hairy," and *pus*, meaning "foot." The translation of "hairy foot" does not apply. It has been speculated that Linnaeus may have meant thick-footed or rough-footed. The specific name, *novemcinctus*, is from two Latin words, *novem*, meaning "nine," and *cinctus*, meaning "banded" or "girdled."

IDENTIFICATION AND DESCRIPTION   The armadillo is medium-sized, about the size of a large opossum, with the dorsal and lateral body enclosed with skin-covered armor consisting of nine movable rings between a shoulder and hip shield. The long, tapering tail is encased in twelve bony ridges. The head is small, with a long, narrow snout. The claws are long and white. The cheek teeth are peg-like, ranging in number from seven to nine on each side of the upper and lower jaws. Coloration is brownish black with scattered whitish hairs above, sides spotted with ivory yellow, tail predominantly yellowish white, ears brown, and yellowish orange below. Males are usually larger than females.

MEASUREMENTS AND DENTAL FORMULA

Total Length:	615–800 mm (20.2–31.5 in)
Tail Length:	245–373 mm (9.6–14.8 in)
Hind Foot:	65–107 mm (2.6–4.2 in)
Ear:	32–43 mm (1.25–1.7 in)
Skull Length:	93–102 mm (3.7–4.0 in)
Weight:	2.5–8 kg (5.5–18 lb)
Dental Formula:	I 0/0, C 0/0, P 4–6/4–6, M 3/3 = 28–36

ARKANSAS DISTRIBUTION AND ABUNDANCE The armadillo was recorded in southwestern Arkansas as early as 1921 (Dellinger and Black 1940), and by 1940 it was apparently well estab-

Dasypus novemcinctus, Nine-banded Armadillo. *David A. Easterla*

lished along the western edge and in the south-western corner of the state. During the last 45 years it has steadily increased its range, possibly in relation to changing agricultural practices, and is now well established statewide.

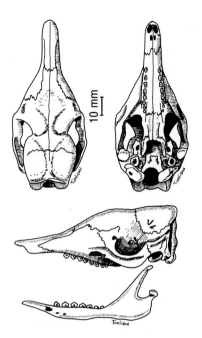

Skull of *Dasypus novemcinctus*

LIFE HISTORY   The armadillo occurs in wooded bottom lands and other habitats such as pine forests, brushy areas, and fields. It prefers areas with a dense ground cover and loose textured soil which provide easy digging. Population densities are usually lower in areas with heavy clay or rocky soils. In areas of rocky terrain, they tend to be more numerous near alluvial stream bottoms and den under exposed tree roots along creek banks or in crannies and crevices in limestone outcroppings.

Armadillos are burrowing animals. They dig burrows 2–8 m (6.6–26 ft) long and about 18–20 cm (7.1–7.9 in) in diameter near stumps or brush piles and in stream banks, old levees, hillsides, or similar places. At the end of the burrow, a slight enlargement is made for a nest which consists of a mass of leaves or grass. In-

dividuals usually dig several burrows. The burrows often are used by other mammals such as rabbits, woodchucks, opossums, and skunks. The nests and burrows are probably of importance in regulating body temperature at both high and low air temperatures since the armadillo is a relatively poor thermoregulator, shows conspicuous overcompensation to cold stress (Johansen 1961), and will not survive freezing temperatures long unless provided with adequate nesting material. Extended cold snaps, especially on the northern periphery of its range, may be responsible for "winter kills" (Fitch et al. 1952) by actual freezing or by starvation resulting from inability to forage at low temperatures (Talmage and Buchanan 1954; Buchanan and Talmage 1954). However, a series of mild winters may be accompanied by range extensions.

In arid regions, armadillos are usually concentrated near streams or water holes. Fitch et al. (1952) reported many dead armadillos during an extended drought in Texas; whether death was due to the limiting effect of drought on the invertebrate food supply or by the armadillo's inability to conserve body water is open to question.

During summer, the armadillo is usually nocturnal in its activity, but in midwinter, it may emerge from its burrow to forage during the warmest part of the day, generally in mid-afternoon. Invertebrates comprise more than 90% of the armadillo's diet, with insects, chiefly beetles, constituting more than four-fifths of the animal food eaten (Kalmbach 1944). In southwestern Arkansas, Sikes et al. (in preparation) found that major food items were earthworms, beetles and their larvae, and fly larvae, but some vertebrate material was noted. They also found that the diet showed a marked seasonal shift, with fly larvae constituting the dominant food item in the winter months while beetles and their larvae were the most heavily consumed in all other seasons.

Armadillos mate in midsummer, in July or August. Spontaneous ovulation usually occurs in late June or early July but may take place as late as November. Implantation of the fertilized egg is delayed until near the end of November or early December (Enders 1966). After a three-month gestation period a litter of four genetically identical young are born (all of one sex). Parturition is usually in late March and early April, although some births may occur as late as May. Very little deviation from the quadruplet condition has been found. At birth, the young resemble miniature adults; their eyes are open and they are able to walk in a few hours. The young remain with the mother until they are several months old (Galbreath 1982).

Distribution of the nine-banded armadillo (*Dasypus novemcinctus*)

IMPORTANCE AND/OR MANAGEMENT   The armadillo is disliked by some farmers because cattle and horses may step into burrows near the surface and injure themselves, dikes and levees may be undermined by burrows, or gardens or row crops may be dug up in the animals' search for insects. It is often accused by sportsmen of destroying eggs and nests of quail, but it does so rarely and only inadvertently. Their burrows, by providing shelter for wildlife, including furbearers, may largely offset any minor damage to ground-nesting birds. Though farmers and gardeners often condemn the armadillo, the benefits it confers by eating large numbers of noxious insects probably far outweigh the relatively small amount of damage it does to crops.

In recent years, the armadillo has been used in genetic and medical research and has become a model laboratory animal for research on leprosy. Ironically, the armadillo is frequently used for food in the southwestern United States. The light-colored flesh, when properly prepared, is considered very tasty and equal to pork in texture and flavor.

The subspecies *D. n. mexicanus* occurs in Arkansas.

SELECTED REFERENCES
Buchanan and Talmage (1954); Clark (1951); Cleveland (1970); Dellinger and Black (1940); Enders (1966); Fitch et al. (1952); Galbreath (1982); Humphrey (1974); Johansen (1961); Kalmbach (1944); Talmage and Buchanan (1954).

Order Lagomorpha *Lagomorphs*

Lagomorphs closely resemble rodents but are distinguished from them by several prominent features. Like rodents, they have a pair of large, chisel-shaped, evergrowing, upper incisor teeth, but differ from them in having a second peg-like pair immediately behind each of the large upper incisors. The hind feet are much larger than the forefeet, and the external ears are very long. Unlike rodents, they have short, fluffy tails that resemble tufts of cotton. All lagomorphs are strict herbivores.

The order includes hares, rabbits, and pikas. Only three species, all in the family Leporidae, are found in Arkansas.

FAMILY LEPORIDAE

HARES AND RABBITS

Members of this family are small- to medium-sized mammals with long, dense pelage. General characteristics of the family are: Hind legs considerably longer than front legs; hind feet large, soles covered with hair; ears long, eyes large; short, recurved tail; tibia and fibula fused; clavicles reduced; skull with elongated muzzle; numerous small openings in sides of the muzzle in front of the eye sockets, giving the bone the appearance of a latticework; and large, hollow tympanic bullae.

WHOLE ANIMALS

1. Top of tail black, with a black stripe extending
   onto rump; general color grayish above, white
   below; ear more than 100 mm (3.9 in) and with
   black patch at tip; length of hind foot more than
   115 mm (4.5 in) .... *Lepus californicus*, Black-tailed Jackrabbit

   Top of tail brownish; general color brownish
   above, white below; length of ear less than 100
   mm (3.9 in); length of hind foot less than 115
   mm (4.5 in) 2

2. Back grayish brown, heavily intermixed with
   black, sometimes giving a spotted effect; nape
   of neck only slightly reddish; pelage short and
   coarse; tail slender and thin-haired; large, total
   length more than 450 mm (17.7 in); length of
   ear more than 65 mm (2.6 in) .... *Sylvilagus aquaticus*, Swamp Rabbit

   Back reddish-brown, sides and rump paler and
   grayer than back; nape of neck bright rusty-red;
   small, total length less than 450 mm (17.7 in);
   length of ear less than 65 mm (2.6 in) .... *Sylvilagus floridanus*, Eastern Cottontail

SKULLS

1. Length 90 mm (3.5 in) or more; interparietal
   bone absent or indistinct in adult (fig. 10a); supraorbital processes triangular and winglike,
   standing well out from braincase (fig. 10c); base
   of braincase with many perforations .... *Lepus californicus*, Black-tailed Jackrabbit

   Length less than 90 mm (3.5 in); interparietal
   bone present and distinct in adult (fig. 10b); supraorbital processes long, narrow, and strap-
   like, frequently fused to the braincase at their
   posterior ends (fig. 10d,e); base of braincase
   with fewer perforations 2

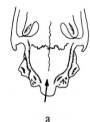
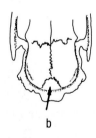
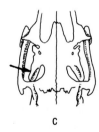
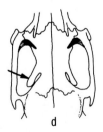
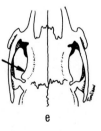

a   b   c   d   e

FIGURE 10.   Dorsal view of leporid skulls showing the lack of an interparietal bone (a); distinct interparietal bone (b); triangular, winglike supraorbital process standing well out from braincase (c); supraorbital process fused or touching braincase forming slit-like opening (d); and supraorbital process
completely fused to braincase (e).

2. Length less than 80 mm (3.2 in); supraorbital process long and narrow, usually fused with or touching braincase and forming a slit-like opening or narrow aperture above (fig. 10d) .... *Sylvilagus floridanus*, Eastern Cottontail

Length more than 80 mm (3.2 in); supraorbital processes completely fused to braincase with no slit-like opening above or only a very small hole (fig. 10e) .... *Sylvilagus aquaticus*, Swamp Rabbit

EASTERN COTTONTAIL

Sylvilagus floridanus

NAME   *Sylvilagus* is of Latin and Greek origin, from *sylva*, meaning "a wood," and *lagos*, meaning "hare," hence meaning "wood hare." The specific name, *floridanus*, is a Latinized word meaning "of Florida," describing the place where the species was first collected.

IDENTIFICATION AND DESCRIPTION   The eastern cottontail is medium-sized with long hind legs, long ears, and a short, recurved tail. It is conspicuously white beneath, and buffy or reddish brown with a grayish wash and a fine sprinkling of black above. It is rusty red behind the ears and on the front and side of its forelegs. Its throat is buffy.

MEASUREMENTS AND DENTAL FORMULA
Total Length: 335–490 mm (13.2–20 in)
Tail Length: 34–75 mm (1.4–3 in)
Hind Foot: 75–111 mm (3–4.4 in)
Ear: 47–71 mm (1.9–2.8 in)
Skull Length: 60–82 mm (2.4–3.2 in)
Weight: 0.6–1.6 kg (1.3–3.5 lb)
Dental   I 2/1, C 0/0, P 3/2, M 3/3
  Formula: = 28

ARKANSAS DISTRIBUTION AND ABUNDANCE
The eastern cottontail occurs statewide and is abundant.

LIFE HISTORY   The eastern cottontail occurs in a wide variety of habitats but is most common in brushy, upland fencerows, thickets, and woodlands, especially along the forest edge. It inhabits old fields and dry bottomlands where blackberry thickets, tangles of honeysuckle, or similar vegetation provide adequate cover. Cottontails usually are absent from wetter habitats frequented by the swamp rabbit.

Cottontails usually are solitary and mainly active at night, but often they are observed feeding near dawn and dusk and on dull, overcast or rainy days. Usually they rest in a "form" (a shallow depression in the ground, usually in good cover) during the day. A wide variety of plants is included in their diet, but in summer they prefer grasses, clover, and broad-leaved

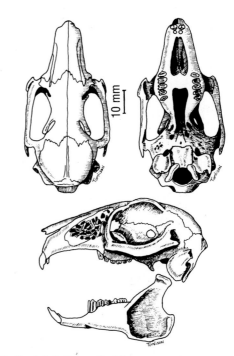

Skull of *Sylvilagus floridanus*

weeds. In winter, they feed on buds, twigs, roots, and bark of shrubs and small saplings.

In northern Arkansas, males and females reach breeding condition in February (January in southern Arkansas), and the peak of the breeding season is in March, when the first litters are produced. Breeding continues through August and September, but it is depressed during late fall and winter, except in the southern part of the range. The eastern cottontail is a prolific breeder, and in northern Arkansas a female may produce three to four litters per year. However, it is probable that as many as five to six litters may be produced annually in southern Arkansas.

The nest is a shallow excavation, often at the base of a tree or shrub, lined with fine grass and hair plucked from the female's breast. The young are naked, blind, and helpless at birth. They grow rapidly and are weaned and leave the nest to fend for themselves in 2–3 weeks. Females have been known to reach adult size

and bear two litters during the breeding season in which they were born (Hill 1972).

Heavy predation by foxes, coyotes, and other predators, parasites, disease, hunting, and other factors combine to keep rabbit populations in check. Although the potential life span of the cottontail may be as long as 10 years (Lord 1963), few individuals survive more than a year in the wild.

IMPORTANCE AND/OR MANAGEMENT   The eastern cottontail is the most abundant small game mammal in Arkansas and provides both sport and food for many people. Populations may vary widely from year to year depending upon the amount of optimal habitat, weather, disease, and other factors. Cottontails often are seriously infected with the bacterial disease, tularemia, which is transmissible to humans. Hunters and other persons should avoid handling rabbits that look sick or show abnormal behavior (Hickie 1940). If the rabbit, when

Sylvilagus floridanus, Eastern Cottontail. *Phil A. Dotson*

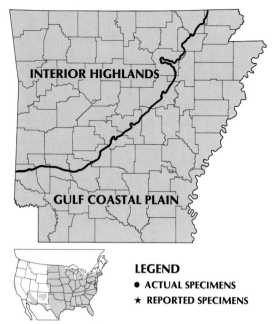

Distribution of the eastern cottontail (*Sylvilagus floridanus*)

The specific name, *aquaticus*, is the Latin word meaning "found in water."

IDENTIFICATION AND DESCRIPTION   The swamp rabbit is relatively large and big-headed, with ears relatively shorter and rounder than those of the cottontail. It has a slender, thinly haired tail. Its pelage is grayish brown, heavily intermixed with black above. Except for a buffy neck and chest, it is white below. The hind feet are reddish brown on the dorsal side.

MEASUREMENTS AND DENTAL FORMULA
Total Length: 452–552 mm (17.8–21.8 in)
Tail Length: 50–74 mm (2–3 in)
Hind Foot: 90–113 mm (3.5–4.5 in)
Ear: 60–80 mm (2.4–3.2 in)
Skull Length: 60–92 mm (2.4–4.5 in)
Weight: 1.2–2.9 kg (2.6–6.4 lb)
Dental Formula: I 2/1, C 0/0, P 3/2, M 3/3 = 28

ARKANSAS DISTRIBUTION AND ABUNDANCE
The swamp rabbit occurs statewide; it is gener-

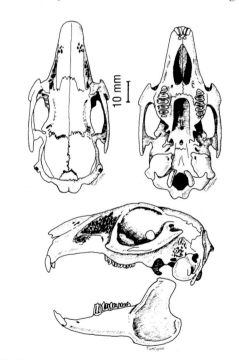

Skull of *Sylvilagus aquaticus*

opened, has many tiny white spots on its liver, it should be discarded. As a further precaution, rubber gloves should be worn when cleaning rabbits because the disease organism may enter the body through small cuts or breaks in the skin. Usually, infected animals die after the first few freezes of the year; hence, hunting seasons usually are during the winter months.

The eastern cottontail in Arkansas belongs to the subspecies *S. floridanus alacer* (Hall 1951a).

SELECTED REFERENCES
Chapman et al. (1982); Hall (1951a); Hickie (1940); Hill (1972); Lord (1963).

SWAMP RABBIT

Sylvilagus aquaticus

NAME   *Sylvilagus* is of Latin and Greek origin, from *sylva*, meaning "a wood," and *lagos*, meaning "hare," hence meaning "wood hare."

Sylvilagus aquaticus, Swamp Rabbit. *Ted Borg*

ally scarce in the Interior Highlands but locally abundant along the Illinois, White, and Black rivers in the Ozarks, and more common in the Gulf Coastal Plain.

LIFE HISTORY   The swamp rabbit lives in hardwood bottomland swamps and in the canebrakes and dense thickets of shrubs, trees, and vines bordering flood plains of rivers and creeks. Its presence may be detected by piles of fecal pellets on logs, stumps, or other elevations.

Swamp rabbits are seldom far from water and readily enter water when pursued. They swim and dive with ease and often will lie still beneath a bush or amid floating debris with only the nose above water. Apparently they often use backtracking maneuvers to outwit pursuers (Terrel 1972). This species is mainly active at night or at dawn or dusk. During the day, it does not use a "form" like a cottontail but usually rests on a log, stump, or other dry spot that is often surrounded by water. The swamp rabbit feeds on emergent vegetation, grasses, sedges, cane, tree seedlings, bark, and leaves. It is fond of young shoots of cane and for this reason is often referred to as the "cane-cutter."

Young may be produced during any month of the year, but most breeding activity occurs from January to September. Fall and winter repro-

duction evidently is minimal (Hill 1967). After a gestation period of 39–40 days, the first litters are produced in mid- to late February. The litter size varies from one to six, averaging three to four, and an average of 2.5 litters is produced annually. The peak breeding season falls between February and May when the vegetation is most lush.

The nest composed of grasses and lined with rabbit fur is a slight excavation in the ground or may be situated in a hollow log or stump. In the southern part of the range, Spanish moss is sometimes used to line the nest. The young are well furred but blind when born; the eyes are open, and they are able to walk in two to three days.

IMPORTANCE AND/OR MANAGEMENT   Much of the optimal habitat of the swamp rabbit in the hardwood swamps and river bottoms of the Gulf Coastal Plain of eastern Arkansas has been destroyed by channelization of streams, drainage of swamps, and clearing of hardwood forests. As in other states, the range of the swamp rabbit in Arkansas has been steadily shrinking

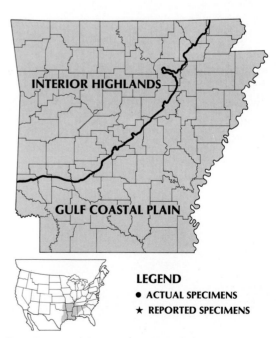

LEGEND
● ACTUAL SPECIMENS
★ REPORTED SPECIMENS

Distribution of the swamp rabbit (*Sylvilagus aquaticus*)

with drainage of the wetlands, and where formerly it was common, it may now be scarce or absent. Unless measures are taken to preserve or restore the habitat in much of its range, the swamp rabbit eventually may become rare or threatened.

The subspecies in Arkansas is *S. a. aquaticus*.

SELECTED REFERENCES
Hill (1967); Terrel (1972).

BLACK-TAILED JACKRABBIT

Lepus californicus

NAME *Lepus* is the Latin word for "hare." The specific name, *californicus*, is Latinized for "of California," the place where it was first collected.

IDENTIFICATION AND DESCRIPTION The black-tailed jackrabbit is a large lagomorph with long ears, tipped with black, which are nearly as long as its hind foot. The tail is black above and grayish white below. The pelage is grayish brown or grayish buffy above and white below. It has a buffy neck and chest, and the rump is whitish or pale gray with a median black stripe extending onto the tail.

MEASUREMENTS AND DENTAL FORMULA
Total Length: 465–630 mm (18.3–25 in)
Tail Length: 50–112 mm (2–4.5 in)
Hind Foot: 112–145 mm (4.5–5.7 in)
Ear: 99–131 mm (3.9–5.2 in)
Skull Length: 92–101 mm (3.6–4 in)
Weight: 1.8–3.6 kg (4–8 lb)
Dental I 2/1, C 0/0, P 3/2, M 3/3
 Formula: = 28

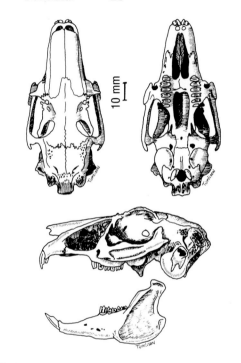

Skull of *Lepus californicus*

ARKANSAS DISTRIBUTION AND ABUNDANCE The black-tailed jackrabbit occurs on the western edge of Arkansas and westernmost portion of Arkansas River Valley and Fourche Mountains. It is not common.

LIFE HISTORY The black-tailed jackrabbit inhabits open grasslands, pastures, and cultivated areas and avoids timberland and cover more than one-half a meter high. In river bottom areas, it occurs to a limited extent in some-

Lepus californicus, Black-tailed Jackrabbit.
Bill Reaves   Texas Parks & Wildlife Department

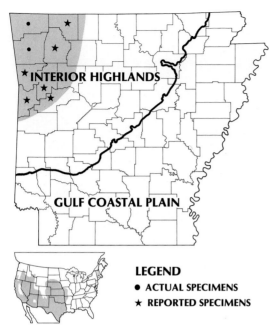

Distribution of the black-tailed jackrabbit (*Lepus californicus*)

LEGEND
• ACTUAL SPECIMENS
★ REPORTED SPECIMENS

tors. They become active at dusk and forage well into the night, eating grasses and herbs as well as cultivated crops including alfalfa, clover, and soybeans. In autumn and winter, they eat dried herbs and grasses, bark, twigs, buds, prickly pears, forage crops, and fruits. In parts of the West, where they are extremely numerous under favorable conditions, it has been estimated that 30 jackrabbits can consume as much forage as one sheep.

Breeding continues the year around, but most activity takes place between December and September. The peak of the breeding season coincides with greening of the vegetation (Lechleitner 1959). The gestation period ranges from 41 to 47 days and averages about 43 days (Haskell and Reynolds 1947). Females produce one to four litters per year; the litter size varies from one to eight, averaging two to three. Lechleitner (1959) reported that the average litter size was one in January, increased to four during the peak of breeding in April, and then declined to one in August. Young females are capable of breeding at about 8 months of age, but most do not breed until the second year.

When cover is abundant, the nest may be only an enlarged form, but it may be below ground level and lined with fur where cover is scarce. The precocious young are well furred and have their eyes open at birth. Weaning occurs when the young are 3 weeks old, but they may begin to supplement their diet with green vegetation at the age of 10 days. Young jackrabbits become independent of their mother at 3–4 weeks of age. They grow rapidly and reach adult size when 7–8 months old. Jackrabbits have a lower reproductive potential than the cottontail or swamp rabbit but appear to have a greater longevity. Lechleitner (1959) estimated that more than 25% of the population he studied was over one year old. Individuals have been known to live as long as 8 years in the wild.

Both young and adult hares are favorite prey of many predators, including coyotes, bobcats, hawks, and owls. In some areas of the West, more than 50% of the coyote's diet consists of jackrabbit.

what brushy habitat. This species was first observed in Franklin County, Arkansas, in 1927, and it was subsequently reported from Benton, Crawford, and Washington counties (Black 1936), where it now is locally common. It may always have been present in small numbers in the prairie peninsulas of western Arkansas since it is a normal component of grassland communities in the southwestern United States. Brown (1908) found remains of a now extinct species of jackrabbit, *Lepus giganteus*, in a Pleistocene bone deposit in the Conard Fissure in Newton County. With widespread clearing of land for agriculture beginning in the 1940s in western Arkansas, the jackrabbit apparently expanded its range as suitable habitat opened up. In recent years, much timberland has been cleared by ranchers in western Arkansas, providing avenues for dispersal, and it is expected that some further range expansion may occur.

Jackrabbits spend most of the day in a shallow "form" scratched out under a shrub or in a clump of tall grass where they are protected from sun and wind and concealed from preda-

IMPORTANCE AND/OR MANAGEMENT At this time no control or management measures are needed.

The subspecies in Arkansas is *L. c. melanotis*.

SELECTED REFERENCES
Black (1936); Brown (1908); Dunn et al. (1982); Haskell and Reynolds (1947); Lechleitner (1959).

Order Rodentia *Rodents*

The order Rodentia is the largest mammalian order with more than 30 families, 488 genera, and over 1,750 species. Rodents are extremely successful: they are nearly cosmopolitan in distribution, they are important members of most terrestrial and many aquatic ecosystems, they often reach extremely high population densities, and they exploit a wide variety of foods. Many rodents resemble members of other orders in terms of life styles and morphological features. Rodents are an extremely complex and fascinating group.

The rodents, as expected, are the largest group of mammals in Arkansas both in number of species and of individuals. They range in size from the tiny eastern and western harvest mice, which may weigh less than 10 g (0.35 oz), to the large beaver, which may weigh more than 25 kg (55 lb). The members of this order are very diverse in form and habits; some are largely aquatic, some mainly arboreal, and others spend most of their lives underground. The majority of species in this group are mainly nocturnal. Fox squirrels, gray squirrels, and chipmunks are diurnal; that is, they are active only during daylight hours. The woodchuck is primarily diurnal but shows some nocturnal activity. Other species are primarily nocturnal but show some daytime activity. Additionally, many display crepuscular patterns: they are active at dawn and dusk.

Rodents are generally small-sized mammals characterized by a single pair of curved, chisel-like, continually growing incisors in both the upper and lower jaws. The absence of canine teeth leaves a wide gap, the diastema, between the incisor and cheek teeth. Several species in the order cause serious economic losses to farmers, and other species constitute a definite health hazard by transmitting diseases to man. On the other hand, others are economically beneficial through their fur or flesh.

WHOLE ANIMALS

1. Tail densely furred, distinctly hairy .... SCIURIDAE (squirrels), page 119

   Tail sparsely furred or naked (or nearly so) 2

2. Size large, total length of adult more than 750
   mm (29.5 in) (head and body usually 500 mm
   [19.7 in] or more) 3

   Size smaller, total length of adult less than 750
   mm (29.5 in) (head and body usually less than
   500 mm [19.7 in]) 4

3. Mammary glands (nipples) located along each
   side of back; tail long, round, nearly naked and
   scaly .... CAPROMYIDAE (nutria), page 186

   Mammary glands located ventrally, tail dorso-
   ventrally flattened and scaly .... CASTORIDAE (beaver), page 134

4. External fur-lined cheek pouches present; claws
   on forefeet greatly enlarged; tail much shorter
   than head and body .... GEOMYIDAE (pocket gopher), page 131

   External fur-lined cheek pouches absent; claws
   on forefeet not greatly enlarged .... MURIDAE (rats and mice), page 138

SKULLS

1. Infraorbital aperture larger than foramen mag-
   num (fig. 11a) .... CAPROMYIDAE (nutria), page 186

   Infraorbital aperture smaller than foramen mag-
   num (fig. 11b,c) 2

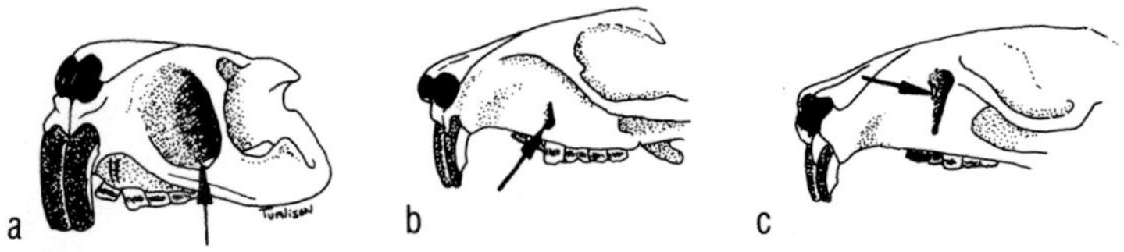

FIGURE 11.   Infraorbital foramen: a) larger than foramen magnum
(Hystricomorpha); b) minute (Sciuromorpha); and c) elongated and vertical (Myomorpha).

2. Total number of teeth 20–22; four or five cheek
   teeth on each side of upper jaw (first cheek
   tooth may be very tiny) 3

   Total number of teeth 16; three cheek teeth on
   each side of upper jaw 4

3. Skull large, more than 100 mm (3.93 in) long;
   four cheek teeth in upper jaw, with flat grinding
   surfaces and transverse enamel loops .... CASTORIDAE (beaver), page 134

Skull smaller, less than 100 mm (3.93 in) long;
four or five cheek teeth in upper jaw, without
transverse enamel loops .... SCIURIDAE (squirrels), page 119

4. External ear canal (auditory meatus) tube-like,
conspicuous .... GEOMYIDAE (pocket gopher), page 131

External ear canal not tube-like, inconspicuous
.... MURIDAE (rats, mice, and voles), page 138

FAMILY SCIURIDAE

SQUIRRELS

Members of this family are mainly active during daylight and are well known to most people. Characteristics which they share in common are: Tail cylindrical, bushy, and long-haired; forefeet with four toes and a knob-like thumb, hindfeet with five nearly equal toes; distinct postorbital processes on skull; small infraorbital aperture; cheek teeth rooted, four on each side of lower jaw and four to five on each side of upper jaw.

This family is represented in Arkansas by five species.

KEY TO SPECIES

WHOLE ANIMALS

1. Fore and hind legs connected by a loose fold of
skin; tail well furred, flattened horizontally,
sides nearly parallel; pelage soft, dense, and
very fine; eyes very large .... *Glaucomys volans*, Southern Flying Squirrel

Fore and hind feed not connected by a loose
fold of skin; tail not flattened horizontally 2

2. Tail short, not more than one-fourth of total
length; feet black, hind foot more than 75 mm
(2.95 in) long; body robust and heavy .... *Marmota monax*, Woodchuck

Tail long, more than one-fourth of total length;
feet not black, hind foot less than 75 mm long
(2.95 in) 3

3. Longitudinal light and dark stripes on back; tail
moderately long, not very bushy .... *Tamias striatus*, Eastern Chipmunk

No longitudinal stripes on back; tail bushy 4

4. Lateral hairs on tail tipped with white; uniformly gray above, grayish white below (occasionally all black); outer side of ear sometimes
white .... *Sciurus carolinensis*, Gray Squirrel

Lateral hairs on tail tipped with straw color to
reddish orange; tawny gray to tawny black above,
reddish orange below (occasionally all black);
ear reddish orange .... *Sciurus niger*, Fox Squirrel

SKULLS

1. Total number of teeth 22; five cheek teeth on
   each side of upper jaw 2

   Total number of teeth 20; four cheek teeth on
   each side of upper jaw 4

2. Front surface of incisors white; length more than
   70 mm (2.8 in); width more than 40 mm (1.6
   in); top of skull flattened or somewhat concave
   (hollowed) .... *Marmota monax*, Woodchuck

   Front surface of incisors yellow or orange; length
   less than 70 mm (2.8 in); width less than 40
   mm (1.6 in); top of skull convex (rounded) 3

3. Length less than 50 mm (2.0 in) (usually about
   34–36 mm [1.3–1.4 in]); first upper cheek tooth
   small but about same height as second and with
   only one cusp; interorbital region deeply notched
   anterior to postorbital process (fig. 12) .... *Glaucomys volans*, Flying Squirrel

FIGURE 12.   Interorbital region of *Glaucomys volans* deeply notched anterior to postorbital process.

FIGURE 13.   Tiny first upper cheek tooth of
Sciurus carolinensis.

Length more than 50 mm (usually about 60 mm
[2.4 in]); first upper cheek tooth tiny and with
only one cusp (fig. 13); interorbital region not
deeply notched anterior to postorbital pro-
cesses .... *Sciurus carolinenis*, Gray Squirrel

4. Length less than 50 mm (2.0 in) (usually about
   38–42 mm [1.5–1.7 in]); upper cheek tooth
   row less than 7 mm (0.28 in) long .... *Tamias striatus*, Eastern Chipmunk

   Length more than 50 mm (usually about 65 mm
   [2.6 in]); upper cheek tooth row more than 7
   mm (0.28 in) long .... *Sciurus niger*, Fox Squirrel

Eastern Chipmunk

Tamias striatus

NAME   *Tamias* is the Greek word for "a storer" and refers to the food-storing habits of this species. The specific name, *striatus*, is the Latin word for "striped."

IDENTIFICATION AND DESCRIPTION   The chipmunk is a small squirrel with well-developed cheek pouches and a flattened, hairy tail. The animal is striped on the sides of its head and on its back. The pelage is reddish brown above with five dark stripes alternating with two light buffy stripes, all ending at a reddish rump patch. The species is generally whitish below, sometimes suffused with buffy tan color.

The skull of the chipmunk is most likely to be confused with that of the southern flying squirrel; however, the chipmunk has four cheek teeth on each side of the upper jaw.

MEASUREMENTS AND DENTAL FORMULA

Total Length:	205–299 mm (8.1–11.8 in)
Tail Length:	69–115 mm (2.7–4.5 in)
Hind Foot:	31–43 mm (1.2–1.7 in)
Ear:	11–22 mm (0.43–0.87 in)
Skull Length:	38–50 mm (1.5–2.0 in)
Weight:	73–126 g (2.6–4.4 oz)
Dental Formula:	I 1/1, C 0/0, P 1/1, M 3/3 = 20

Tamias striatus, Eastern Chipmunk. *Lynn Rogers*

ARKANSAS DISTRIBUTION AND ABUNDANCE
The chipmunk is primarily confined to Interior Highlands. It is scarce or rare on the western edge of the West Gulf Coastal Plain, and apparently absent or rare in most of the eastern half of the West Gulf Coastal Plain and the Mississippi Alluvial Plain. Although locally abundant in some areas of the Ozarks, chipmunks are not common throughout their range.

LIFE HISTORY   The chipmunk occurs in rocky, wooded ravines, along wooded limestone escarpments or old stone fences, and in brushy woodlands where there are numerous fallen logs, rockpiles, or woodpiles that provide shelter for escape and lookout posts. It is primarily a ground dweller but occasionally climbs trees in search of fruits, nuts, or buds. Its burrow is dug at the base of old stumps, among tree roots, or under rocks and logs. In addition to a nest chamber, the burrow may have one or more storage chambers for the winter food supply.

Chipmunks are active during daytime and generally emerge from their burrows in early morning and late afternoon. Daily activity consists mainly of gathering food, and chipmunks make frequent trips to the burrow with their cheek pouches crammed with seeds, nuts, cherry pits, and other food items. Several storage chambers may be filled with food which they live on during the period of food scarcity in winter. Wherever the chipmunk is common, its soft call may be heard on balmy days during spring and fall. When alarmed or startled, chipmunks utter a trilling sound. Their vocal repertoire also includes a loud chip repeated at short intervals, sometimes for several minutes at a time.

The eastern chipmunk remains active throughout the year in Arkansas, but it spends much less time above ground during the winter months. Unlike other ground squirrels, it does not enter into lengthy periods of hibernation, but during cold winter days it undergoes bouts of torpor in its burrow, awakening periodically to feed. The duration of torpor periods varies with the ambient temperatures and may last from one to six days (Pivorun 1976). On warm, sunny days, it may be seen above ground during any winter month. Chipmunks do not become excessively fat in autumn like other hibernators; instead, they rely on their food stores for needed energy during cold weather.

Breeding activity begins from late February to March, and the first litters are born in April and May after a 31-day gestation period (Smith and Smith 1975; Yerger 1955). Females may produce one or two litters annually, and summer litters usually are born in July and August. The litter size ranges from one to eight, averaging four to five. Females born in the spring may breed later in the same year, but apparently most do not breed until they are about 1 year old. The naked and blind young are reared in an underground nest chamber and first appear above ground at the age of 5–6 weeks. When 2 months old, they are able to shift for themselves. The potential life span of the chipmunk may be as long as 8 years, but the maximum

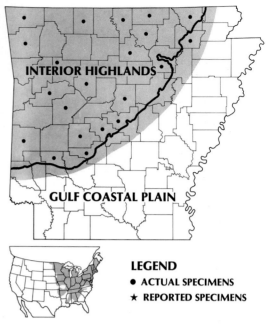

LEGEND
- ● ACTUAL SPECIMENS
- ★ REPORTED SPECIMENS

Distribution of the eastern chipmunk (*Tamias striatus*)

longevity in the wild is probably about 2–3 years.

IMPORTANCE AND/OR MANAGEMENT   No management or control measures are needed.

The subspecies that occurs in Arkansas is *T. s. venustus*, sometimes called the southwestern chipmunk.

SELECTED REFERENCES
Pivorun (1976); Smith and Smith (1975); Yerger (1955).

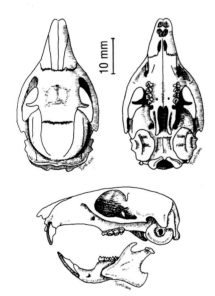

Skull of *Tamias striatus*

WOODCHUCK

Marmota monax

NAME   *Marmota* is the Latin name for "marmot." The specific name, *monax*, is an American Indian name for "the digger." Woodchucks are also known as groundhogs, marmots, and whistling pigs.

IDENTIFICATION AND DESCRIPTION   The woodchuck is a large, heavy-bodied rodent. It has a

Marmota monax, Woodchuck. *Herb Troester*

short, blunt muzzle; small, rounded ears; a stubby, furry tail; and short, powerful legs. Its toes have long, slightly curved claws, and the front teeth are white. The fur is thick and coarse. The pelage is a grizzled yellowish gray to dark brown or nearly black above and lighter below (often with a reddish wash). The feet and tail are dark brown to black. Males are somewhat larger than females.

MEASUREMENTS AND DENTAL FORMULA

Total Length:	418–665 mm (16.5–26.2 in)
Tail Length:	100–189 mm (3.9–7.4 in)
Hind Foot:	61–74 mm (2.4–2.9 in)
Ear:	23–25 mm (0.91–0.98 in)
Skull Length:	73–95 mm (2.9–3.7 in)
Weight:	2–60 kg (4.4–32 lb)(heaviest in autumn)
Dental Formula:	I 1/1, C 0/0, P 2/1, M 3/3 = 22

ARKANSAS DISTRIBUTION AND ABUNDANCE
The woodchuck is primarily confined to the In-terior Highlands. It is scarce or rare on the Mississippi Delta and almost absent from the West Gulf Coastal Plain (except perhaps on its extreme western edge).

LIFE HISTORY   The woodchuck usually occurs near the forest edge, in open fields, or along brushy fencerows, and seldom inhabits dense woodlands. It is sometimes found near the base of limestone escarpments where it burrows beneath rocks or makes its den in natural crevices or caves. Woodchucks dig extensive burrows, usually in sloping ground, which have 2–3 entrances, one of which may be concealed and serves as an escape hole. A nest chamber located in a dry portion of the burrow contains a nest of dried grass or leaves.

Woodchucks are active in daytime, especially in early morning and late afternoon, but they also exhibit considerable nighttime activity (Hayes 1976). Hayes monitored woodchucks telemetrically in northwestern Arkansas and found that they have a unimodal activity cycle from May to mid-June and from October through late November; a bimodal midsummer pattern was found from mid-June through September. During the time of year when the unimodal pattern was evident, more than 50% of the activity was underground. Nighttime activity is especially prevalent during the mating season in February and March.

Hayes (1977) also found that home ranges averaged 1.99 ha (4.9 acres) in northwestern Arkansas. Smith (1972) showed that woodchucks may migrate from winter to summer dens with corresponding shifts in home ranges. Woodchucks exhibit little territoriality except in the immediate area of the home den (Hamilton 1934; Grizzell 1955).

The diet of the woodchuck includes grasses, legumes, clover, and various succulent green herbs. Only a small amount of animal matter (less than 1%), such as insects and snails, is eaten. Occasionally woodchucks can be a nuisance in a garden when it is near their burrow.

Breeding follows emergence from hibernation in the spring. Woodchucks usually do not breed until they are 2 years of age (Grizzell 1955). In northern Arkansas, mating probably occurs from late January or early February to early March. Most litters are born in February, March, or early April after a gestation period of 31–33 days. A young woodchuck in the University of Arkansas at Fayetteville vertebrate collection weighed 396 g (13.9 oz) when collected on 21 May in Fayetteville, Arkansas. Extrapolating from growth data on young woodchucks (Hamilton 1934), its birth date would have been about 4 April and conception would have taken place about 4 or 5 March. Only one litter per year is produced, which averages four to five young (although the litter size may vary from two to nine) weighing 22–39 g (0.78–1.38 oz) at birth. They are weaned when about 4 weeks old. Although the potential longevity is 8–10 years, it is probable that most woodchucks survive no longer than 4–5 years in the wild.

In late summer, before entering hibernation, woodchucks accumulate a large reserve of body

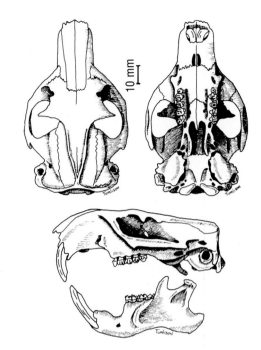

Skull of *Marmota monax*

fat. In northern latitudes, woodchucks usually begin hibernation earlier (in October) and emerge later (in February or early March) than farther south (Davis 1967). In northern Arkansas, the hibernating period appears to be fairly short, probably not longer than 6–8 weeks, with entry into hibernation around mid- or late November and emergence in January or early February. Anthony (1962) reported that few woodchucks hibernate in southern Illinois. The hibernating den is usually located beneath a stump or tree roots which provide maximum protection from predators and seeping water.

IMPORTANCE AND/OR MANAGEMENT Woodchuck burrows are frequently used as den or refuge sites by rabbits, raccoons, skunks, and other mammals. Most problems concerning crop or garden depredation or burrowing activities are localized and often are the work of one or two individuals. No management or control measures are needed in Arkansas.

The subspecies in Arkansas is *M. m. monax*.

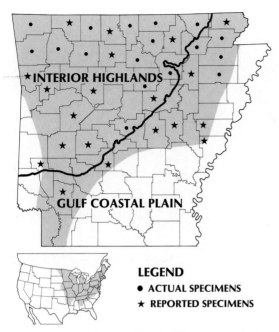

LEGEND
● ACTUAL SPECIMENS
★ REPORTED SPECIMENS

Distribution of the woodchuck (*Marmota monax*)

SELECTED REFERENCES
Anthony (1962); Davis (1967); Grizzel (1955); Hamilton (1934); Hayes (1976, 1977); Lee and Funderburg (1982); Smith (1972).

GRAY SQUIRREL

Sciurus carolinensis

NAME *Sciurus* is the Latin name for "squirrel." The specific name, *carolinensis*, is Latinized for "of Carolina," for the place from which this species was first collected and described.

IDENTIFICATION AND DESCRIPTION The gray squirrel is a medium-sized squirrel with a long, flattened, bushy tail. Hairs on the body are tipped with white, and the general pelage is grayish, washed with yellowish brown above. The head and back are darker, and the belly is white or light gray. There is a buff or white ring around the eye, and tufts of white behind the ears are common in some individuals. Black (melanistic) and pure white (albino) color phases are not uncommon in this species.

The skull of the gray squirrel can be distinguished from that of the fox squirrel by the presence of a small upper premolar. In a very few individuals, this tooth may be absent.

MEASUREMENTS AND DENTAL FORMULA
Total Length: 390–653 mm (14.1–25.7 in)
Tail Length: 180–300 mm (7.1–11.8 in)
Hind Foot: 45–75 mm (17.7–29.5 in)
Ear: 24–35 mm (0.95–1.4 in)
Skull Length: 60–63 mm (2.4–2.5 in)
Weight: 317–710 g (11.2–25.0 oz)
Dental Formula: I 1/1, C 0/0, P 2/1, M 3/3 = 22

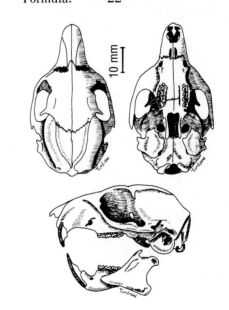

Skull of *Sciurus carolinensis*

ARKANSAS DISTRIBUTION AND ABUNDANCE
The gray squirrel occurs statewide and is abundant in wooded areas.

LIFE HISTORY The gray squirrel occurs in deciduous, chiefly oak-hickory, forests and stands of mixed conifers and hardwoods, especially those with mature, nut-bearing trees. It also is common in parks and suburban yards. Gray squirrels and fox squirrels normally do not share the same habitat. In cities, gray squirrels are

Sciurus carolinensis, Gray Squirrel. *Phil A. Dotson*

more common in suburban yards while fox squirrels are more often found in parks. Gray squirrels seem to be more adept climbers and spend more time in trees than fox squirrels. They descend to the ground mainly to collect food, to bury nuts, and play or engage in mating chases. This squirrel is strictly diurnal and is most active during early morning or late afternoon.

Foods eaten by gray squirrels include acorns, nuts, seeds and fruits of various trees in its habitat, fungi, and buds. They occasionally raid gardens for green tomatoes, berries, and other produce, and they often become pests at bird feeders. They are especially fond of sunflower seeds and shelled corn. Squirrels do not hibernate; however, they often store quantities of food for winter use. During spells of severe cold or rainy weather, they may remain inactive in their nests. Populations vary with the abundance of food. When there is a good crop of

acorns and nuts, mortality of young is low and a high population survives through the winter. A poor mast crop in the following year may be accompanied by a population decline through starvation or migration in search of food.

The home ranges of gray squirrels are generally smaller than those of fox squirrels. Several authors (Flyger 1960; Cordes and Barkalow 1973; and Hougart 1975) reported that home ranges of gray squirrels varied from 0.5 to 1.8 ha (1.2–4.4 acres), with males having slightly larger ranges than females.

Fox and gray squirrels are noticeably more active in September and early October. During this season, they bury acorns and nuts for winter. Some dispersal occurs at this time (predominantly by subadults from the spring litters), and the "fall reshuffle" also occurs. During this "fall reshuffle," individuals may move 10–20 km (6.2–12.4 mi) into entirely new locations (Flyger and Gates 1982).

This species has two kinds of nests: a temporary leaf and twig nest situated high above ground in a crotch or outer branches of a tree and more permanent nests constructed of shredded bark and plant fibers in a hollow den tree. The young usually are reared in the latter type of nest if den trees are available. Gray squirrels often take over and use large bird houses or nest boxes.

In northern Arkansas, there are two breeding seasons, each lasting about three and one-half months (Forsyth 1963; Jester 1957). The first season extends from late December and early January until mid-May, and the second extends from June to mid-October. Most males are in rut from late December to late February and again from early June to mid-August; however, some males may be in breeding condition during any month of the year with the possible exception of July. In most males, the testes regress in size from April until late May and again from July to August. The peak of the rut occurs in January and February. Reproductively active males chase females for 1–3 days before mating. After a gestation period, which averages 44 days, the litter of three to five young is born. The first litters are produced from mid-February until April. Second litters are born from June through September and rarely in October. The breeding season is probably somewhat longer in southern Arkansas. Young squirrels are weaned at about 6 weeks of age. They mature rapidly and females are capable of producing young when about a year old.

IMPORTANCE AND/OR MANAGEMENT In Arkansas, the gray squirrel is an important small game mammal. The best management tools appear to be regulation of the annual kill through bag limits, restriction of hunting during peaks in breeding activity, and conservation of mature den and nut-bearing trees (Uhlig 1956). Many squirrels are killed by cars in cities; in the wild, they are preyed upon by red-tailed hawks, bobcats, foxes, and other predators which do not, however, seriously affect population levels.

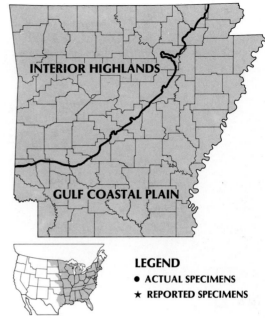

Distribution of the gray squirrel (*Sciurus carolinensis*)

The subspecies which occurs in Arkansas is *S. c. carolinensis*.

SELECTED REFERENCES
Cordes and Barkalow (1973); Flyger (1960); Flyger and Gates (1982); Forsyth (1963); Hougart (1975); Jester (1957); Uhlig (1956).

Fox Squirrel

Sciurus niger

NAME *Sciurus* is the Latin name for "squirrel." The specific name, *niger,* is the Latin word for "black," and apparently refers to the fact that many fox squirrels are melanistic.

IDENTIFICATION AND DESCRIPTION The fox squirrel is relatively large, heavy-bodied, and has a squarish profile. Its ears are rather short. It has a long, bushy tail that is edged with buffy brown. The pelage is rusty-yellow, grizzled with gray above, and pale yellow to orange below. Its nose and feet are yellowish brown to rusty-orange. A black or blackish (melanistic) color phase is common in this species, particularly in bottomland areas.

Sciurus niger, Fox Squirrel. *Phil A. Dotson*

MEASUREMENTS AND DENTAL FORMULA

Total length:	454–698 mm (17.9–27.5 in)
Tail Length:	180–330 mm (7.1–12.9 in)
Hind Foot:	47–83 mm (1.9–3.3 in)
Ear:	20–32 mm (0.79–1.3 in)
Skull Length:	63–69 mm (2.5–2.7 in)
Weight:	425–1000 g (15–35.3 oz)
Dental Formula:	I 1/1, C 0/0, P 1/1, M 3/3, = 20

ARKANSAS DISTRIBUTION AND ABUNDANCE

Fox squirrels occur statewide in wooded areas. Fox squirrels are less abundant than gray squirrels in many areas and are found more often in upland than in bottomland forests.

LIFE HISTORY

The fox squirrel occurs in open stands of oak, hickory, and other hardwoods, as well as mixed pine and hardwood stands, which provide its basic food items. This species is also common in city parks. Open stands of timber are well tolerated by fox squirrels but seem to be avoided by gray squirrels. Perhaps because of the larger size of fox squirrels, they appear to be less agile climbers than gray squirrels. Fox squirrels leap from tree to tree less often and spend more time foraging on the ground. Like gray squirrels, they are strictly diurnal but have a somewhat different activity pattern. Fox squirrels do not become active until an hour or more after sunrise (Lowery 1974; Moore 1957); their activity decreases in mid-morning, but they become active again around midday. Another activity period occurs in late afternoon before sunset.

In general, the life history of the fox squirrel is quite similar to that of the gray squirrel (see gray squirrel account). Its diet includes the same kind of food items, and the annual reproductive cycle differs very little from that of the gray squirrel. Females produce two litters of three to five young annually after a gestation period which averages 45 days (Asdell 1964). However, a well-nourished female may give birth to as many as six to seven young.

IMPORTANCE AND/OR MANAGEMENT   See comments on gray squirrel.

The race *S. n. rufiventer* occurs over most

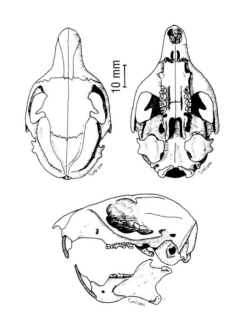

Skull of *Sciurus niger*

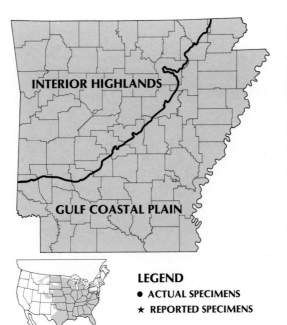

LEGEND
- ● ACTUAL SPECIMENS
- ★ REPORTED SPECIMENS

Distribution of the fox squirrel (*Sciurus niger*)

of the northern two-thirds of the state. It is probable that the race *subauratus* occurs in southeastern Arkansas and that intergradation between two races occurs. In addition, intermediates between the races of *rufiventer* and *ludovicianus* probably occur in southwestern Arkansas—a specimen from Delight, Pike County, has been referred to the race *ludovicianus* (Lowery and Davis 1942).

SELECTED REFERENCES
Asdell (1964); Lowery (1974); Lowery and Davis (1942); Moore (1957).

SOUTHERN FLYING SQUIRREL

Glaucomys volans

NAME   *Glaucomys* is from two Greek words, *glaukos*, meaning "gray," and *mys*, meaning "mouse." The specific name, *volans*, is the Latin word for "flying." It should be noted that this squirrel does not exhibit true flight, but instead it glides from spot to spot.

IDENTIFICATION AND DESCRIPTION   The southern flying squirrel is a small squirrel that has a furred "gliding" membrane extending on each side from its wrist to its ankle. It has a well-furred, flattened tail and large eyes. The fur is soft, dense, and silky. It is gray to brown or pinkish cinnamon above (the fur is slate colored at its base), and creamy white below (the fur is white to its base). The underside of the gliding membrane is bordered by a pinkish cinnamon color.

The skull is most likely to be confused with that of the chipmunk; however, the flying squirrel has five cheek teeth on each side of the upper jaw.

MEASUREMENTS AND DENTAL FORMULA
Total Length: 198–253 mm (7.8–9.9 in)
Tail Length: 75–120 mm (2.9–4.7 in)
Hind Foot: 21–33 mm (0.83–1.3 in)
Ear: 16–21 mm (0.63–0.83 in)
Skull Length: 31–34 mm (1.2–1.3 in)
Weight: 40–98 g (1.4–3.5 oz)
Dental   I 1/1, C 0/0, P 2/1, M 3/3
  Formula: = 22

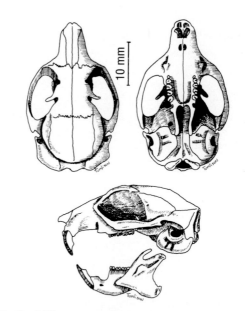

Skull of *Glaucomys volans*

Glaucomys volans, Southern Flying Squirrel. *Phil A. Dotson*

ARKANSAS DISTRIBUTION AND ABUNDANCE
The flying squirrel occurs statewide in wooded areas.

LIFE HISTORY   The flying squirrel usually is found in heavily forested areas not far from water. In the Arkansas Ozarks, somewhat open oak-hickory woodlands with numerous den trees or old dead trees containing woodpecker holes that provide nesting sites are preferred. Elsewhere in the state, other forest types with mature trees that have suitable nest cavities are utilized.

Because of their largely nocturnal habits, flying squirrels are seldom seen by the average person, even though they may be common in an area. They are most often observed gliding from tree to tree on bright moonlit nights or in the dim light of predawn or dusk. Their large eyes, which glow red in the beam of a lantern, are well adapted for night vision. Before launching into a glide, the legs are spread so that the lat-eral "gliding" membranes are fully extended. The downward course and speed of the glide can be controlled by the tail and membranes. The flying squirrel is capable of executing right angle turns and changing the glide angle during "flight." The momentum is checked by an up-ward swoop just before it lands feet first, and it alights head up at the base of a tree, then scam-pers upward to forage or to launch into another glide to a neighboring tree. Flying squirrels seldom forage on the ground or at any great dis-tance from a tree.

The favorite food of the flying squirrel is hickory nuts, although it readily eats acorns, buds, seeds of various trees, fruits, berries, mushrooms, insects, and occasionally bird eggs and nestlings. It is also fond of meat and will feed on the carcasses of dead animals; it is frequently caught in traps baited with meat, which are set for furbearing animals. Flying squirrels often may be detected by the birdlike chirps and twitters they utter while foraging. In the northern portion of the flying squirrel's range, a winter supply of nuts and seeds is stored in tree cavities. In the southern portions, however, milder winters, alternate food, and greater ease in obtaining mast do not necessitate any sort of food caching (Heidt 1977).

The nest is situated in a tree cavity 4.5–10 m (15–35 ft) above ground and usually is lined with finely shredded inner bark, grasses, moss, hair, and leaves. In the southern part of its range, Spanish moss is sometimes used to line the nest (Moore 1947). Occasionally flying squirrels usurp old bird nests and abandoned leaf nests of fox and gray squirrels and make them over for their own use (Dolan and Carter 1977). Flying squirrels are very gregarious, and in winter as many as a dozen or more may occupy one large tree cavity. In suburban yards, bluebird and martin houses are sometimes appropriated by flying squirrels, and they may visit bird feeders at night for a feast of peanut butter or sunflower seeds.

Mating occurs in late January or early February and again from late May through July, although the second breeding period is not as intense. In extreme southern Arkansas, mating may occur through August, and some litters are born from late September to early October (Goertz 1965). After a gestation period of 39–40 days, females produce a litter of two to three (which may range from one to seven) tiny, blind, and hairless young. Young flying squirrels grow rapidly and are weaned and able to shift for themselves when 5–6 weeks old. They do not breed until at least one year of age.

IMPORTANCE AND/OR MANAGEMENT Flying squirrels often are kept as pets. They are docile, easily tamed, and seldom bite unless roughly handled. In the wild they have few enemies except house cats, rat snakes, and owls.

The subspecies *G. v. saturatus* occurs in most of the state. It may possibly intergrade with the race *volans* in the extreme northernmost tier of counties since the demarcation between the races is not well marked (Dolan and Carter 1977). The race *texensis* may possibly occur in the extreme southwestern corner of

Distribution of the southern flying squirrel (*Glaucomys volans*)

the state, but Lowery (1974) questions whether animals in this range belong to that race.

SELECTED REFERENCES
Dolan and Carter (1977); Goertz (1965); Heidt (1977); Lowery (1974); Moore (1947).

FAMILY GEOMYIDAE

POCKET GOPHERS

Members of this family are meduim-sized rodents adapted for an underground existence. General characteristics of the family are: external ears inconspicuous and extremely short; eyes tiny; external fur-lined cheek pouches; nearly naked tail very sensitive to touch; fur soft and fine, without conspicuous markings; forefeet enlarged, with long claws adapted for digging; thumb a mere knob with a nail; skull large, angular, with widespreading zygomatic arches; front teeth long, upper one grooved on anterior faces; total number of teeth 16.

The family is represented in Arkansas by one species.

BAIRD'S POCKET GOPHER

Geomys breviceps

NAME *Geomys* is from two Greek words, *ge*, meaning "earth," and *mys*, meaning "mouse." The specific name, *breviceps*, is from the Latin words, *brevis*, meaning "short," and *cepha*, meaning "head," referring to its short head.

IDENTIFICATION AND DESCRIPTION The pocket gopher is a stocky rodent that is well adapted for digging and living underground. Its ears are round and extremely short; the eyes are tiny; the tail is short and nearly naked; and the front legs are stout and strongly clawed. It has external, fur-lined cheek pouches. The upper front teeth are orange on the outer face and have prominent grooves (the lateral [outermost] groove on each tooth is deeper and more prominent than the medial [innermost] groove). The pelage is pale brown to slate gray or blackish above and paler below. The tail is brownish near the body, but pale buff to whitish as it extends away from the body. Males are larger than females.

Individuals with mottled white on the head, throat, belly, or back (piebald) are occasionally seen. Black (melanistic) individuals also are fairly common.

There is one molt annually (from spring to fall). The new fur appears first on the rump and gradually moves forward. There is generally a very noticeable molt line separating the old fur from new fur.

MEASUREMENTS AND DENTAL FORMULA
Total Length: 173–357 mm (6.8–14.1 in)
Tail Length: 45–102 mm (1.8–4.0 in)
Hind Foot: 20–40 mm (0.79–1.6 in)
Ear: 3–4 mm (0.12–0.16 in
Skull Length: 34–63 mm (1.3–2.5 in)
Weight: 74–530 g (2.6–19.0 oz)
Dental I 1/1, C 0/0, P 1/1, M 3/3
Formula: = 20

ARKANSAS DISTRIBUTION AND ABUNDANCE
Baird's pocket gopher is found in the West Gulf Coastal Plain, the Ouachita Mountains division of the Interior Highlands, and the extreme western and southern portions of the Ozark Mountains division of the Interior Highlands. It is scarce in the Mississippi Alluvial Plain.

LIFE HISTORY The pocket gopher ordinarily is solitary and antisocial, lives almost its entire life below ground, and seldom travels any great distance overland. It comes to the surface only to deposit earth excavated from its burrow or to forage briefly for food. The mounds of loose soil associated with its burrows often are the only sign of its presence. The principal regulatory factor determining pocket gopher populations is the suitability of the habitat—food, cover, soil type, and moisture (Chase et al. 1982). Pocket gophers occur only in soils with a low clay (less than 30%) and a high sand (more than 40%) content (Downhower and Hall 1966). The amount of silt in the soil does not seem to be critical. Areas where the water table is within about 1.5 m (4.9 ft) of the surface apparently

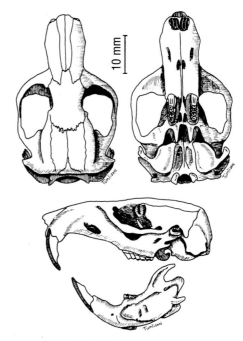

Skull of *Geomys breviceps*

Geomys breviceps, Baird's Pocket Gopher. *Edward F. Pembleton*

exclude this species from places where the soil type is suitable. It also may be excluded from thin soils where low temperatures in winter freeze the ground several inches deep.

About 90% of the burrow system consists of shallow subsurface runways and associated food storage chambers. These subsurface burrows, which are excavated in their search for food (Miller 1964), lie 15–25 cm (5.9–9.8 in) below the surface and may be several hundred meters long. A deeper tunnel system which may reach a depth of 1.5 m (4.9 ft) is not connected to the ground surface except through the subsurface runs. These tunnels end blindly or lead to a chamber containing a spherical grasslined nest 30 cm (11.8 in) or more above the deepest part of the tunnel. Several sanitation chambers, used for depositing excrement, are usually constructed in the burrow system.

The vegetarian diet of the pocket gopher consists chiefly of fleshy roots and stems of various weeds and grasses. The pocket gopher also consumes tubers, bulbs, acorns, and occasional white grubs and insect pupae. Considerable quantities of roots and tubers may be stored underground in the northern part of its range, but it seems probable that the pocket gopher stores only small amounts of food in the milder climate of the southern part of its range.

Breeding begins in late January or early February and may continue through August. At this time males and females may occupy the same burrow system. After a gestation period of four to five weeks (Wilks 1963), females produce a litter of one to eight young (and average three to four), generally in March and April. In southern Arkansas, older females probably produce a second litter in July or August. The young weigh about 5 g (0.18 oz) at birth (Vaughan 1962) and grow rapidly; females reach puberty

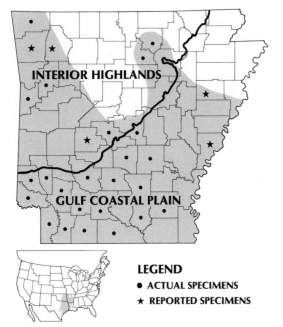

Distribution of Baird's pocket gopher (*Geomys breviceps*)

when about 3 months old (Wilks 1963) and may reach sexual maturity and produce a litter before the end of the breeding season.

The pocket gopher has relatively few natural enemies and maintains relatively stable populations. Predators including bobcats, badgers, coyotes, snakes (bull snakes, rat snakes, and rattlesnakes), weasels, and owls capture pocket gophers in their burrows or at night on the surface, but they do not significantly affect populations of this species.

IMPORTANCE AND/OR MANAGEMENT Pocket gophers may cause economic losses to the farmer, rancher, and forester. They are also a nuisance to the home gardener or golf course manager. Their gnawing can damage plastic irrigation pipe and buried cables (Capp 1976; Connolly and Landstrom 1969). They do, however, deepen the soil, may aid in improving drainage and retarding runoff of surface water, build up humus content of the soil, and destroy weeds.

Barnes (1973) reviewed methods of pocket gopher control. Included are various traps, the placing of poison baits in tunnels, and the less effective method of inserting poison gases and gas bombs into pocket gopher burrows. Since all entrances are plugged, gas does not penetrate rapidly in all of the tunnels. Also, the pocket gopher may wall off areas where the gases are present. The use of toxic bait is probably the most effective method of control.

Heaney and Timm (1983) recently determined that the pocket gopher found in Arkansas should be identified as *G. breviceps* rather than as *G. bursarius*. We concur with their decision and have thus made the specific change. The subspecies which occurs in Arkansas is *G. b. sagittalis*.

SELECTED REFERENCES
Barnes (1973); Davis (1940); Capp (1976); Chase et al. (1982); Connolly and Lanstrom (1969); Downhower and Hall (1966); Heaney and Timm (1983); Miller (1964); Vaughan (1962); Wilks (1963).

FAMILY CASTORIDAE
BEAVERS

Beavers are large, heavy-bodied, aquatic rodents. General characteristics of the family are: A broad, scaly, horizontally flattened tail; fully webbed hind feet; short legs; short ears; a massive skull; large, powerful front teeth, deep orange-red on anterior faces; rootless cheek teeth; total number of teeth 20.

The family is represented in Arkansas by one species.

BEAVER
Castor canadensis

NAME *Castor* is the Greek word for "beaver." The specific name, *canadensis*, is Latinized for "of Canada," referring to the country where the first specimen was taken.

Castor canadensis, Beaver. *Phil A. Dotson*

IDENTIFICATION AND DESCRIPTION   The beaver is a large, heavy-bodied rodent with a flat, paddle-shaped, scaly tail and webbed hind feet. The two inside toes of each hind foot have movable, doubled, or split nails, which the beaver uses as combs for grooming. It has small, valvular ears and valvular nostrils. The underfur is dense and silky, while the guard hairs are long, coarse, and glossy. The pelage is cinnamon-brown above and lighter below without a reddish tinge; the tail and feet are black.

MEASUREMENTS AND DENTAL FORMULA

Total Length: 875–1212 mm (34.4–47.7 in)
Tail Length: 230–440 mm (9.1–17.3 in)
Hind Foot: 156–192 mm (6.1–7.6 in)
Ear: 33–37 mm (1.3–1.5 in)
Skull Length: 114–139 mm (4.5–5.5 in)
Weight: 11–35 kg (24.2–77 lb)
Dental Formula: I 1/1, C 0/0, P 1/1, M 3/3 = 20

ARKANSAS DISTRIBUTION AND ABUNDANCE
The beaver occurs statewide. The beaver was exterminated in Arkansas soon after 1900. Efforts by the Arkansas Game and Fish Commission to restock beaver in the state began in 1926, but the early transplants were largely failures. More than 50 beaver were released in Arkansas between 1943 and 1945. All of these releases were at least partially successful (Holder 1951; Sealander 1956). A large and growing beaver population is present throughout the state today, due in part to a poor market for beaver pelts. The species is classed as a nuisance animal by the Arkansas Game and Fish Commission.

LIFE HISTORY   Over most of the state the beaver lives in burrows dug into the banks of streams or impoundments. The burrow entrance is hidden from sight beneath the water, and since the beaver is seldom active during daylight hours, its presence in an area often goes unnoticed. In flat, bottomland areas, low dams may be constructed behind which water is impounded to form a beaver pond. The den is usually built into the bank of the stream leading to the dam, and the large lodges used for food storage and protection that are typical of northern beaver are rarely built.

The beaver feeds on a variety of aquatic and terrestrial vegetation including sedges, rushes, cattails, and the bark, leaves, and twigs of many kinds of shrubs and trees. The most heavily utilized tree species in northwestern Arkansas are black willow, water locust, sweet gum, silver maple, buttonbush, and speckled alder; these six species comprise over 75% of the beaver's diet (Money 1977). Where it occurs, sweet gum is the preferred food followed by speckled alder and buttonbush. Sycamore and witch hazel are avoided by beavers. Many other trees and shrubs also make up the beaver's diet. In Arkansas, Money also found that in summer the diet is mainly herbaceous vegetation, leaves, and only small amounts of bark. Giant ragweed (*Ambrosia trifida*) and several species of sunflower (*Helianthus* spp.) are

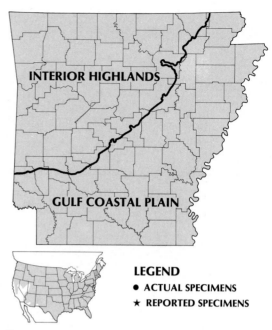

Distribution of the beaver (*Castor canadensis*)

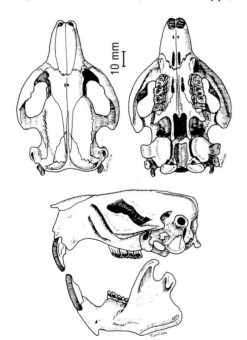

Skull of *Castor canadensis*

heavily utilized and appeared to be preferred food, since beavers often traveled quite far from water to secure them. Because of year-round availability, southern beavers do not store twigs and branches on the bottoms of ponds or in burrows as northern beavers do.

Beavers usually are monogamous and live in colonies that consist of an adult male and female together with young of the year and the litter of the previous year. Mating occurs in January and February, and the young are born in April, May, and June after a 128-day gestation period (Bradt 1939). The average litter size is three to five (but ranges from one to eight), and when born the kits are fully furred and have their eyes open. The young grow rather slowly and do not begin breeding until the second breeding season following birth. Although most authorities agree that females produce only one litter annually, some females in the southern part of the range apparently produce a second litter in August or September (Moore and Martin 1949). In Arkansas, the beaver has few enemies except man and may live for 15 or more years in the wild.

A beaver dam. Beaver use dams to impound water to create suitable habitat. *Joe Clark*

IMPORTANCE AND/OR MANAGEMENT   Perhaps no other mammal in Arkansas is as valuable as the beaver and, at the same time, creates more problems and economic losses. Its activities often conflict with man's vested interests, and damage to agricultural and timber lands presents difficult problems in proper wildlife management for game and fish commissions. In the flat Delta country of Arkansas, beavers cause flooding of agricultural land by damming canals, drainage ditches, and pipes. They also fell or girdle valuable timber near water or cause timber kills in flat, bottomland forests by submerging the roots of trees behind their dams in water for prolonged periods.

On the other hand, the beaver provides several important "services" to humans. Because of their construction of ponds, beavers provide water storage for a variety of uses, retard soil erosion, enhance conditions for warm water fishes, and create wildlife habitat through the formation of standing water, edge, and plant di-versity in close proximity (Hill 1982). Perhaps the greatest beneficiary of the beaver in Arkansas has been the river otter (*Lutra canadensis*). Recent studies (Tumlison et al. 1982; Karnes and Tumlinson 1984; Polechla 1987) have demonstrated a positive relationship between the two species. Furthermore, river otter populations have been able, due in large part to the beaver, to recover from near extirpation.

Historically, beaver have been the mainstay of the fur industry. Before their extirpation in Arkansas, beaver were an important fur resource. However, it was not until the 1960s, following re-establishment, that beaver again became important. In spite of this near extirpation, between 1942 and 1982, beaver ranked seventh in terms of total pelts sold, The Mississippi Delta ranked first (37%) in total harvest, followed by the Ozark Mountains (22%), the West Gulf Coastal Plain (21%), and the Ouachita Mountains (20%) (Peck et al. 1985). In addition, the secretions from the castor

Trees gnawed by beavers, Devil's Den State Park. *Gene R. Ploskey*

glands (castoreum), which open into the urethra, are quite valuable and are used in the perfume and trapping industries.

Beaver have been infected by tularemia, which not only decimates the beaver population but may be transmitted to trappers and others handling the carcasses (Stenlund 1953; Heidt et al. 1985a). Beaver have also been implicated as a reservoir for the waterborne parasite, *Giardia* (Davies and Hibler 1979). In Arkansas, a recent survey (Heidt et al. 1985b) demonstrated that 9 of 78 beaver (11.5%) had the parasite. We would caution that stream and pond water should be purified before drinking.

It is not possible to assign subspecific rank to the present beaver population in Arkansas since beaver introduced by the Arkansas Game and Fish Commission for restocking came from so many parts of the beaver's range in the United States.

SELECTED REFERENCES

Bradt (1939); Davies and Hibler (1979); Heidt et al. (1985a and b); Hill (1982); Holder (1951); Karnes and Tumlison (1984); Money (1977); Moore and Martin (1949); Novak (1987); Peck et al. (1985); Polechla (1987); Sealander (1956); Stenlund (1953); Tumlison et al. (1982).

FAMILY MURIDAE
RATS, MICE, AND VOLES

American mammalogists have long divided members of this group into two families: the Cricetidae (new world rats and mice) and the Muridae (old world rats and mice). This separation has been debated for many years (Simpson

1945:206), and some authorities (e.g., Ellerman 1940–49) have never recognized such a separation. The weight of recent taxonomic evidence favors the views of Ellerman and others (Anderson 1972; Hooper and Musser 1964; Musser 1969). A reluctance on the part of most American mammalogists to depart from traditional classification, rather than unfamiliarity with new evidence, probably accounts for continuing the older familial separation in most recent mammal books. In this text we have grouped both families under the family Muridae.

Members of the family Muridae in America are included in three subfamilies. The Cricetinae, which includes most small ground dwelling forms with long tails, large ears, and large eyes; the Microtinae, which includes most small ground dwelling forms with short tails (except the muskrat), small ears, and small eyes; and the Murinae, which includes mostly small ground dwelling and arboreal forms with long tails, large ears, and small eyes. The cheek teeth of cricetines either have two longitudinal rows of enamel-covered cusps or may be flat-crowned with enamel arranged in S-shaped loops. The microtines have flat-crowned cheek teeth with prismatic patterns, and the murines have cheek teeth with three longitudinal rows of enamel-covered cusps. Cricetines and microtines possess a post-caecal spiral which is absent in murines (Lange and Staaland 1970).

The muskrat is the only largely aquatic species in the family, but the semiaquatic rice rat and bog lemming also are closely associated with water, and they swim and dive quite readily. Other species in the family have terrestrial habitat preferences which range from open grassland to upland and lowland forests and rocky outcrops. Species included in the subfamily Murinae originally were not present in North and South America but were introduced by man. Wherever they occur, they are closely associated with humans, and they have inflicted tremendous agricultural losses through their consumption and fouling of stored grains and feeds. Besides the direct losses attributable to the familiar house mouse and Norway rat, the cost of control measures employed against them is very high. They are also a serious threat to the health of human populations since they harbor fleas and lice that transmit plague, typhus, and other diseases to man. On the beneficial side, the albino strains of the house mouse and Norway rat are used widely in genetic and medical research.

Some native murids are almost exclusively vegetarian, whereas a good deal of animal matter is included in the diet of others. Introduced murids are voracious feeders and consume all types of food. When well fed, they reproduce prolifically and their numbers often reach troublesome proportions. Most murids are active mainly at night or during twilight hours.

KEY TO SPECIES

WHOLE ANIMALS

1. Tail compressed laterally, scaly and scantily haired; hind feet partly webbed and toes with fringe of stiff hairs; front feet with five clawed toes; size large, total length more than 500 mm (19.7 in) . . . . *Ondatra zibethicus*, Muskrat

Tail rounded in cross section; feet not webbed;
front feet with four clawed toes (a small, nailed
thumb is present in *Synaptomys*); size small,
total length less than 400 mm (15.7 in)... 2

2. Tail very short, usually less than one-third of
the total length... 3

Tail relatively long, more than one-third of the
total length... 5

3. Tail shorter than or about as long as hind foot;
small, nailed thumb on each front foot in addition to four clawed toes; heels of hind feet with
tuft of blackish hairs; back brownish mixed
with gray, black, and yellow; grizzled head,
gray below; upper front teeth with a shallow
groove .... *Synaptomys cooperi*, Southern Bog Lemming

Tail distinctly longer than hind foot; upper
front teeth smooth 4

4. Tail sharply bicolored; fur relatively coarse;
back grayish to blackish brown, grizzled with
tan or whitish-tipped hairs, buffy below..................... *Microtus ochrogaster*, Prairie Vole

Tail not sharply bicolored, usually of same
color as back; fur soft and smooth; back bright
russet-brown to brownish chestnut; gray tipped
with buff or cinnamon below............................ *Microtus pinetorum*, Woodland Vole

5. Tail usually well haired, annulations nearly or
completely concealed by hair; small- to me-
dium-sized.. 6

Tail sparsely haired, annulations not concealed by hair, giving scaly appearance; small-
to medium-sized.. 16

6. Rat-sized, total length of adults usually more
than 250 mm (9.8 in); tail distinctly bicolored,
longer than 120 mm (4.7 in); grayish brown
above, white or grayish white below .... *Neotoma floridana*, Eastern Woodrat

Mouse-sized, total length of adults usually less
than 200 mm (7.9 in); tail shorter than 120
mm (4.7 in) 7

7. Eyes small; front teeth grooved 8

Eyes larger; front teeth smooth *(Note: Species
included here may be difficult to tell apart, and
a combination of characters must be used for
certain identification; when in doubt, consult
an authority.)*.. 11

8. Tail longer than head and body (projects beyond nose when laid forward along back), usually more than 70 mm (2.8 in); tail brown above, grayish white below; total length usually more than 135 mm (5.3 in); golden brown (sides reddish or orangish yellow) above, grayish white (usually washed with buff) below .... *Reithrodontomys fulvescens*, Fulvous Harvest Mouse

Tail shorter than or about as long as head and body, less than 70 mm (2.8 in); total length usually less than 135 mm (5.3 in) *(Note: Species included here are difficult to tell apart, and a combination of characters must be used for certain identification; when in doubt, consult an authority.)* 9

9. Tail distinctly bicolored, top with median stripe; pale gray to buffy gray washed with buff and sprinkled with black hairs above (middle of back darker), dull white beneath .... *Reithrodontomys montanus*, Plains Harvest Mouse

Tail not distinctly bicolored, stripe on top of tail wide, covering top surface and not contrasting strongly with underside. 10

10. Brownish or gray mixed with black (sometimes blackish down middle of back) above, ashy gray below; ears blackish; total length usually less than 125 mm (4.9 in). .... *Reithrodontomys humulis*, Eastern Harvest Mouse

Brownish-buff with intermixture of blackish hairs above, grayish-white below; ears pale, flesh color, or buffy; total length usually more than 125 mm (4.9 in). .... *Reithrodontomys megalotis*, Western Harvest Mouse

11. Tail well haired and distinctly bicolored 12

Tail usually thinly haired and not distinctly bicolored. 14

12. Tail with prominent tuft of hair at tip (penciled), usually about equal to or longer than head and body .... *Peromyscus attwateri*, Texas Mouse

Tail only slightly or not at all tufted at tip, nearly equal to or shorter than head and body 13

13. Tail sharply bicolored and usually shorter than head and body; hind foot usually less than 21 mm (0.83 in); ear usually less than 17 mm (0.67 in); size small; grayish to rich red-brown above, with blackish area along middle of back, whitish fur below; ears thinly margined with white. .... *Peromyscus maniculatus*, Deer Mouse

Tail bicolored but not always with sharp division, usually equal to or slightly longer than head and body; hind foot usually about 22–24 mm (0.87–0.95 in); ear usually about 18 mm (0.71 in); size medium to large; dark brown with a wide blackish area along middle of back above, dull white below . . . . *Peromyscus gossypinus*, Cotton Mouse

14. Fur long, wide blackish area along middle of back; hind foot usually 22–24 mm (0.87–0.95 in); ear usually about 18 mm (0.71). . . . . *Peromyscus gossypinus*, Cotton Mouse (see above)

Fur short, no blackish area along middle of back, hind foot usually less than 22 mm (0.87 in); ear usually less than 18 mm (0.71 in). 15

15. Ears same color as body, usually about 16–17 mm (0.63–0.67 in); hind foot usually about 17–19 mm (0.67–0.75 in); golden brown or orange-brown above, mixed with blackish hairs in some pelage phases, white below tinged with pinkish cinnamon . . . . *Ochrotomys nuttalli*, Golden Mouse

Ears contrasting with body color, generally gray or blackish; usually shorter than 16 mm (0.63 in); hind foot usually about 20–22 mm (0.79–0.87 in) pale to rich reddish brown above, white or grayish white below . . . . *Peromyscus leucopus*, White-footed Mouse

16. Mouse-sized; no color contrast between upper and lower surfaces of body; mixed yellowish brown and black above, ashy gray below; total length rarely more than 180 mm (7.1 in). . . . . *Mus musculus*, House Mouse

Rat-sized, color of upper and lower surfaces of body contrasting; total length usually more than 200mm (7.9 in) 17

17. Tail bicolored, usually equal to or longer than head and body; feet whitish; fur soft, short, smooth to touch; grayish brown and somewhat grizzled above, whitish or grayish white below . . . . *Oryzomys palustris*, Marsh Rice Rat

Tail nearly uniform in color, thinly haired or nearly naked 18

18. Tail usually longer than head and body; ears large (usually about 21 mm [0.83 in] or more), relatively hairless, standing out from fur; muzzle pointed; grayish brown to blackish above, gray below . . . . *Rattus rattus*, Black Rat

Tail usually shorter than head and body; ears relatively short, half buried in neck fur. 19

19. Grizzled buff and black above, grayish or buffy below; fur coarse, long, rough to touch; feet grayish. . . . . *Sigmodon hispidus*, Hispid Cotton Rat

Grayish brown above, gray below; fur coarse; feet brownish. . . . . *Rattus norvegicus*, Norway Rat

SKULLS

1. Cheek teeth flat-crowned and with numerous triangles or transverse folds on grinding surface 2

   Cheek teeth not flat-crowned and with two or three longitudinal rows of enamel-covered tubercles (cusps) on grinding surface (cusps apparent even when worn) 7

2. Length more than 50 mm (2.0 in); triangles on grinding surfaces of cheek teeth . . . . *Ondatra zibethicus*, Muskrat

   Length less than 50 mm (2.0 in); triangles or transverse folds on grinding surfaces of cheek teeth. 3

3. Length more than 30 mm (1.2 in) 4

   Length 30 mm (1.2 in) or less 5

4. Grinding surfaces of cheek teeth with S-shaped transverse ridges of enamel (lophs) (fig. 14) . . . . *Sigmodon hispidus*, Hispid Cotton Rat

FIGURE 14.   Grinding surfaces of cheek teeth of *Sigmodon hispidus* with S-shaped transverse ridges of enamel.

   Grinding surfaces of cheek teeth with enamel in triangular folds (prisms). . . . . *Neotoma floridana*, Eastern Woodrat

5. Upper front teeth with longitudinal groove on face (fig. 15a). . . . . *Synaptomys cooperi*, Southern Bog Lemming

   Upper front teeth smooth on face (fig. 15b). 6

a   b

FIGURE 15.   Upper front incisors grooved (a) and smooth (b).

6. Least interorbital constriction usually 4 mm (0.16 in) or less; loph 3 of second upper cheek tooth rounded (fig. 16a) . . . . *Microtus ochrogaster*, Prairie Vole

FIGURE 16.   Upper cheek tooth row of *Microtus ochrogaster* (a) and *M. pinetorum* (b). Inner loop 3 of second upper cheek tooth rounded in *ochrogaster* and squarish in *pinetorum*.

Least interorbital constriction usually more than 4 mm (0.16 in); loph 3 of second upper cheek tooth squarish (fig. 16b) . . . . *Microtus pinetorum*, Woodland Vole

(Note: The two species above are very difficult to tell apart solely on the basis of skull characteristics because measurements overlap; whenever possible, compare pelages, which are distinctive.)

7. Cheek teeth with two longitudinal rows of enamel-covered cusps 8

Cheek teeth with three longitudinal rows of enamel-covered cusps 17

8. Upper front teeth with longitudinal groove on face; length less than 30 mm (1.2 in) 9

Upper front teeth smooth on face. 12

9. First and second lower cheek teeth with a distinctive labial shelf or ridge on the side near the cheek, sometimes with distinct cusplets (fig. 17). . . . . *Reithrodontomys humulis*, Eastern Harvest Mouse

FIGURE 17.   First and second lower cheek teeth of *Reithrodontomys humulis* with distinct labial shelf.

First and second lower cheek teeth without a distinct labial shelf or ridge. 10

10. First primary fold (pf1) in last upper cheek tooth as long as or longer than second primary fold (pf2) and extending more than halfway across tooth, major fold (mf) clearly visible (fig. 18a); major fold of last lower cheek tooth

equal to or longer than first primary fold (fig. 19a) .... *Reithrodontomys fulvescens*, Fulvous Harvest Mouse

First primary fold in last upper cheek tooth distinctly shorter than second fold and extending less than halfway across tooth, major fold indistinct or absent (fig. 18b); main fold of last lower cheek tooth shorter than first primary fold (fig. 19b).. 11

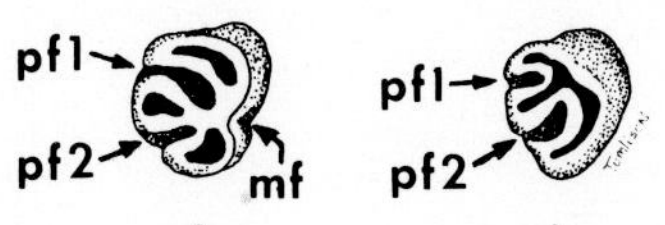

FIGURE 18.   Last upper cheek teeth of *Reithrodontomys fulvescens* (a) and *R. montanus* and/or *R. megalotis* (b). pf1 = first primary fold, pf2 = secondary primary fold, and mf = major fold.

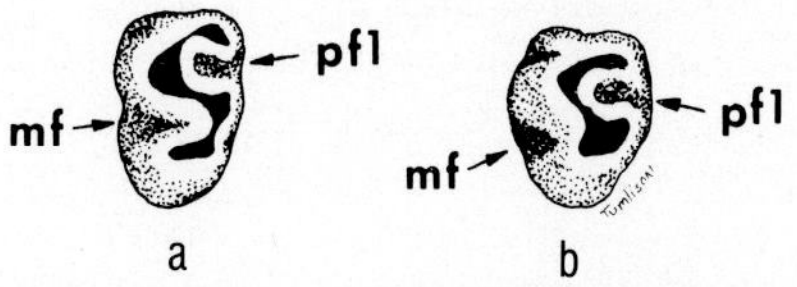

FIGURE 19.   Last lower cheek teeth of *Reithrodontomys fulvescens* (a) and *R. montanus* and/or *R. megalotis* (b). pf1 = first primary fold and mf = major fold.

11. Rostrum short and broad; braincase narrow, usually less than 9.5 mm (0.37 in)............. *Reithrodontomys montanus*, Plains Harvest Mouse

Rostrum longer and narrower; braincase broader, usually more than 9.5 mm (0.37 in) ... *Reithrodontomys megalotis*, Western Harvest Mouse

(Note: Skulls of Reithrodontomys *are very difficult to tell apart even by a professional mammalogist; whenever possible, use a combination of all possible characteristics for certain identification. For more information consult Hooper [1952].)*

12. Distinct ridges present above eye sockets, forming a distinct bead on the side of the skull (fig. 20); length 30 mm (1.2 in) or more.................... *Oryzomys palustris*, Marsh Rice Rat

Ridges above eye sockets absent... 13

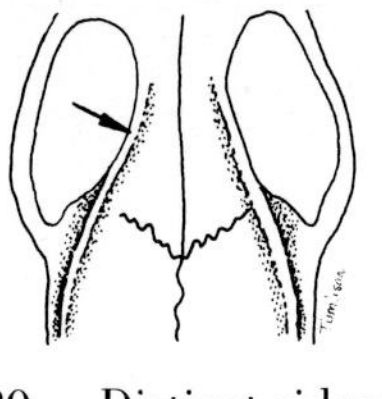

FIGURE 20.   Distinct ridges above eye sockets of *Oryzomys palustris*.

13. Length more than 26 mm (1.0 in); zygomatic breadth more than 14 mm (0.55 in); upper cheek tooth row 4 mm or more (0.16 in); length of palatine slits more than 5 mm (0.20 in) 14

Length less than 26 mm (1.0 in); zygomatic
breadth less than 14 mm (0.55 in); upper
cheek tooth row less than 4 mm; length of pal-
atine slits 5 mm or less (0.20 in). 15

14. Nasals usually larger than 11 mm (0.43 in);
zygomatic breadth usually more than 15 mm
(0.59 in); length about 27–30 mm (1.10–1.14
in) or more . . . . *Peromyscus gossypinus*, Cotton Mouse

Nasals usually smaller than 11 mm (0.43 in);
zygomatic breadth usually less than 15 mm
(0.59 in); length about 28–29 mm (1.10–1.14
in). . . . . *Peromyscus attwateri*, Texas Mouse

*(Note: Skull measurements of the two species
above frequently overlap; whenever possible,
combine with body measurements and pelage
coloration characteristics for positive
identification.)*

15. Posterior palatine foramina (small holes) closer
to posterior edge of palate than to palatine slits
(fig. 21a); palate not extending to the back
edge of the last cheek tooth. . . . . *Ochrotomys nuttalli*, Golden Mouse

Posterior palatine foramina approximately halfway between palatine slits and posterior edge
of palate (fig. 21b); palate extending to or be-
yond back edge of last cheek tooth 16

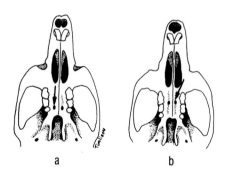

FIGURE 21.   Ventral view of skulls showing positions of the posterior palatine foramina in
relation to the palatine slits or anterior palatine foramina on *Ochrotomys nuttalli* (a) and *Peromyscus* sp. (b).

16. Palatine slits essentially parallel; braincase
flattened, more or less parallel; rostrum nar-
row; length usually less than 24 mm (0.95 in). . . . . *Peromyscus maniculatus*, Deer Mouse

Palatine slits bowed out in middle; braincase
rounded, not parallel-sided; rostrum shorter

and broader; length usually more than 24 mm (0.95 in) and usually less than 27 mm (1.1 in) . . . . *Peromyscus leucopus*, White-footed Mouse

(Note: Skull measurements of O. nuttalli, P. maniculatus, *and* P. leucopus *frequently overlap; whenever possible, combine with body measurements and pelage coloration characteristics for positive identification.)*

17. Length less than 22 mm (0.87); no heavy ridges on skull; upper incisors notched (fig. 22a). . . . . *Mus musculus*, House Mouse

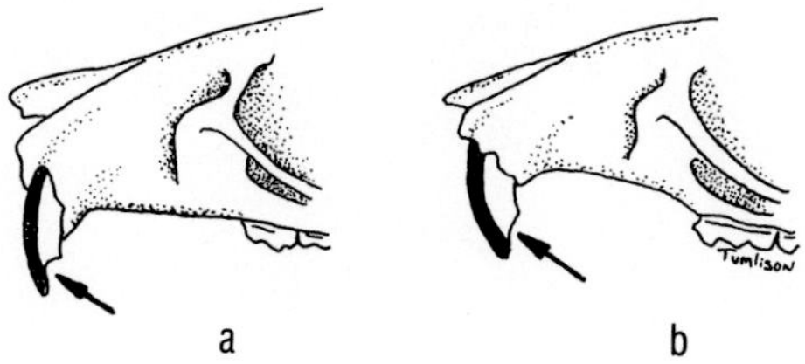

FIGURE 22.   Upper incisors of *Mus musculus* notched (a) and upper incisors not notched (b).

Length more than 30 mm (1.2 in); heavy ridges over orbit and posteriorly on skull; upper incisors not notched (fig. 22b) 18

18. Temporal ridges on skull strongly bowed outward posteriorly (fig. 23a), diastema much less than twice as long as cheek tooth row; distinct notches on anterior row of cusps on first cheek tooth . . . . *Rattus rattus*, Black Rat

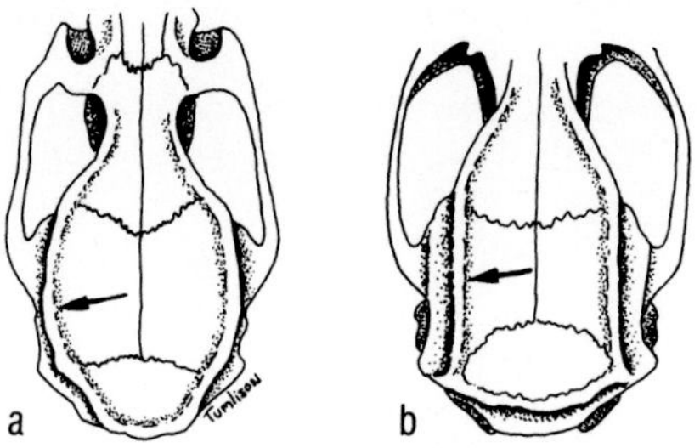

FIGURE 23.   Bowed temporal ridges of *Rattus rattus* (a) and parallel ridges of *R. norvegicus* (b).

Temporal ridges of skull approximately parallel (fig. 23b); diastema slightly less than twice as long as cheek tooth row; no distinct notches on anterior row of cusps on first cheek tooth. . . . . *Rattus norvegicus*, Norway Rat

Marsh Rice Rat

Oryzomys palustris

NAME *Oryzomys* is from two Greek words meaning "rice mouse"; *oryza* means "rice," and *mys* means "mouse." The specific name, *palustris*, is the Latin word for "marshy."

IDENTIFICATION AND DESCRIPTION The rice rat is small- to medium-sized with a sparsely haired, long, slender tail which is not sharply bicolored. The tail is nearly one-half the total length. It has prominent ears, moderately large eyes, and white feet. It is grayish brown to brown above and grayish white to grayish buff below.

Superficially the rice rat resembles the Norway rat. It may be distinguished by its smaller size, bicolored tail, longer and softer fur, and different cusp pattern on the molar teeth.

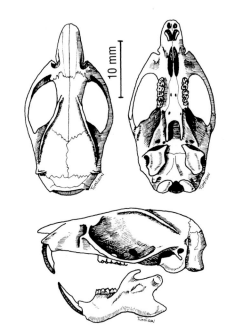

Skull of *Oryzomys palustris*

Oryzomys palustris, Marsh Rice Rat.
Richard K. Laval

MEASUREMENTS AND DENTAL FORMULA

Total Length:	186–305 mm (7.3–12.0 in)
Tail Length:	84–156 mm (3.3–6.1 in)
Hind Foot:	21–39 mm (0.83–1.5 in)
Ear:	10–18 mm (0.39–0.71 in)
Skull Length:	28–31 mm (1.1–1.2 in)
Weight:	31–78 g (1.1–2.8 oz)
Dental Formula:	I 1/1, C 0/0, P 0/0, M 3/3 = 16

ARKANSAS DISTRIBUTION AND ABUNDANCE
The rice rat occurs statewide, except for a few northern counties adjacent to Missouri. It is not generally distributed but may be locally abundant.

LIFE HISTORY The semiaquatic rice rat inhabits wet meadows and the dense vegetation bordering marshes, swamps, bayous, streams, ditches, drainage canals, and ponds. It is sometimes found in submarginal habitat, such as densely vegetated old fields, pinelands, and bottomland forests. The rice rat is an adept swimmer and diver, often swimming for some distance under water (Hamilton 1946). In northwestern Arkansas, this species is not common but may be locally abundant in isolated localities where the habitat is suitable.

Rice rats show around-the-clock activity but are more active and show a wider range of movement at night. More daytime activity is apparent when the cover is dense. They feed on seeds and succulent parts of a variety of plants and also dine on insects, snails, crayfish, and other animals. In marshy areas, the rice rat constructs feeding platforms of freshly cut stems of marsh grasses. These may be as large as dinner plates and are a sure sign of the rice rat's presence.

Globular grapefruit-sized nests of closely woven dry grasses and leaves are constructed in a chamber at the end of a shallow burrow above high-water level or in a shallow depression amid tangled vegetation. In wet, marshy areas the nest is sometimes suspended well above water level in interlaced marsh grasses or clumps of cattails.

The length of the breeding season is quite variable, depending upon population density, climate, and other factors (Negus et al. 1961). In the southern part of its range, reproductive activity may continue throughout the year under favorable conditions. In northern Arkansas, the breeding season probably extends from February through October or early November. Females bear litters of one to seven young after a 25-day gestation period. Older females generally produce four to five young per litter whereas the average litter size for young females is three. The litter size and number of litters produced annually also vary with population density, weather, and nutritional state (Negus et al. 1961). Fewer litters are produced during periods of food scarcity and inclement weather, and the litter size is reduced when the population density is high. Young rice rats attain sexual maturity when about 6 to 8 weeks old.

The average life span of the rice rat in the wild is about 7 months. Under natural conditions predators and disease take a heavy toll. Water moccasins and owls prey heavily upon rice rats; other predators include feral housecats, mink, foxes, raccoons, and weasels.

IMPORTANCE AND/OR MANAGEMENT Rice rats can cause serious economic losses to rice growers when ample cover is present on levees surrounding rice fields. In most rice growing areas of Arkansas, however, populations may be declining due to the lack of sufficient cover as a result of management practices that involve control of vegetation on levees by mowing or with herbicides.

The subspecies present in Arkansas is *O. p. texensis*.

SELECTED REFERENCES
Hamilton (1946); Negus et al. (1961).

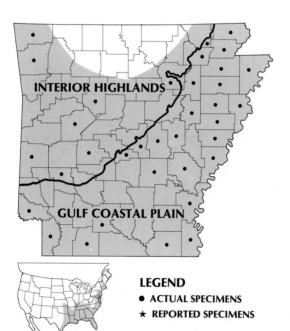

Distribution of the marsh rice rat (*Oryzomys palustris*)

Plains Harvest Mouse
Reithrodontomys montanus

NAME *Reithrodontomys* is from three Greek words and means "groove-toothed mouse." *Re-*

ithron means "groove," *odous* means "tooth," and *mys* means "mouse." The specific name, *montanus*, comes from the Latin word, *mons*, meaning "mountain." This description, "belonging to the mountain," is not accurate for this plains dwelling mammal.

IDENTIFICATION AND DESCRIPTION   The plains harvest mouse is a small rodent that has a distinctly bicolored tail with a narrow black stripe on its upper surface (the tail is less than one-half of the total length). There is a buffy patch usually present behind the ear. This mouse is pale gray to buffy-gray above (sprinkled with black hairs) and dull white below. The upper front teeth (incisors) are grooved.

The plains harvest mouse may be confused with the eastern harvest mouse, which is darker and does not have a distinctly bicolored tail with a narrow black stripe on top. It also resembles the western harvest mouse, which is larger and grayer. It may sometimes be confused with the house mouse which does not have grooved front teeth. The house mouse is also larger and grayer and has a long, scaly, nearly naked tail.

Reithrodontomys montanus, Plains Harvest Mouse. *Charles R. Preston*

MEASUREMENTS AND DENTAL FORMULA
Total Length: 95–143 mm (3.7–5.6 in)
Tail Length: 41–63 mm (1.6–2.5 in)
Hind Foot: 14–20 mm (0.55–0.79 in)

Ear: 12–16 mm (0.47–0.63 in)
Skull Length: 19 mm (0.75 in)
Weight: 5–15 g (0.18–0.53 oz)
Dental Formula: I 1/1, C 0/0, P 0/0, M 3/3 = 16

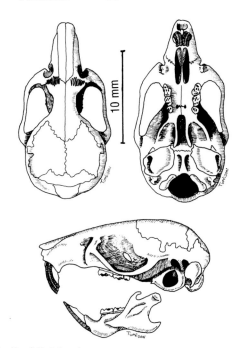

Skull of *Reithrodontomys montanus*

ARKANSAS DISTRIBUTION AND ABUNDANCE
The plains harvest mouse is known only from Washington and Benton counties; it is uncommon. Washington and Benton counties, Arkansas, and McDonald County, Missouri (Long 1961a), are probably at the eastern limit of this species range.

LIFE HISTORY   The life history of the plains harvest mouse is poorly known. It is usually associated with dry upland areas covered with short grasses (Blair 1939; Goertz 1963; Hooper 1952), but in Washington County, Arkansas, this species also has been found in an old hay field originally planted with fescue and Bermuda grass but subsequently invaded by broom sedge, Johnson grass, foxtail, and other grasses. In Brazos County, Texas, this mouse occurs most commonly in blackland prairies dominated by bluestem grass (Davis 1974).

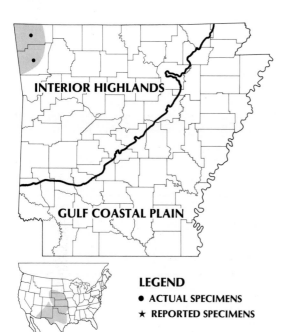

Distribution of the plains harvest mouse (*Reithrodontomys montanus*)

The food of this mouse consists of the stems and seeds of a variety of plants, including small grains.

The nest composed of fine grass is situated in a tussock of grass or beneath the ground in a burrow. Apparently this species breeds throughout the year but is probably more prolific during the warmer months. Females give birth to a litter of two to five young (an average of three) after a 21-day gestation period. The young are weaned at about 2 weeks of age, reach adult size in 5 weeks, and are sexually mature when 2 months old (Davis 1974).

IMPORTANCE AND/OR MANAGEMENT   No control or management measures are required. However, prairie habitat in northwest Arkansas should be preserved wherever possible.

The subspecies which occurs in Arkansas is *R. m griseus*.

SELECTED REFERENCES
Blair (1939); Davis (1974); Goertz (1963); Hooper (1952); Long (1961a).

EASTERN HARVEST MOUSE

Reithrodontomys humulis

NAME   *Reithrodontomys* is from three Greek words and means "groove-toothed mouse." *Reithron* means "groove," *odous* means "tooth," and *mys* means "mouse." Lowery (1974) feels that the specific name, *humulis*, was an error, and that Audubon and Bachman, who were responsible for naming the mammal, actually meant *humilis*. *Humilis* is the Latin word for "small," which would be more descriptive. Lowery also points out that in their *Quadrupeds of North America* (1851–1854), they spelled it *humilis*.

Reithrodontomys humulis, Eastern Harvest Mouse. *Roger W. Barbour*

IDENTIFICATION AND DESCRIPTION The eastern harvest mouse is a small rodent with a tail which is less than one-half of its total length and not distinctly bicolored. It has small, beady eyes. The pelage is dark brown, brownish gray, or gray heavily mixed with black above and grayish white, buffy, or gray below. The upper front teeth are grooved.

MEASUREMENTS AND DENTAL FORMULA
Total Length: 107–150 mm (4.2–5.9 in)
Tail Length: 45–70 mm (1.8–2.8 in)
Hind Foot: 11–20 mm (0.43–0.79 in)
Ear: 8–12 mm (0.31–0.47 in)
Skull Length: 18–21 mm (0.71–0.83 in)
Weight: 6–16 g (0.21–0.56 oz)
Dental I 1/1, C 0/0, P 0/0, M 3/3
Formula: = 16

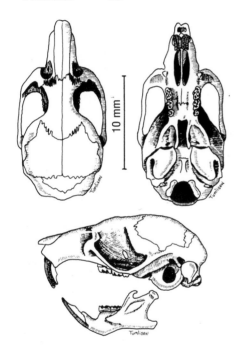

Skull of *Reithrodontomys humulis*

ARKANSAS DISTRIBUTION AND ABUNDANCE Hall (1981) includes most of Arkansas within the eastern harvest mouse's geographic range. However, specimens have only been recorded from Sebastian, Mississippi, and Columbia counties (Sealander 1956, 1977; Tumlison et al. 1988). It appears that this species is uncommon and widely scattered. Tumlison et al. (1988), however, suggest that it may be locally abundant.

LIFE HISTORY The eastern harvest mouse lives in old fields where tall grasses and early herbaceous stages of old-field succession are present. It is found most often in fields dominated by broom sedge, fescue, Johnson grass, goldenrod, and other herbaceous plants (Dunaway 1968) but sometimes occurs in cultivated grain fields. Honeysuckle thickets and roadside ditches where there are thick stands of tall grasses or sedges are also frequented by this mouse. Tumlison et al. (1988) captured 32 individuals in a Bermuda grass field in Columbia County. Additional plants present included wild oats, rushes, and other grasses.

This mouse is seldom seen since it is largely nocturnal. It eats weed and grass seeds, green vegetation, grain, and insects. This species builds a baseball-sized, round nest of shredded grass and plant fibers. The nest is usually situated on the ground in a clump of tall grass or beneath a rock; sometimes it is placed above ground in a clump of grass or sedges or in a small shrub.

The breeding season extends from late spring to late fall. A reduction in breeding activity occurs during midsummer. In southern Arkansas, this species probably breeds throughout the year, as it does in Louisiana (Lowery 1974). After a 21–22-day gestation period (Kaye 1961), females give birth to two to five young (Layne 1959; Kaye 1961). The litter size averages two to three, but it is occasionally as high as seven or eight. The young are weaned at 2–4 weeks of age and become sexually mature and capable of breeding when 11–12 weeks old.

IMPORTANCE AND/OR MANAGEMENT No management or control measures are needed.

The subspecies present in Arkansas have not been definitely determined. Tentatively, the race in eastern Arkansas is *R. h. humulis*. Hooper (1943) refers specimens from west of

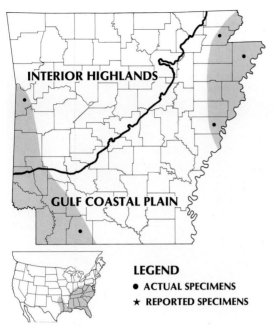

LEGEND
- ● ACTUAL SPECIMENS
- ★ REPORTED SPECIMENS

Distribution of the eastern harvest mouse (*Reithrodontomys humulis*)

the Mississippi River in Louisiana to the race *merriami*, and if this race extends northward, it is probable that specimens from western Arkansas and eastern Oklahoma (Jones and Anderson 1959; Smith 1964) belong to this race rather than representing a westward extension of the race *humulis* through the Arkansas River Valley where they have never been taken.

SELECTED REFERENCES
Dunaway (1968); Hall (1981); Hooper (1943); Kaye (1961); Layne (1959); Lowery (1974); Sealander (1956, 1977); Tumlison et al. (1988).

Western Harvest Mouse
Reithrodontomys megalotis

NAME *Reithrodontomys* is from three Greek words and means "groove-toothed mouse." *Reithron* means "groove," *odous* means "tooth," and *mys* means "mouse." The specific name,

megalotis, is from two Greek words, *megas*, meaning "large," and *ous*, meaning "ear."

IDENTIFICATION AND DESCRIPTION The western harvest mouse is a medium-sized harvest mouse with a tail which is about equal in length to its head and body (the tail is darker on top with a decided grayish cast). It has prominent eyes and large, flesh-colored (or buffy-cinnamon) ears. It is buffy, brownish buff, or brownish gray above with numerous black-tipped hairs and grayish washed with buff hairs below. The fur is rather long, soft, and silky. The upper front teeth are grooved.

MEASUREMENTS AND DENTAL FORMULA
Total Length: 118–170 mm (4.7–6.7 in)
Tail Length: 55–96 mm (2.2–3.8 in)
Hind Foot: 14–20 mm (0.55–0.79 in)
Ear: 10–16 mm (0.39–0.63 in)
Skull Length: 19–23 mm (0.75–0.91 in)
Weight: 8–16 g (0.28–0.56 oz)
Dental Formula: I 1/1, C 0/0, P 0/0, M 3/3 = 16

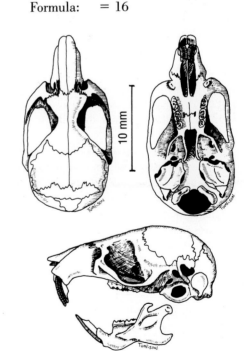

Skull of *Reithrodontomys megalotis*

Reithrodontomys megalotis, Western Harvest Mouse. *Phil A. Dotson*

ARKANSAS DISTRIBUTION AND ABUNDANCE
The western harvest mouse occurs in the upper portion of the Mississippi Alluvial Plain as far south as Phillips County (McDaniel et al. 1978).

Presently the western harvest mouse does not appear to coexist with the larger fulvous harvest mouse (*R. fulvescens*) in forested areas of Arkansas, although both species occupy the same general habitat in eastern Arkansas and have been caught side by side (McDaniel et al. 1978). The western harvest mouse may be extending its range southward in the Delta as the result of large-scale deforestation of this region. Railroad rights-of-ways appear to be serving as avenues of dispersal.

LIFE HISTORY   The western harvest mouse is associated with a wide variety of habitat types over its extensive range in the United States, Mexico, and Central America. It is seldom found in forested areas and prefers early successional stages of abandoned fields and open areas with thick stands of grasses which bear large seeds, such as brome, fescue, foxtail, switch grass, side-oats grama, bluestem, and purple top (Svendsen 1970). Often it occurs in weedy and brushy fencerows bordering cultivated fields and grain fields and along ditch banks where adequate food is available.

This mouse is almost strictly nocturnal (Carley et al. 1970). It feeds on grass and weed seeds, succulent stems of grasses, and insects when available. When searching for food, the mouse readily climbs grass stems and may travel for some distance in thick stands of grass without descending to the ground. On the ground, it often uses runways of voles, cotton rats, pocket gophers, and other rodents.

The globular nest, consisting of finely shredded grass and plant fibers, is usually placed on the ground beneath the shelter of a clump of

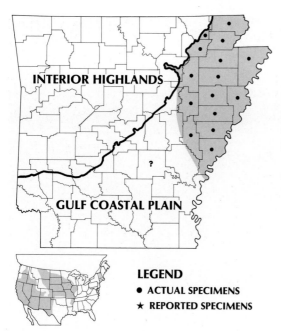

Distribution of the western harvest mouse
(*Reithrodontomys megalotis*)

grass, but sometimes it is built above the ground in a tangle of weeds or grasses. In winter the nest is usually underground.

The breeding season of this mouse extends through most of the year, but more litters are produced in April and October. Females may produce as many as seven litters per year in the wild. The gestation period is 22–33 days, and litter size ranges from one to nine, with an average of three to four young per litter. Mature females produce larger litters than young or old females (Richens et al. 1974). Young weigh about 1.0–1.5 g (0.03–0.05 oz) at birth and are completely weaned when 19–22 days old. Females are capable of breeding and producing litters when 6–8 weeks old.

IMPORTANCE AND/OR MANAGEMENT   No management or control measures are needed.

The subspecies present in Arkansas is *R. m. dychei*.

SELECTED REFERENCES
Carley et al. (1970); McDaniel et al. (1978); Richens et al. (1974); Sealander (1954); Svendsen (1970).

FULVOUS HARVEST MOUSE
Reithrodontomys fulvescens

NAME   *Reithrodontomys* is from three Greek words and means "groove-toothed mouse." *Reithron* means "groove," *odous* means "tooth," and *mys* means "mouse." The specific name, *fulvescens*, is from the Latin word, *fulvus*, and means "reddish yellow." This refers to the color on the sides of the body.

IDENTIFICATION AND DESCRIPTION   This species is a medium-sized harvest mouse with a tail which is longer than its head and body (the tail is not sharply bicolored). It is golden brown above with a mixture of black hairs along the center of its back. It is grayish-white and strongly washed with buff below. The sides are cinnamon or reddish yellow and the ears are cinnamon. The upper front teeth are grooved.

MEASUREMENTS AND DENTAL FORMULA
Total Length:	125–200 mm (4.9–7.9 in)
Tail Length:	66–100 mm (2.6–3.9 in)
Hind Foot:	15–22 mm (0.59–0.87 in)
Ear:	9–17 mm (0.35–0.67 in)
Skull Length:	22 mm (0.87 in)
Weight:	7–18g (0.25–0.63 oz)
Dental Formula:	I 1/1, C 0/0, P 0/0, M 3/3 = 16

ARKANSAS DISTRIBUTION AND ABUNDANCE
The fulvous harvest mouse occurs statewide; it is less common on the Gulf Coastal Plain.

LIFE HISTORY   The fulvous harvest mouse occurs in neglected fields with dense stands of various species of tall grasses such as broom sedge, Johnson grass, and purple top, along fencerows with tangles of grasses, vines, and shrubs, and in transitional areas of mixed grass and brush, often along creek bottoms. The fulvous harvest mouse frequently is found in the same habitat with cotton rats, least shrews, and rice rats. In the southern part of its range, which extends into Mexico, this mouse is found in dry, desert-like areas associated with vegetation such as mesquite and prickly pear cactus.

This species is primarily nocturnal. It feeds

Reithrodontomys fulvescens, Fulvous Harvest Mouse. *Dick T. Stalling*

mainly on the seeds and succulent parts of various grasses, sedges, and weeds. The nest, which has an opening on one side, is usually constructed above ground in thick stands of tall grasses. It is not much larger than a baseball and is composed of shredded grass and weed stems. Sometimes the nest is built in an abandoned bird nest.

The breeding season extends from February to October over most of the range, but in the southern United States and Mexico it may breed throughout the year (Dalquest 1953). Peak breeding occurs in March and July (Packard 1968). Females produce an average litter of two to four young after a gestation period of 22–23 days. Litter size may range from one to seven. The young weigh slightly more than 1 g at birth. Growth is rapid and the young are weaned at 3 weeks of age. They leave the nest when about 5 weeks old. Sexual maturity is reached when the young are 2–3 months old.

IMPORTANCE AND/OR MANAGEMENT This species is of little economic importance and seldom attains high population levels. No man-

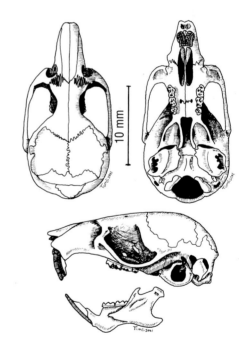

Skull of *Reithrodontomys fulvescens*

INTERIOR HIGHLANDS

GULF COASTAL PLAIN

LEGEND
● ACTUAL SPECIMENS
★ REPORTED SPECIMENS

Distribution of the fulvous harvest mouse (*Reithrodontomys fulvescens*)

agement or control measures are needed.

The subspecies in Arkansas is *R. f. aurantius*.

SELECTED REFERENCES
Dalquest (1953); McDaniel et al. (1978); Packard (1968).

Deer Mouse

Peromyscus maniculatus

NAME   *Peromyscus* is from two Greek words, *pera*, meaning "pouch," and *myskos*, meaning "little mouse." It should be noted that the first part of the name may also be from the Latin *pero*, meaning "pointed," referring to the pointed shape of the skull. The specific name, *maniculatus*, is from the Latin word meaning "small handed," and indicates the size of the front foot.

IDENTIFICATION AND DESCRIPTION   The deer mouse is small, with a relatively short tail which is distinctly bicolored. It has large, black eyes, white feet, and ears edged with buff or white. The ears are usually shorter than the hind foot. It is a pale grayish buff to deep reddish-brown above and white below.

Peromyscus maniculatus, Deer Mice. *John R. MacGregor*

MEASUREMENTS AND DENTAL FORMULA   This species shows wide variation in body dimensions over an extensive range in North America. Measurements given here are for the races *ozarkiarum* and *bairdii*.

Total Length:	116–154 mm (4.6–6.1 in)
Tail Length:	40–66 mm (1.6–2.6 in)
Hind Foot:	15–20 mm (0.59–0.79 in)
Ear:	12–20 mm (0.47–0.79 in)
Skull Length:	22–25 mm (0.87–0.98 in)
Weight:	16–26 g (0.56–0.92 oz)
Dental Formula:	I 1/1, C 0/0, P 0/0, M 3/3 = 16

ARKANSAS DISTRIBUTION AND ABUNDANCE
The deer mouse is present in most of the state, but it is apparently rare or absent in most of the West Gulf Coastal Plain.

LIFE HISTORY   The deer mouse always inhabits open areas including weedy fields, fencerows, roadsides and railroad rights-of-way, pastures, hay meadows, and cropland. It is absent from dense forests. Underground burrows of moles, gophers, and other nocturnal rodent species are used by this mouse during the

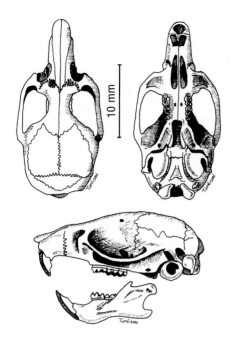

Skull of *Peromyscus maniculatus*

birth, grow rapidly, and are weaned at about 4 weeks of age. Females may begin breeding when they are 5–10 weeks old.

Deer mice are a staple food item of feral cats, bobcats, hawks, owls, weasels, mink, foxes, and snakes. The young are also preyed upon by short-tailed shrews. This species seldom lives more than a year in the wild.

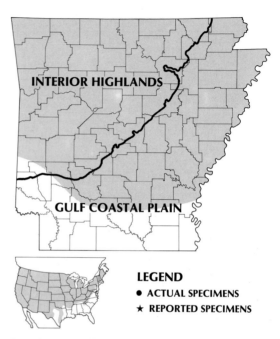

Distribution of the deer mouse (*Peromyscus maniculatus*)

daytime. It is nocturnal and prefers early evening and predawn hours for feeding.

The bulky nest of the deer mouse usually is constructed underground but may be placed beneath a rock, in a grass clump above ground, or under a large clod of earth (Dice 1932). It is about 25 cm (9.8 in) in diameter and made of coarse grass stems and roots of grasses and weeds outside; the inside is generally lined with soft plant down.

Deer mice feed on grass and weed seeds, insects when available, berries, nuts, waste grain, fungi, and small invertebrates. In the northern part of their range, large quantities of seeds and nuts may be stored underground for winter use during inclement weather.

This species breeds throughout the year in Arkansas, but most breeding activity occurs from March until November. Females produce four to six litters per year in the wild after a gestation period of 22–27 days. The litter size ranges from one to nine and averages about three to four. Females often breed again immediately after giving birth to a litter. The young weigh between 1 and 2 g (0.03–0.07 oz) at

IMPORTANCE AND/OR MANAGEMENT   No management or control measures are needed.

Two subspecies occur in Arkansas: the prairie deer mouse, *P. m. bairdii*, and the Ozark white-footed mouse, *P. m. ozarkiarum* (Black 1935). The area of intergradation between the two races in Arkansas is not definitely known.

SELECTED REFERENCES
Black (1935); Dice (1932).

White-footed Mouse
Peromyscus leucopus

NAME *Peromyscus* is from two Greek words, *pera*, meaning "pouch," and *myskos*, meaning "little mouse." It should be noted that the first part of the name may also be from the Latin *pero*, meaning "pointed," referring to the pointed shape of the skull. The specific name, *leucopus*, is from two Greek words, *leukon*, meaning "white," and *pous*, meaning "foot."

IDENTIFICATION AND DESCRIPTION The white-footed mouse is a small- to medium-sized mouse with a tail about equal to or shorter than its head and body (the tail is not distinctly bicolored). The ears are large (dusky brown, edged with white), the eyes are large, and the feet are white. It is grayish brown to rich reddish brown above and white below.

MEASUREMENTS AND DENTAL FORMULA

Total Length:	132–205 mm (5.2–8.1 in)
Tail Length:	51–98 mm (2.0–3.9 in)
Hind Foot:	15–24 mm (0.59–0.95 in)
Ear:	13–19 mm (0.51–0.75 in)
Skull Length:	25–27 mm (0.98–1.0 in)
Weight:	13–36 g (0.46–1.3 oz)
Dental Formula:	I 1/1, C 0/0, P 0/0, M 3/3 = 16

ARKANSAS DISTRIBUTION AND ABUNDANCE The white-footed mouse occurs statewide and is abundant.

LIFE HISTORY The white-footed mouse occurs in woodlands having adequate cover in the form of fallen logs, brush piles, rock piles, and brushy fencerows. Old outbuildings, seldom-used cabins, and other man-made structures situated in wooded rural and urban areas are

Peromyscus leucopus, White-footed Mouse. *Darryl B. Little*

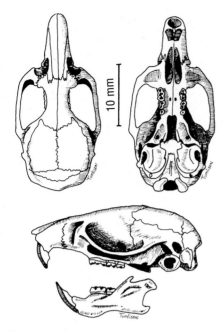

Skull of *Peromyscus leucopus*

frequently occupied by this mouse. It is one of the most common small mammals in wooded portions of the state, but it is seldom seen due to its generally nocturnal activity.

White-footed mice nest in rotten stumps, under fallen logs, beneath stones, in rock crevices or caves, under trash piles, and in underground burrows. They are excellent climbers and frequently nest in tree cavities, abandoned squirrel and bird nests, or bird houses well above ground. The globular nest is composed of grasses, dry leaves, and other plant material. The inside of the nest may be lined with milkweed floss or other plant down.

The food of the white-footed mouse consists of various seeds, nuts, insects, snails, and other small invertebrates. The summer diet includes much plant material such as grass and weed seeds, fruits, berries, clover, and other herbaceous matter. Large quantities of seeds and nuts may be cached in autumn for winter use.

In Arkansas, the breeding season extends throughout the year, but reproduction slackens in late summer. Females rear four to five litters per year in the wild. Litter size ranges from one to seven and averages about four. The gestation period is 22–25 days but may be prolonged as much as 14 days when females are lactating. The young weigh 1.5 to 2 g (0.05–0.07 oz) at birth and are usually weaned when 22–28 days old.

Natural predators of the white-footed mouse include bobcats, foxes, feral housecats, owls, and snakes. If these predators are not destroyed, the white-footed mouse is seldom destructive to stored or shocked grain.

IMPORTANCE AND/OR MANAGEMENT   No management or control measures are needed.

Two subspecies occur in Arkansas: the northern white-footed mouse, *P. l. noveboracensis*, which occurs in the northern tier of counties, and the southern white-footed mouse, *P. l. leucopus*, which occurs over most of the state. The race *noveboracensis* is larger and paler than *leucopus*, often has a more reddish brown color, and has a hairier tail. The two races intergrade, but the zone of intergradation is not definitely known.

Distribution of the white-footed mouse (*Peromyscus leucopus*)

Female white-footed mouse feeding young. *John R. MacGregor*

SELECTED REFERENCES
Brown (1964); Nicholson (1941); Rintamaa et al. (1976).

COTTON MOUSE

Peromyscus gossypinus

NAME   *Peromyscus* is from two Greek words, *pera*, meaning "pouch," and *myskos*, meaning "little mouse." It should be noted that the first part of the name may also be from the Latin *pero*, meaning "pointed," referring to the pointed shape of the skull. The specific name, *gossypinus*, is derived from the Latin words *gossyp*, meaning "cotton," and *inus*, a suffix meaning "belonging to." This implies a relationship to cotton fields, where the cotton mouse is not regularly found. It also has been suggested that this may refer to the cottony nest material used by the animal.

IDENTIFICATION AND DESCRIPTION   This species is a medium- to large-sized mouse with a sparsely-haired tail equal to or slightly longer than the head and body (the tail may or may not be bicolored). It has a large, white hind foot (usually 22 mm [0.87 in] or more), large ears (usually about 18 mm [0.71 in]), and large eyes. It is dark brown to dusky brown above with a wide darker area along the middle of the back and whitish below.

MEASUREMENTS AND DENTAL FORMULA
    Total Length: 141–206 mm (5.6–8.1 in)
    Tail Length: 55–97 mm (2.2–3.8 in)
    Hind Foot: 18–26 mm (0.71–1.0 in)
    Ear: 15–22 mm (0.59–0.87 in)
    Skull Length: 27–30 mm (1.0–1.2 in)
    Weight: 20–51 g (0.71–1.8 oz)
    Dental   I 1/1, C 0/0, P 0/0, M 3/3
        Formula: = 16

ARKANSAS DISTRIBUTION AND ABUNDANCE
The cotton mouse occurs nearly statewide, with

Peromyscus gossypinus, Cotton Mouse.
Roger W. Barbour

the exception of the western half of the Springfield and Salem plateaus where it appears to be absent.

LIFE HISTORY   The cotton mouse inhabits dense underbrush along stream banks and in bottomland hardwood forests. It occupies habitat simlar to that of *P. leucopus* but generally is not found in the drier upland woods occupied by the white-footed mouse. The habitat of white-footed and cotton mice frequently overlaps, and natural hybridization is possible (McCarley 1954). However, behavioral and ecological isolating mechanisms apparently serve to maintain the distinctiveness of the two species in the wild (Bradshaw 1965; Lowery 1974). Wolfe and Linzy (1977) believe that the two species only rarely hybridize under natural conditions.

Cotton mice are nocturnal and nest beneath fallen logs or stumps and in buildings. They climb trees readily, and the nest often is placed in a hollow stump or tree cavity.

Animal food, including adult and larval insects, spiders, slugs, and snails, makes up a large part of its diet. Spores of the fungus *Endogone* are frequently eaten; seeds and other plant material comprise the remainder of the diet.

Cotton mice apparently breed throughout the year in Arkansas, but reproduction may fall off during late spring and summer. Litter size ranges from one to seven and averages about four. The gestation period is 23 days, and the young weigh about 2 g (0.07 oz) when born (Pournelle 1952). Development is rapid: the young are weaned in 20–25 days and begin foraging for themselves. Males reach sexual maturity in 6–8 weeks, and breeding may begin at about 10 weeks of age.

IMPORTANCE AND/OR MANAGEMENT   No management or control measures are needed.

The subspecies *P. g. megacephalus* occurs over most of this species range in Arkansas, with the possible exception of the southeastern corner of the state (see St. Romain 1976). Lowery (1974) believes that all Louisiana specimens can be assigned to the race *gossypinus*, but his opinion is not shared by St. Romain.

SELECTED REFERENCES
Bradshaw (1965); Lowery (1974); McCarley (1954); Pournelle (1952); St. Romain (1976); Wolfe and Linzey (1977).

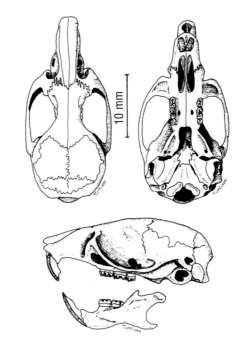

Skull of *Peromyscus gossypinus*

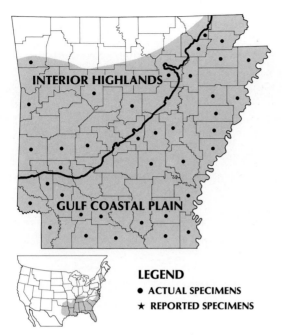

LEGEND
- ● **ACTUAL SPECIMENS**
- ★ **REPORTED SPECIMENS**

Distribution of the cotton mouse (*Peromyscus gossypinus*)

MEASUREMENTS AND DENTAL FORMULA

Total Length:	160–218 mm (6.3–8.6 in)	
Tail Length:	68–111 mm (2.7–4.4 in)	
Hind Foot:	20–26 mm (0.79–1.0 in)	
Ear:	17–22 mm (0.67–0.87 in)	
Skull Length:	28–29 mm (1.1–1.2 in)	
Weight:	19–41 g (0.67–1.5 oz)	
Dental	I 1/1, C 0/0, P 0/0, M 3/3	
Formula:	= 16	

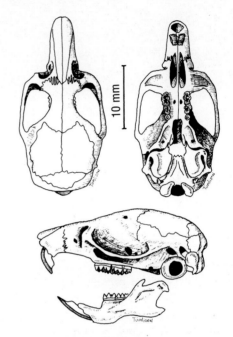

Skull of *Peromyscus attwateri*

TEXAS MOUSE

Peromyscus attwateri

NAME *Peromyscus* is from two Greek words, *pera*, meaning "pouch," and *myskos*, meaning "little mouse." It should be noted that the first part of the name may also be from the Latin *pero*, meaning "pointed," referring to the pointed shape of the skull. The specific name, *attwateri*, is the patronym for Attwater.

IDENTIFICATION AND DESCRIPTION The Texas mouse is a medium- to large-sized mouse with a moderately well-haired tail equal to or longer than its head and body. The tail is bicolored and prominently tufted (penciled) at its tip, a diagnostic characteristic in identifying the species. It has large ears (usually 19–20 mm [0.75–0.79 in] or more), large, white feet (usually about 24 mm [0.95 in]), and large eyes. It is grayish brown to fairly dark brown above, buffy or tawny on the sides, and white or creamy white below.

ARKANSAS DISTRIBUTION AND ABUNDANCE The Texas mouse is restricted to the Interior Highlands.

LIFE HISTORY The Texas mouse (formerly called the brush mouse) is found along rocky outcroppings or cliffs of limestone or sandstone, often near the base of an escarpment. In the Missouri Ozarks, this species is strongly associated with cedar glades growing in shallow soils overlying beds of dolomite (Brown 1964). In the Ouachita Mountains, the Texas mouse is also closely associated with rock outcroppings or talus-like slopes found in open pine-oak-hickory forest or woodland on steep, dry, south

Peromyscus attwateri, Texas Mouse. *Gary A. Heidt*

facing slopes and in predominantly red cedar woods occurring in dry, rocky ravines and upon exposed beds of shale (Montgomery 1974). Sugg (1988) has recently found, using morphological and genetic traits, that there is very little genetic interchange between populations found on different ridges and mountaintops. This implies that this species is fairly habitat specific and that the ridges and mountaintops act as islands, while the intervening valleys act as barriers to dispersal.

The nest is situated under tumbled rocks, in rock crevices, or in other natural cavities. It is a globular structure of grasses, plant fibers, and dry leaves. The report (Black 1937) that this mouse builds a miniature replica of a woodrat nest made of brush and sticks thus far has not been substantiated (Long 1961b).

The Texas mouse is an excellent climber and may feed to a considerable extent on food obtained in trees, such as hackberries and cedar berries. The chief food appears to be acorns; other foods utilized extensively by this mouse are camel crickets, beetle larvae, pine seeds, and grass seeds.

Very little is known about reproduction in this species. Breeding may occur throughout the year, but apparently peak breeding occurs

in the spring and fall with a lull in breeding activity during hotter summer months. Litter size ranges from two to six; the usual litter size is three.

IMPORTANCE AND/OR MANAGEMENT   No management or control measures are needed.

The taxonomic status of *P. attwateri* has recently been clarified by Lee et al. (1972) and Schmidly (1973), who elevated the subspecies *P. boylii attwateri* to its present specific rank.

SELECTED REFERENCES
Black (1937); Brown (1964); Lee et al. (1972); Long (1961b); Montgomery (1974); Schmidly (1973); Sugg (1988).

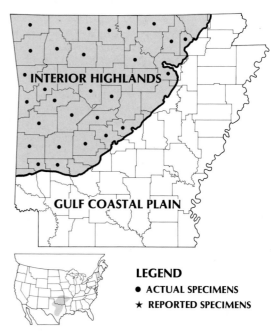

Distribution of the Texas mouse (*Peromyscus attwateri*)

GOLDEN MOUSE
Ochrotomys nuttalli

NAME   *Ochrotomys* comes from two Greek words, *ochra*, meaning "pale yellow," and *mys*, meaning "mouse," thus describing its general

Ochrotomys nutalli, Golden Mouse. *John R. MacGregor*

coloration. The specific name, *nuttalli*, is a patronym for Thomas Nuttall, an early American naturalist.

IDENTIFICATION AND DESCRIPTION   The golden mouse is a small mouse the tail of which is slightly shorter than its body and is not distinctly bicolored. Its ears are the same color as its body, and they are usually about 16–17 mm (0.63–0.67 in) long; the hind foot is usually about 17–19 mm (0.67–0.75 in) long. This mouse is golden-brown or orange-brown above (mixed with blackish hairs in some pelage phases) and white below, tinged with pinkish cinnamon.

MEASUREMENTS AND DENTAL FORMULA
   Total Length: 132–210 mm (5.2–8.3 in)
Tail Length: 57–93 mm (2.2–3.7 in)
Hind Foot: 15–21 mm (0.59–0.83 in)
Ear: 14–20 mm (0.55–0.79 in)
Skull Length: 23–26 mm (0.91–1.0 in)
Weight: 12–31 g (0.42–12.2 oz)
Dental   I 1/1, C 0/0, P 0/0, M 3/3
   Formula: = 16

ARKANSAS DISTRIBUTION AND ABUNDANCE
The golden mouse occurs statewide; it is more common in southern and eastern Arkansas.

LIFE HISTORY   The golden mouse occurs in forested areas. It prefers woodlands with a dense, brushy understory or underbrush bordering streams. Favorite habitats are tangles of honeysuckle vines, canebrakes, and thickets of wild grapevines, greenbrier, or blackberry.

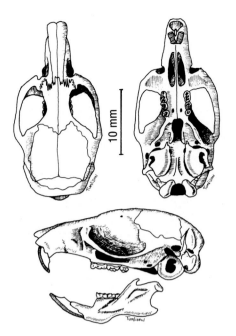

Skull of *Ochrotomys nuttalli*

They are more common in moist, lowland forests having dense underbrush but also occur in dry, upland forests of pine and cedar with a sparse understory (Linzey and Packard 1977).

Golden mice are highly arboreal and often build nests 1–5 meters (3.3–16.5 ft) above ground level in thickets of grapevine, honeysuckle, or greenbrier. The globular nest is made of leaves, grasses, plant fibers, and a lining of plant down, fur, or feathers (Goodpaster and Hoffmeister 1954). In open woodlands, nests are frequently placed in hollow stumps or under fallen logs. From one to eight may occupy the nest. Nest-like feeding platforms also may be constructed in the crotch of a shrub or in the crown of a fallen tree near ground level; sometimes they are placed in a tree fork as high as 15 m (50 ft) above ground.

This mouse is nocturnal and forages only at night. The diet consists of seeds, fruits, herbaceous materials, and some insects. Preferred seeds are those of dogwood, sumac, and wild cherry. These are gathered and transported to the feeding platform in cheek pouches.

Breeding possibly occurs throughout the year in southern Arkansas, but it is probably limited to the period from March to October in northern counties and at higher elevations in the Ouachita Mountains. The gestation period is 25–30 days (Linzey and Linzey 1967), and the litter size varies from one to four. Two to three young comprise the usual litter. Fall litters tend to be larger than spring litters. Growth is rapid and weaning usually occurs in about three weeks.

IMPORTANCE AND/OR MANAGEMENT   No control or management measures are needed.

The subspecies *O. n. flammeus* occurs over most of the species range in Arkansas. The subspecies *O. n. lisae* occurs in southeastern and northeastern Arkansas (Packard 1969). The golden mouse is extremely docile. It readily adjusts to captivity and makes an interesting pet.

SELECTED REFERENCES
Goodpaster and Hoffmeister (1954); Linzey and Linzey (1967); Linzey and Packard (1977); Packard (1969).

Distribution of the golden mouse (*Ochrotomys nutalli*)

Hispid Cotton Rat

Sigmodon hispidus

NAME   *Sigmodon* is from two Greek words, *sigma*, which is the equivalent of the Greek letter "S," and *odous*, meaning "tooth." This refers to the S-shaped cusp pattern on the last molar teeth. The specific name, *hispidus*, is the Latin word for "rough," referring to the texture of its fur.

IDENTIFICATION AND DESCRIPTION   The cotton rat is medium-sized and robust. Its sparsely haired tail is shorter than its head and body and indistinctly bicolored. The ears are blackish or grayish, relatively short, and half buried in neck fur. The pelage is grayish brown to blackish brown above (grizzled with pale buff) and grayish or buffy below.

MEASUREMENTS AND DENTAL FORMULA

Total Length:	177–365 mm (7.0–14.4 in)
Tail Length:	58–166 mm (2.3–6.5 in)
Hind Foot:	24–35 mm (0.95–1.4 in)
Ear:	16–24 mm (0.63–0.95 in)
Skull Length:	28–39 mm (1.1–1.5 in)
Weight:	52–211 g (1.8–7.4 oz)
Dental Formula:	I 1/1, C 0/0, P 0/0, M 3/3 = 16

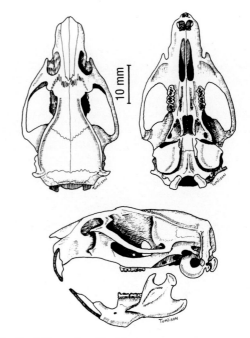

Skull of *Sigmodon hispidus*

ARKANSAS DISTRIBUTION AND ABUNDANCE
The cotton rat occurs statewide and is abundant.

LIFE HISTORY   The cotton rat is a very common small mammal in Arkansas wherever suitable cover is present. It inhabits uncultivated

Sigmodon hispidus, Hispid Cotton Rat. *William R. Teska*

FAMILY MURIDAE   167

fields, grassy roadside ditches, brushy fence-rows, and railroad rights-of-way. It is quite common in fields of broom sedge and other grasses where there is a heavy mat of dead vegetation that provides a protective canopy against aerial predators. It seldom occurs in forested areas but is found near the forest edge. This species exhibits wide population fluctuations. At times it undergoes explosive population increases and becomes extremely abundant in favorable habitat. Such outbreaks may be followed by years when population densities are very low. In general, populations tend to be low in spring, then they build up and reach peak densities in autumn.

The nest is a crude mass of grasses and plant fibers placed in shallow surface depressions among clumps of coarse grasses or underground. From the nest, runways radiate outward to feeding areas beneath the mat of dead grasses and herbs. Shallow burrow systems may be constructed where vegetational cover is light. The runways and burrows of cotton rats are extensively used by other small mammals including shrews, voles, deer mice, harvest mice, and house mice. The diet consists of herbaceous plants, grasses, rice and other grain, insects, crayfish, and eggs of ground-nesting birds.

Breeding occurs throughout the year. In northwestern Arkansas, the major breeding periods apparently are from February through July and from September through November (Sealander and Walker 1955). Cotton rats are extremely prolific and produce litters of 2–15 young after a gestation period of 27 days (Kilgore 1970). Growth of the young is very rapid and they may be weaned when 5–10 days old. Sexual maturity is attained at the age of 40–50 days. Females produce six or more litters per year, and the average litter size varies from five to seven.

Predators such as foxes, coyotes, bobcats, owls, and hawks consume large numbers of cotton rats, which may serve in an important buffering capacity against predation upon desirable species of wildlife. Cotton rats harbor

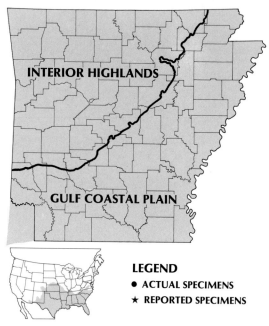

Distribution of the hispid cotton rat (*Sigmodon hispidus*)

numerous kinds of parasites and constitute a potential reservoir for diseases such as typhus and plague (Meyer and Meyer 1944).

IMPORTANCE AND/OR MANAGEMENT   The cotton rat damages truck crops and is particularly destructive to the eggs and chicks of bobwhite quail; it also competes with quail for food. When present in large numbers, these rats are sometimes troublesome in orchards and meadows and may damage crops such as cotton, sugar cane, squash, and sweet potatoes. Plowing and cultivation of land and heavy grazing of pastures by livestock often effectively reduce their numbers.

Two subspecies occur in Arkansas. The nominate race, *S. h. hispidus*, is found over most of the state but apparently intergrades with the race *texianus* on the western edge of the state. However, the subspecific status of the cotton rat in western Arkansas will remain questionable until a thorough study is undertaken.

SELECTED REFERENCES
Kilgore (1970); Meyer and Meyer (1944); Sealander and Walker (1955).

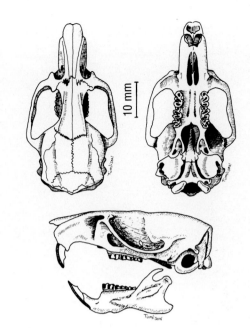

Skull of *Neotoma floridana*

Eastern Woodrat

Neotoma floridana

NAME   *Neotoma* is from two Greek words, *neos*, meaning "new," and *tomos*, meaning "cut." This refers to the fact that it was a new kind of mammal with cutting teeth, thus distinguishing it from *Mus*, to which it was originally assigned. The specific name, *floridana*, means "of Florida," signifying where it was first collected.

IDENTIFICATION AND DESCRIPTION   The eastern woodrat is a medium-sized rodent with a distinctly bicolored and fairly well-haired tail which is slightly shorter than its head and body. It has large, nearly naked ears, large, black eyes, and white feet. The pelage is brown or brownish gray to dull buffy or dusky above (mixed with black) and white or grayish white below.

Neotoma floridana, Eastern Woodrat.
James N. Layne

MEASUREMENTS AND DENTAL FORMULA
Total Length: 297–441 mm (11.7–
17.4 in)
Tail Length: 128–210 mm (5.0–8.3 in)
Hind Foot: 32–43 mm (1.4–1.7 in)

Ear:	20–30 mm (0.79–1.2 in)
Skull Length:	47–50 mm (1.9–2.0 in)
Weight:	147–428 g (5.2–15.1 oz)
Dental Formula:	I 1/1, C 0/0, P 0/0, M 3/3 = 16

ARKANSAS DISTRIBUTION AND ABUNDANCE
The eastern woodrat occurs statewide; it is less common in the Gulf Coastal Plain where extensive clearing of bottomland forests has destroyed much of its habitat.

LIFE HISTORY   The eastern woodrat (also called the pack rat or cave rat) is common in the Ozark and Ouachita mountain regions where there are numerous caves and rock outcroppings. They live in caves, fissures, and crevices within cliffs and bluffs and in rocky litter near the bases of escarpments. Woodrats are locally distributed and scarce in bottomland regions of the Gulf Coastal Plain, where they may occur in dense brush bordering streams, fencerows, deserted buildings, and timberlands with a dense understory of shrubs and vines.

In mountainous regions, the woodrat makes

Woodrat nests such as this one can often be found in old buildings and sheds. *Gary A. Heidt*

piles of sticks and twigs under overhanging rock ledges and in cracks and crevices of the rock. Miscellaneous articles such as rocks, bones, jar lids, broken glass, tin cans, empty shell casings, and other man-made objects are often placed in the pile. The spherical nest of shredded bark, leaves, and grass is about 15 cm (6 in) in diameter and is placed further back in a crevice. In bottomland areas, woodrat houses are built on the ground at bases of trees, against fallen logs, or in underground burrows along wooded stream banks. Houses also are constructed in hollow logs and uninhabited buildings. Woodrats have sanitary habits; there are usually one or more toilet areas near the nest where fecal material is deposited.

Woodrats are strictly nocturnal and feed upon a wide variety of plant material including leaves and twigs of various shrubs and trees, berries, fruits, mushrooms, seeds, acorns, and other nuts. Animal food, such as insects and snails, is seldom eaten. In autumn, woodrats store leaves, twigs, seeds, and nuts in one or

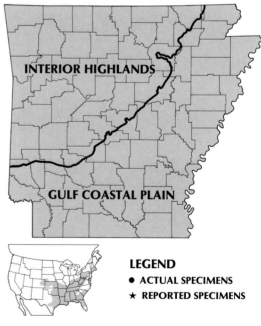

LEGEND
- ● ACTUAL SPECIMENS
- ★ REPORTED SPECIMENS

Distribution of the eastern woodrat (*Neotoma floridana*)

more galleries of their houses for winter use. The leaves and seeds of osage orange trees are stored more often and in greater quantities than other food (Rainey 1956). Dogwood leaves are also favored.

The breeding season probably extends throughout the year in southern Arkansas. Breeding may be confined to the period from March to October in northern Arkansas. The litter size varies from one to six, and females have two to three litters per year. The usual number of young in a litter is two or three. The length of gestation is not definitely known but appears to be 30–39 days. Young woodrats weigh 10–15 g (0.4–0.5 oz) when born and are weaned when between 3 and 4 weeks old. Woodrats do not reach adult size until they are about 8–9 months of age. Females probably do not begin breeding until they are about a year old. Woodrats have a low reproductive potential but apparently compensate with greater longevity than other small mammals. In the wild, they may attain an age of 3 or 4 years.

IMPORTANCE AND/OR MANAGEMENT   No management or control measures are needed. Its flesh is edible and is reported to be superior to that of squirrels, but it is seldom eaten by man.

Two subspecies occur in Arkansas: the Osage woodrat, *N. f. osagensis*, which is found in the Interior Highlands, and the Illinois woodrat, *N. f. illinoensis*, which occurs in the Gulf Coastal Plain. The zone of intergradation between the races has not been definitely determined.

SELECTED REFERENCES
Hamilton (1953); Rainey (1956).

Prairie Vole

Microtus ochrogaster

NAME   *Microtus* is from two Greek words, *mikros*, meaning "small," and *ous*, meaning "ear." The specific name, *ochrogaster*, is also from two Greek words, *ochro*, meaning "yellow," and *gaster*, meaning "belly."

Microtus ochrogaster, Prairie Vole.
John R. MacGregor

IDENTIFICATION AND DESCRIPTION   The prairie vole is a small rodent with a short tail (somewhat less than twice the length of the hind foot) that is sharply bicolored. Its ears are almost concealed in relatively coarse fur, and its eyes are small. It is grayish to blackish brown above (grizzled with tan or whitish-tipped hairs) and buffy below.

The prairie vole can be distinguished from the woodland vole by its longer, bicolored tail,

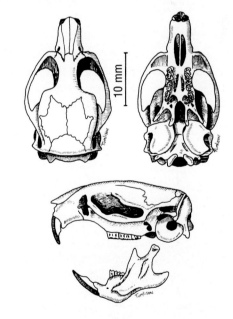

Skull of *Microtus ochrogaster*

and from the southern bog lemming by the absence of grooved incisors.

MEASUREMENTS AND DENTAL FORMULA
Total Length: 116–172 mm (4.6–6.1 in)
Tail Length: 23–49 mm (0.91–2.0 in)
Hind Foot: 15–22 mm (0.60–0.87 in)
Ear: 9–17 mm (0.35–0.67 in)
Skull Length: 23–30 mm (0.91–1.2 in)
Weight: 27–60 g (0.95–2.1 oz)
Dental   I 1/1, C 0/0, P 0/0, M 3/3
  Formula: = 16

ARKANSAS DISTRIBUTION AND ABUNDANCE
The prairie vole is found across the northern tier of counties and southward on the Gulf Coastal Plain to near the southern boundary of Arkansas County.

LIFE HISTORY   The prairie vole inhabits grassy roadsides, railroad rights-of-way, pastures, and meadows wherever cover is dense enough to conceal it from enemies. It also lives in cultivated fields of clover, alfalfa, and lespedeza. This animal occurs in grassy areas near the forest edge but does not invade woodlands.

Prairie voles are generally tolerant of each other and have extensive runway systems beneath the grass canopy. Runways are approximately 45–55 mm (1.7–2.2 in) wide and, depending on their use, they may be deep and devoid of vegetation or mere imprints on the grass. Runways in active use can be identified by small piles of fresh grass cuttings and brownish black droppings. Prairie voles also maintain an underground system of burrows, and often these burrows form large mounds (0.6–1.2 m [2–4 ft] in diameter) which are catacombed with tunnels and may have numerous entrances. Excavation of these mounds often reveals food caches and nests. Where the grass is tall, a globular nest of coarse grasses, lined with finer grass or finely shredded vegetation, is built above ground among grass roots. Nests are about 15–20 cm (6–8 in) in diameter and have one or two openings.

Prairie voles feed mainly upon grasses and other green vegetation. They do not climb tall vegetation, but rather clip it at the base so

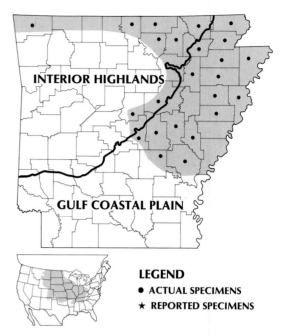

Distribution of the prairie vole (*Microtus ochrogaster*), Arkansas map modified from Moore and Heidt 1981.

they can obtain the nutritious portion. Insects, snails, and vegetable matter may be eaten occasionally when available. This species forages both day and night, with alternating periods of eating and sleeping. Seeds, bulblets, tubers, and plant roots may be cached in underground chambers near the nest.

Prairie voles tend to be monogamous and breeding continues throughout the year, with peaks of breeding activity in spring and fall (Getz and Hofmann 1986). Females produce three to four litters per year. Litter size ranges from one to nine, with three to five young comprising the usual litter. The gestation period is about 21 days, and the young weigh about 3 g (0.11 oz) at birth (Fitch 1957). The young develop rapidly and are weaned when about 3 weeks old. They reach sexual maturity and begin breeding when 4–6 weeks old. Prairie voles, like microtines in general, are subject to population fluctuations. These population shifts may result in densities ranging from a few to over 200 voles per acre.

IMPORTANCE AND/OR MANAGEMENT   No management or control measures are needed.

With the advent of railways after the settlement of Arkansas, colonization of outlying areas surrounding the Grand Prairie probably was facilitated by the railroad rights-of-way which provided convenient avenues of dispersal. Recent evidence suggests that linkage of populations in central and northern Arkansas has occurred in this way (Moore and Heidt 1981). However, fairly extensive collecting in central Arkansas by Trusten H. Holder in the late 1930s failed to turn up any specimens of *M. ochrogaster*. It is possible that reduced maintenance of railroads in recent years, coupled with less frequent burning of rights-of-way along the tracks, may have favored dispersal by permitting sufficient cover to develop along the rights-of-way. No prairie voles were collected in the vicinity of Pine Bluff, Jefferson County, in the mid-1950s although extensive trapping was conducted for a period of more than 3 years. The prairie vole was first reported in central Arkansas by Kee and Enright (1970). Thus, it appears that range extension of this vole has taken place in comparatively recent times. As with other species of *Microtus*, power line transmission corridors and medians of interstate highways are probably also relatively recent means of dispersal for this vole (Getz et al. 1978). One of the authors (Heidt) is currently monitoring westerly movement along Interstate 40 and has recently (March 1988) recorded this species in Faulkner County.

Since the exact historical background of this species is not known for sure, its subspecific status is not clear.

SELECTED REFERENCES
Fitch (1957); Getz et al. (1978); Getz and Hofmann (1986); Johnson and Johnson (1982); Kee and Enright (1970); Moore and Heidt (1981); Tamarin (1985).

WOODLAND VOLE
Microtus pinetorum

NAME   *Microtus* is from two Greek words, *mikros*, meaning "small," and *ous*, meaning "ear." The specific name, *pinetorum*, is derived from the Latin, *pinetum*, meaning "a pine woods," and *orium*, meaning "belonging to a place of." This refers to the Georgia pine forests where the species was first collected. The woodland vole is sometimes called the pine vole.

IDENTIFICATION AND DESCRIPTION   The woodland vole is small with a short tail (slightly longer than the hind foot) that is not sharply bicolored. It has small ears, partially concealed by fur, and tiny eyes. The fur is soft, dense, and a bright russet-brown to brownish chestnut above (sprinkled with blackish hairs) and grayish washed with buff or cinnamon below.

The woodland vole can be distinguished from the prairie vole by its shorter tail, and from the southern bog lemming by the absence of grooved incisors.

MEASUREMENTS AND DENTAL FORMULA
Total Length: 80–148 mm (3.2–5.8 in)
Tail Length: 15–25 mm (0.60–0.98 in)
Hind Foot: 15–19 mm (0.60–0.75 in)
Ear: 7–11 mm (0.28–0.43 in)
Skull Length: 24–27 mm (0.95–1.1 in)
Weight: 21–56 g (0.74–1.98 oz)
Dental   I 1/1, C 0/0, P 0/0, M 3/3
  Formula: = 16

ARKANSAS DISTRIBUTION AND ABUNDANCE
The woodland vole occurs statewide; it is locally common, but it may be sporadic in occurrence due to somewhat restricted habitat requirements.

LIFE HISTORY   Woodland voles occur in a variety of habitats ranging from grassy, overgrown areas in fields and fencerows to orchards and moist woodlands where there is sufficient ground cover in the form of grasses or thick leaf mold to provide concealment from terrestrial predators. They spend much of their time burrowing below the soil surface and seldom leave their burrows except at night. The burrows are usually just beneath the leaf litter or matted grass and generally are only 8–10 cm (3–4 in) deep, but they may be as deep as 30 cm (12 in). Surface runways may be used where there is dense grass cover, but most of their activity is underground. Hot summer weather may greatly reduce observable activity (Paul 1970).

The globular nest of dead leaves and grasses usually is just below the ground surface or under the shallow roots of a stump; sometimes it is located beneath a partially buried log. It is usually 15–18 cm (5.9–7.1 in) in diameter and may have three or four openings. This species appears to be quite social (Paul 1970), and as many as three females with litters have been found in one nest (Raynor 1960).

The diet consists mainly of roots, tubers,

bulbs, and bark of various shrubs and trees. Seeds, fruit, nuts, insects, and other animal matter are also eaten. In orchards, fallen apples and pears are relished. The voles burrow to the fallen fruit and feed from beneath it. Large quantities of roots and tubers may be stored in the burrow system for winter use.

The woodland vole probably breeds throughout the year in Arkansas as it does in Oklahoma (Goertz 1971). However, breeding activity may be reduced in the hot summer months. The gestation period is not definitely known but is probably about 21 days (Asdell 1964). Litter size ranges from one to eight, and usually there are about two to four young in a litter. Females produce from one to six litters per year. The young weigh about 2 g (0.07 oz) at birth. They develop rapidly and are weaned when between 16 and 21 days old. Adult size is reached 12–15 weeks after birth.

Microtus pinetorum, Woodland Vole. *Richard K. Laval*

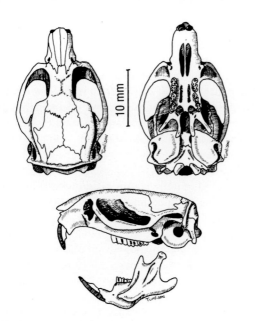

Skull of *Microtus pinetorum*

LEGEND
• ACTUAL SPECIMENS
★ REPORTED SPECIMENS

Distribution of the woodland vole (*Microtus pinetorum*)

Probable distributions in Arkansas of: 1. M.p. nemoralis; 2. M.p. auricularis; and 3. zone of intergradation between nemoralis and auricularis.

IMPORTANCE AND/OR MANAGEMENT When abundant, this species may severely damage orchards. Most of the damage is underground, where the voles eat rootlets and girdle larger roots, killing the trees. They sometimes do serious damage to young pine plantations as well.

Two subspecies occur in Arkansas. The race *M. p. nemoralis* is found in the Interior Highlands and the race *M. p. auricularis* occupies the Gulf Coastal Plain. The zone of intergradation between the two races is not definitely known but probably occurs near the foothills of the Ozark and Ouachita mountains.

SELECTED REFERENCES
Asdell (1964); Goertz (1971); Johnson and Johnson (1982); Paul (1970); Raynor (1960); Tamarin (1985).

MUSKRAT

Ondatra zibethicus

NAME   *Ondatra* is the Indian name for this animal. The specific name, *zibethicus*, is from the Latin, meaning "musky-odored."

IDENTIFICATION AND DESCRIPTION   The muskrat is a large microtine with a long, blackish, laterally flattened, and nearly naked tail. It has short legs and large, partly webbed hind feet. The toes have a fringe of stiff hairs to aid in swimming. Its ears are nearly concealed by fur, and the eyes are small. The pelage is dense and waterproof, consisting of soft underfur overlaid by long, smooth guard hairs. The muskrat is dark brown above, with lighter sides, and pale buff to cinnamon brown below.

MEASUREMENTS AND DENTAL FORMULA
Total Length: 409–635 mm (16.1–25.0 in)
Tail Length: 180–295 mm (7.1–11.6 in)
Hind Foot: 63–88 mm (2.5–3.5 in)
Ear: 15–25 mm (0.60–0.98 in)
Skull Length: 60–69 mm (2.4–2.7 in)
Weight: 541–1814 g (19.1–64.0 oz)
Dental Formula: I 1/1, C 0/0, P 0/0, M 3/3 = 16

ARKANSAS DISTRIBUTION AND ABUNDANCE
The muskrat occurs statewide; it is very common in the Gulf Coastal Plain.

LIFE HISTORY   The muskrat lives in slow-moving streams, canals, drainage ditches, borrow pits, farm ponds, minnow ponds, reservoirs, and swamps where there is an ample supply of aquatic plants and animals. During the growing season, rice fields in Arkansas serve as an excellent substitute for marshland. In marsh-type habitat, the muskrat typically builds large, dome-shaped houses or lodges of cattails, bulrushes, sedges, or other vegetation. In Arkansas, muskrats most often construct burrows in banks of streams, ditches, or levees surrounding ponds and rice fields. The underwater opening of the burrow, or "plunge hole," is 15–30 cm (6–12 in) below water level. There may be several entrances to the burrow system, and tunnels from the entrance holes lead upward to one or more dry nest chambers.

Muskrats feed mainly on bulbs, roots, stems, and leaves of aquatic vegetation but include a small amount of animal food such as crayfish, frogs, clams, and various kinds of dead animal matter in the diet. Favorite foods are cattails, bulrush tubers, pickerelweed, smartweed, sedges, water lilies, willows, and rice. If their preferred foods are not available, they will eat almost any kind of vegetation growing in or near water.

Although chiefly nocturnal, muskrats are active during daytime and often may be observed in early morning or from mid to late afternoon swimming across ponds or streams. They are excellent swimmers and divers and can remain submerged for as long as 15 minutes. Occasional forays are made to feed away from water in nearby gardens or cornfields. During peak breeding periods in spring and fall, adult muskrats often travel overland to establish new homes. Muskrats found at considerable distances from water often are sexually mature

Ondatra zibethicus, Muskrat. *Phil A. Dotson*

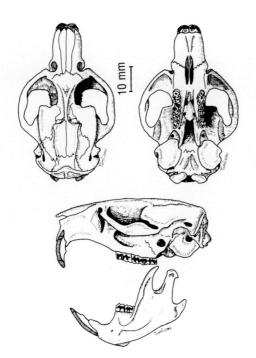

Skull of *Ondatra zibethicus*

The musk-rat is a serious agricultural pest in some parts of the state. It is more than a nuisance to fish farmers due to its burrowing activities in levees and pond banks. Habitat reduction by lowering water levels during winter months and the elimination of aquatic vegetation is one of the most effective methods for reducing muskrat populations.

On the positive side, the muskrat has long been one of the most important furbearers in the Southeastern United States (Boutin and Birkenholz 1987). Likewise, it has traditionally been one of the mainstays of the Arkansas fur trade, ranking third in total number of pelts sold. The general trend of muskrat harvests has been to increase harvest sizes. This is expected, because the major factor limiting muskrat populations is available habitat. As land use patterns have changed in Arkansas to include large acreages of rice and fish farms, particularly in the Mississippi Delta, prime muskrat habitat has increased proportionately. Thus, the Mississippi Delta leads in muskrat

young dispersing to new homes after being evicted by the parents when a new litter reaches the kit stage. Forced overland movements also may take place when drought dries up the hábitat. When traveling on land away from water, muskrats are highly vulnerable to predation and are frequently killed by motor vehicles on highways.

Breeding continues throughout the year in Arkansas, with peaks of breeding activity from March through April and from October through November. Muskrats are very prolific and have a high reproductive potential. Females usually breed in the spring following the year of birth and for about two years thereafter. The gestation period is about 29–30 days (Smith 1938), and in Arkansas females produce two to four litters per year. It is probable that a breeding female may produce as many as six litters per year in a productive habitat in southernmost Arkansas. Litter size varies from one to eleven, but the usual number in a litter is around four or five. Muskrat kits are weaned and able to shift for themselves when about one month old (Errington 1939).

Distribution of the muskrat (*Ondatra zibethicus*)

Aggregation of mussel shells indicating a muskrat feeding area. *Keith Sutton*

production (72%), followed by the Ozarks (19%), the Ouachitas (7%), and the West Gulf Coastal Plain (1%). It might also be expected that the West Gulf Coastal Plain, with its abundant waterways, should also produce a greater percentage of the total harvest. However, the introduced nutria seem to be firmly established in that region, and some data seem to suggest that nutria may displace muskrats in marginal habitats like those found in the West Gulf Coastal Plain (Peck et al. 1985). At present, the extent to which this introduced rodent has displaced or reduced muskrat populations in the state is not known. Of course, the substitution of one agricultural pest for another offers little consolation to the farmer.

The subspecies found in Arkansas belongs to the nominate race *O. z. zibethicus.*

SELECTED REFERENCES
Boutin and Birkenholz (1987); Errington (1939); Peck et al. (1985); Smith (1938).

SOUTHERN BOG LEMMING
Synaptomys cooperi

NAME *Synaptomys* is derived from two Greek words, *synapto*, meaning "to unite," and *mys*, meaning "mouse." This name probably implies the link that the bog lemming provides between true lemmings and voles. The specific name, *cooperi*, is a patronym honoring William Cooper, who collected the first specimen.

IDENTIFICATION AND DESCRIPTION The southern bog lemming is a small, robust rodent which has a very short (shorter than or about equal in length to the hind foot), indistinctly bicolored tail. Its ears are short (almost concealed in long fur), and the eyes are small. There is a small nailed thumb on each front foot. The upper front teeth are broad, bright orange, and have a shallow groove (this characteristic easily distinguishes it from *Microtus*).

Synaptomys cooperi, Southern Bog Lemming. *Roger W. Barbour*

Its fur is long and loose and brownish mixed with gray, black, and yellow above (the head is grizzled) and gray below.

MEASUREMENTS AND DENTAL FORMULA

Total Length: 98–154 mm (3.9–6.1 in)
Tail Length: 13–25 mm (0.5–0.98 in)
Hind Foot: 16–26 mm (0.63–1.0 in)
Ear: 8–16 mm (0.32–0.63 in)
Skull Length: 22–30 mm (0.87–1.2 in)
Weight: 21–50 g (0.74–1.8 oz)
Dental
Formula:
I 1/1, C 0/0, P 0/0, M 3/3
= 16

ARKANSAS DISTRIBUTION AND ABUNDANCE
The southern bog lemming is locally distributed in small colonies in the northeastern and east central part of the state. Bog lemmings are colonial and occur in small groups that are rather sporadic in occurrence.

LIFE HISTORY   The bog lemming is primarily an inhabitant of wet meadows, bogs, various

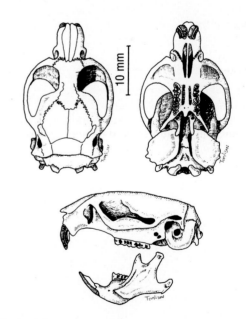

Skull of *Synaptomys cooperi*

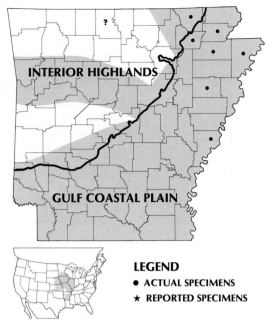

LEGEND
- **ACTUAL SPECIMENS**
- ★ **REPORTED SPECIMENS**

Distribution of the southern bog lemming (*Synaptomys cooperi*)

types of grassland, weedy fields, and marshes. However, it also occurs in moist woodlands and in orchards (Connor 1959). The chief requirement of this species seems to be the presence of green, succulent sedges and grasses, which are its main source of food. It constructs runways through thick, heavily matted stands of grass and makes piles of fresh grass cuttings in the runways that resemble those of the prairie vole. However, the presence of bright green droppings in the runway indicates the presence of bog lemmings. They also dig burrows underground to a depth of about 15 cm (6 in) or more that are connected with the surface runways. Lemmings are active at all hours of the day and night, but most activity is during late afternoon and at night.

The nest of dry leaves and grass is lined with soft material such as fine grass, fur, or feathers. It is about 10–20 cm (3.9–7.9 in) in diameter and is usually placed in an underground chamber adjoining the burrow system. During warmer months, the nest is sometimes built above ground in thick mats of grass.

The breeding season extends throughout the year. Very little is known about the reproduction of this species in Arkansas, but peaks in breeding activity probably occur in spring and fall. Litter size varies from one to seven; the usual litter size is two to five. The gestation period is 23 days (Connor 1959) and the young weigh 3–4 g (0.10–0.15 oz) at birth. They are weaned when about 3 weeks old.

IMPORTANCE AND/OR MANAGEMENT   No management or control measures are needed.

The subspecies present in Arkansas is *S. c. gossii*.

SELECTED REFERENCES
Connor (1959).

BLACK RAT
Rattus rattus

NAME   Both the generic and specific name, *rattus*, is Latin for "rat." This species is also known as the roof rat.

IDENTIFICATION AND DESCRIPTION   The black rat is medium-sized with a relatively slender body and a tail longer than its head and body.

Rattus rattus, Black Rat. *Walter E. Howard*

The almost naked ears are large and can be extended over the eyes. It has a pointed muzzle. The fur is soft and mixed with many long, harsh, bristly hairs. It is grayish brown to black above and gray to yellowish white or white below.

MEASUREMENTS AND DENTAL FORMULA
Total Length: 325–455 mm (12.8–
                17.9 in)
Tail Length: 160–255 mm (6.3–10.0 in)
Hind Foot: 27–42 mm (1.1–1.7 in)
Ear: 17–27 mm (0.67–1.9 in)
Skull Length: 41–48 mm (1.6–1.9 in)
Weight: 115–350 g (4.1–12.3 oz)
Dental I 1/1, C 0/0, P 0/0, M 3/3
  Formula: = 16

ARKANSAS DISTRIBUTION AND ABUNDANCE
The black rat probably occurs statewide in and around human habitations. The black rat is not particularly abundant, but it is more common in the southern portion of the state and along the Arkansas and Mississippi rivers where it might be transported by river traffic.

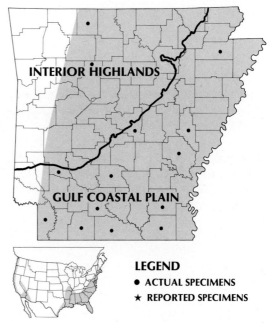

Distribution of the black rat (*Rattus rattus*)

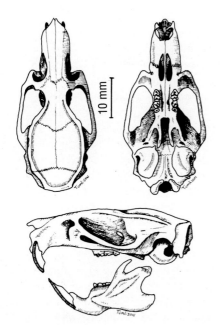

Skull of *Rattus rattus*

LIFE HISTORY   The black rat or roof rat is a nonnative species that was first introduced into the United States in the early seventeenth century. It was once abundant in many parts of North America, but with the introduction of the Norway rat in the late eighteenth century, black rat populations declined to the point where this species became rare or extinct in many areas. Wherever they occur together, the larger, more aggressive Norway rat has displaced or driven out the black rat. They sometimes occur together but are behaviorally and ecologically separated. The roof rat, which is a much better climber, occupies the upper stories of buildings, and the Norway rat lives in lower levels of buildings, underground, and in sewer systems and garbage dumps of cities. Like the Norway rat, the black rat is omnivorous and eats a wide variety of vegetable and animal matter.

Black rats breed throughout the year. The gestation period is about 21 days, and the average litter size ranges from six to nine. Young rats are weaned when about 3 weeks old and become sexually mature and capable of breeding when about 3 months old.

IMPORTANCE AND/OR MANAGEMENT Both the black rat and its relative, the Norway rat, constitute a serious public health problem where they live in close proximity to humans. They not only contaminate foodstuffs but also harbor numerous species of parasites and infectious organisms. They transmit such diseases as typhus, plague, leptospirosis, trichinosis, and rat-bite fever to humans through the parasites they harbor. For control measures, see the discussion in the Norway rat account.

The subspecies in Arkansas is *R. r. alexandrinus*.

SELECTED REFERENCES
Davis (1953); Lowery (1974); Worth (1950).

NORWAY RAT

Rattus norvegicus

NAME *Rattus* is from the Latin *rattus*, meaning "rat." The specific name, *norvegicus*, is a Latinized word meaning "of Norway," indicating the country for which the species was named.

IDENTIFICATION AND DESCRIPTION The Norway rat is a large, robust rat with a tail which is conspicuously annulated and shorter than its head and body. The small, hairy ears do not reach the eyes, and the muzzle is blunt. The fur is soft with few harsh, bristly hairs. The pelage is grayish brown or reddish brown above and pale gray to grayish brown below.

MEASUREMENTS AND DENTAL FORMULA
    Total Length: 294–460 mm (11.6–18.1 in)
    Tail Length: 122–220 mm (4.8–8.7 in)
    Hind Foot: 30–46 mm (1.2–1.8 in)
    Ear: 15–25 mm (0.60–0.98 in)
    Skull Length: 38–50 mm (1.5–2.0 in)
    Weight: 168–485 g (5.9–17.1 oz)
    Dental Formula: I 1/1, C 0/0, P 0/0, M 3/3 = 16

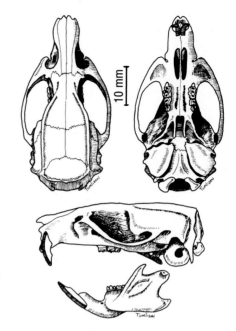

Skull of *Rattus norvegicus*

ARKANSAS DISTRIBUTION AND ABUNDANCE
The Norway rat is common statewide; it generally lives in or near buildings.

LIFE HISTORY The Norway rat lives in close association with man and his dwelling places. It is found in warehouses, commercial buildings, wharves, feed stores, farm buildings, and private residences. This species also is common in garbage dumps and sewers of cities, and it frequently lives apart from buildings in cultivated fields and meadows during the summer months. This rat is primarily nocturnal and during daytime lives in nests underground or in the walls, floors, and foundations of buildings. The nest is constructed of shredded paper, rags, and trash of various kinds.

Norway rats will eat virtually anything that is edible. This species is primarily vegetarian but will readily eat animal food of various kinds. In poultry houses, it often eats eggs and young chickens. In crowded tenements of large cities, hungry rats often bite children and adults while they are sleeping. Garbage of all kinds and grain are favored foods.

Rattus norvegicus, Norway Rat. *Phil A. Dotson*

This species is extremely prolific and breeds throughout the year. The gestation period is 21–23 days, and litters of from two to fifteen young are produced. The usual litter size is six to eight. The young are weaned when 3 weeks old, and they may begin breeding and producing litters when 3–4 months old. Under favorable conditions, a single female may produce from six to eight litters per year. The average life span is estimated to be between 2 and 3 years.

IMPORTANCE AND/OR MANAGEMENT   The Norway rat is one of the worst scourges of mankind. It consumes or fouls tremendous quantities of human food, does great damage to property, and causes much human misery, suffering, and death by transmitting diseases and parasites.

While no one method can provide total control of rats, maintenance of cleanliness, and the elimination of cover and food may be the most effective long-term measures. Other control

Young of the Norway rat. *John R. MacGregor*

FAMILY MURIDAE   183

Distribution of the Norway rat (*Rattus norvegicus*)

IDENTIFICATION AND DESCRIPTION The house mouse is small and has a long, nearly naked, scaly tail. It has moderately large, naked ears and a rather pointed rostrum. Its eyes are small. The pelage is mixed yellowish brown and black above and ashy gray below. There are a number of color variations, including the albino mouse, which is used in laboratories.

The house mouse can be easily distinguished from harvest mice by its lack of grooved upper incisors; from members of the genus *Peromyscus* by the lack of sharp color differences between the dorsal and ventral sides; and from the golden mouse by its coloration.

MEASUREMENTS AND DENTAL FORMULA

Total Length:	125–198 mm (4.9–7.8 in)
Tail Length:	58–102 mm (2.3–4.0 in)
Hind Foot:	15–24 mm (0.60–0.94 in)
Ear:	10–18 mm (0.39–0.71 in)
Skull Length:	19–23 mm (0.74–0.91 in)
Weight:	10–30 g (0.35–1.1 oz)
Dental Formula:	I 1/1, C 0/0, P 0/0, M 3/3 = 16

measures include shooting, gassing, trapping, and poison bait. Poisons should be used with caution as they are also toxic to humans, domestic animals, and innocent wildlife. In addition, some populations of rats are demonstrating immunity to various poisons, particularly those which cause internal bleeding. Rats also rapidly learn to avoid poison bait.

The common laboratory rat which is used extensively in medical, biological, and behavioral research is the albino variety of the Norway rat.

SELECTED REFERENCES
Calhoun (1962); Davis (1953).

HOUSE MOUSE

Mus musculus

NAME *Mus* is the Latin word for "mouse." The specific name, *musculus*, is the Latin word for "little mouse" and refers to its size.

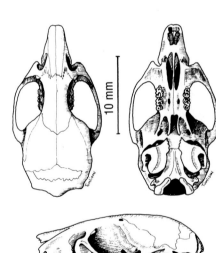

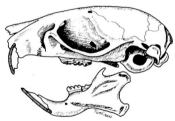

Skull of *Mus musculus*

Mus musculus, House Mouse. *Phil A. Dotson*

ARKANSAS DISTRIBUTION AND ABUNDANCE
The house mouse is extremely common state-wide. It may be found in or near buildings, as well as in open fields and brushy areas, especially during spring and summer.

LIFE HISTORY   The introduced house mouse is closely associated with humans and lives in dwellings, warehouses, commercial buildings, restaurants, factories, and other buildings. Barns, granaries, and feed stores are its favorite habitat and often support large populations if control measures are not taken. The nest is made of soft materials and is placed under floors and in the walls of buildings. In the wild, the nest is placed under piles of trash, stones, or logs, or in some other protected place. In the field, house mice often use runways of other small native mice such as deer mice, harvest mice, and voles. When present in large numbers, they may exclude native mice from favorable habitat, even though other species may be competitively superior (Dueser and Porter 1986).

House mice are obnoxious and destructive pests in houses where they gnaw holes in woodwork, chew books and clothing, consume food stores, and contaminate them with their droppings. On farms and in feed stores, house mice are particularly destructive to stored grain. They will eat almost any food eaten by humans or their domestic animals, but they are not completely dependent on such fare, since in the field they feed on weed seeds, insects, and other plant and animal matter.

This species is extremely prolific and breeds year-round. Some decrease in breeding activity occurs during winter and midsummer (Smith 1954). Females may produce as many as 13 litters in one year. The litter size varies from three to ten but is usually between four and seven. After a gestation period of 18–20 days, the young are born blind and naked. They grow rapidly and are fully weaned at the age of 3 weeks. Sexual maturity is attained and breeding may begin when they are 6–8 weeks old.

IMPORTANCE AND/OR MANAGEMENT   House mice which become a nuisance in dwellings are most easily eliminated with snap traps. Poisons are also effective, but frequently poisoned mice die within walls and other inaccessible places where they create an undesirable stench.

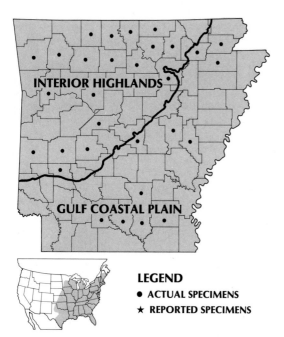

Distribution of the house mouse (*Mus musculus*)

SELECTED REFERENCES
Catlett and Shellhammer (1962); DeLong (1967); Dueser and Porter (1986); Smith (1954).

FAMILY CAPROMYIDAE

CAPROMYIDS

The only member of the family Capromyidae in Arkansas is the nutria, or coypu, which was introduced into the United States from South America. The nutria is adapted for aquatic life and is an excellent swimmer. It is the only species in the genus *Myocastor*. General characteristics of the family are: Size large, form robust; tail moderately long, round, scaly, and poorly haired; head somewhat triangular; eyes and ears small; hind feet webbed; claws large and sharp; fur soft, thick, and silky; infraorbital canal greatly enlarged; incisors broad, strong, orange to orange-red; mandible with a reduced coronoid process and an enlarged, laterally deflected angular process.

NUTRIA

Myocastor coypus

NAME   *Myocaster* is from two Greek words, *mys*, meaning "mouse," and *kastor*, meaning "beaver," thus meaning "mouse beaver." The specific name, *coypus*, is the Latinized form of "coypu," meaning "an aquatic mammal" in the language of the Araucanian Indians of south central Chile and adjacent parts of Argentina.

IDENTIFICATION AND DESCRIPTION   The nutria is a large, beaver-sized rodent with a tail which is shorter than its head and body. The tail is long, round, scaly, and sparsely haired except at its base. Its ears are small, round, and almost hidden in the fur. The eyes are small and the hind feet webbed, and there are four or five teats located along each side of its back. The pelage is glossy, black, or dark amber to light rusty or brownish blond above (the back is usually darker than the sides) and paler below. Its front teeth are orange to orange-red.

MEASUREMENTS AND DENTAL FORMULA
Total Length: 800–1050 mm (31.5–41.3 in)
Tail Length: 300–450 mm (11.8–17.7 in)
Hind Foot: 100–150 mm (3.9–5.9 in)
Ear: 20–30 mm (0.79–1.2 in)
Skull Length: 105–130 mm (4.1–5.1 in)
Weight: 7–11 kg (15–24 lb)
Dental Formula: I 1/1, C 0/0, P 1/1, M 3/3 = 20

ARKANSAS DISTRIBUTION AND ABUNDANCE
The nutria is well established in the West Gulf Coastal Plain, the southern and eastern portions of the Mississippi Delta, and it is colonizing in the Arkansas River Valley.

LIFE HISTORY   In most respects, the habitat occupied by the nutria is similar to that of the muskrat. It lives in marshy or swampy areas, streams, farm and minnow ponds, oxbow lakes, and other bodies of water wherever there is ample aquatic and semiaquatic vegetation.

The nutria is almost exclusively vegetarian but has been reported to eat shellfish occasionally. Preferred foods are three-cornered grass, cattails, sedges, and bulrushes, but when these are not available, it will eat a wide variety of other plant material. Nutrias are fond of alfalfa, clover, and various legumes; in summer, they will graze heavily on Bermuda grass and other soft grasses. In ponds, the nutria feeds on water plants such as duckweed, and in agricultural areas, it eats weeds and cultivated crops such as rice, soybeans, and sugar cane. Nutrias are active throughout the day and night. Feeding activity alternates with periods spent sunning, sleeping, grooming, or swimming (Warkentin 1968). Nutria are quite vocal and emit sounds that may resemble a woman screaming, laughing, or cackling. These vocalizations can be quite disconcerting when one is near a swamp at night.

The nest of the nutria is a crude affair consisting of a loose pile of sedges, reeds, and other vegetation. It is usually placed near the water's edge or in a burrow close to water, but occasionally the nest is located in a burrow at some distance from water. Burrows commonly are made in densely vegetated banks and levees that have a vertical or rather steep slope with a burrow entrance near water level. Nutrias often appropriate the burrow of a muskrat or an armadillo and enlarge it for their own use. Burrows are usually short tunnels which extend 1–2 m (3–6.5 ft) into the bank, but they may be rather complex with several entrances and may be as deep as 10–15 m (33–50 ft) or more. This species also accumulates large plat-

Myocaster coypus, Nutria. *Martin T. Fulter*
Texas Parks & Wildlife Department

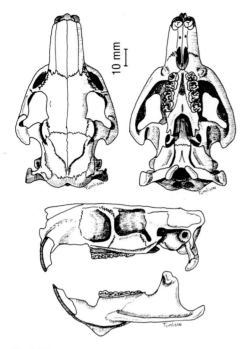

Skull of *Myocastor coypus*

forms of uneaten plant parts wherever it lives or feeds. These platforms are used for resting, feeding refuge, and nesting. In marshy areas, the platforms may float on the water's surface and resemble houses built by muskrats.

In the South, nutrias breed continuously and are very prolific. The gestation period is 130–134 days, and the number of young per litter ranges from two to eleven. The average litter size is about four to five. Females breed when about a year old and produce two to three litters per year. Miscarriages of whole litters or parts of litters are frequent, and embryo resorptions are also common. In some years, fewer than one-half of the developing embryos survive (Evans 1970). The young have their eyes open and are fully furred when born; they weigh from 165–225 g (6–8 oz) and are able to swim shortly after birth (Newson 1966). The young are weaned when 6–8 weeks old.

IMPORTANCE AND/OR MANAGEMENT The first successful introduction of the nutria in the South was in Louisiana in 1938. Since then, it has become well established through natural dispersal and by transplantations along the Gulf Coast and inland to Oklahoma, Arkansas, Tennessee, and northern Mississippi and Alabama. Transplantations have also resulted in the establishment of feral populations in many coastal states of the Southeast.

Its burrowing activities may cause serious damage to drainage canals, irrigation ditches, and levees in rice-growing areas and on fish farms. The nutria was introduced in many areas as a natural control against aquatic vegetation choking ponds and waterways, but its value for this purpose is greatly overrated since it more often feeds on desirable vegetation, especially in waterfowl habitat, and avoids water hyacinth, bladderwort, algae, and other unwanted vegetation. Nutria have few natural enemies, and, except for trapping, no control measures appear to be very effective. It is claimed that their numbers may be reduced or held in check by alligators where these are indigenous or introduced.

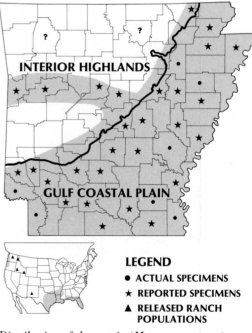

Distribution of the nutria (*Myocastor coypus*), Arkansas map modified from Bailey and Heidt 1978.

Nutria do not represent a very valuable fur resource in Arkansas. They are, however, becoming more important as evidenced by the fact that 94% of nutria harvesting from 1950 through 1982 occurred in the late 1970s and early 1980s. As would be expected, 90% of the nutria taken were from the West Gulf Coastal Plain and the Mississippi Delta (Peck et al. 1985).

SELECTED REFERENCES
Bailey and Heidt (1978); Evans (1970); Kinler et al. (1987); Newson (1966); Peck et al. (1985); Warkentin (1968).

Order Carnivora *Carnivores*

The name carnivore means "flesh-eater," and members of the order are characterized by having specialized teeth—the carnassials—in the upper and lower jaws which are adapted for cutting and tearing flesh. Many members of the order are exclusively flesh eaters, but this is by no means true of all. Some carnivores found in Arkansas, such as raccoons, skunks, and bears, include a considerable quantity of plant material in their diet as well as flesh of various kinds of animals. This order includes many valuable furbearers (e.g., mink, fox, raccoon, and otter) which provide an important source of income for trappers in the state. Most carnivores are active chiefly at night, although coyotes, skunks, raccoons, and other species often are abroad in daylight hours; such species chiefly seem to avoid activity during the hottest parts of the day, and in winter months, they may be active even at midday.

Five families of carnivores are found in Arkansas. Members of the order are mostly medium-sized and terrestrial. The mink and otter, however, spend much of their time in or near water. Carnivores have large, recurved fangs (canine teeth) which project decidedly beyond the small incisors and the adjoining cheek teeth (premolars and molars). In most carnivores, except in bears and raccoons, the cheek teeth are adapted for shearing rather than crushing or grinding food. The condyle of the dentary bone and the glenoid fossa of the squamosal bone are transversely elongated and thus allow no rotary jaw action and only limited transverse movement. Most carnivores have well-developed senses of smell, hearing, and sight.

1. Five clawed toes on each front and hind foot 2

   Four clawed toes on hind foot, five toes on front foot (inner toe—"dewclaw"—reduced and high on foot, often without a claw) 4

2. Tail very short and concealed in long fur of rump; total number of teeth 41 (number may be less since anterior premolars are often lost); larger molars flat-crowned, adapted for crushing; feet plantigrade; size very large, weight 100–230 kg (220–507 lb); skull length more than 250 mm (9.8 in) .... URSIDAE (bears), page 206

   Tail long; total number of teeth 40 or less; size small to medium, weight usually less than 10 kg (22 lb) 3

3. Total number of teeth 40; tail with series of buff and black rings, tip black .... PROCYONIDAE (raccoons and allies), page 210

   Total number of teeth less than 40; tail not ringed .... MUSTELIDAE (weasels and allies), page 216

4. Claws short, sharp, strongly curved and retractile, concealed in fur; short, rounded muzzle; tail not bushy; total number of teeth 30 or 32 .... FELIDAE (cats), page 233

   Claws blunt, moderately curved and not retractile, well exposed; elongated muzzle; tail bushy; total number of teeth 42; body doglike .... CANIDAE (dogs, foxes, and allies), page 191

FAMILY CANIDAE

DOGS, FOXES, AND ALLIES

Members of this family are medium-sized, doglike carnivores distinguished by long legs adapted for running on the toes (digitigrade) and a dentition that is specialized for cutting and tearing flesh. Wild canids all have bushy tails and an elongated muzzle which belies their well-developed sense of smell. The color pattern of each species also is quite uniform. Some breeds of the domestic dog, which have been derived from wolf stock by selective breeding, may have shortened muzzles, short legs, non-bushy tails, and a wide variety of color patterns. Some dogs, however, closely resemble coyotes or wolves in general appearance. Wolves and coyotes also frequently interbreed with domestic dogs, and the resulting hybrids often are very difficult to distinguish from their wild progenitors.

The genera *Vulpes* and *Urocyon* were included in the genus *Canis* by Mivart (1890), Winge (1941), and Van Gelder (1978) on morphological grounds. The karyotypes of the three genera are, however, quite different, with a chromosome number of 78 in *Canis*, 66 in *Urocyon*, and 38 and 50 in *Vulpes* (Ewer 1973). The view for combining the genera has not been well accepted, and we continue to maintain the established separation.

WHOLE ANIMALS

1. Tail to end of last vertebra more than half as
   long as the head and body and less than 1050
   mm (41.3 in); hind foot less than 160 mm (6.3
   in); nosepad less than 19 mm (0.75 in) wide 2

   Tail to end of last vertebrae less than half as
   long as head and body and total length more
   than 1050 mm (41.3 in); hind foot more than
   160 mm (6.3 in); nosepad more than 19 mm
   wide (0.75 in) 3

2. Grizzled-gray above, buff below; legs and feet
   reddish brown; outer side of ears yellowish red;
   throat white; top of tail with black stripe, tipped
   with black .... *Urocyon cinereoargenteus*, Gray Fox

   Yellowish red above, white, or grayish white below; legs and feet blackish; outer side of ears
   and muzzle sometimes blackish; throat white;
   top of tail without stripe, tipped with white .... *Vulpes vulpes*, Red Fox

3. Total length usually less than 1350 mm (53.1
   in); ear usually less than 120 mm (4.72 in);
   foreleg about 630 mm (25 in) at shoulder;
   muzzle narrow, nosepad less than 25 mm (0.98
   in) wide; gray to tawny mixed with black above
   (occasionally black), throat and belly white;
   weight 8–16 kg (17.6–35.3 lb) .... *Canis latrans*, Coyote

   Total length usually more than 1350 mm (53.1
   in); ear usually longer than 120 mm (4.72 in);
   foreleg about 690 mm (27.2 in) at shoulder;
   muzzle broad, nosepad more than 25 mm wide
   (0.98 in); gray to tawny or reddish mixed with
   black above, creamy or buffy below (sometimes
   all black except for white feet and pectoral
   spot); sides of muzzle buffy red; legs longer and
   more slender in proportion to body size, and ear
   larger in proportion to head size than *C. latrans*;
   weight 16–41 kg (35.3–90.4 lb) .... *Canis rufus*, Red Wolf

   *(Note: Although the red wolf is extinct in Arkan-
   sas, dog × wolf, dog × coyote, and coyote ×
   wolf hybrids still present in some parts of the
   state may show the typical size and color characteristics of red wolves. Careful examination of
   skulls is usually necessary to verify that such individuals are hybrids.)*

SKULLS

1. Relatively small, less than 150 mm (5.9 in)
   long; postorbital processes of frontal thin and
   dished out (concave) on top surface 2

   Relatively large, more than 150 mm long (5.9
   in); postorbital processes of frontal thick and
   rounded (convex) on top surface 3

   Cranial ridges in the form of a broad "U" and
   not forming a median crest posteriorly (fig. 24a);
   sides of braincase rough; upper incisors not
   lobed; contour of lower jaw not curved, with
   notch on lower border (fig. 24c) .... *Urocyon cinereoargenteus*, Gray Fox

2. Cranial ridges in the form of a narrow "V" and
   meeting posteriorly to form a median crest (fig.
   24b); sides of braincase smooth; upper and
   lower outer incisors lobed; contour of lower jaw
   curved, with no notch on lower border (fig.
   24d) .... *Vulpes vulpes*, Red Fox

FIGURE 24.   Cranial ridges of *Urocyon cinereoargenteus* forming a broad "U" (a) and cranial ridges of *Vulpes vulpes* forming a narrow "V" (b). Lower jaw of *U. cinereoargenteus* with notch on lower border (c) and lower jaw of *V. vulpes* with no notch (d).

3. Length usually less than 210 mm (8.3 in); width
   of skull across zygomatic arches usually less
   than 110 mm (4.3 in); upper canine tooth with
   greatest diameter at base 10.5 mm (0.41 in) or
   less .... *Canis latrans*, Coyote

Length usually more than 215 mm (8.5 in); width of skull across zygomatic arches usually more than 110 mm (4.3 in); upper canine tooth with greatest diameter at base usually more than 10.5 mm (0.41 in) .... *Canis rufus*, Red Wolf

(Note: Skull measurements of large, male coyotes and small, female red wolves often overlap; furthermore, dog × coyote, dog × wolf, and coyote × wolf hybrids show intermediate skull characteristics between dogs, coyotes, and wolves—in such cases, both body and skull measurements may be required for positive identification, and the opinion of a professional mammalogist may be needed.)

Dog, Coyote, or Wolf?

In Arkansas and other states, crosses between domestic dogs and coyotes are common. In the past, dogs and coyotes also interbred with red wolves. Hybrids resulting from such crosses, especially where crosses involve German shepherd dogs, often closely resemble coyotes or wolves. Dogs abandoned by their owners often revert to a semi-wild state, and offspring of such dogs that are reared in the wild without human influence are referred to as feral dogs. In behavior and appearance, feral offspring of German shepherd dogs or of dog × wolf and coyote × wolf crosses often are difficult to distinguish either from coyotes or wolves. The following characteristics are presented as an aid to distinguishing between feral dogs, dog × coyote or dog × wolf hybrids, and coyote × red wolf hybrids. Often it is impossible to positively identify these canids without the help of a taxonomist familiar with their characteristics.

WHOLE ANIMALS

1a. Ears always erect; eyes greenish yellow (rarely blue); dew claws absent on hind feet; muzzle elongated; profile slopes gently above eyes or is more or less flat; tail usually bottle-shaped, bushy; underfur well developed and thick; middle toes on front feet register (track) close together (see tracks in Appendix C); pelage color uniform, ranging from gray to tawny mixed with black (or all black); weight seldom more than 11–14 kg (24–31 lb) (coyote) or may be 20 kg (44 lbs) or more (red wolf)........ *Canis latrans*, Coyote; *Canis rufus*, Red Wolf; *C. latrans* × *C. rufus* hybrids.

1b. Ears sometimes flopped over or drooped; eye color variable, if brown, not a coyote or wolf; dew claws may be absent, but if present, not a coyote or wolf; muzzle may be elongated, but if short and broad, not a coyote or wolf; profile may show a definite rise ("stop") above eyes; tail seldom bottle-shaped, usually brushlike; underfur may be poorly developed, thin, or absent; middle toes on front feet tend to spread apart in register (see tracks in Appendix B); pelage color highly variable but may resemble coyote or wolf; weight variable, ranging from 11 to more than 20 kg (24–44 lb)............ *Canis familiaris*, Domestic Dog; *C. familiaris* × *C. latrans*, or *C. familiaris* × *C. rufus* hybrids.

SKULLS

1a. Upper incisors always close-set and even; rostrum elongated and narrow (somewhat broader in *C. rufus*); width of rostrum less than 18% of greatest skull length; inner lobe of fourth upper premolar poorly developed, smooth, or absent; length of upper molar row divided by width of palate between inner margins of alveoli of first upper molars is equal to 3.1 or more; profile flat or gently sloping above eyes...... *Canis latrans*, Coyote; *Canis rufus*, Red Wolf; *C. latrans* × *C. rufus* hybrids.

1b. Upper incisors usually (but not always) with spaces between teeth; rostrum may be elongated and narrow or short and broad; width of rostrum usually more than 18% of greatest skull length; inner lobe of fourth upper premolar sometimes has weak cusp; length of upper molar row divided by width of palate between inner margins of alveoli of first upper molars usually 2.7 or less; first lower premolars sometimes absent; profile may show distinct rise ("stop") above eyes................ *Canis familiaris*, Domestic Dog; *C. familiaris* × *C. latrans* or *C. familiaris* × *C. rufus* hybrids.

(Note: Skull characters of different breeds of the domestic dog are extremely variable, but a pronounced rise in the profile above the eyes ("stop") is usually, but not always, indicative of dog ancestry. German shepherd skulls or husky skulls are very similar to those of coyotes and red wolves. Detailed measurements often are necessary to make positive identifications; whenever possible, all available combinations of skull and body characters should be used.)

COYOTE

Canis latrans

NAME   *Canis* is the Latin word for "dog." The specific name, *latrans*, is the Latin word for "a barker."

IDENTIFICATION AND DESCRIPTION   The coyote is slender and medium-sized, resembling a small German shepherd dog. The tail is bushy and tipped with black. It has a long, narrow, reddish brown or gray muzzle; erect, pointed ears; and long legs. The pelage is grizzled buff or gray overlaid with black-tipped hairs above and whitish, cream, or pale gray with yellowish tint below.

Melanistic coyotes, which resemble the black phase of the red wolf in all respects except size, occur in Arkansas, and it seems possible that red wolf genes have become incorporated into the gene pool of the predominant coyote population through introgressive hybridization (Gipson et al. 1974; Gipson 1976). Melanistic individuals that are pure coyotes are also possible.

MEASUREMENTS AND DENTAL FORMULA
Total Length: 1000–1350 mm (39.4–53.1 in)
Tail Length: 267–440 mm (10.5–17.3 in)
Hind Foot: 166–220 mm (6.5–8.7 in)
Ear: 91–120 mm (3.6–4.7 in)
Skull Length: 171–219 mm (6.7–8.6 in)
Weight: 9–16 kg (19.8–35.3 lb)
Dental   I 3/3, C 1/1, P 4/4, M 2/3
  Formula: = 42

ARKANSAS DISTRIBUTION AND ABUNDANCE The coyote occurs statewide; it is more common in western Arkansas.

LIFE HISTORY   Coyotes inhabit open fields, brushlands, second-growth woodlots, and forest edge habitat. In Arkansas, the coyote originally was found mainly in the more open areas of western Arkansas, but with changing agricultural practices, which involved clearing of timberlands and creation of more open lands, it had extended its range to the central part of the state or beyond by the early 1950s and over the entire state by the early 1960s. Eastward expansion of the coyote population was accompanied by extensive hybridization with red wolves.

Although mainly nocturnal, coyotes are sometimes observed in the daytime along highways and in open fields. Their principal activity peak begins near sunset, and a smaller activity peak occurs near daybreak (Gipson and Sealander 1972).

Rabbits, various rodent species, and other animal food make up the principal part of the diet, but coyotes also eat considerable plant food, especially during summer and fall (Gipson 1974). Persimmons, muscadines, and melons, when available, are evidently relished by coyotes. Coyotes are opportunists, and their diet is composed of foods that are most abundant and easily available. Prior to the 1930s, no large-scale commercial poultry industry existed in Arkansas, and poultry made up only a small percentage of the coyote's diet. By 1950, poultry production in the state had expanded tremendously, poultry dumps were common, and poultry made up a large share

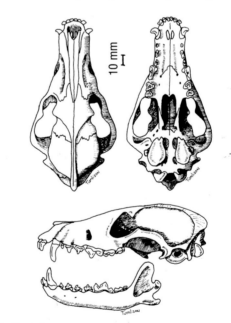

Skull of *Canis latrans*

Canis latrans, Coyote. *Phil A. Dotson*

of the coyote's menu (Gipson and Sealander 1976). Deer and domestic livestock are sometimes found in coyote stomachs and, along with poultry, such remains mainly represent carrion.

Female coyotes produce one litter per year which averages about six pups (Gier 1968). Litter size ranges from two to twelve, but a litter of 19 has been recorded from Utah. The average litter in Arkansas is four to five pups. In Arkansas, females are bred from mid-February through the first week of March, and males are capable of breeding from late November through March (Gipson et al. 1975). The gestation period is about 63 days (between 58 and 65 days), and litters are born from late April through early May. Pups are weaned when about 5–7 weeks old (Bekoff 1977).

Gier (1968) reported a close correlation between food supply, especially rodents, and breeding success, because the condition in which female coyotes enter the breeding season determines the number of females that will breed and the number of eggs ovulated. During good "mouse years," up to 80% of the old females produce litters. Usually females do not breed until their second year, but when rodents are plentiful in the diet, one-half or more of yearling females become pregnant.

IMPORTANCE AND/OR MANAGEMENT
The status of the coyote in Arkansas and other states is highly controversial. Coyotes are thoroughly disliked by farmers, stockmen, and some sportsmen who complain of coyote predation on poultry, livestock, especially calves, and game animals. Some complaints are justified, but in many cases packs of wild dogs are the real culprits. On the other hand, the coyote is highly esteemed by predator hunters and by sportsmen who enjoy pursuing coyotes and foxes with hounds.

Poultry and livestock eaten by coyotes often

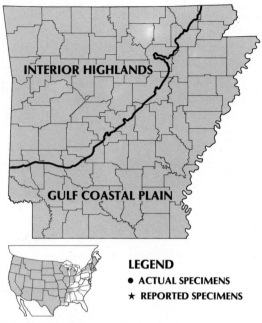

LEGEND
● ACTUAL SPECIMENS
★ REPORTED SPECIMENS

Distribution of the coyote (*canis latrans*)

are carrion including dead chickens and turkeys dumped by growers or calves that have died through bad weather, disease, or outright neglect during the calving season. Deer remains in coyote stomachs are most often found during late fall and winter when deer are crippled during hunting seasons and become easy prey. A few fawns may be caught in spring when they are first dropped, and deer remains in some coyote stomachs consist of carrion obtained from road kills. The overall impact of the coyote on deer populations in the state appears to be minor.

As a furbearer, coyotes were not harvested until the 1950s, and 98% of the total harvest before 1983 occurred in the 1970s and early 1980s. The coyote ranked ninth in both size and value of the total furbearer harvests. Regionally, 37% of coyotes were harvested from the Ozark Mountains, 27% from the Mississippi Delta, 19% from the Ouachita Mountains, and 17% from the West Gulf Coastal Plain (Peck et al. 1985).

Any assessment of the economic effects of coyotes must take into account not only the damage they do but also their beneficial role in consuming large numbers of rodents and rabbits, scavenging dead animals, and removing diseased and injured animals from deer populations. Large-scale control measures against the coyote generally are very costly and ineffective, whereas selective removal of nuisance animals by professional trappers is a more effective way of dealing with the problem.

Coyotes readily hybridize with domestic dogs, and the fertile offspring of such crosses are often referred to as "coydogs." When coyotes mate with German shepherd dogs, their offspring often are difficult to distinguish from either coyotes or red wolves. Extensive hybridization of coyotes and red wolves, which began in the 1930s and 1940s, resulted in the demise of the red wolf as a viable species over most of its former range. Occasional specimens which resemble red wolves in size, coloration, and other characteristics could result from crosses between hybrid parents (Gipson et al. 1974).

The subspecies present in the state is *C. l. frustror*.

SELECTED REFERENCES
Bekoff (1977, 1982); Gier (1968); Gipson (1974, 1976); Gipson and Sealander (1972, 1976); Gipson et al. (1974, 1975); Peck et al. (1985).

RED WOLF
Canis rufus

NAME   *Canis* is the Latin word for "dog." The specific name, *rufus*, is the Latin name for "reddish."

IDENTIFICATION AND DESCRIPTION   The red wolf is larger and more robust than the coyote, and its head, nose, and nosepad are broader. The legs are longer and the feet are larger; the ears are much larger; and its pelage is coarser. The red wolf has a bushy tail that is tipped with black. Its muzzle, ears, nape, and outer surfaces of the legs are tawny. The remainder of

Canis rufus, Red Wolf. *Phil A. Dotson*

the pelage is a mixture of cinnamon-buff and tawny interspersed with gray and black above (the back is heavily overlaid with black) and whitish to pinkish-buff below (the nose and throat are sometimes whitish). A color phase occurs which is largely black except for a white pectoral spot, white feet, white on the chin and throat, and white hairs in the inguinal region and inner surface of the legs.

MEASUREMENTS AND DENTAL FORMULA

Total Length: 1355–1650 mm (53.3–64.9 in)
Tail Length: 343–432 mm (13.5–17.0 in)
Hind Foot: 210–254 mm (8.3–10.0 in)
Ear: 120–130 mm (4.7–5.1 in)
Skull Length: 206–257 mm (8.1–10.1 in)
Weight: 16–41 kg (35–90 lb)
Dental Formula: I 3/3, C 1/1, P 4/4, M 2/3 = 42

ARKANSAS DISTRIBUTION AND ABUNDANCE

The red wolf formerly occurred throughout the state, but it is now considered to be extinct in Arkansas and over most of its former range (Gipson et al. 1974; Nowak 1970; Paradiso and Nowak 1971, 1972). Red wolves apparently were exterminated in a large part of the Gulf Coastal Plain during the first two decades of the present century, but pure red wolves persisted in the Interior Highlands until about 1940. The decline of the red wolf population began during the 1920s and was accelerated during the 1930s. Humans played a major role in the demise of the red wolf through habitat alteration, extensive hunting by farmers, ranchers, and sportsmen, and through State and Federal trapping operations.

A breakdown of ecological isolation between red wolves and coyotes apparently began during the 1930s, accompanied by extensive hybridization and the appearance of large numbers of specimens intermediate in size between red wolves and coyotes. With the eastward expansion of the coyote's range during the 1940s and 1950s, such hybridization became more general, and specimens showing characteristics of hybrids were found in easternmost Arkansas by the early 1960s. A few specimens showing some of the size characteristics of the red wolf still occur in isolated pockets on the West Gulf Coastal Plain of southern Arkansas but are smaller than red wolves present in the state during the 1920s. Coyote × red wolf and coyote × dog hybrids occur in the same areas, and specimens showing red wolf characteristics, which are at the lower end of the red wolf size spectrum, probably represent progeny of such hybrids. In hybrid canid populations, offspring that physically resemble one of the original parent stocks are occasionally produced. This does not mean that the red wolf still exists as a distinct species in Arkansas. The opinion of most competent workers concerned with the preservation of the endangered red wolf is that it has been exterminated over most of its range, with the exception of the coastal prairies and

marshes of the Gulf Coast counties of Texas and Louisiana (Paradiso and Nowak 1972). Hybrid specimens with red wolf characteristics are also rapidly disappearing. Hybridization of red wolves in Texas and Louisiana has occurred, and they are now probably extinct there also.

The U.S. Fish and Wildlife Service is conducting an extensive red wolf recovery program. Included is a captive breeding program at Tacoma, Washington, and a releasing program at the Alligator National Wildlife Refuge in North Carolina. As of the summer of 1988, a total of 14 red wolves had been released. Other potential release sites were being investigated.

Lawrence and Bossert (1967) believe that the red wolf should be considered just another subspecies of *Canis lupus*. This view is still shared by other investigators.

SELECTED REFERENCES
Gipson et al. (1974); Lawrence and Bossert (1967); Nowak (1970); Paradiso and Nowak (1971, 1972).

INTERIOR HIGHLANDS

GULF COASTAL PLAIN

LEGEND
● ACTUAL SPECIMENS
★ REPORTED SPECIMENS

Historical range of the red wolf (*Canis rufus*)

FERAL DOG

Canis familiaris

NAME *Canis* is the Latin word meaning "dog." The specific name, *familiaris*, means "to be familiar," referring to its domesticated state.

REMARKS Feral dogs of the German shepherd breed are often difficult for untrained observers to distinguish from coyotes or red wolves. In the wild state, crosses between dogs and coyotes frequently occur, and the feral offspring of such crosses often cannot be positively identified in the field.

Free-ranging feral dogs generally are more destructive to wildlife than coyotes. The blame for predation on white-tailed deer and domestic livestock, which is commonly attributed to coyotes, more often should be placed on packs of wild dogs or hybrid "coydogs." In many instances, various breeds of domestic dogs running free are not truly feral but have been abandoned by their owners. Many abandoned dogs die from disease, starvation, and exposure, or become highway casualties, but some join wild dog packs and run down the easiest prey available, which often is domestic livestock. Frequently, free-running farm dogs become temporary members of such packs. Free-running dogs are extremely common in Arkansas and have resulted in some severe problems for wildlife (e.g., the chasing of pregnant deer).

The ancestry of the domestic dog is lost in antiquity. Various species of wild canids have been domesticated by man for thousands of years to serve as hunting companions, watchdogs, beasts of burden, and even food. Domestication of the dog is believed to have taken place as far back as the Mesolithic Era. Present-day breeds of dogs have apparently descended from at least two and possibly four subspecies of the gray wolf, *C. lupus*. The subspecies involved are the Asian wolf, the northern wolf, possibly the Tibetan mountain wolf or Chinese wolf, and the Arabian wolf (Fiennes 1976; Olsen and Olsen 1977). Dingos, pariah dogs, and Alsatians are obviously derived from wolves. Jackals may also be implicated in the domestic dog's ancestry.

SELECTED REFERENCES
Fiennes (1976); Olsen and Olsen (1977).

RED FOX

Vulpes vulpes

NAME   Both the generic and specific name, *vulpes*, is from the Latin name for "fox."

IDENTIFICATION AND DESCRIPTION   The red fox is medium-sized and has the general appearance of a small dog. Its tail is long and bushy with the terminal portion black and tipped with white. The muzzle is pointed; the ears are prominent and black in back; and the feet are black. The pelage is reddish yellow to tawny above and whitish or grayish below.

MEASUREMENTS AND DENTAL FORMULA

Total Length:	900–1140 mm (35.4–44.9 in)
Tail Length:	300–432 mm (11.8–17.0 in)
Hind Foot:	130–175 mm (5.1–6.9 in)
Ear:	76–110 mm (2.9–4.3 in)
Skull Length:	133–158 mm (5.2–6.2 in)
Weight:	2.7–8.6 kg (6–18 lb)
Dental Formula:	I 3/3, C 1/1, P 4/4, M 2/3 = 42

ARKANSAS DISTRIBUTION AND ABUNDANCE
The red fox occurs statewide; it is scarce in the southwestern part of the state. Apparently red foxes have been declining over the past 20 years. This may be correlated with expanding coyote populations. Sargeant (1982) found that in the prairie states, increased populations of coyotes meant a decrease in populations of the red fox. Voigt and Earle (1983) and Sargeant et al. (1987) found that the red fox avoided coyotes although coexistence could occur.

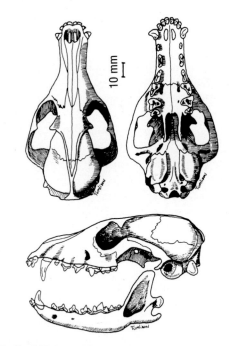

Skull of *Vulpes vulpes*

Vulpes vulpes, Red Fox. *Phil A. Dotson*

LIFE HISTORY The red fox prefers upland woods and farmlands with meadows, cultivated fields, pastures, and woodlots. Thick cover is usually avoided. It is not often seen during daytime because it is mainly nocturnal, but occasionally it may be observed sitting on a high vantage point or hunting for mice in open fields or along roadsides, especially during early morning and at dusk. Foxes center their activity around a pup-rearing den during spring and summer. Some resting sites and most foraging sites are away from the den. Red foxes travel away from the den largely between dusk and dawn (Ables 1975). Daily traveling distances by resident adults within their territories rarely exceeds 10 km (6 mi). Although foxes are not often predictable in their patterns, they may visit the same sites during many consecutive nights (Macdonald 1981).

The major part of the diet consists of small mammals, but the red fox also eats substantial quantities of small birds, insects, and a variety of plant food. Staple foods of the red fox are cottontail rabbits, cotton rats, deer mice, and voles (Korschgen 1959; Scott 1943). Fruits, such as persimmons and mulberries, and other plant foods are eaten when available but comprise only a small portion of the diet. Red foxes feed on quail occasionally, but there is little objective support for the contention that they are destructive to quail nests and chicks (Korschgen 1959). Carrion, such as road kills and discarded poultry, is readily eaten, but there is apparently little predation upon well-husbanded live poultry. Red foxes have been known to store food in caches. Caching is necessary when prey becomes scarce because foxes feed on a regular basis (Samuel and Nelson 1982).

The den is usually located in a wooded area adjoining a field or along wooded rivers and streams. It is excavated in a cut bank or gully

A fox den. *Joe Clark*

or may be situated in a natural cavity or crevice in a rocky outcrop. Woodchuck burrows are frequently appropriated and enlarged for use as dens. Burrows may have several entrances and ordinarily are 6–9 m (23–30 ft) or more long and a little more than 1 m (3 ft) in depth. The den is primarily used for rearing young but may be used to bed down in during severe winter weather.

Red foxes are monogamous and have reputedly remained mated for several years. They pair off and mate from late December or early January into February. Females produce one litter per year after a gestation period of 51–53 days. Litter size varies from one to eleven, with four to five being the usual number. The young are born in March to April; at birth, the young are blind and weigh about 10 g (0.35 oz), and their eyes open at the age of 1 week (Stanley 1963). The pups first appear outside the den when about 3 weeks old. Both parents partici-

pate in the care and feeding of the young. Pups are weaned when about 2 months old and leave the den and forage for themselves when 6 months old. Females reach sexual maturity and first breed when about 10 months old. Red foxes may live as long as 5 years.

IMPORTANCE AND/OR MANAGEMENT   The red fox is much admired by sportsmen who love the chase. It has greater speed and stamina than the gray fox and has less of a tendency to "tree." Hunters consider it an excellent quarry for testing the trailing capability, speed, and endurance of their hounds. Poultry raisers despise the red fox since they occasionally kill poultry, especially when the poultry is raised on an open range. However, most poultry consumed by red foxes appears to be discarded poultry carrion. Some sportsmen also detest the red fox because of its alleged destruction of eggs and young and adult quail; feeding habit

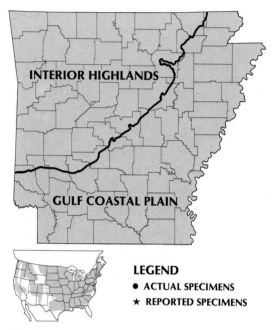

LEGEND
• ACTUAL SPECIMENS
★ REPORTED SPECIMENS

Distribution of the red fox (*Vulpes vulpes*)

introduced many times by sportsmen and the Arkansas Game and Fish Commission, but it is by no means certain that introduced foxes belonged to the European subspecies. The weight of evidence now favors the view that European red foxes never became well established in the United States and that the present-day red fox population consists of various subspecies of the native red fox (Paradiso 1969). The subspecies that occurs in Arkansas is *V. v. fulva*.

SELECTED REFERENCES
Ables (1975); Korschgen (1959); Macdonald (1981); Paradiso (1969); Samuel and Nelson (1982); Sargeant (1982); Sargeant et al. (1987); Scott (1943); Stanley (1963); Voigt and Earle (1983); Voigt (1987).

analyses by various investigators indicate that such damage is slight. Any harm that this species does is largely balanced by the large quantities of more harmful rats and mice that it eats. On the debit side of the ledger is the fox's susceptibility to rabies, which is often epidemic in fox populations (Voigt 1987).

The red fox has traditionally been a much sought-after furbearer; this has been particularly true over the past 15 years, when longhair fur has been in demand. However, the Arkansas Game and Fish Commission recognized declining red fox populations and banned the trapping of red fox in 1975.

There has been a continuing debate over the years concerning whether the red fox in the East and parts of the West is the introduced European subspecies or the native American red fox. Originally the red fox was not present over most of the state when it was heavily forested, although it may have been present in prairie peninsulas on the western edge of the state. Clearing of land for agriculture provided suitable habitat, and the red fox extended its range into Arkansas from the North. It has been

GRAY FOX

Urocyon cinereoargenteus

NAME *Urocyon* is from two Greek words, *oura*, meaning "tail," and *kyon*, meaning "dog." The specific name, *cinereoargenteus*, is from two Latin names, *cinereus*, meaning "ash colored" or "gray," and *argenteus*, meaning "silvery," thus the name means "silvery gray."

IDENTIFICATION AND DESCRIPTION The gray fox is medium-sized and slightly smaller and shorter legged than the red fox. It has a long and bushy tail with a black stripe on the upper side and a black tip. The muzzle is pointed; the ears are prominent; the fur is coarse; its claws are long, sharp, and curved. The dorsal pelage is a mixture of color, including reddish brown or reddish yellow on the sides of the neck, back of the ears, and the sides of the legs and feet. Blackish patches occur on the end of the muzzle and chin, and the throat and cheeks are white. It is grizzled salt-and-pepper gray above. The venter is whitish along the center of the belly, and it is tawny along the sides and underside of the tail.

Urocyon cinereoargenteus, Gray Fox.
Texas Parks & Wildlife Department

with interspersed fields, woods, and brushy fencerows. Rocky wooded areas with dense underbrush are preferred.

Gray foxes usually den in hollow trees or logs, rock crevices, brush piles, and occasionally in a ground burrow. The den is sometimes located in a hollow tree at a height of 5–9 m (16–30 ft) above ground. The gray fox is an adept climber, and it not only climbs leaning trees but also ascends vertical trunks with catlike ease by virtue of its long, sharp, curved claws. When pursued it will often jump from branch to branch. Because of its lack of stamina and tendency to tree early in a chase, it is not a favorite of fox hunters.

The gray fox is mainly nocturnal and usually spends the day holed up in a hollow tree or log, in a natural rock crevice, or in a brush pile. It occasionally forages during daytime, but it is seldom seen because of its use of protective cover, its secretive habits, and its concealing coloration. Gray foxes tend to avoid open fields.

MEASUREMENTS AND DENTAL FORMULA

Total Length:	800–1125 mm (31.5–44.3 in)
Tail Length:	275–443 mm (10.8–17.4 in)
Hind Foot:	100–150 mm (3.9–5.9 in)
Ear:	60–83 mm (2.4–3.3 in)
Skull Length:	120–130 mm (4.7–5.1 in)
Weight:	2.5–6.4 kg (5.5–14 lb)
Dental Formula:	I 3/3, C 1/1, P 4/4, M 2/3 = 42

ARKANSAS DISTRIBUTION AND ABUNDANCE
The gray fox occurs statewide; it is less common in the Delta.

LIFE HISTORY
The gray fox inhabits hardwood forests, wooded bottomlands, and farmlands

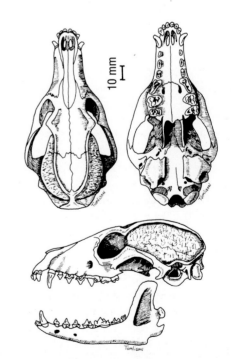

10 mm

Skull of *Urocyon cinereoargenteus*

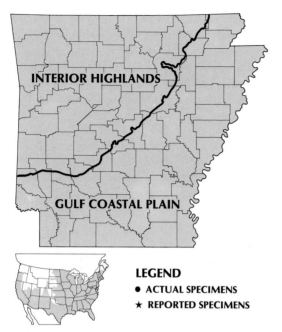

Distribution of the gray fox (*Urocyon cinereoargenteus*)

Foods eaten by the gray fox are similar in most respects to those in the red fox's diet. Cottontail rabbits are eaten to a greater extent and make up nearly one-half of the gray fox's diet (Korschgen 1957a). Cotton rats are another important food item, followed by white-footed mice and voles. Other mice and rats, squirrels, songbirds, insects, fruit, and other plant foods round out the diet. Gray foxes consume more plant foods, such as persimmons and corn, than either the red fox or coyote. Gray foxes are seldom a major predator of poultry but on occasion will take unpenned chickens, ducks, and young turkeys.

The breeding season in Arkansas probably extends from about mid-January through March, with a peak in mating activity from mid-February to early March (Layne and McKeon 1956, Layne 1958). Females give birth to one litter per year which varies from one to ten young, with an average of three to five in the litter. Most litters are whelped from late March through May. The gestation period is from 51 to 63 days, and at birth the young are blind and weigh about 8–9 g (0.28–0.32 oz). The pups grow rapidly and leave the den when about 3 weeks old. They are provided with food by both parents and begin to forage for themselves when about 3 months old. Young gray foxes begin breeding in the year following their birth.

IMPORTANCE AND/OR MANAGEMENT Gray foxes are very susceptible to rabies, distemper, leptospirosis, mange, and other diseases, and they undergo periodic population fluctuations. Few foxes have been reported with rabies in Arkansas (Heidt 1982). They have few predators besides humans, dogs, and possibly coyotes.

The gray fox is an important furbearer in Arkansas. Over the past 40 years in the state, gray foxes have averaged sixth in numbers of pelts harvested and third in value. Regionally, the Ozark Mountains have produced the most pelts, followed by the Mississippi Delta, the West Gulf Coastal Plain, and the Ouachita Mountains (Heidt et al. 1984; Peck et al. 1985). Currently the Arkansas Game and Fish Commission prohibits trapping in a portion of the Mississippi Delta and the West Gulf Coastal Plain.

SELECTED REFERENCES
Ewer (1973); Fritzell (1987); Heidt (1982); Heidt et al. (1984); Korschgen (1957a); Layne (1958); Layne and McKeon (1956); Peck et al. (1985).

FAMILY URSIDAE
BEARS

Members of this family are large, heavy, thick-set mammals. They have a rudimentary tail, plantigrade feet with five well-developed toes on each foot, a long snout, and rounded, medium-sized ears. The molar teeth are adapted for crushing with broad, flat, tuberculated crowns. The last upper molar is elongated and very large. The tympanic bullae are not inflated. Members of this family are omnivorous.

One species occurs in Arkansas.

BLACK BEAR

Ursus americanus

NAME *Ursus* is the Latin word for "bear." The specific name, *americanus*, is the Latinized form "of America," for eastern North America where this species was first described.

IDENTIFICATION AND DESCRIPTION The black bear is large and heavily built. It has a well haired but very short tail; a straight facial profile; a broad nosepad; small eyes; and toes armed with strong nonretractile claws. The pelage is deep glossy black to cinnamon-brown above with a brownish snout (sometimes there is a white patch on the chest).

MEASUREMENTS AND DENTAL FORMULA
Total Length:	1270–1980 mm (50–78 in)
Tail Length:	80–280 mm (3.2–11.0 in)
Hind Foot:	184–280 mm (7.2–11.0 in)
Ear:	132–142 mm (5.2–5.6 in)
Skull Length:	254–336 mm (10.0–13.2 in)
Weight:	100–227 kg (220–500 lb)
Dental Formula:	I 3/3, C 1/1, P 4/4, M 2/3 = 42

ARKANSAS DISTRIBUTION AND ABUNDANCE
The black bear formerly occurred statewide; it was reduced to a remnant population in the late 1940s and early 1950s that was scattered throughout the Ouachita Mountains, parts of the Ozarks, and chiefly along the Mississippi bottoms in and around the White River National Wildlife Refuge (Sealander 1956).

A successful restocking program was initiated by the Game Division of the Arkansas

Ursus americanus, Black Bear. *John R. MacGregor*

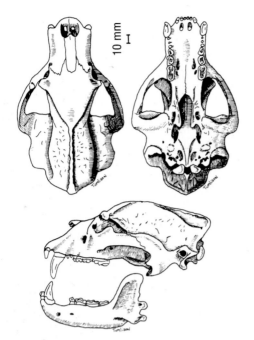

Skull of *Ursus americanus*

active in broad daylight. Bears tend to be solitary except for sows with cubs. They are expert climbers, and bear cubs often take refuge in trees when frightened. During the day, bears bed down in dense thickets, canebrakes, or rock caves. They usually begin foraging near dusk.

Bears are omnivorous and feed on a wide variety of foods. They eat nuts, fruits, mice, insects (especially ants), fish, grass roots, and other animal and plant food that may be available. Acorns and other nuts are important food items in autumn and winter; berries, fruits, grasses, and roots are eaten in large quantities during spring and summer. The bulk of the diet during most of the year consists of vegetable matter. Overturned rotten logs, diggings around rotten stumps, and the presence of large, soft droppings filled with berry seeds are signs of foraging activity by black bears.

The litter size varies from one to five. An average litter size is one to two cubs, but triplets are not uncommon. However, litters of four are rare and litters of five are exceptional

Game and Fish Commission in 1959 with bears obtained from Minnesota and Canada. A total of 154 black bears had been released in the Ozark National Forest by 1967, and by 1973, the population was estimated to be around 600–700. Numerous sightings in recent years and a current large-scale study on the ecology of the black bear indicate that resident populations have been established in the Ozark and Ouachita National Forests. The most recent estimate by personnel of the Arkansas Game and Fish Commission is that the bear population in Arkansas is in excess of 2,000

LIFE HISTORY   Black bears prefer remote, heavily forested areas and impenetrable thickets and canebrakes along rivers and streams in bottomlands. They seldom adapt well to the presence of humans and tend to be restricted to more inaccessible forest and swampland. Suitable habitat in Arkansas is now mainly in the Ozark and Ouachita National Forests and in the White River National Refuge area in eastern Arkansas.

The black bear is nocturnal but is sometimes

Distribution of the black bear (*Ursus americanus*)

A black bear and cubs. *Lynn Rogers*

(Rowan 1945). Black bears normally mate in alternate years during June or July, after which males and females go their separate ways. After a gestation period of about seven months, the young are born in January or February. Delayed implantation occurs in the black bear, and the blastocysts do not implant until late November or early December (Wimsatt 1963). At birth, cubs are naked and blind and weigh 170–280 g (6–10 oz). Growth is slow at first, and their eyes open when they are about 40 days old. The cubs usually follow the sow until the spring of their second year. Females may fail to produce young in the year following a poor mast crop. Young females do not reach sexual maturity and breed until they are about 3 years old, although there is some variation (Pelton 1982). Black bears have a life expectancy of about 25 years.

The size and shape of a black bear's home range is determined by the richness of its habitat. In addition, factors such as sex, age, season, and population density may influence the size and boundary configuration. Since these factors often change, so do individual home ranges. For example, Rogers (1977) noted that some bears have moved more than 160 km (100 mi) to take advantage of available food.

It is generally agreed that bears do not undergo true hibernation. However, a number of unique physiological changes do occur. Body temperature drops only 7–8°C (12.6–14.4°F), metabolism drops 50–60%, heart rate drops from 40 to 50 beats per minute to 8 to 19, and the bear exhibits a weight loss of 20–27%. The animals do not eat, drink, defecate, or urinate during the denning period. True hibernators reduce the above body functions even further. In addition, while true hibernators can be handled during hibernation without arousal, bears are easily aroused (Pelton 1982). Bears begin to enter dens (hollow trees, caves, and abandoned mines) in late November or early December in Arkansas. They are less lethargic than their northern cousins and may become active during the winter months.

IMPORTANCE AND/OR MANAGEMENT One of the bear's favorite foods is honey, and unprotected bee yards may sometimes be severely damaged. Where good bear habitat adjoins good bee range, bears are highly unpopular with beekeepers. However, apiaries can be protected with electric fences and bear-proof beehive platforms at relatively little expense. Predation by bears on livestock is not too common in Arkansas since most of the population is concentrated in the national forests, well away from most human habitations. As populations have increased, reports on orchard and berry patch depredations have become more numerous. In response to nuisance bears, personnel from the Arkansas Game and Fish Commission live trap and translocate problem bears. Transplanted bears have been known to move long distances, and several bears released in Arkansas are known to have traveled as far as 160–418 km (99.4–260 mi) from the release site (Wilson and Gipson 1975).

At one time bears were extremely common in Arkansas, which earned it the unofficial designation of the "bear state." McKinley (1962) cites an early account by Turnbo, who related that in 1814 an early settler named Jim Coker saw eleven adult bears swim single file across West Sugar Loaf Creek near the White River in Marion County, Arkansas. Turnbo also recounted that another pioneer in the same region sometimes had stored as much as a thousand pounds of bear "bacon" at one time. It is said that Oil Trough (Independence County) received its name from the storage of bear oil there (in troughs made from hollow logs) before shipment down the White River.

The original black bears in Arkansas were probably assignable to the race *U. a. lutreolus*, which may still exist in the White River area. However, the bears stocked from Minnesota and Canada belong to the race *U. a. americanus*.

SELECTED REFERENCES
Conley (1977); Folk et al. (1976); McKinley (1962); Pelton (1982); Rogers (1977); Rowan (1945); Sealander (1956); Wilson and Gipson (1975); Wimsatt (1963).

FAMILY PROCYONIDAE

PROCYONIDS

This family includes the raccoons, ring-tailed cats, and their relatives. As with bears, omnivorous feeding habits and climbing are predominant characteristics of this family. Procyonids occupy much of the temperate and tropical parts of North America. They are known from the late Oligocene to the Recent Epoch in North America, from the late Miocene to the late Pliocene Epoch in Europe, and from the late Pliocene to the Recent Epoch in Asia.

Members of this family are small to medium-sized carnivores with plantigrade feet, nonretractile or semiretractile claws, fairly long limbs, broad and tuberculate molar teeth adapted for crushing, and a long, bushy tail.

Two species occur in Arkansas.

KEY TO SPECIES

WHOLE ANIMALS

1a. Tail as long as or longer than head and body, with 14–16 alternating black and yellowish white rings (incomplete below); prominent white eye patches surrounding a black eye ring; no black facial mask; hind foot less than 80 mm (3.2 in); thick fur between pads of feet . . . . *Bassariscus astutus*, Ringtail

1b. Tail shorter than head and body, with 5−7 black rings alternating with buff; prominent black facial mask; hind foot more than 90 mm (3.5 in) . . . . *Procyon lotor*, Raccoon

SKULLS

1a. Length less than 100 mm (3.9 in); palate not extending behind posterior edge of last molars more than palatal width; canine teeth rounded; cheek teeth with pointed cusps . . . . *Bassariscus astutus*, Ringtail

1b. Length more than 100 mm (3.9 in); palate extending behind posterior edge of last molars more than palatal width; canine teeth laterally flattened; cheek teeth with heavy conical cusps. . . . . *Procyon lotor*, Raccoon

Ringtail

Bassariscus astutus

NAME   *Bassariscus* is derived from two Greek words, *bassaris*, meaning "fox," and the suffix, *iskos*, meaning "little." The specific word, *astutus*, is a Latin word meaning "cunning."

IDENTIFICATION AND DESCRIPTION   The ringtail is a small, somewhat catlike carnivore with a flattened tail that is as long as or longer than the head and body, banded with 14−16 alternating black and yellowish white rings (incomplete below), and tipped with black. It has five toes, armed with sharp, curved, semiretractile claws on each foot; the soles of the feet are hairy between the pads; the ears are large, erect, and round; the muzzle is sharp; the eyes are large; and there are black eye rings surrounded by prominent white eye patches. The pelage is a light buff overcast with black and dark brownish overhairs above and grayish white hairs tinged with pale buff below.

MEASUREMENTS AND DENTAL FORMULA

Total Length: 616−811 mm (24.2−32.0 in)
Tail Length: 310−440 mm (12.2−17.3 in)
Hind Foot: 57−78 mm (2.2−3.1 in)
Ear: 44−50 mm (1.7−2.0 in)
Skull Length: 75−84 mm (3.0−3.3 in)
Weight: 728−1100 g (25.6−39.0 oz)
Dental   I 3/3, C 1/1, P 4/4, M 2/2
  Formula: = 40

ARKANSAS DISTRIBUTION AND ABUNDANCE   The ringtail is quite rare; only one specimen record from Warren, Bradley County, exists. Other reports are not represented by specimens (see map).

Bassariscus astutus, Ringtail. *Phil A. Dotson*

LIFE HISTORY The ringtail prefers brushy, boulder-strewn slopes and rock bluffs where it dens in well-protected crevices and cavities. It is less commonly found in woodland areas where it lives in hollow trees and logs. It usually lives no more than 0.5 km (0.3 mi) from water. This species is seldom seen since it is almost strictly nocturnal and is active mainly during the middle of the night, well after dusk and long before dawn. It is an agile climber, easily scaling vertical rock or building walls, and is capable of leaps of 3 m (9.8 ft) or more.

Ringtails are mainly carnivorous and eat a wide variety of foods. In summer, insects comprise more than one-half of the ringtail's diet, followed by mammals and plant material. Its winter diet consists mainly of rats, mice, birds, and a substantial quantity of insects (Taylor 1954). Plant food eaten includes such items as persimmons, cedar berries, hackberries, acorns, and a variety of fruits.

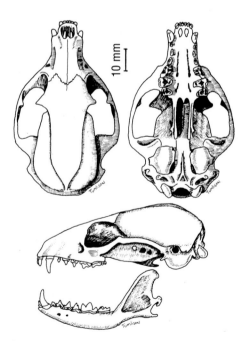

Skull of *Bassariscus astutus*

Mating occurs in April, and females produce a single annual litter of one to five young in May or June throughout the range. The usual litter size is three or four. The length of gestation may be 45–50 days, and the young weigh about 28 g (1 oz) at birth. They are fully haired and their eyes open at the age of 4–5 weeks. At this time, solid food becomes a part of their diet, but they may not be fully weaned until well into August when they are about 4 months old. Foraging with the parents begins when the young are 2 months old (Walker et al. 1968).

IMPORTANCE AND/OR MANAGEMENT   Ringtails received the name "miner's cat" in early days in parts of the western United States when they were tamed by miners and kept around their cabins as mousers. This species sometimes takes up residence in buildings occupied by humans because they are attracted by infestations of rats and mice.

This species is a well-known hitchhiker on railroad cars and may have extended its range into Arkansas and elsewhere by this means of dispersal. It rarely conflicts with human interests and, over most of its range in the United States, is considered an attractive component of the mammal fauna despite its relatively minor economic importance.

SELECTED REFERENCES
Kaufmann (1987); Taylor (1954); Walker et al. (1968).

Distribution of the ringtail (*Bassariscus astutus*)

RACCOON

Procyon lotor

NAME   *Procyon* is derived from two Greek words, *pro*, meaning "before," and *kyon*, meaning "dog." It is not known why this name was given to the raccoon. The specific name, *lotor*, is from the Latin, *lutor*, meaning "a washer," referring to the raccoon's habit of often manipulating its food in water.

IDENTIFICATION AND DESCRIPTION   The raccoon is medium-sized and heavily built, and has a long bushy tail ringed with five to seven black rings terminating in a black band. The head is broad behind and tapers forward to a short, pointed muzzle. The ears are rounded, furred, and moderate in size; the feet are plantigrade with naked soles; and the toes are free and capable of being widely spread. The claws are nonretractile. There is a conspicuous black mask across the eyes and cheeks which is outlined with white. The pelage is grizzled gray, brown, and black above with paler sides, and dull grayish brown tinged with yellowish gray or white below.

MEASUREMENTS AND DENTAL FORMULA

Total Length:	603–1180 mm (23.7–46.5 in)
Tail Length:	190–300 mm (7.5–11.8 in)
Hind Foot:	82–138 mm (3.2–5.4 in)
Ear:	42–66 mm (1.7–2.6 in)
Skull Length:	107–127 mm (4.2–5.0 in)
Weight:	4–14 kg (8.8–30.9 lb)
Dental Formula:	I 3/3, C 1/1, P 4/4, M 2/2 = 40

Procyon lotor, Raccoon. *C. C. Lockwood*

ARKANSAS DISTRIBUTION AND ABUNDANCE
The raccoon occurs statewide and is common.

LIFE HISTORY Raccoons prefer bottomland hardwood stands with a plentiful supply of den trees. They are also common in wooded uplands and in a variety of other habitats including bottomland swamps, farmlands (especially those with cornfields), and heavily wooded residential areas in cities. They are seldom found far from water, which has an important influence upon their distribution.

The den is usually in a hollow tree, in crevices in rock outcrops, in cavities beneath tree roots, and in old woodchuck or armadillo burrows. Raccoons are nocturnal and spend most of the daylight hours sleeping in the den. During cold winter weather, raccoons may "hole up" in the den for several days, living off their reserves of body fat, but they do not hibernate.

Raccoons are omnivorous and opportunistic in their feeding habits. Plant foods include a variety of wild fruits and berries, acorns and other nuts, osage oranges, corn, and other garden produce. Animal foods include grasshoppers and other insects, crayfish, clams, fish, frogs, snakes, occasional small mammals, and eggs of turtles and birds. Fruits, insects, acorns, and crayfish are the main dietary constituents during fall and winter (Johnson 1970).

The mating season extends from December to June with peak breeding activity in February and March. The gestation period is 63 days, and the young are born from April to August. Females produce one litter of one to seven young per year. Most litters are born in April or May, but those from late matings may be born from June to August. The usual number of young in a litter is three or four, but there is a tendency for larger litters to be produced in the northern part of the species range (Johnson 1970). The young leave the den when about 10

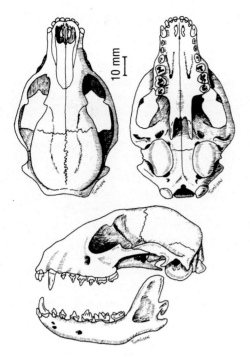

Skull of *Procyon lotor*

weeks old and begin foraging with their mother
(Stuewer 1943). They are not completely
weaned until about the age of 12–14 weeks.
Young females are capable of breeding near the
end of their first year, but males are not successful breeders until their second year.

IMPORTANCE AND/OR MANAGEMENT   The raccoon is a favorite object of the chase in Arkansas and other southern states, where it provides
exciting sport for coon hunters and their dogs.
It has remarkable physical stamina, and its
ability to defend itself is well known. In the
water, it is a match for any dog.

The raccoon is the most important furbearer
in Arkansas. Since the 1940s, raccoons have
been harvested in greater numbers than any
other species. Overall, this species has accounted for 36% of the total state harvest. Regionally, the Mississippi Delta has produced the
highest number (42%), followed by the West
Gulf Coastal Plain (23%), the Ozark Mountains
(20%), and the Ouachita Mountains (12%).
The reasons for the high harvests include the

ubiquitous nature of raccoons, their high population levels, and their high reproductive potential. They are also easily caught, there is great
demand because of the high quality of their fur,
and they are pursued by both trappers and
sportsmen. In addition, attempts at ranching
raccoons have failed (Peck et al. 1985; Sanderson 1987).

On the negative side, raccoons are among
the animals most frequently reported as nuisance animals by wildlife agencies in urban
and suburban areas of the United States (de
Almeida 1987). Nuisance raccoons result in
expenditures by government agencies and private citizens for removal and repairs to damaged property. Raccoons are also known predators of waterfowl and other birds (Llewellyn and
Webster 1960). Raccoons are also known to
harbor distemper and rabies. During the early
1980s, raccoon rabies reached epidemic proportions in the southeast and middle Atlantic
states. In Arkansas, only two raccoons have
been reported rabid from 1976 through 1987
(Heidt 1982, Arkansas Department of Health,
unpublished records).

Distribution of the raccoon (*Procyon lotor*)

Raccoons have adapted extremely well to urban areas and can often be observed around decks and patios, particularly where there is pet food or other edible material available. People often feed raccoons and find they can be quite tame and amusing. However, it should be remembered that raccoons, no matter how tame they may appear, are wild animals that may literally bite the hand that feeds them. As with other wild animals, raccoons are better observed from a distance.

Most of the raccoons in the state are members of the subspecies *P. l. hirtus*, although those occurring along the southern and eastern borders of the state possibly may belong to the race *varius*.

SELECTED REFERENCES

de Almeida (1987); Heidt (1982); Johnson (1970); Kaufmann (1982); Llewellyn and Webster (1960); Peck et al. (1985); Sanderson (1987); Stuewer (1943).

FAMILY MUSTELIDAE
WEASELS AND ALLIES

This is a large family including weasels, mink, badgers, skunks, and otters. Mustelids can be found in virtually every type of terrestrial habitat, from the tropics to the arctic, and live in rivers, lakes, and oceans. In terms of distribution, they can be said to be cosmopolitan. In North America, mustelids appear in the fossil records in the early Oligocene.

Members of this family are small- to medium-sized carnivores, usually with an elongated body and short legs. They have five-toed feet with either partially retractile or nonretractile claws and are either plantigrade or digitigrade. Most species in the family have well-developed anal scent glands. Dietary habits of mustelids range from strictly carnivorous to largely omnivorous. Many members of the family are valuable furbearers.

Six species are found in Arkansas.

KEY TO SPECIES

WHOLE ANIMALS

1. Toes fully webbed; total length more than 800 mm (31.5 in); tail long, tapering, and noticeably thickened at base, more than 250 mm (9.8 in) long . . . . *Lutra canadensis*, River Otter

 Toes only partly webbed or not webbed; total length less than 800 mm (31.5 in); tail not thickened at base, less than 250 mm (9.8 in) long 2

2. Tail about as long as hind foot, about one-fifth to one-sixth length of head and body; claws on front foot much longer than those on hind foot; body thickset, heavy; single whitish stripe on top of head and neck . . . . *Taxidea taxus*, Badger

 Tail much longer than hind foot; about one-half length of head and body 3

3. Color some shade of brown or yellowish brown; body elongated; legs short; claws not retractile 5

Color black or black with conspicuous white markings; body not elongated; claws not retractile 4

4. Upperparts black with two continuous white stripes variable in extent, or entirely black except for white patch on top of head; hind foot more than 60 mm (2.4 in) long .... *Mephitis mephitis*, Striped Skunk

   Upperparts black with broken white stripes or spots variable in extent; small white spot on forehead; hind foot less than 60 mm (2.4 in) long .... *Spilogale putorius*, Eastern Spotted Skunk

5. Total length more than 500 mm (19.7 in); uniformly dark brown above and below (except for occasional white spot on throat and/or chest) at all seasons; toes of hind foot partly webbed .... *Mustela vison*, Mink

   Total length less than 500 mm (19.7 in); brown or yellowish brown above, buffy or yellowish white below; tail tipped with black; toes of hind feet not webbed .... *Mustela frenata*, Long-tailed Weasel

SKULLS

1. Five cheek teeth behind canines on each side of upper jaw; rostrum broader than long; skull nearly as wide at middle of braincase as at zygomatic arch; postorbital region constricted (fig. 25); total number of teeth 36 .... *Lutra canadensis*, River Otter

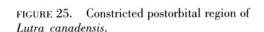

FIGURE 25.   Constricted postorbital region of *Lutra canadensis*.

   Four cheek teeth behind canines on each side of upper jaw; rostrum longer than broad; skull not as wide at middle of braincase as at zygomatic arch; postorbital region not as constricted; total number of teeth fewer than 36 2

2. Braincase triangular in outline viewed from above; last tooth on each side of upper jaw large and triangular (fig. 26a); length more than 90 mm (3.5 in) .... *Taxidea taxus*, Badger

Braincase elongated viewed from above, not flared posteriorly; last tooth of upper jaw squarish or dumbbell-shaped (fig. 26b); length less than 90 mm (3.5 in) 3

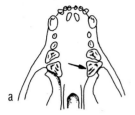

FIGURE 26. Large triangular molar of *Taxidea taxus* (a) and dumbbell-shaped molar of *Mustela frenata* and/or *M. vison* (b).

3. Last tooth on each side of upper jaw large and squarish, distinctly larger than tooth anterior to it; bony palate terminates at or slightly beyond last upper cheek teeth 4

   Last tooth on each side of upper jaw narrower and dumbbell-shaped or almost triangular; bony palate terminates well beyond last upper cheek teeth 5

4. Length less than 70 mm (2.8 in); profile almost flat; last upper cheek tooth wider than long .... *Spilogale putorius*, Eastern Spotted Skunk

   Length more than 70 mm (2.8 in); profile rounded; last upper cheek tooth square .... *Mephitis mephitis*, Striped Skunk

5. Length less than 55 mm (2.2 in); auditory bulla longer than upper cheek tooth row .... *Mustela frenata*, Long-tailed Weasel

   Length more than 55 mm (about 70 mm [2.8 in]); auditory bulla about as long as upper cheek tooth row .... *Mustela vison*, Mink

LONG-TAILED WEASEL

Mustela frenata

NAME *Mustela* is the Latin word for "weasel." The specific name, *frenata*, is from the Latin word, *frenum*, meaning "bridle." This refers to the facial marking seen in the races found in the southern parts of the range.

IDENTIFICATION AND DESCRIPTION The long-tailed weasel is small, and its body is long and slender. It has a small head with a long neck; large, rounded ears; short legs; and partially retractile claws. The tail is long and well furred with the terminal one-fourth or one-third black. The pelage is light brown above and yellowish or yellowish white below, except for a white chin. Males are considerably larger than females.

MEASUREMENTS AND DENTAL FORMULA Lower limits represent females.

Total Length: 290–495 mm (11.1–19.5 in)

Tail Length:	80–153 mm (3.2–6.0 in)
Hind Foot:	25–50 mm (0.98–2.0 in)
Ear:	15–27 mm (0.60–1.1 in)
Skull Length:	31–50 mm (1.2–2.0 in)
Weight:	70–260 g (2.5–9.2 oz)
Dental Formula:	I 3/3, C 1/1, P 3/3, M 1/2 = 34

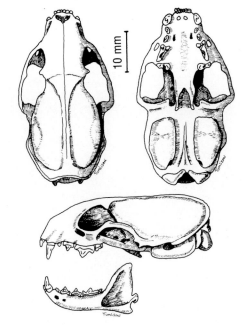

ARKANSAS DISTRIBUTION AND ABUNDANCE

The long-tailed weasel occurs statewide, but it is rare. Because of its secretive habits and low fur value, the long-tailed weasel may be more common than suspected.

LIFE HISTORY   Long-tailed weasels occur in brushlands, fencerows, upland woods, forest edges, and bottomland hardwoods near watercourses. Occasionally they will live in close proximity to humans; for instance, they might live under a house or barn if prey species are abundant in the vicinity. The weasel may appropriate the burrow of a chipmunk, pocket

Skull of *Mustela frenata*

Mustela frenata, Long-tailed Weasel. *Phil A. Dotson*

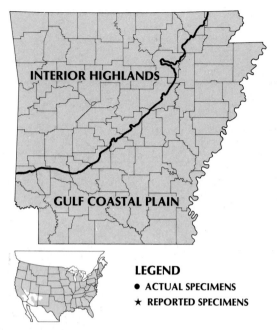

Distribution of the long-tailed weasel (*Mustela frenata*)

gopher, or other rodent; it may also den under tree roots, stumps, logs, or in a rockpile. The nest is made of grass and leaves and may be lined with rodent and rabbit fur.

The bulk of the weasel's diet consists of small mammals including cotton rats, deer mice, voles, pocket gophers, woodrats, chipmunks, shrews, and rabbits. On occasion small birds, reptiles, amphibians, earthworms, and insects are also eaten (Hall 1951b; Polderboer et al. 1941). The only carrion eaten by weasels apparently consists of carcasses stored in their burrows. Weasels are notoriously vicious killers and sometimes kill more than they can eat. Surplus kill may be cached but often decomposes before it can be eaten. The prey is killed by a bite at the base of the skull or in the neck (Hall 1951b). The brain is usually eaten first, after which the heart, lungs, and other parts of the carcass are eaten.

Mating occurs in July and August and females produce a single annual litter in April or May. The total length of gestation is between 205 and 337 days, averaging 279 days, but during most of this time, the fertilized eggs remain quiescent in the blastocyst stage before implantation in the uterus. After implantation, development of the embryo resumes and is completed in 27 days or less (Wright 1948). The litter size varies from one to twelve but usually numbers between five and eight. The young, which weigh about 3 g (0.1 oz) at birth, are weaned when 6–8 weeks old and begin feeding on solid food. Shortly after weaning, the young begin foraging with their mother until nearly full grown. Females reach sexual maturity and mate during their first summer, when they are 3–4 months old. Males do not attain sexual maturity and breed until they are about a year old.

In the northern part of its range, this species turns white in winter except for the black tip on its tail. In Arkansas, weasels do not change color, but the winter coat may be lighter brown than in summer.

IMPORTANCE AND/OR MANAGEMENT   Very little is known about this interesting mammal in Arkansas because of its scarcity, which may be more apparent than real due to its elusiveness, secretive nature, and the difficulty involved in trapping it. Weasels occasionally gain entry into poultry houses and kill young poultry, but they generally play a beneficial role around farm buildings by destroying a great many mice and rats. They are more active at night but often hunt during daylight hours.

The subspecies found in Arkansas is *M. f. primulina*.

SELECTED REFERENCES
Hall (1951b); Hamilton (1933); Polderboer et al. (1941); Wright (1948).

MINK

Mustela vison

NAME   *Mustela* is the Latin word for "weasel." The specific name, *vison*, is obscure. It may come from the Swedish, *vison*, for "a kind of weasel."

Mustela vison, Mink. *Phil A. Dotson*

IDENTIFICATION AND DESCRIPTION   The mink is medium-sized, slender, and considerably heavier-bodied than the long-tailed weasel. The head is small and flattened with a long neck. Its tail is long, well furred, brown basally, and blacker toward the tip. Mink have short legs and short, rounded ears. The pelage is uniformly dark, chestnut-brown above and paler brown below, except for white patches on chin, chest, and occasional white spots on the belly and anal region. Females are about one-fourth smaller than males.

MEASUREMENTS AND DENTAL FORMULA   Lower limits represent females.

Total Length: 425–700 mm (17.0–28.0 in)
Tail Length: 130–230 mm (5.1–9.1 in)
Hind Foot: 50–80 mm (2.0–3.2 in)
Ear: 19–27 mm (0.75–1.1 in)
Skull Length: 57–69 mm (2.2–2.7 in)
Weight: 560–1620 g (19.8–57.1 oz)
Dental Formula: I 3/3, C 1/1, P 3/3, M 1/2 = 34

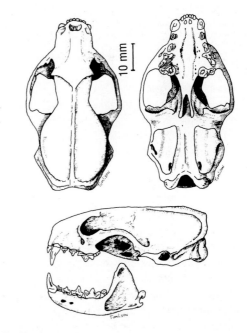

Skull of *Mustela vison*

A mink feeding on a mallard. *Phil A. Dotson*

ARKANSAS DISTRIBUTION AND ABUNDANCE
The mink occurs statewide and is common.

LIFE HISTORY   The mink is a semiaquatic species which is seldom found far from permanent
bodies of water. It occurs along rivers, bayous,
sloughs, reservoirs, and lakes where it pro-
cures much of its food. Brushy stream borders
and streams partly blocked by windfalls and
other debris are preferred habitat. Mink den
under the tree roots along stream banks, in hollow trees, beneath logs or stumps, or in old
muskrat or nutria burrows. The nest chamber is
lined with grass, leaves, fur, and feathers.

Male mink range over a wide area in search of
food. Their linear range along stream banks
ranges from 1.8 to 5 km (1.1–3.1 mi). Females
and juvenile males have a much more restricted
range (Gerell 1970; Marshall 1936). Mink are
chiefly nocturnal but daytime activity is not
uncommon. The occurrence of characteristic

scat, frequently containing crayfish remains,
on rocks or logs and easily identified footprints
in mud along streambanks are signs of the
mink's presence.

The carnivorous diet of the mink includes both
aquatic and terrestrial animals. Favorite foods
of the mink are frogs and crayfish, which make
up a large part of its diet (Korschgen 1957b).
The mink is an accomplished swimmer and
fully capable of catching fish in water, but fish
usually are not an important component of its
diet. Where muskrats are abundant they sometimes make up the bulk of the diet (Hamilton
1940; Sealander 1943). However, the mink is
an opportunist and will eat whatever is most
available. Rabbits, rats, mice, and other mammals are eaten more often in winter in northern
areas; but in the South, frogs, fish, crayfish, insects, clams, and other items are important
constituents of the diet throughout the year.
Larger male mink may consume larger prey, in-

cluding muskrats and rabbits, than do smaller females.

The breeding season extends from January through March. Delayed implantation of the fertilized eggs in the wall of the uterus occurs as in other mustelids, and the gestation period varies from 40 to 75 days with a mean of 51 days (Enders 1952). After implantation, development of the embryo to term takes 29–31 days. The number of young in the single annual litter ranges from one to eleven, with three to four in the usual litter. The kits are weaned 5–6 weeks after birth and begin foraging for themselves when about 8 weeks old. They reach adult size in 5 months. The young accompany the mother until autumn when dispersal occurs.

Like all mustelids, mink possess a pair of anal scent glands that emit a liquid with a very strong, musky odor. The scent may be discharged when the animal is overly excited or aggravated. In addition, the scent may be emitted during conflict with conspecifics. The scent is especially strong during breeding season (Linscomb et al. 1982).

IMPORTANCE AND/OR MANAGEMENT   Mink fur has long had a mystique associated with it. Because of this, the demand for mink pelts has always been high. The influence of mink ranching has also influenced the demand for its fur. Even though mink ranches produce millions of pelts annually, there is still a high demand for wild fur. In Arkansas between 1942 and 1984, mink ranked fourth in pelts harvested and second in total value; however, in recent years this has decreased somewhat, presumably due to commercial ranching operations. Regionally, mink are primarily harvested from the Mississippi Delta and the West Gulf Coastal Plain (Peck et al. 1985).

Two subspecies occur in Arkansas, according to Hall (1981). The race *M. v. mink* occurs in western and northeastern Arkansas, and the race *M. v. vulgivaga* is found in the central and southern portions of the state. However, geographic variation in this species has been studied very little in southern states, and the wide size and color variations due to age, sex, and season need additional study.

SELECTED REFERENCES
Eagle and Whitman (1987); Enders (1952); Gerell (1970); Hall (1981); Hamilton (1940); Korschgen (1957b); Linscomb et al. (1982); Marshall (1936); Peck et al. (1985); Sealander (1943).

BADGER

Taxidea taxus

NAME   *Taxidea* is from Latin and Greek origins, *taxus*, meaning "badger," and *eidos*, meaning "like." The specific name, *taxus*, is the Latin for "badger."

IDENTIFICATION AND DESCRIPTION   The badger is a large, squat, heavy-bodied mustelid. The head is broad and slightly flattened with a short, thick, muscular neck. The eyes are small; ears are small and rounded; the tail is short, bushy, and yellowish brown; the legs are short; and the forefeet are large and powerful with ex-

LEGEND
● ACTUAL SPECIMENS
★ REPORTED SPECIMENS

Distribution of the mink (*Mustela vison*)

Taxidea taxus, Badger. *Phil A. Dotson*

ceptionally long, curved claws. The pelage is
shaggy, longer on the sides than on the back,
with a white medial stripe extending from near
the nose over the head to the shoulder and back
region. Its cheeks are white with a prominent
black patch in front of each ear, and it is grizzled grayish or brownish above (frosted with long
white tips on overhairs) and yellowish white below. The feet are black or brown. Males are
larger than females.

MEASUREMENTS AND DENTAL FORMULA

Total Length:	629–870 mm (24.8–34.3 in)
Tail Length:	100–155 mm (3.9–6.1 in)
Hind Foot:	89–130 mm (3.5–5.1 in)
Ear:	38–60 mm (1.5–2.4 in)
Skull Length:	107–130 mm (4.2–5.1 in)
Weight:	4–12 kg (8.8–26.5 lb)
Dental Formula:	I 3/3, C 1/1, P 3/3, M 1/2 = 34

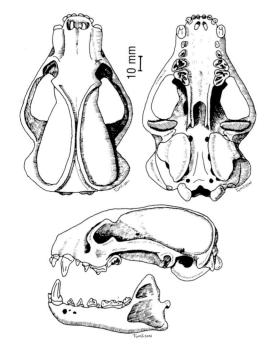

Skull of *Taxidea taxus*

ARKANSAS DISTRIBUTION AND ABUNDANCE

The badger is rare; only one specimen record from near Fayetteville, Washington County (Sealander and Forsyth 1966), exists. There have been several reliable sight records (see map), and one or two badgers from unknown localities are sold annually by Arkansas trappers.

LIFE HISTORY   The badger prefers open country and is more common in areas with loose, sandy soils. Rocky soils and heavily wooded areas are avoided. Badgers are exceptionally well adapted for digging with their heavy, muscular bodies, powerful forelegs, and feet armed with long, heavy claws. They are master excavators that can dig faster than a man with a shovel. Badgers can easily outdig ground-dwelling rodents upon which they depend for food.

Badgers are more active at night but often may be observed foraging in daytime. They are almost exclusively carnivorous and prey mainly upon mammals, including woodchucks, pocket gophers, and other rodents. Rabbits, bird eggs and nestlings, snakes, and insects are also eaten. Where pocket gophers and woodchucks are agricultural pests, the badger can be a definite asset to farmers.

Mating occurs in late summer and early autumn. After the mating season, males become solitary. Implantation of the fertilized egg is delayed until about January or February, and the single annual litter is produced in March and early April (Long 1973, Wright 1966), sometimes as late as May or June. Litter size varies from one to five with the usual number being three. The grass-lined nest chamber is in an enlarged part of the home burrow about 1 m (3 ft) below the surface. The young appear at the mouth of the burrow in June or July and are weaned when about 8 weeks old. They stay in the vicinity of the home burrow until autumn.

The potential life span of the badger is about 15 years, but it probably has a much shorter life span in the wild. The badger has few natural enemies except humans.

Badgers are not true hibernators, but during severe winter weather at higher latitudes and altitudes they may stay in their burrows and sleep for several days subsisting on stored body fat.

IMPORTANCE AND/OR MANAGEMENT   On western livestock ranges, ranchers value the badger's assistance in controlling destructive rodents but do not hold the coyote in similar high esteem. Cahalane (1950) and others have reported that badgers sometimes team up with coyotes to catch prairie dogs and other rodents.

Although Long (1973) placed the Arkansas specimen in the subspecies boundary of *T. t. berlandieri*, the short white stripe on the head, general pelage coloration, and measurements appear to be more characteristic of *T. t. taxus*.

SELECTED REFERENCES
Cahalane (1950); Long (1973); Sealander and Forsyth (1966); Wright (1966).

INTERIOR HIGHLANDS

GULF COASTAL PLAIN

LEGEND
● **ACTUAL SPECIMENS**
★ **REPORTED SPECIMENS**

Distribution of the badger (*Taxidea taxus*)

Eastern Spotted Skunk
Spilogale putorius

NAME *Spilogale* is derived from two Greek words, *spilos*, meaning "spot," and *gale*, meaning "weasel." The specific name, *putorius*, is from the Latin *putor*, which means "a foul odor."

Spilogale putorius, Eastern Spotted Skunk.
Phil A. Dotson

IDENTIFICATION AND DESCRIPTION The spotted skunk is small and slender, not much larger than a large squirrel. It has a long, bushy tail tipped with white. The eyes and ears are small; the legs are short; and the fore and hind feet have many pads. The pelage is black with a triangular white patch on the forehead, a white patch in front of each ear, and four interrupted stripes on the neck, back, and sides. Males are larger than females.

MEASUREMENTS AND DENTAL FORMULA
Total Length:	410–585 mm (16.1–23.0 in)
Tail Length:	138–240 mm (5.4–9.5 in)
Hind Foot:	38–55 mm (1.5–2.2 in)
Ear:	17–25 mm (0.67–0.98 in)
Skull Length:	52–60 mm (2.0–2.4 in)
Weight:	453–1260 g (15.9–44.0 oz)
Dental Formula:	I 3/3, C 1/1, P 3/3, M 1/2 = 34

ARKANSAS DISTRIBUTION AND ABUNDANCE
The spotted skunk is assumed to occur statewide, although it is much more common in the Interior Highlands. It was formerly absent along most of the western border of the Mississippi River, but it may have extended its range in the Gulf Coastal Plain to the banks of the Mississippi River with clearing and drainage of bottomland forest for the production of soybeans and cotton (Van Gelder 1959). There have, however, been very few records and/or sightings in the Gulf Coastal Plain, and its status in that part of the state is questionable.

LIFE HISTORY Spotted skunks occur in a variety of habitats including open fields, prairies, croplands, fencerows, farmyards, forest edges, and woodlands. Wetlands and dense timber stands are avoided. A preference is shown for areas with rocky outcrops and ledges where natural rock cavities and crevices provide shelter and den sites. It also dens in deserted woodchuck or armadillo burrows, brush piles, woodpiles, hollow trees or logs, and under buildings. The den contains a nest of grass or hay. During the non-breeding season, dens may be used by several skunks (Crabb 1948).

Spilogale is mainly nocturnal and usually is not seen during daytime. It is omnivorous and feeds upon small mammals, insects, birds, and to a lesser extent upon fruits, corn, nuts, small

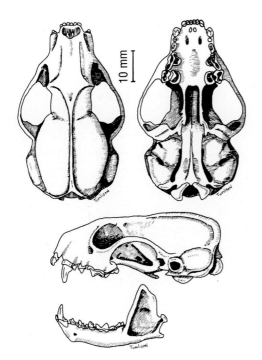

Skull of *Spilogale putorius*

lizards, and snakes. The summer and fall diet consists predominantly of insects and other arthropods, whereas in winter and spring, rabbits, mice, and other small mammals comprise the bulk of the diet. Spotted skunks are efficient "mousers" and will quickly rid a barn of rats. They are agile climbers and can run up and down trees like squirrels. Their climbing ability enables them to occasionally feed upon fruits and the eggs or nestlings of songbirds.

The reproductive patterns of eastern and western forms of the spotted skunk have been documented by Mead (1968a, 1968b). In the eastern spotted skunk, mating occurs in March and April. Most females come into heat in late March and fertilization occurs in April. Nearly all females are bred by the end of April. In the South, some females possibly mate again in July or August and produce a second litter. The gestation period is estimated to be 50–65 days. There may be delays of two weeks or more before the fertilized eggs are implanted in late April and May, but the period of delayed im-

plantation is not definitely known. Females produce a litter of two to nine, with the usual litter consisting of four to five young (Crabb 1944; Mead 1968a). The young weigh about 10 g (0.4 oz) at birth and are weaned when about 8 weeks old. Females come into heat and breed when 9–10 months old.

The defensive behavior of spotted skunks is well known; it consists of a rapid series of handstands which serve as a warning to potential aggressors. If approached too closely, they drop to all fours, assume a horseshoe-shaped stance, with the tail lifted and the anus and head directed toward the potential aggressor. The musk may be accurately discharged for a distance of 4–5 m (13–16 ft) (Manaro 1961).

IMPORTANCE AND/OR MANAGEMENT Spotted skunks occasionally raid poultry houses and kill chickens and eat eggs, but more often chicken carrion is consumed. Van Gelder (1953) describes an interesting egg-opening technique employed by this species in which the hen's egg is straddled, passed back by the forelegs, and given a quick kick with the hind legs that pro-

LEGEND
- ● ACTUAL SPECIMENS
- ★ REPORTED SPECIMENS

Distribution of the eastern spotted skunk (*Spilogale putorius*)

pels it with considerable force against a wall or other object. This procedure may be repeated several times until the egg breaks.

The subspecies found in Arkansas is *S. p. interrupta*.

SELECTED REFERENCES
Crabb (1944, 1948); Manaro (1961); Mead (1968a, 1968b); Van Gelder (1953, 1959).

STRIPED SKUNK

Mephitis mephitis

NAME   *Mephitis* is a Latin word meaning "bad odor," referring to the extremely strong scent of this species.

IDENTIFICATION AND DESCRIPTION   The striped skunk is medium-sized, heavy-bodied, and about the size of a house cat. The head is slender with a pointed muzzle; the ears are short and rounded; the eyes are small; the legs are short; the feet are semi-plantigrade and the front feet are armed with long claws. The fur is dense and coarse. The pelage is black or brownish black with a narrow stripe on the middle of the forehead and white on the nape, which usually divides into two white stripes continuing for part or all of the body length. The pattern of white is highly variable and can be used to identify individual animals. Some specimens are almost entirely black, others are mainly white on the back. Females are as much as 15% smaller than males.

MEASUREMENTS AND DENTAL FORMULA

Total Length:	540–760 mm (21.3–29.9 in)
Tail Length:	200–280 mm (7.9–11.0 in)
Hind Foot:	57–82 mm (2.2–3.2 in)
Ear:	17–30 mm (0.67–1.2 in)
Skull Length:	57–79 mm (2.2–3.1 in)
Weight:	0.5–5.4 kg (1.1–12.0 lb)
Dental Formula:	I 3/3, C 1/1, P 3/3, M 1/2 = 34

Mephitis mephitis, Striped Skunk. *Phil A. Dotson*

ARKANSAS DISTRIBUTION AND ABUNDANCE
The striped skunk occurs statewide and is abundant.

LIFE HISTORY   The striped skunk lives in open meadows, brushlands, areas with rock outcrops, forest edges, and in farmlands with a mixture of pastures, cultivated fields, fencerows, and open woodlots. It is seldom found at any great distance from water. Normally nocturnal, the striped skunk may occasionally be observed in daytime. Foraging for food ordinarily begins near sundown.

Rock cavities and crevices are favorite den

sites when this type of habitat is present. Skunks sometimes dig their own burrows but ordinarily appropriate abandoned woodchuck, armadillo, or fox burrows. Often dens are located beneath old outbuildings or abandoned houses.

Striped skunks are omnivorous and eat a wide variety of animal and vegetable matter. In general, their feeding habits are beneficial to farmers. More than one-half of the summer diet consists of insects (Kelker 1937) plus fruits and berries, but in winter, rats, mice, and other small mammals become important dietary constituents. Carrion from road kills or hunting cripples is frequently eaten. Skunks become very fat in late fall. They do not hibernate but may den up and sleep for several days during severe winter weather. Several individuals sometimes occupy the same den (Allen and Shapton 1942).

Breeding apparently occurs in late February and early March (Verts 1967). The gestation period usually varies from 62 to 66 days but may be as long as 75 days. The litter size ranges from two to ten, and the usual number of kits in a litter is six or seven. Young are born in late April or in May, and the average weight is about 35 g (1.2 oz); their subsequent growth is rapid. The young are able to eat solid food at about 6 weeks old when they begin to accompany their mother on hunting trips. Weaning apparently occurs when they are 8–10 weeks old. Most young skunks have broken the family ties by about mid-August.

The senses of sight and hearing are poor to fair. Striped skunks are not particularly social, although they will den communally. They occasionally utter low growls, grunts, snarls, churring, short squeals, shrill screeches, or hissing noises (Godin 1982).

They are relatively docile animals, but when provoked, they give warnings of displeasure and assume a defensive posture before discharging their scent. Warnings include arching the back, stamping the front feet, and shuffling backward. In addition, they may click their teeth, growl, or hiss. Immediately before scenting, a skunk raises its tail and bends into a U-shaped position, with both the head and tail

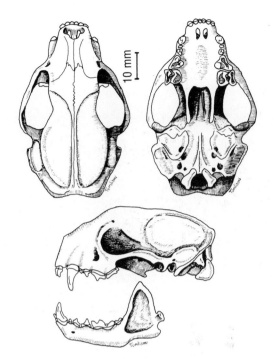

Skull of *Mephitis mephitis*

facing the enemy. It discharges its scent rapidly and can aim behind, to either side, or in front of itself. It can do this by changing the position of the two nipples just inside the anus. The jet of musk may be atomized as a fine mist or as a short stream of rain-sized droplets. It can spray accurately for a distance of about 3 m (10 ft) and can reach a distance of about 5 m (16.5 ft). The spray covers an arc of 30–45° (Verts 1967; Godin 1982).

Skunks generally avoid spraying themselves and will refrain from spraying if their tails are held tightly over the anus. A striped skunk can be handled if it is grasped around the neck with one hand and by the tail with the other. Contrary to popular belief, a skunk can spray while suspended by its tail. Furthermore, they do not scatter the scent with the tail.

Skunks have few natural predators, with the possible exception of the great horned owl. Most potential predators soon learn not to molest them after one encounter with their potent defense mechanism.

Distribution of the striped skunk (*Mephitis mephitis*)

IMPORTANCE AND/OR MANAGEMENT   Skunks may occasionally raid poultry houses; however, they usually take one bird at a time. Wanton killing of poultry is usually done by some other species. Most complaints about skunks are a result of their denning under houses and other buildings. These animals can be trapped and transported to other areas (if one is careful, skunks will seldom spray when in a trap); a liberal dose of moth crystals placed under the building will often cause the skunks to leave, or the entrances may be closed after it has been ascertained that the animals have left. One-way doors can be placed over the entrance so that the skunk can leave but may not return, or one can tell by the tracks if the skunk has left by sprinkling flour around the entrance. The only problem with the latter technique is that an entire family of unknown numbers may be present.

Skunks are the major vector of wildlife rabies in the United States, averaging between 40–50% of all reported cases. In Arkansas, as would be expected, skunks also account for most of the reported rabies cases, averaging around 65% of the total reported cases since 1950 (80% or more in each of the years since 1980). Between 1977 and 1979, Arkansas experienced a severe epidemic of skunk rabies. In 1979, at the peak of the epidemic, 301 laboratory-confirmed cases were reported; this ranked Arkansas first in the nation in reported cases per square mile. Previous to 1980, skunk rabies seemed to be confined to the Interior Highlands, but since then, cases have been reported from the Gulf Coastal Plain. A survey of human contacts with known rabid skunks in Arkansas revealed that, "the rabid skunk coming in contact with humans generally will be solitary, aggressive or unafraid, and found around buildings in the country during daylight hours (usually in the morning)" (Ferguson and Heidt 1980; Heidt 1982; Heidt et al. 1982).

Skunks tame easily and make interesting pets. Since the rabies virus may be latent for over a year and may become active when the animal experiences some type of stress, however, it is strongly advised that persons neither purchase pet skunks nor remove them from the wild. In addition, due to the incidence of rabies in Arkansas, the Arkansas Game and Fish Commission has banned the possession of skunks.

Until the late 1970s, striped skunks represented one of the major furbearers in Arkansas. Since that time, however, skunk harvests have drastically declined. This may be due, in part, to low prices and the justified fear of rabies (Peck et al. 1985).

Apparently two subspecies occur in Arkansas (Hall 1981). The race *M. m. mesomelas* occurs over most of the state, and the somewhat larger race, *M. m. nigra*, possibly occurs in the northeastern corner of the state. There has been insufficient study to determine where the zone of intergradation between the races occurs or whether both races are actually present.

SELECTED REFERENCES

Allen and Shapton (1942); Ferguson and Heidt (1980); Godin (1982); Hall (1981); Heidt et al. (1982); Heidt (1982); Kelker (1937); Verts (1967).

RIVER OTTER

Lutra canadensis

NAME   *Lutra* is the Latin word for "otter." The specific name, *canadensis*, is Latinized for "of Canada," the country from which the first specimen was collected.

IDENTIFICATION AND DESCRIPTION   The river otter is a large, long-bodied mustelid with a small, flattened head and a broad muzzle. It has small, close-set ears; small eyes; short legs; feet with fully webbed toes; and a tail that is long, tapered, muscular, and thick at the base (about one-third of total length). The fur is thick, dense, and glossy, a dull brown or reddish brown above and paler brown or grayish below. The throat and muzzle are silvery-gray or brownish white. Males are larger than females.

MEASUREMENTS AND DENTAL FORMULA
Total Length: 889–1300 mm (35.0–51.2 in)
Tail Length: 300–507 mm (11.8–19.9 in)
Hind Foot: 100–146 mm (3.9–5.7 in)
Ear: 17–25 mm (0.67–0.98 in)
Skull Length: 98–107 mm (3.9–4.2 in)
Weight: 4.5–14 kg (9.9–30.9 lb)
Dental Formula: I 3/3, C 1/1, P 4/3, M 1/2 = 36

ARKANSAS DISTRIBUTION AND ABUNDANCE
The otter occurs statewide with increasing populations (Polechla 1987).

LIFE HISTORY   The otter occurs in rivers, creeks, bayous, and lakes that are mostly bordered by timber. It usually follows watercourses but may occasionally travel as much as 15 km (9.3 mi) over land. Male otters may traverse as much as 9–10 km (5–6 mi) of stream course in a night. Where food is plentiful, individuals and family groups may range over no more than

Lutra canadensis, River Otter. *C. C. Lockwood*

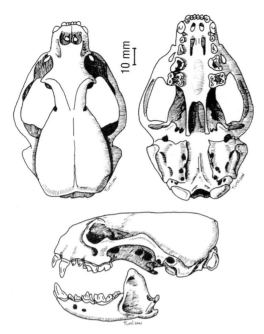

Skull of *Lutra canadensis*

12–20 km (7.5–12.5 mi) of stream course per year (Wilson 1959), but individuals have been reported to range over as much as 80–95 km (50–60 mi) of stream in the course of a year (Liers 1951). The home range of family groups may be limited to about 6 sq km (3.7 sq mi) while the kits are growing up, but may be extended to as much as 15 sq km (9.3 sq mi) by the time the young leave the parents. Several studies in Arkansas have demonstrated the close relationship between the presence of otters and beaver (Karnes et al. 1984; Polechla 1987).

Otters are well adapted for living much of the time in water, where they procure most of their food. They are exceptionally fine swimmers and divers and often swim long distances underwater. The bulk of their diet consists of game and forage fishes, frogs, and crayfish (Lagler and Ostenson 1942; Ryder 1955). Clams, turtles, snakes, muskrats, water insects, and occasionally waterfowl make up the balance of its diet. Many sport fishermen detest the fish-eating habits of otters, but various studies indicate that they eat mainly rough fish that are easier to catch. They sometimes become entangled in the nets of commercial fishermen and are unwelcome around fish hatcheries.

Female river otters generally do not reach sexual maturity until they are 2 years of age. Breeding occurs in most temperate regions during late winter or early spring, following parturition. Copulation normally occurs in the water, and otters may copulate several times a day and on consecutive days (Liers 1951; McDaniel 1963; Park 1971). Delayed implantation of the blastocyst results in a total gestation period of 290–380 days; actual developmental time is 60–63 days. The earliest parturition date in the wild is in early January and extends through May; the peak seems to be in March or April (Lauhachinda 1978). The litter size varies from one to six, with an average of two or three cubs per litter. The burrow is most often found in a stream bank with the entrance underwater or beneath exposed tree roots along the bank. Abandoned beaver, nutria, or muskrat burrows are frequently appropriated. The cubs are born toothless and blind and remain helpless until 5–6 weeks old. They first appear outside the nest when 10–12 weeks old and must be taught to swim by the mother. Females do not tolerate males near the young until they are about 6 months old. The young accompany the mother until they are about 1 year old and full grown.

Otters are more social than most mustelids. The basic social group consists of an adult female and her juvenile offspring. There have been conflicting reports as to the inclusion of males in the social group; however, groups of bachelor males have been observed at times other than the breeding season (see Melquist and Dronkert 1987).

River otters communicate primarily through olfactory, auditory, and tactile signals. Unlike many carnivores, their visual senses are not acute. Olfactory communication is achieved by scent-marking with feces, urine, and anal sac secretions, and is probably the major mode of intergroup communication (Melquist and Hornocker 1983).

INTERIOR HIGHLANDS

GULF COASTAL PLAIN

LEGEND
- ● ACTUAL SPECIMENS
- ★ REPORTED SPECIMENS

Distribution of the river otter (*Lutra canadensis*)

IMPORTANCE AND/OR MANAGEMENT Heavy trapping combined with the demise of the beaver greatly reduced otter populations in Arkansas, and they were scarce or rare in many streams in the state around the turn of the century. With the imposition of a legal trapping season, numbers slowly increased but fluctuated over the years with changes in trapping pressure as prices paid for pelts increased or decreased. Otters have always been more numerous in rivers and other bodies of water in the Gulf Coastal Plain, but clearing of bottomland forests in the Delta and other parts of the Coastal Plain for the cultivation of row crops has had a detrimental effect on the otter population. In recent years, however, there appears to have been an increase in the otter

population which has paralleled the increases in muskrat, beaver, and nutria populations.

The subspecies in Arkansas is *L. c. lataxina* (van Zyll de Jong 1972).

SELECTED REFERENCES
Karnes et al. (1984); Lagler and Ostenson (1942); Lauhachinda (1978); Liers (1951); McDaniel (1963); Melquist and Hornocker (1983); Melquist and Dronkert (1987); Park (1971); Polechla (1987); Ryder (1955); Tumlison and Karnes (1987); van Zyll de Jong (1972); Wilson (1959).

FAMILY FELIDAE
CATS

Members of the family Felidae are the most proficient predators among the carnivores. Some species regularly kill prey as large as themselves, and they often kill prey several times heavier. Throughout the history of the order, the cats have been the most highly specialized for a predacious style of life.

Members of this family are medium- to large-sized carnivores. They are digitigrade and have five toes on the front and four on the hind feet. The feet are large, and the retractile claws are sharp and strongly curved. Cats have large eyes that are well suited for night vision and their largely nocturnal habits. In addition, cats have, next to primates, the most highly developed binocular vision, which enables them to accurately perceive depths of field. The canine teeth are large, and the large shearing cheek teeth are adapted for a diet consisting largely of flesh. Only two native species occur in Arkansas.

KEY TO SPECIES

WHOLE ANIMALS

1. Tail longer than hind foot; ears not tufted 2

Tail about the length of hind foot; ears tufted; gray to brown spotted and blotched with black above, whitish with black blotches below; a conspicuous black bar on inside of front legs .... *Felis rufus*, Bobcat

2. Tail more than 500 mm (19.7 in); weight more than 45 kg (99.2 lb); gray brown to pale buff above, pale white or tan below .... *Felis concolor*, Mountain Lion

Tail usually less than 350 mm (13.8 in); weight variable, usually less than 10 kg (22 lb); color variable .... *Felis catus*, Feral House Cat

SKULLS

1. Total number of teeth 28; three cheek teeth on each side of upper jaw .... *Felis rufus*, Bobcat

Total number of teeth 30; four cheek teeth on each side of upper jaw 2

2. Skull length more than 130 mm (5.1 in) .... *Felis concolor*, Mountain Lion

Skull length less than 130 mm (5.1 in) .... *Felis catus*, Feral House Cat

---

MOUNTAIN LION

Felis concolor

NAME   *Felis* is the Latin word for "cat." The specific name, *concolor*, is the Latin word for "one color," referring to the uniform color pattern. The mountain lion is also known as the cougar or panther.

IDENTIFICATION AND DESCRIPTION   The mountain lion is a large, powerfully built cat with a long tail (slightly more than one-third of the total length) that is tipped with dusky black. It has a relatively small, rounded head. The ears are blackish externally, relatively small, rounded and without tufts. Its claws are long, sharp, curved, and retractile. The pelage is uniformly pale brown to reddish brown above and dull white below; the inner ear, chin, lips, and lower cheeks are whitish. Females are smaller than males.

MEASUREMENTS AND DENTAL FORMULA
    Total Length: 1500–2743 mm (59.1–
                   108.0 in)

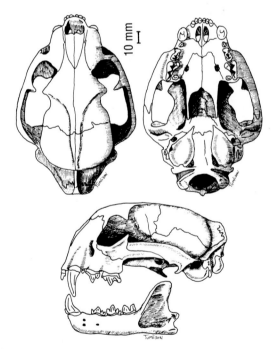

Skull of *Felis concolor*

Felis concolor, Mountain Lion. *Phil A. Dotson*

Tail Length:	534–900 mm (21.0–35.4 in)
Hind Foot:	220–295 mm (8.7–11.6 in)
Ear:	75–100 mm (2.9–3.9 in)
Skull Length:	155–234 mm (6.1–9.2 in)
Weight:	36–103 kg (79.4–227.0 lb)
Dental Formula:	I 3/3, C 1/1, P 3/2, M 1/1 = 30

ARKANSAS DISTRIBUTION AND ABUNDANCE
The mountain lion is on the Federal Endangered Species list and is rare. The present cougar populations in Arkansas are centered near the Saline and Ouachita River bottomlands in south central Arkansas, the White River National Wildlife Refuge near the confluence of the White and Arkansas rivers, the western Ozark Mountains north of the Arkansas River, and the Ouachita Mountains in west central Arkansas south of the Arkansas River (Lewis 1969, 1970; Noble 1971; Sealander and Gipson 1973). Scattered occurrences in other areas may indicate dispersing young or an occasional individual or mated pair. No mountain lions have been reported from the northeastern section of the Delta, which has been largely cleared for agriculture.

LIFE HISTORY   The mountain lion or cougar lives in a variety of habitats but usually tends to avoid the vicinity of humans. It occurs in rough, rocky, wooded uplands, large tracts of bottomland forest and swamps, and remote, mountainous regions of the national forests. Although this cat sometimes lives close to human habitations, it is rarely seen due to its silent and secretive habits.

The mountain lion's expert stalking ability enables it to capture large prey, chiefly the white-tailed deer in Arkansas, which is its staple food. The largest concentrations of cougar sightings in the state have been from areas with high deer populations. However, the cougar population in the state appears to be sub-

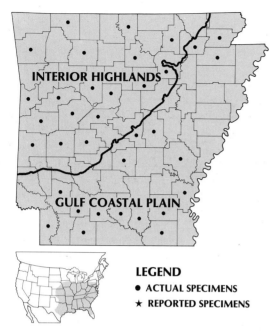

Distribution of the mountain lion (*Felis concolor*)

LEGEND
● ACTUAL SPECIMENS
★ REPORTED SPECIMENS

INTERIOR HIGHLANDS

GULF COASTAL PLAIN

Cougars apparently have no regular breeding season, and females may come into heat at various times of the year. Females do not breed until they are at least 2 or 3 years old and then mate only every 2 or 3 years thereafter. Adults are tolerant of each other only during the brief breeding period, and shortly after mating males leave the females to care for themselves and their offspring. The gestation period is about 90–96 days and the usual litter consists of two to three kittens but may range from one to six. Although births may occur at any time of year, most litters are born in the spring. The den is usually situated under an overhanging ledge, in a natural rock crevice, or in a dense thicket, but seldom in a cave. When about 2–3 months old, lion kittens are weaned and begin accompanying the mother on night hunting trips. They weigh about 20 kg (45 lb) at the age of 8 months and may remain with their mother for over a year.

Cougars have been known to live for as long as 19 years in captivity, but their life span is probably about 10 years in the wild (Johnson and Couch 1954). Although the cougar sometimes lives for several years in the vicinity of human habitations, it is rarely seen due to its silent, extremely secretive habits and largely nocturnal activity. Tracks in mud around stream margins or beside stockponds and its occasional characteristic "scream" are usually the only signs of its presence.

IMPORTANCE AND/OR MANAGEMENT Hornocker (1969, 1970) found that female cougars occupied ranges of 13–52 sq km (8–32 sq mi) and that males ranged over 39–78 sq km (24–48 sq mi) or more. In his opinion, territoriality is one of the most important regulators of mountain lion numbers. Although there are still a number of sufficiently large, rugged wilderness areas with large deer populations in Arkansas, such areas are rapidly disappearing. The remaining areas providing suitable habitat for the mountain lion are in urgent need of preservation if this endangered species is to be preserved as part of our wildlife heritage for future generations.

stantially lower than could be supported by the present deer population, and suitable habitat remote from human activities seems to be the most important limiting factor at present. Cougars will eat smaller prey such as rabbits, raccoons, opossums, and foxes when larger prey is not available. Feral pigs and domestic livestock may be eaten occasionally, but reports of such predation in Arkansas are largely unconfirmed.

Cougars spend most of their time on the ground but readily climb trees to escape pursuing dogs or to gain an advantageous position when hunting. Once a cougar has eaten its fill of a kill, the remainder of the carcass may be covered with dry leaves, grass, or brush and may serve as a food cache for several days; but unless the cat is old, such carrion is most often eaten by coyotes. The mountain lion has tremendous strength and has been known to drag a 270 kg (600 lb) heifer as far as 200 m (660 ft) up the side of a mountain (Young and Goldman 1946). It lacks stamina, however, and when pursued rarely runs more than 300–400 m (985–1300 ft) before seeking refuge in a tree.

There have been persistent but unverified reports of black panthers in Arkansas over a period of many years. Most reports can be discounted because sightings occurred against contrasting snow backgrounds, in poor lighting conditions, or during brief glimpses. It is suspected that most of these sightings may have actually been of rapidly moving otters or large feral house cats. Melanism is known from South American races of the species, but no authentic record of this color phase is known in North America.

The subspecies *F. c. coryi* occurs in Arkansas.

SELECTED REFERENCES
Hornocker (1969, 1970); Johnson and Couch (1954); Lewis (1969, 1970); Noble (1971); Sealander and Gipson (1973); Young and Goldman (1946).

FERAL HOUSE CAT
Felis catus

NAME   *Felis* is the Latin word for "cat." The specific name, *catus*, is a Latinized English word meaning "cat," referring to the house cat.

REMARKS   Feral house cats are domestic cats that have strayed away from farms or cities and reverted to a wild or semi-wild state. Cats that have been reared away from human influence in the wild may be considered truly feral, but many house cats found in the wild should be considered semi-feral or free-ranging since they are not permanently resident but return to human habitations during colder weather. Feral or semi-feral house cats are numerous throughout the state. There are many varieties or breeds of house cats, and colors are highly variable depending upon the breed or mixture of breeds. Feral house cats are usually about one-half the size of bobcats, although large toms occasionally reach a comparable size. Generally they are not confused with bobcats because of their long tails, smaller size, and variable coloration.

The house cat is most closely related to the African wildcat (*Felis silvestris lybica*) and the forest wildcat of Europe (*Felis silvestris silvestris*). It is believed that the house cat is descended primarily from the race *lybica*, which subsequently crossed with the race *silvestris* in Europe. These races are sometimes accorded specific rank (Ewer 1973; Guggisberg 1975). The domestic cat has been associated with man for about 4,000 years and was figured in Egyptian art as far back as 1600 B.C.

Hybrids between bobcats and domestic cats have been produced in captivity but have proved to be sterile (Eaton 1976). There are only a few authenticated records of such hybrids occurring in the wild (Gashwiler et al. 1961; Young 1958), although unverifiable reports of such crosses are not uncommon. In a litter of such hybrids reported by Gashwiler et al. (1961), three had short tails and closely resembled bobcats in all but size, and two looked like ordinary house cats. In Europe, the lynx is considered to be a deadly enemy of the forest wildcat. If the closely related bobcat shows similar animosity toward house cats, hybridization in the wild would appear to be an exceptional event.

Feral house cats are a serious threat to many native species of wildlife. Songbirds, game birds, and rabbits are important constituents of their diet during some seasons, and they may be responsible for some of the predation on domestic poultry that is most often attributed to bobcats and coyotes. Although feral house cats consume large numbers of small rodents (Hubbs 1951; McMurry and Sperry 1941), their destructiveness to game species may outweigh their benefits to farmers where they occur in or adjacent to primary game areas. Feral house cats also pose the danger of carrying rabies and other diseases to humans or their domestic animals.

SELECTED REFERENCES
Eaton (1976); Ewer (1973); Gashwiler et al. (1961); Guggisberg (1975); Hubbs (1951); McMurry and Sperry (1941); Young (1958).

Bobcat

Felis rufus

NAME   *Felis* is the Latin word meaning "cat." The specific name, *rufus*, is the Latin word for "reddish," referring to the body color.

IDENTIFICATION AND DESCRIPTION   The bobcat is medium-sized and about twice the size of a domestic cat. The tail is very short (usually shorter than the hind foot) with a black tip above and white below. Its ears are prominent with short black tufts (sometimes absent); the eyes are large with elliptical pupils; hair on the sides of the face is long, forming a ruff ("sideburns"). The pelage is reddish brown, olive-brown, or smoky gray (spotted or streaked with black) above and whitish, spotted with black below.

MEASUREMENTS AND DENTAL FORMULA

Total Length: 787–1015 mm (31–40 in)

Tail Length: 122–180 mm (4.8–7.1 in)
Hind Foot: 155–197 mm (6.1–7.8 in)
Ear: 61–76 mm (2.4–3.0 in)
Skull Length: 101–139 mm (4.0–5.5 in)
Weight: 4.5–20 kg (9.9–44.1 lb)
Dental Formula: I 3/3, C 1/1, P 2/2, M 1/1 = 28

ARKANSAS DISTRIBUTION AND ABUNDANCE
Bobcats occur statewide and have good stable populations (Rucker et al. 1985).

LIFE HISTORY   Bobcats occur in a wide variety of habitats but prefer rocky outcrops and canyons where such terrain is available. They are also found in heavily wooded uplands and bottomland forests, brushy areas, swamps, and semi-open farmlands. In the Ouachita Mountains, they seem to prefer 0–20 year regeneration areas and hardwood forests (Rucker et al. 1985). This species is primarily solitary and be-

Felis rufus, Bobcat. *C. C. Lockwood*

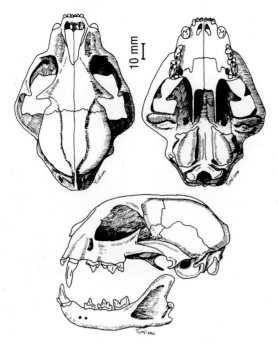

Skull of *Felis rufus*

cause of its covert habits is seldom sighted even where it is abundant. The bobcat is mainly nocturnal and is seldom active in daytime. Occasionally one may be fortunate to obtain a glimpse of a bobcat sunning on a log or on a ledge.

The bobcat is almost exclusively carnivorous. Statewide during all seasons and for both sexes, the most important food is rabbit (Fritts and Sealander 1978a; Tumlison 1983). Squirrels are an important supplementary food in the Interior Highlands, and rats and mice are important food items on the Gulf Coastal Plain. Rodents included in the diet, besides fox and gray squirrels, are chipmunks, flying squirrels, woodrats, cotton rats, white-footed mice, harvest mice, and pine voles. Deer, mostly carrion, are eaten mainly during autumn and winter following deer hunting season. Although capable of killing deer, the bobcat is not a significant cause of deer mortality in Arkansas. Rabbits and rodents apparently serve as buffers against such predation. Other minor items in the bobcat's diet include opossum, raccoon, skunk, birds, and snakes.

In Arkansas, peak breeding activity occurs from early December to late February and then tapers off in March and April. Some breeding may occur as early as November or as late as August (Fritts and Sealander 1978b; Tumlison 1983). These findings are similar to those of Crowe (1975). Late summer litters could represent second litters of early breeding females or litters of females that failed to conceive during the early breeding season. Males are apparently in breeding condition all year. Most litters are produced from March through early May; parturition may occur from early February to as late as October. Litters are born after a gestation period of about 62 days. They consist of one to six (usually two or three) blind, well-furred kittens weighing about 140–340 g (4.9–12 oz) each. The nest of dead leaves, moss, and dried grass in which they are born is usually in an inaccessible recess under a large rock ledge, in a hollow tree or log, or in a cavity beneath roots of a tree. Kittens are weaned when 60–70 days old and are able to fend for themselves when about 6 months old. Family ties are

Distribution of the bobcat (*Felis rufus*)

not completely broken until the female mates and becomes pregnant again. In Arkansas, young females come into heat during their first year, but a high percentage does not conceive during this first estrus (Fritts and Sealander 1978a). Most young females apparently mate successfully when between 1 and 2 years old; most males become potential breeders by their second winter.

Density estimates vary considerably depending on various habitat types and relative prey density (McCord and Cardoza 1982). Rucker et al. (1989) conducted a two year study of bobcat ecology in the Ouachita Mountains and found the minimum density to average one bobcat/9.6 sq km (one bobcat/6 sq mi). While these estimates were lower than some in the southeastern United States, they were similar to those reported in the Ozark Mountains of southwestern Missouri—one bobcat/10–15 sq km (Hamilton 1982) and the Ouachita Mountains in Oklahoma—one bobcat/11 sq km (Rolley 1985).

Rucker et al. (1989) reported home ranges of 64.2 sq km (39.9 sq mi) for an adult male and an average of 24.5 sq km (15.2 sq mi). Home ranges varied in size in different seasons, but the animals remained in their general area throughout the study. These home range sizes fall within those reported in other studies (McCord and Cardoza 1982).

IMPORTANCE AND/OR MANAGEMENT Bobcats sometimes kill domestic poultry but generally render a service to farmers by reducing rabbit and rodent populations. The meat of the bobcat is quite edible, and this cat has provided a tasty meal to many hunters.

Historically, the bobcat in Arkansas was considered a predator with no closed season. In 1968, bobcats, together with coyotes and red wolves, were classed as furbearers even though there was not a closed season on these mammals. This was modified in 1973, when bobcats could be taken during specified hunting seasons. Beginning in 1978, bobcats could only be taken during the regular furbearer season.

The total value and number of bobcat pelts sold varied considerably between 1942 and 1984. However, 89% of the pelts were harvested after 1970, reflecting the increased value of bobcat in markets influenced by the international trade in felids. Regionally, bobcat harvests have been slightly higher in the Ozark Mountains and the Mississippi Delta (31% and 28%, respectively) and evenly balanced in the Ouachita Mountains and the West Gulf Coastal Plain (21% and 20%, respectively) (Peck et al. 1985).

Two subspecies of the bobcat occur in Arkansas. The race *F. r. floridanus* occurs over most of the Gulf Coastal Plain (Peterson and Downing 1952), and the race *F. r. rufus* occurs in the Interior Highlands (Hall 1981). Presumably the races intergrade through the foothills of the Ozarks and the Ouachita Mountains.

SELECTED REFERENCES
Crowe (1975); Fritts and Sealander (1978a, 1978b); Hall (1981); Hamilton (1982); McCord and Cardoza (1982); Peck et al. (1985); Peterson and Downing (1952); Rolley (1985); Rollings (1945); Rucker et al. (1985, 1989); Tumlison (1983).

Order Perissodactyla *Odd-toed Ungulates*

The term "ungulate" has no taxonomic status but refers to all hoofed mammals. Ungulates are typically herbivorous and are adapted to rapid cursorial locomotion. Among the ungulates are some of the most graceful and beautiful mammals, and also some that are in grave danger of extinction.

Members of the Order Perissodactyla have an odd number of hoofed toes on each foot. The central (third) toe is much larger than the others and carries most of the animal's weight; this condition is termed *mesaxonic.* The smaller, lateral toes may or may not be present.

There are no native living members of this order in Arkansas. The order includes horses, rhinoceroses, and tapirs. Skulls of the familiar domestic horse of Old World origin are sometimes found in the field, and for this reason the order is included in this guide. Identifying characteristics of the skull and teeth are included in the key to orders.

Horses and tapirs were found in Arkansas during Pleistocene times but became extinct long before the arrival of white men in North America. The Andean tapir (*Tapirus terrestris*), which is still living in South America, was once an inhabitant of Arkansas and is discussed in the section dealing with prehistoric mammals.

Order Artiodactyla   *Even-toed Ungulates*

The artiodactyls (pigs, camels, deer, antelope, cattle, and their kin) far overshadow the perissodactyls, both in diversity and numbers. In mammals of this order, the third and fourth toes of each foot have a large, hard hoof, and the main axis of the foot passes between these toes; this condition is referred to as *paraxonic*. The other toes are absent or greatly reduced in size. All native members of the order lack upper incisor teeth.

When Arkansas was first settled by white men, the native mammal fauna included buffalo, elk, and white-tailed deer. Buffalo and elk were exterminated in the state during the early part of the nineteenth century (elk reintroductions were discussed under "Extirpated Recent Mammals of Arkansas").

Several well-known domestic species of artiodactyls are found in Arkansas, for which keys to whole animals are not needed. Skulls of these species often are found in fields or woods and frequently mistaken for wild species. Therefore, the skull key includes both wild and domesticated species of the order which occur in Arkansas.

WHOLE ANIMALS

1a. Size large, more than 1.2 m (4 ft) high at shoulders; tail straw-colored . . . . *Cervus elaphus*, Wapiti or Elk

1b. Size smaller, less than 1.2 m (4 ft) high at shoulders; tail brown above, white below . . . . *Odocoileus virginianus*, White-tailed Deer

SKULLS

1. Front teeth present in upper jaw; canine teeth present in upper and lower jaw, triangular in cross section; eye sockets incompletely encircled by bone (FAMILY SUIDAE, pigs) . . . . *Sus scrofa*, Feral Pig

   Front teeth absent in upper jaw; upper canine teeth present or absent; eye sockets completely encircled by bone 2

2. Skull with large space in front of each eye socket exposing inner bones (FAMILY CERVIDAE, cervids) 3

   Skull without space in front of each eye socket (FAMILY BOVIDAE, bovids) 4

3. Knob-like canine teeth present on each side of upper jaw; length of upper cheek tooth row more than 110 mm (4.3 in) . . . . *Cervus elaphus*, Wapiti or Elk

   Upper canine teeth normally absent; length of upper cheek tooth row less than 110 mm (4.3 in) . . . . *Odocoileus virginianus*, White-tailed Deer

4. Skull length more than 350 mm (13.8 in) 5

   Skull length less than 350 mm (13.8 in) (usually less than 315 mm [12.4 in]) 6

5. Skull elongated viewed from above; prominent ridge on top of skull between horns or horn cores . . . . *Bos taurus*, Domestic Cow

   Skull roughly triangular viewed from above; no prominent ridge on top of skull between horns or horn cores . . . . *Bison bison*, Bison

6. Deep, pit-like depression in front of each eye socket; no groove on top of skull; horns usually absent, but if present horns (or horn cores) curved downward and outward . . . . *Ovis aries*, Domestic Sheep

Deep, pit-like depression not present in front of each eye socket; groove on top of skull forming a "V" or "U" on forehead; horns (or horn cores) usually present, nearly parallel, and directed backward. . . . . *Capra hircus*, Domestic Goat

FAMILY SUIDAE

PIGS

Characteristics of this family are: limbs with four toes on each foot (lateral toes not touching ground); elongated, mobile snout with an expanded, nearly flat terminal surface and terminal nostrils; upper canine teeth recurved and visible externally as tusks.

This family is represented in Arkansas by the domestic pig, which exists in small numbers in a wild state.

Feral Pig

Sus scrofa

Feral pigs need little description since their appearance is quite similar to that of the domestic pig, but they are leaner and rangier. At one time it was a common practice in Arkansas to turn pigs loose in the fields and woods to feed upon acorns, roots, tubers, amphibians, reptiles, rodents, bird eggs, and other food. After the pigs were allowed to fatten through the spring and summer, they were rounded up in the fall and claimed by their owners according to brands or markings. Some of these free-ranging pigs reverted to a wild or semi-wild state. With the passage of a law prohibiting use of open range in Arkansas, the feral or razorback hog population underwent a marked decline.

A few feral hogs still range through the national forests, bottomland forests, and swamps in the state. These hogs may travel in bands of six or more and are sometimes hunted for sport and meat. The Arkansas Game and Fish Commission requires a valid hunting license but otherwise does not regulate hunting of feral pigs.

Feral pigs have been blamed by sportsmen and nature lovers for the extinction of the ruffed grouse and wild turkey in Arkansas through destruction of nests and eggs. In recent years, these two species have been successfully restocked in the Ozark and Ouachita mountains.

FAMILY CERVIDAE

CERVIDS

Members of this family include the elk, deer, caribou, and moose. They occur throughout the New World, Europe, Asia, and northwestern Africa; they have been widely introduced in other areas.

Probably the most widely recognized characteristic of this family are antlers. Antlers are bony outgrowths on the skull of cervid males, except for caribou, and are shed annually. They may attain massive size and have intricate designs. Other characteristics of the family are: Upper incisors absent; upper canines may be present but are generally reduced; lower canines are incisor-like; ears large; muzzle long; tail short or medium-sized; lateral hooves nearly always present on all feet; gall bladder absent.

White-tailed Deer

Odocoileus virginianus

NAME *Odocoileus* comes from two Greek words, *odous*, meaning "tooth," and *koilos*, meaning "hollow;" referring to the prominent depressions in the molar teeth. The specific name, *virginianus*, is the Latinized meaning "of Virginia," for the locality where the species was first named.

IDENTIFICATION AND DESCRIPTION The white-tailed deer is a large, even-toed hoofed mammal with large ears and a tail that is long, bushy, and conspicuously white beneath. It has long legs. Large, conspicuous antlers in the male have the main beams directed forward and bearing unforked tines. Glands include oval metatarsal glands on the outside of the lower hind legs, tarsal glands on the inside of the hind legs at the hock (marked by bands or tufts of white hair), and pedal glands between the two main toes on all four feet. The pelage is gray or grayish brown above (reddish brown in summer) and white below. The throat and inside of the legs are white. Males are larger than females.

MEASUREMENTS AND DENTAL FORMULA

Total Length:	1600–2150 mm (63.0–84.6 in)
Tail Length:	230–360 mm (9.1–14.2 in)
Hind Foot:	400–500 mm (15.7–19.7 in)
Ear:	140–230 mm (5.5–9.1 in)
Height at Shoulder:	660–1066 mm (26.0–42.0 in)
Skull Length:	230–320 mm (9.1–12.6 in)
Weight:	40–136 kg (88.2–300.0 lb)
Dental Formula:	I 0/3, C 0/1, P 3/3, M 3/3 = 32

Odocoileus virginianus, White-tailed Deer. *Phil A. Dotson*

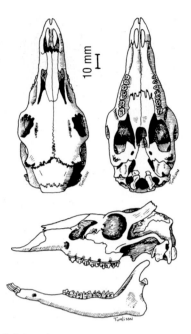

Skull of *Odocoileus virginianus*

ARKANSAS DISTRIBUTION AND ABUNDANCE
The white-tailed deer occurs statewide and is abundant.

LIFE HISTORY   The white-tailed deer is an inhabitant of forest edges, open woodland, brushland, and second-growth deciduous forest succession. Cutover and burned-over areas with a dense growth of young hardwoods, shrubs, and herbs providing ample browse are favored habitat. Deer are less common in heavily forested areas that shade out young trees, shrubs, and herbs upon which they depend for food.

In northwestern Arkansas, white-tailed deer are most active in midmorning, mid-afternoon, and early evening (Cartwright 1975). In southeastern Arkansas, deer are active in early evening and from dawn to about 9 AM but are less active during midmorning than in northern Arkansas (Pledger 1975). Greater activity is shown during the early stages of gestation, and some shifts in time of greatest activity occur during the breeding and fawning seasons and between sexes. Deer usually seek cover and bed down during late afternoon and in the middle of the night.

White-tailed deer are mainly browsers, feeding upon leaves, twigs, and shoots of various kinds of trees and shrubs, but they also graze upon grass and broad-leaved herbs. Acorns are important food in autumn, and fruits, berries, and mushrooms are relished when available. The white-tailed deer is one of the most adaptable animals in the world. This adaptability is reflected in the diversity of foods that it eats. It has been called both a "grazer" and a "browser" (Hesselton and Hesselton 1982).

White-tailed deer are ruminants; that is, they have four chambers through which food passes before it enters the small intestine. The first three chambers—the rumen, reticulum, and omasum—are actually modifications of the esophagus. The fourth chamber, the abomasum, is the true stomach. By passing through these various chambers, the food is acted on by bacteria and other microorganisms, which greatly enhance the digestion process; the microorganisms also synthesize certain essential amino acids and vitamins needed by the deer. In addition, food is regurgitated from the rumen

Distribution of the white-tailed deer (*Odocoileus virginianus*)

A deer rub. Male deer use trees and shrubs to rub the velvet from their antlers and to let other male deer know of their presence. *Keith Sutton*

and rechewed, further increasing mechanical breakdown.

Individual deer have limited home ranges; males generally have larger ranges than females. In the Ozark Mountains, home ranges of buck deer vary from 253 to 1652 ha (625–4082 acres) and average between 520 and 781 ha (1284–1930 acres); does have smaller home ranges which vary from 31 to 797 ha (77–1970 acres) and average between 278 and 560 ha (690–1385 acres) (Cartwright 1975). In the coastal plain of southeastern Arkansas, buck home ranges varied from 544 to 1610 ha (1350–3980 acres) and averaged 1077 ha (2661 acres); home ranges of does varied from 29 to 748 ha (72–1850 acres) and averaged 427 ha (1055 acres) (Pledger 1975).

The breeding season of Arkansas white-tails ranges from late September through February. The peak breeding season in northern Arkan-

sas is from October through mid-November—about three weeks earlier than in the southern part of the state (Wilson and Sealander 1971). Fawns are born from late March through June or later, after a gestation period ranging from 195 to 212 days. Young does generally produce a single fawn, but older does often give birth to twins and sometimes to triplets. Fawns are weaned when 3–4 months old and reach sexual maturity in 1 to 1.5 years. Some doe fawns breed in their first winter.

Most deer harvested in Arkansas fall in the 2.5- 3.5-year age class, although in some areas of the state the average age of harvested bucks does not exceed 1.5 years. A few deer in the wild survive for as long as 15 years, but most do not survive much more than 7–8 years (Dahlem 1975).

The antlers of the white-tailed deer are among its most fascinating characteristics. These are

Cedar tree with deer rub. The size of this rub would indicate a large buck. *Keith Sutton*

deciduous bony structures that grow out from permanent pedicles of the frontal bones. Antlers are covered with skin and some hair (the velvet) only as they grow and are continuous with the skull. This skin, which is highly vascularized, provides nourishment to the bone as it grows. Antlers are grown annually and shed following the breeding season, or rut. New antler growth starts in April due to an increased level of male hormones stimulated by increasing daylight. As spring and summer pass, increased levels of testosterone stimulate further antler growth as well as growth of the testes. This culminates in the rut, which usually peaks in November. Prior to the rut, antler growth ceases, the velvet membrane dries up and splits, and this material is often rubbed off on small trees and bushes. These occurrences prepare the

antlers for becoming sparring weapons, which are used in rutting behavior. Following the rut, antlers are shed, usually by mid-January (Hesselton and Hesselton 1982). Contrary to popular vernacular terms, antlers are not horns; horns are permanent bony outgrowths covered by a hard sheath.

IMPORTANCE AND/OR MANAGEMENT White-tailed deer were present in substantial numbers in Arkansas until the turn of the century when expansion of agricultural, lumbering, and livestock production in the state, as well as widespread slaughter by market hunters, contributed to a rapid decline in numbers (Donaldson et al. 1951; Holder 1951). In most areas of the state, deer became extinct between 1910 and 1920. Scattered bands remained in some counties, and a low point of less than 500 head was reached in 1927–30, when federal and state refuge systems were established in the state. A population upturn then began which was accelerated by importations of deer from Wisconsin, Louisiana, North Carolina, and Texas by the Arkansas Game and Fish Commission and by sportsmen's organizations. An extensive restocking program involving movement of deer from areas of deer concentration to unoccupied range was carried on for more than a decade.

At present, the deer herd in the state is extremely numerous. During the 1987–88 hunting season, 103,511 deer were killed. In addition, there is no way of knowing how many thousands more were killed illegally by poachers. Some areas of the state, especially the coastal plain of south Arkansas, have become overpopulated to the point that large die-offs have occurred from epizootic hemorrhagic disease, bluetongue, parasitic infections, and other causes. Such die-offs, as well as hunting, tend to restore the balance between deer numbers and available habitat and usually reduce the incidence of disease and parasitic infections to a normal level.

Recently, Karlin et al. (1989) examined the genetic structure of the deer herd in the West Gulf Coastal Plain and the southern Mississippi

Delta. They found that genetic heterozygosity was depressed, particularly in the West Gulf Coastal Plain. Depressed heterozygosity means that genetic variation has decreased. Other researchers have demonstrated that, among other things, decreased genetic variation results in poorer reproduction, depressed growth and weight of fawns, smaller deer, and poorer antler growth (Johns et al. 1977; Smith et al. 1982). 1977; Smith et al. 1982).

The subspecies originally present in the state was *O. v. macrourus*. However, due to transplantations from other states followed by interbreeding, it is not possible at present to assign Arkansas white-tails to any specific race.

SELECTED REFERENCES
Holder (1951); Cartwright (1975); Dahlem (1975); Donaldson et al. (1951); Hesselton and Hesselton (1982); Johns et al. (1977); Karlin et al. (1989); Pledger (1975); Smith et al. (1982); Wilson and Sealander (1971).

Species of Unverified Occurrence

In addition to the 71 naturally occurring wild mammals, the reintroduced elk, the extirpated bison, the extinct red wolf, and the several domestic species, there are several species which have either not yet been observed in the state or for which a presumably accidental record exists. These species are listed here because they may possibly exist in Arkansas in low numbers or may extend their ranges into the state. All have ranges that closely approach the borders of Arkansas.

THIRTEEN-LINED GROUND SQUIRREL
Spermophilus tridecemlineatus

This species may occur in prairie areas in extreme northwestern Arkansas. S. C. Dellinger (personal communication) claimed that he observed this species on at least two occasions in Benton and Washington counties in the early 1930s. Nearby records are from northeastern Oklahoma and southwestern Missouri. The species was present in northeastern Arkansas from about A.D. 900–1300, as evidenced by skeletal remains in an archaeological site (Guilday and Parmalee 1971).

FRANKLIN'S GROUND SQUIRREL
Spermophilus franklinii

J. D. Black (*in litt.* 1951) reported that he observed this squirrel twice near Huntsville, Madison County, at close range and obtained a glimpse of one near Goshen, Washington County. The nearest recent records are from the southeastern corner of Kansas.

HISPID POCKET MOUSE
Perognathus hispidus

Hall (1981) shows the range of this species in southeastern Oklahoma and northeastern Texas as near the extreme southwestern corner of Arkansas in the Red River Valley of Texas. However, Lowery (1974) reported only seven specimens from five localities in west central Louisiana. None of the records is very near Arkansas.

Meadow Jumping Mouse
Zapus hudsonius

Bryan P. Glass collected this species from Adair County, Oklahoma, which lies adjacent to Crawford and Washington counties on the western edge of Arkansas. The species range also closely approaches the border of Arkansas in extreme northeastern Arkansas (Hall 1981; Severinghaus and Beaseley 1973) near the Missouri boot heel. Presumably this mouse may be discovered at some time in northeastern or northwestern Arkansas.

Porcupine
Erethizon dorsatum

Clark (1985) reported on a female porcupine that was killed near the town of Ben Lomond in Sevier County. It is thought that this animal may have rafted down the Red River into Arkansas. Dodge (1982) and Hall (1981) report that the range of the porcupine extends into central Texas and Oklahoma.

GLOSSARY

The following list of terms includes those often used in the descriptions or discussions of mammals. Not all of the entries have been used in the foregoing text; likewise, the list is not all-inclusive. Where a term has several meanings, only the one applying to mammals is used. The glossary from Jones and Birney (1988) was used extensively.

AESTIVATION. Torpidity in summer.

AGOUTI HAIR. Hair with alternate pale and dark bands of color.

ALBINO. An animal lacking all external pigmentation.

ALLOPATRIC. Pertaining to two or more populations that occupy disjunct or nonoverlapping geographic areas.

ALTRICIAL. Pertaining to young that are blind, frequently naked, and entirely dependent on parental care at birth; opposed to precocial.

ALVEOLUS (pl. alveoli). A pit or socket in the jaw bone which receives the root or roots of a tooth.

ANNULATION. A ring or ring-shaped structure.

ANTLER. A bony growth on the head of a cervid which is shed annually.

ARBOREAL. Pertaining to activity in trees.

AUDITORY BULLA (pl. bullae). A hollow, rounded bony capsule at the base of the braincase which encloses the bones of the inner ear.

AUDITORY MEATUS. A tube-like passage leading from the outer ear to the ear drum.

BACULUM. Sesamoid bone (*os penis*) in penis of males of certain mammalian groups.

BEAM. Main trunk of antler.

BICOLORED. Of two colors; contrasting colors.

BICUSPID. A tooth with two major cusps.

BIFID. A tooth with two cusps.

BIFURCATE. Divided into two branches.

BIPEDAL. Pertaining to locomotion on two legs.

BLASTOCYST. In embryonic development of mammals, a ball of cells produced by repeated division (cleavage) of fertilized egg; stage of implantation in uterine wall.

BOREAL. Northern, of high latitudes.

BRAINCASE. A part of the skull enclosing the brain.

BUCCAL. Pertaining to cheek.

BUNODONT. Low-crowned, rectangular grinding teeth, typical of omnivores.

CALCAR. In bats, a bony extension from the heel

which partially supports the tail membrane.

CANINE or CANINE TOOTH. The tooth situated between the front cutting teeth (incisors) and the first cheek tooth (premolar). Also referred to as the "eyetooth."

CARNASSIAL. Specially adapted shearing or cutting teeth in carnivores; the last premolar in the upper jaw and the first molar in the lower jaw.

CARNIVOROUS. Meat-eating; feeding on other animals.

CARPAL. Any one of group of bones in the wrist region, distal to the radius and ulna and proximal to the metacarpals.

CAUDAL. Pertaining to tail or toward tail (caudad).

CAVERNICOLOUS. Living in caves (or mines).

CECUM. A blind pouch or diverticulum near the junction of the small and large intestine.

CHEEK TEETH. The premolar and molar teeth.

CLAVICLE. The collar bone.

CLAW. Sheath of keratin on digits; usually long, curved, and sharply pointed.

CLINE. Gradual change in morphological character through a series of interbreeding populations; character gradient.

COPROPHAGY. Feeding on feces.

COSMOPOLITAN. Common to all the world; not local or limited, but widely distributed.

CRANIAL. Pertaining to the skull enclosing the brain.

CRANIUM. The braincase or part of the skull enclosing the brain.

CREPUSCULAR. Pertaining to periods of dawn and dusk (twilight); active by twilight.

CROWN. Part of the tooth not covered by gum tissue in the living animal.

CURSORIAL. Pertaining to running; running locomotion.

CUSP. A point or prominence on the crown of a tooth.

DECIDUOUS DENTITION. Juvenile or "milk" teeth, those that appear first in lifetime of a mammal, consisting of incisors, canine, and premolars; generally replaced by adult dentition.

DELAYED IMPLANTATION. Postponement of embedding of blastocyst (embryo) in uterine wall for several days, weeks, or months.

DENTAL FORMULA (pl. formulae). A way of expressing the number and kinds of teeth of mammals. The kinds of teeth are indicated by the abbreviations I (incisor), C (canine), P or PM (premolar), and M (molar). The number in the numerator represents the number of teeth in one side of the upper jaw and the denominator represents the number of teeth in one side of the lower jaw.

DENTARY BONE. One of two bones that make up the lower jaw of mammals.

DENTITION. Collectively, the teeth of a mammal.

DEWCLAW. Vestigial digit on foot.

DEWLAP. Pendulous fold of skin under neck.

DIASTEMA. A distinct space between adjacent teeth. For example, the space between the incisor and cheek teeth in species lacking canine teeth.

DICHROMATISM. Having two distinct color phases.

DIGITIGRADE. Walking on the toes with the wrist and ankle bones held off the ground, as in dogs or cats.

DISTAL. Away from base or point of attachment, or from any named reference point; opposed to proximal.

DIURNAL. Active by day; opposed to nocturnal.

DORSAL. Pertaining to the back of an animal; opposed to ventral.

ECTOPARASITE. Parasite living on and feeding from external surface of an animal (e.g., fleas, lice, ticks).

ENAMEL. Hard outer layer of tooth consisting of calcareous compounds and a small amount of organic matrix.

ENDEMIC. Native to a particular region and living nowhere else.

ENDOPARASITE. Parasite living within a host (e.g., tapeworm, fluke, roundworm).

EPIPHYSIS. Secondary growth center near end of long bone.

ESTROUS CYCLE. Recurring growth and development of uterine lining, culminating in a time when the female is sexually receptive to the male.

ESTRUS. Stage of estrous cycle when female is sexually receptive to male; "heat."

EXTIRPATION. Extinction, usually specific to a certain geographic area.

FAMILIAL NAME. Name applying to a group of organisms of family rank among animals, ending in -idae (names of subfamilies end in -inae).

FECES. Excrement.

FECUNDITY. Rate of producing offspring; fertility.

FENESTRATE. Having openings.

FERAL. Domestic animal that has reverted to wild state.

FETUS. Embryo in later stages of development (still in uterus).

FIBULA. The outer shinbone or smaller of the two leg bones located on the side of the leg. This bone is sometimes fused with the tibia.

FLANK. Sides of animal between ribs and hips.

FORAMEN (pl. foramina). An opening in the skull through which nerves or blood vessels pass.

FORAMEN MAGNUM. The large opening at the back of the skull through which the spinal cord passes.

FOSSA. Pit or depression in bone.

FOSSORIAL. Pertaining to life underground.

GESTATION PERIOD. The period of pregnancy; measured from conception to delivery or birth of the young. Where delayed implantation is involved, this may be measured from the time of implantation of the fertilized egg in the uterus until birth.

GRANIVOROUS. Subsisting on diet of grains and seeds.

GRAVID. Pregnant.

GUANO. Excrement of bats or birds.

GUARD HAIRS. The coarser, longer hairs that project beyond and protect the shorter and finer underfur.

HALLUX. First (most medial) digit of hind foot.

HERBIVORE. Animal that consumes plant material as main component of its diet.

HETERODONT. Dentition differentiated into incisor, canine, premolar, and molar teeth.

HIBERNACULUM. Shelter in which animal hibernates.

HIBERNATE. To pass the winter in an inactive (torpid or dormant) state.

HOLARCTIC. North America and temperate Eurasia considered together as one zoogeographical realm.

HOME RANGE. The area on which a mammal carries out its normal activities.

HOOF. The horny covering which protects the front end of the digit and supports the weight of the mammal in members of the orders Perissodactyla and Artiodactyla.

HORN. The hollow sheath covering an outgrowth of bone from the skull.

HORN CORE. The permanent bony spike which serves as a base for a permanent horn. It normally is a projection from the frontal bone.

HYPSODONT. Pertaining to particularly high-crowned tooth; such teeth have shallow roots.

IMPLANTATION. Process by which blastocyst embeds in uterine lining.

INCISOR or INCISOR TEETH. Tooth or teeth set in the anteriormost part of the lower jaw and in the premaxillary bone of the upper jaw; front teeth.

INFRAORBITAL APERTURE or INFRAORBITAL FORAMEN. A passage or opening in the skull in front of the eye socket to the side of the rostrum.

INGUINAL. Pertaining to or in the region of the groin.

INSECTIVORE. Animal that primarily eats insects.

INTERFEMORAL MEMBRANE. The fold of skin in a bat which stretches from the hind legs to the tail; also called the tail membrane or uropatagium.

INTERGRADATION. To merge gradually, one into another, as different species through evolution.

INTERORBITAL CONSTRICTION. The least distance across the top of the skull between the eye sockets.

INTERORBITAL REGION. The area on top of the skull between the eye sockets.

INTERPARIETAL. An unpaired bone which lies between the parietal bones at the top and back of the skull.

INTERSPECIFIC. Between or among species.

INTRASPECIFIC. Within a species.

KARYOTYPE. Morphological description of chromosomes of a cell, including size, shape, position of centromere, and number.

KEEL. Ridge that provides expanded surface for attachment.

KERATIN. Tough, fibrous protein, especially abundant in epidermis and epidermal derivatives.

LABIAL. Pertaining to the lips.

LACTATION. The secretion of milk by the mammary gland.

LATERAL. At or near the side away from the midline.

LINGUAL. Pertaining to the tongue.

LITTER. Two or more young delivered at one birth by a female mammal.

LOPH. A transverse ridge of enamel across the grinding surface of a tooth, as in rodents.

MAMMARY GLAND or MAMMA (pl. mammae). Milk-producing gland.

MANDIBLE. Lower jaw; in mammals composed single pair of bones, the dentaries.

MARSUPIUM. An abdominal pouch formed by a fold of skin that encloses the mammary glands in marsupials and serves as an incubation chamber.

MASTICATE. To chew.

MAXILLA (pl. maxillae) or MAXILLARY BONE. One of a pair of bones which bear the upper canine, premolar, and molar teeth.

MEDIAL. Situated in or occurring in the midline or middle.

MEDIAN CREST or SAGITTAL CREST. A raised ridge of bone on top of and extending from front to back of the braincase in the midline.

MELANISTIC. Having more than the normal amount of dark pigment; black or blackish.

MESIC. Pertaining to habitats or areas with available water or moisture; moderately moist or humid.

METACARPALS. Bones of forefoot exclusive of phalanges.

METATARSALS. Bones of hindfoot exclusive of phalanges.

METATARSAL GLAND. A gland located on the inside of the hind leg of a deer between the toes and heel.

MOLAR or MOLAR TOOTH. One of the posteriormost or back teeth of the upper and lower jaw, often adapted for grinding, that is not preceded by a temporary (deciduous) or "milk" tooth.

MOLT. Process by which hair is shed and replaced.

MONESTROUS. Having a single estrous cycle per year.

MONOTYPIC. Pertaining to taxon that contains only one immediately subordinate taxon (e.g., genus with only one species).

MUZZLE. Projecting snout.

NAPE. Back of neck.

NARES. Openings of nose.

NASAL or NASAL BONE. One of a pair of bones on the top of the skull that form the roof of the nasal passage.

NATAL. Pertaining to birth.

NEONATAL. Newborn.

NOCTURNAL. Active by night; opposed to diurnal.

NOMINATE. Of a subordinate taxon (subspecies, subgenus, etc.) which contains the type of the subdivided higher taxon and bears the same name.

NOSEPAD. The bare part of the nose of a mammal.

NOTCH OF EAR. An indentation at the lower portion of the external ear or pinna.

OCCIPITAL. Pertaining to the part of the skull surrounding the foramen magnum.

OCCIPITAL CREST. Ridges which extend to the side from the median crest at the back of the braincase.

OCCLUSAL. Pertaining to contact surfaces of upper and lower teeth.

OMNIVOROUS. Eating both plant and animal food.

ORBIT. The bony socket in the skull in which the eyeball is situated.

ORDINAL NAME. Name applying to an order of organisms.

OS CLITORIDIS. Small sesamoid bone in clitoris of females of some mammalian species; homologous to baculum in males.

PALATE. The bony roof of the mouth.

PALATINES. Paired bones forming the posterior part of the hard palate.

PALATINE SLITS or ANTERIOR PALATINE FORAMINA. Paired perforations at the anterior end of the hard palate where the premaxillary and maxillary bones join.

PAPILLA. Any blunt, rounded, or nipple-shaped projection.

PARAPATRIC. Pertaining to two or more populations that occupy locally contiguous geographic areas in which they are ecologically isolated.

PARTURITION. The act of giving birth.

PATAGIUM. Web of skin; in bats, the wing membrane.

PATRONYM. Scientific name based on name of person or persons.

PECTORAL. Pertaining to the chest.

PEDAL GLAND. A gland located on the hind foot of a deer between toes 3 and 4.

PELAGE. Collectively, all the hairs on a mammal.

PELVIC. Pertaining to the region of the hip girdle.

PENCILLED. Ending of a mammal's tail in a tuft of fur or hair (like a pencil).

PHALANGES. Bones of fingers and toes, distal to metacarpals and metatarsals.

PINNA. Externally projecting part of ear.

PLACENTA. Structure formed by maternal and fetal tissues across which materials are exchanged between the mother and fetus.

PLACENTAL SCAR. Scar that remains on uterine wall after deciduate placenta detaches at parturition.

PLANTIGRADE. Walking or standing on the sole of the foot with the heel touching the ground, as in bears and humans.

POLLEX. Thumb; most medial digit on hand.

POLYESTROUS. Having more than one estrous cycle per year.

POSTERIOR. Pertaining to or toward rear end.

POSTERIOR PALATINE FORAMINA. Paired perforations on the posterior part of the hard palate.

POSTORBITAL PROCESS. A process projecting out from the top of the frontal bone of the skull and forming a part of the posterior border of the eye socket.

POSTPARTUM ESTRUS. Ability of female to become sexually receptive to male directly after giving birth.

PRECOCIAL. Pertaining to young that are born at a relatively advanced stage, capable of movement shortly after birth, and usually capable of some feeding without parental assistance.

PREHENSILE. Adapted for grasping by curling or wrapping around.

PREMAXILLA (pl. premaxillae). One of a pair of bones in the front of the upper jaw that bear the incisor teeth.

PREMAXILLARY BONES. Bones in the upper jaw that bear the incisor teeth.

PREMOLAR or **PREMOLAR TOOTH.** A tooth or teeth on each side of the upper and lower jaw which is preceded by deciduous or "milk" teeth. In the upper jaw, these teeth are confined to the maxillary bone. When canine teeth are present, premolars are behind these teeth. They are in front of the molars.

PRISM. Sharply-angled area of dentine surrounded by enamel on the grinding surface of cheek teeth, as in rodents; geometric-shaped area on grinding surface of tooth.

PROGENY. Offspring.

PROXIMAL. Situated toward or near a point of reference or attachment; opposed to distal.

RACE. Informal name for subspecies.

RANGE. Geographic area inhabited by a particular taxon.

RECURVED. Curved downward and backward.

REFUGIUM. Geographic area to which species retreats in times of stress.

REGISTER. The imprint of a mammal's foot or feet in mud, sand, or snow.

RETRACTILE. Capable of being drawn back or in, as in the claws of cats.

RIPARIAN. Referring to flood plains or valleys of watercourses.

ROOT. Portion of tooth that lies below gum and fills alveolus.

ROOTED TOOTH. Tooth with definite growth; not evergrowing.

ROOTLESS TOOTH. Tooth that is evergrowing, having a continuously open root canal.

ROSTRUM. The anteriorly projecting part of the skull in front of the eye sockets; the nose or snout muzzle.

RUMEN. First "stomach" of ruminant animals; modification of the esophagus.

RUMINANT. Any of the Artiodactyls that possess a rumen; cud-chewing.

RUT. Season of sexual activity when mating occurs, particularly in deer and other Artiodactyls.

SAGITTAL CREST. A median, longitudinal raised ridge of bone on top of the braincase.

SALTATORY. Adapted for leaping; usually with elongated and unusually well-developed hind legs.

SCAPULAR. Pertaining to the shoulder blade or shoulder region.

SCAT. A dropping of excrement.

SEXUAL DIMORPHISM. Difference in sexual or other (secondary sexual, such as size) features between males and females of species.

SPECIES. Group of naturally or potentially interbreeding populations reproductively isolated (or mostly so) from other such groups.

SUBSPECIES. Relatively uniform and genetically distinctive population of a species that represents a separately or recently evolved lineage with its own evolutionary tendencies, definite geographic range, and actual or potential zone of intergradation with another such group or groups.

SUPRAORBITAL PROCESS. A process on the top rim of each eye socket.

SUPRAORBITAL RIDGE. A beadlike ridge bordering the top of the eye socket.

SYMPATRIC. Pertaining to two or more populations that occupy overlapping geographic areas.

TARSAL GLAND. A gland on the inside of the hind leg of a deer, slightly below the hock or ankle.

TAXON. Any group distinctive from other groups at the same taxonomic level.

TEAT. Protuberance of a mammary gland in which numerous small ducts empty into a common collecting structure that in turn opens to the exterior through one or few pores.

TEMPERATE. As a climatic term, referring to middle latitudes between boreal and tropical regions.

TEMPORAL RIDGES. Ridges which transverse the top or sides of the braincase, usually arise near the postorbital processes and converge posteriorly to form the median or sagittal crest.

TERRITORY. Portion of home range that an individual defends against members of the same and sometimes different species.

TIBIA. The shin or large bone of the lower leg.

TINE. Spike on antler.

TORPOR. A state of inactivity or dormancy accompanied by a reduction in heart rate, body temperature, and metabolism.

TRAGUS. In bats a leathery projection of skin near the bottom of the external ear opening.

TRIFID. Tooth with three points or cusps.

TUBERCLE. A small knotlike prominence which may be either hard or soft.

TUBERCULATED. In teeth, used synonymously with cusps; raised appearance on the surface of a bone or tooth.

TUSK. An enlarged and elongated tooth, usually a modified incisor or canine tooth.

TYMPANIC BULLA (pl. bullae). *See* auditory bulla.

TYPE SPECIMEN. Specimen (holotype) on which a species or subspecies name is based.

UNDERFUR. Short hairs of mammal that serve primarily as insulation.

UNGULIGRADE. Walking on tips of toes; usually toes surrounded by a hoof, as in horses and cows.

UNICUSPID. A tooth with a single cusp.

VALVULAR. Capable of being closed, as in a valvular nostril.

VENTRAL. Pertaining to the under or lower surface; opposed to dorsal.

VERNACULAR NAME. Common name; opposed to scientific name.

VERNAL. Seasonal term pertaining to spring.

VIBRISSAE. Long, stiff hairs that serve primarily as tactile receptors.

VOLANT. Able to fly.

VULVA. External genitalia of female.

XERIC. Pertaining to dry habitats or areas.

ZYGOMATIC ARCH. The bony arch which borders the outside of the eye socket.

ZYGOMATIC BREADTH or **WIDTH.** The width of the skull across the zygomatic arches at the widest part.

APPENDIX A

The Mammalian Skull

GENERAL STRUCTURE

The bones and general structural features of the mammalian skull are relatively constant. Due to the wide variety of habits and habitats occupied, however, the size, shape, and modifications of the basic structure are highly variable. Knowledge of the skull is important because it gives clues to the many habits of the mammal in question, particularly its feeding habits. Furthermore, comparing cranial characteristics is an invaluable way of distinguishing many species. To acquaint the reader with various bones as well as with differences between mammals, the following figures illustrate a bobcat (*Felis rufus*), a member of the Order Carnivora, and the eastern woodrat (*Neotoma floridana*), a member of the Order Rodentia.

Features of a Carnivore (Bobcat) Skull

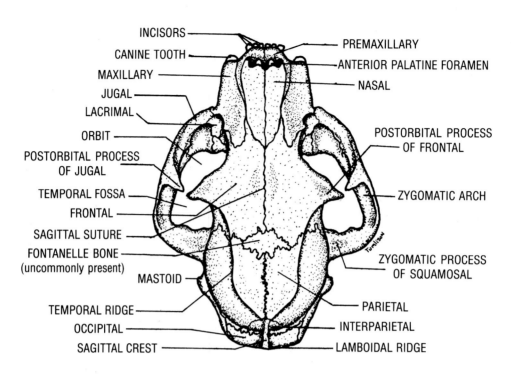

INCISORS — PREMAXILLARY
CANINE TOOTH — ANTERIOR PALATINE FORAMEN
MAXILLARY — NASAL
JUGAL
LACRIMAL
ORBIT — POSTORBITAL PROCESS OF FRONTAL
POSTORBITAL PROCESS OF JUGAL
TEMPORAL FOSSA — ZYGOMATIC ARCH
FRONTAL
SAGITTAL SUTURE
FONTANELLE BONE (uncommonly present) — ZYGOMATIC PROCESS OF SQUAMOSAL
MASTOID
TEMPORAL RIDGE — PARIETAL
OCCIPITAL — INTERPARIETAL
SAGITTAL CREST — LAMBOIDAL RIDGE

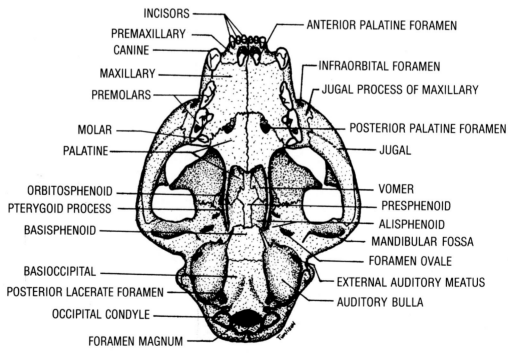

INCISORS — ANTERIOR PALATINE FORAMEN
PREMAXILLARY
CANINE — INFRAORBITAL FORAMEN
MAXILLARY — JUGAL PROCESS OF MAXILLARY
PREMOLARS
MOLAR — POSTERIOR PALATINE FORAMEN
PALATINE — JUGAL
ORBITOSPHENOID — VOMER
PTERYGOID PROCESS — PRESPHENOID
BASISPHENOID — ALISPHENOID
MANDIBULAR FOSSA
FORAMEN OVALE
BASIOCCIPITAL — EXTERNAL AUDITORY MEATUS
POSTERIOR LACERATE FORAMEN — AUDITORY BULLA
OCCIPITAL CONDYLE
FORAMEN MAGNUM

Features of a Carnivore (Bobcat) Jaw

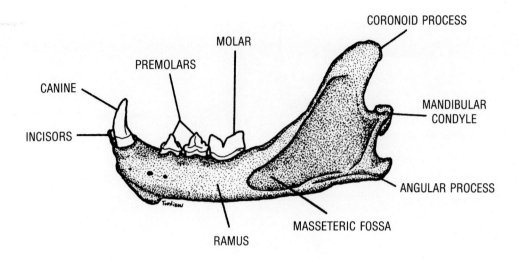

CORONOID PROCESS

MOLAR

PREMOLARS

CANINE

INCISORS

MANDIBULAR
CONDYLE

ANGULAR PROCESS

MASSETERIC FOSSA

RAMUS

Features of a Rodent (Eastern Woodrat) Jaw

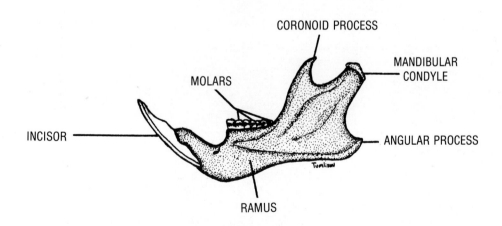

CORONOID PROCESS

MANDIBULAR
CONDYLE

MOLARS

INCISOR

ANGULAR PROCESS

RAMUS

Features of a Rodent (Eastern Woodrat) Skull

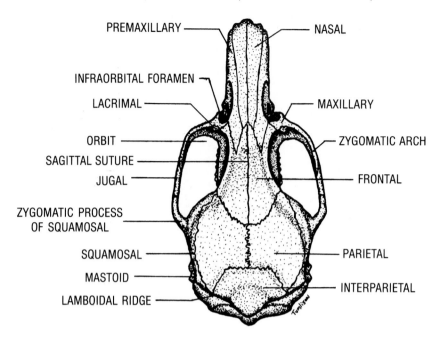

PREMAXILLARY — NASAL

INFRAORBITAL FORAMEN — MAXILLARY

LACRIMAL —

ORBIT — ZYGOMATIC ARCH

SAGITTAL SUTURE —

JUGAL — FRONTAL

ZYGOMATIC PROCESS OF SQUAMOSAL —

SQUAMOSAL — PARIETAL

MASTOID —

LAMBOIDAL RIDGE — INTERPARIETAL

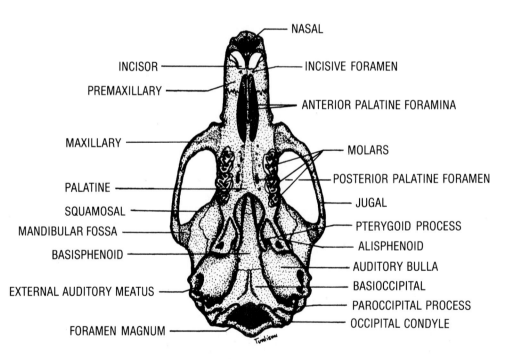

NASAL

INCISOR — INCISIVE FORAMEN

PREMAXILLARY — ANTERIOR PALATINE FORAMINA

MAXILLARY — MOLARS

PALATINE — POSTERIOR PALATINE FORAMEN

SQUAMOSAL — JUGAL

MANDIBULAR FOSSA — PTERYGOID PROCESS

BASISPHENOID — ALISPHENOID

AUDITORY BULLA

EXTERNAL AUDITORY MEATUS — BASIOCCIPITAL

PAROCCIPITAL PROCESS

OCCIPITAL CONDYLE

FORAMEN MAGNUM

MEASUREMENTS

A number of somewhat standardized measurements are used for illustrating variations in the mammalian skull. Since the skull is a complex structure it can vary in many ways; thus, different measurements are often used for different groups of mammals. Measurements are taken in a straight line between two points and are recorded in millimeters. In most cases, calipers of some type are used. Some of the most common measurements are identified below.

Basal length—From the anterior edge of the premaxillae to the anteriormost point on the lower border of the foramen magnum.

Condylobasal length—From the anterior edge of the premaxillae to the posteriormost projection of the occipital condyles.

Greatest length of skull—From the most anterior part of the rostrum (excluding teeth) to the most posterior point of the skull.

Breadth of braincase—Greatest width across the braincase posterior to the zygomatic arches.

Least interorbital breadth—Least distance dorsally between the orbits.

Postorbital constriction—Least distance across the top of the skull posterior to the postorbital process.

Zygomatic width—Greatest distance between the outer margins of the zygomatic arches.

Maxillary tooth row—Length from the anterior edge of the alveolus of the first tooth present in the maxillae to the posterior edge of the alveolus of the last tooth.

Palatal length—From the anterior edge of the premaxillae to the anteriormost point on the posterior edge of the palate.

Palatal width—Usually the width of the palate between alveoli of any specified tooth. Occasionally includes alveoli.

Tympanic bullae length and width—Greatest length and width of bulla.

Mandible length—Greatest length of the mandible usually excluding teeth.

Mandibular tooth row—Length from the anterior edge of the alveolus of the canine or first cheek tooth to the posterior edge of the alveolus of the last tooth. Incisors are not included in this measurement.

APPENDIX B

Selected Mammal Tracks

As pointed out in the chapter on observing and studying mammals, tracks often provide key clues as to what species of mammals are in an area. However, reading tracks is a difficult job because their legibility varies greatly with the substrate, weather, and gait of the mammal. Tracks are best represented in soft mud along rivers, streams, ponds, or lakes. Dusty or sandy trails and, in the winter, fresh fallen snow are also good substrates. Once tracks are discovered, one should first assess the size and shape of the prints. Are there claws present? Do they resemble a hand? What type of gait was used? Did the animal drag its tail? Where do the tracks begin and end? One may rule out one mammal after another by close observation of the surroundings, and one may possibly arrive at the exact species. One should remember the tracks alone should not be used to assess the presence of a particular mammal. Other signs and indicators of activity (e.g., tunnels, feces, scrapes, and scratches) can provide a great deal of information.

Included in the following figures are the tracks of 28 commonly encountered native species and six domestic species. Average size, gait, and often a diagram of typical fecal material are included. The tracks are phylogenetically arranged. Murie's (1974) field guide to tracks is suggested for more detailed study.

VIRGINIA OPOSSUM

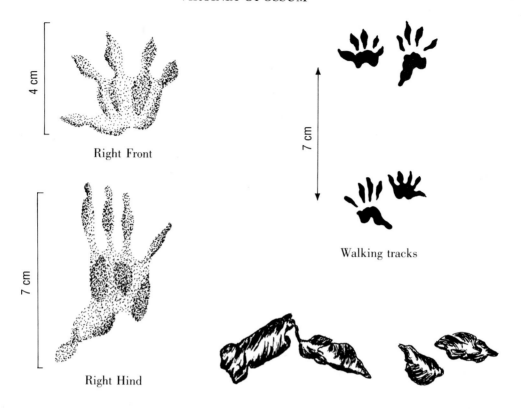

4 cm

Right Front

7 cm

Right Hind

7 cm

Walking tracks

SOUTHERN SHORT-TAILED SHREW

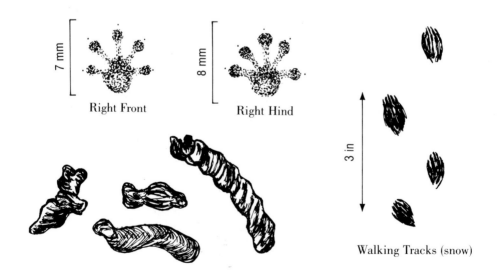

7 mm

Right Front

8 mm

Right Hind

3 in

Walking Tracks (snow)

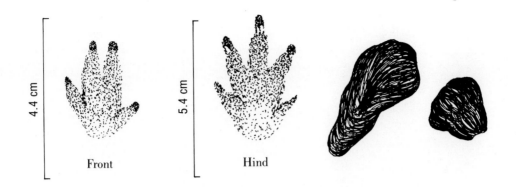

4.4 cm

Front

5.4 cm

Hind

EASTERN COTTONTAIL

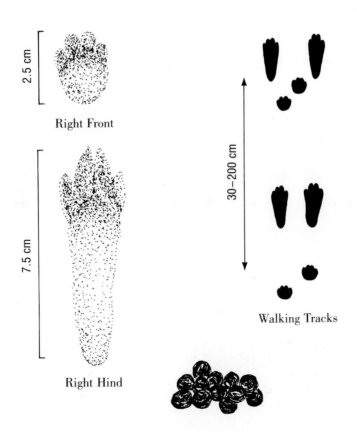

2.5 cm

Right Front

7.5 cm

Right Hind

30–200 cm

Walking Tracks

EASTERN CHIPMUNK

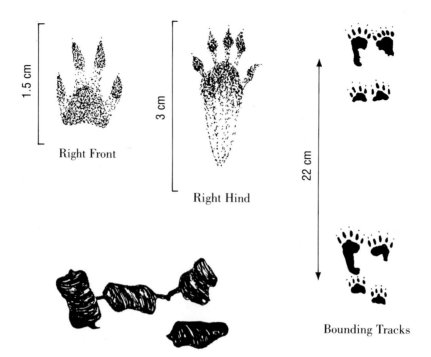

1.5 cm

Right Front

3 cm

Right Hind

22 cm

Bounding Tracks

WOODCHUCK

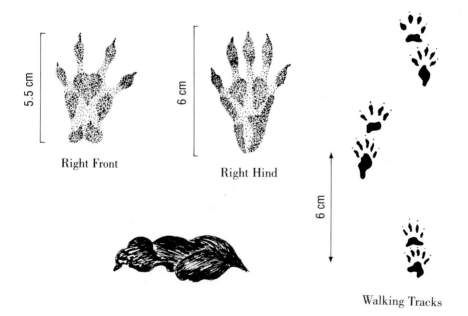

5.5 cm

Right Front

6 cm

Right Hind

6 cm

Walking Tracks

Gray Squirrel

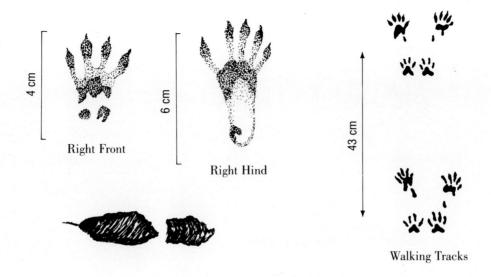

4 cm

Right Front

6 cm

Right Hind

43 cm

Walking Tracks

Beaver

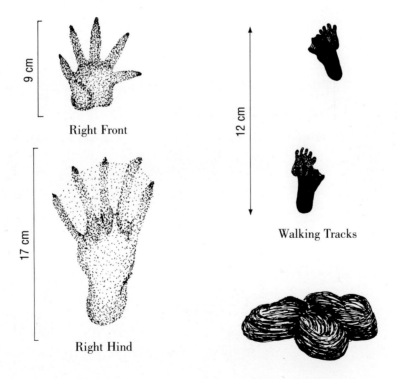

9 cm

Right Front

17 cm

Right Hind

12 cm

Walking Tracks

MARSH RICE RAT

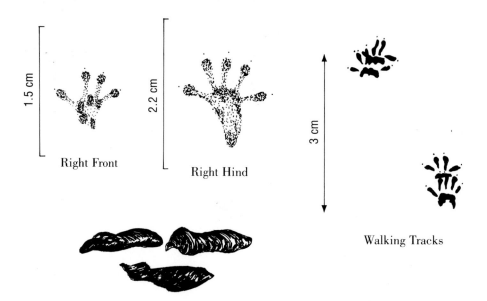

1.5 cm

Right Front

2.2 cm

Right Hind

3 cm

Walking Tracks

DEER MOUSE

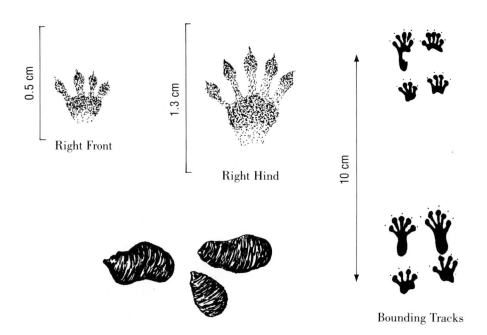

0.5 cm

Right Front

1.3 cm

Right Hind

10 cm

Bounding Tracks

EASTERN WOODRAT

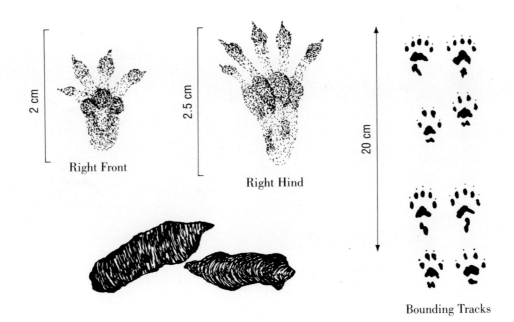

2 cm

Right Front

2.5 cm

Right Hind

20 cm

Bounding Tracks

PRAIRIE VOLE

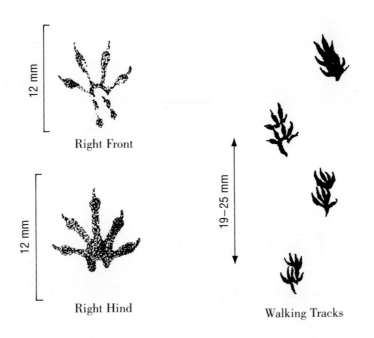

12 mm

Right Front

12 mm

Right Hind

19–25 mm

Walking Tracks

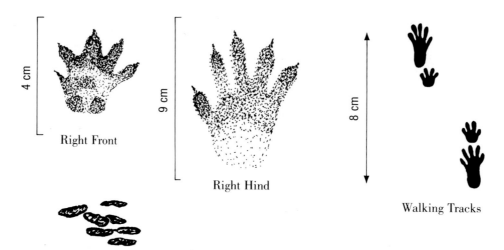

4 cm

Right Front

9 cm

Right Hind

8 cm

Walking Tracks

NORWAY RAT

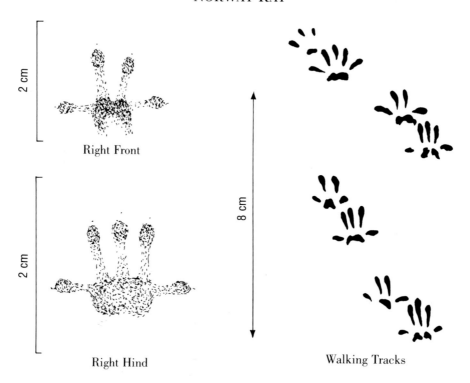

2 cm

Right Front

2 cm

Right Hind

8 cm

Walking Tracks

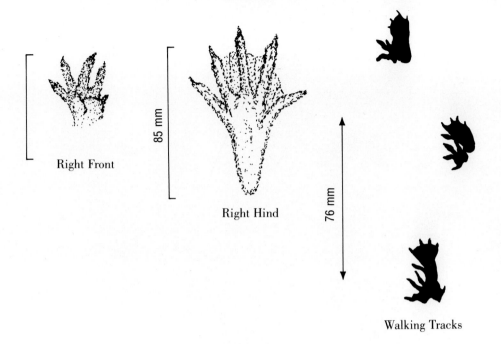

Right Front

85 mm

Right Hind

76 mm

Walking Tracks

COYOTE

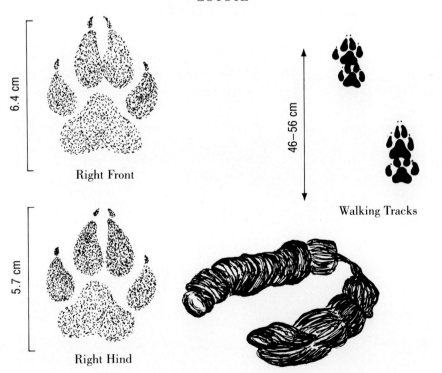

6.4 cm

Right Front

46–56 cm

Walking Tracks

5.7 cm

Right Hind

RED FOX

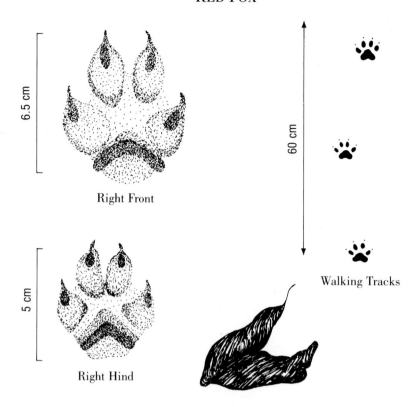

6.5 cm

Right Front

5 cm

Right Hind

60 cm

Walking Tracks

GRAY FOX

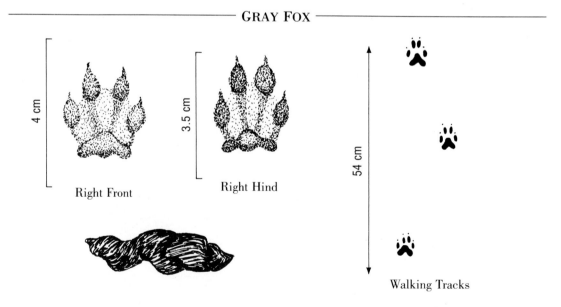

4 cm

Right Front

3.5 cm

Right Hind

54 cm

Walking Tracks

BLACK BEAR

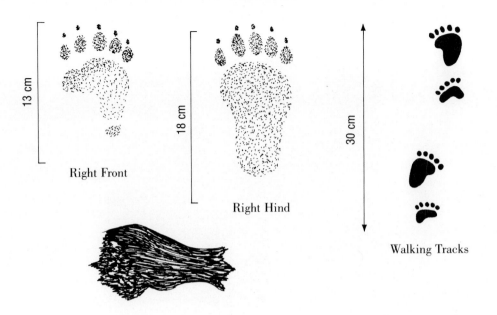

13 cm

Right Front

18 cm

Right Hind

30 cm

Walking Tracks

RACCOON

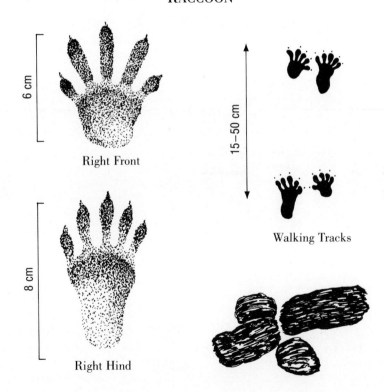

6 cm

Right Front

8 cm

Right Hind

15–50 cm

Walking Tracks

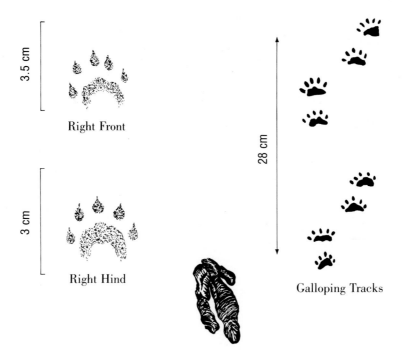

3.5 cm

Right Front

3 cm

Right Hind

28 cm

Galloping Tracks

EASTERN SPOTTED SKUNK

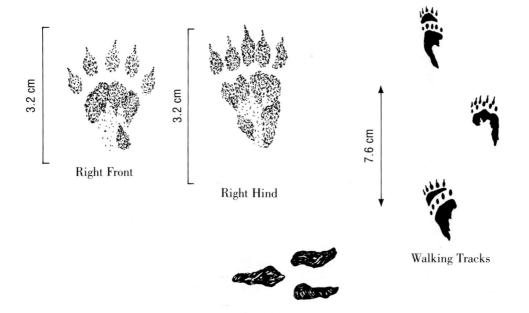

3.2 cm

Right Front

3.2 cm

Right Hind

7.6 cm

Walking Tracks

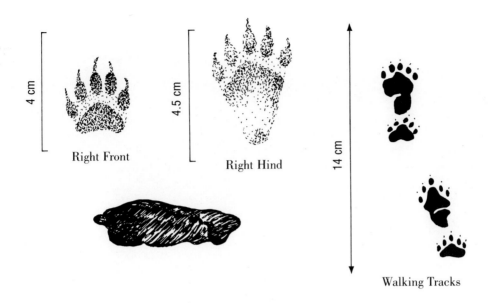

4 cm

Right Front

4.5 cm

Right Hind

14 cm

Walking Tracks

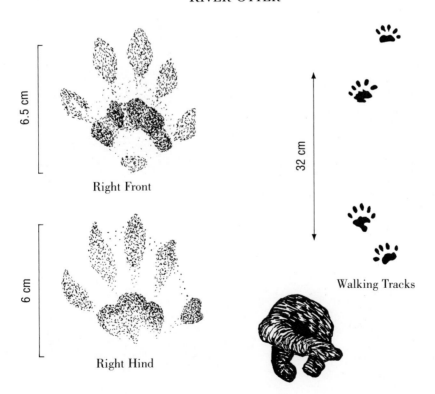

6.5 cm

Right Front

6 cm

Right Hind

32 cm

Walking Tracks

SELECTED MAMMAL TRACKS   277

MOUNTAIN LION

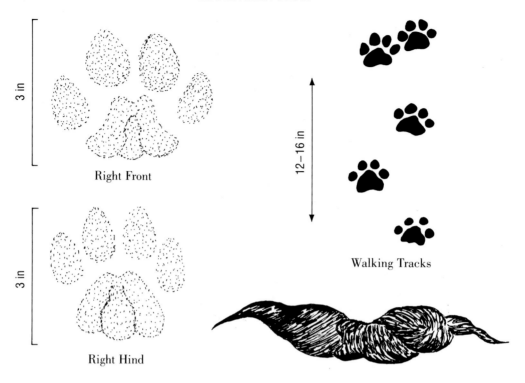

3 in

Right Front

3 in

Right Hind

12–16 in

Walking Tracks

BOBCAT

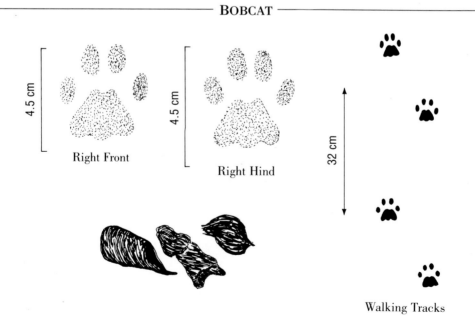

4.5 cm

Right Front

4.5 cm

Right Hind

32 cm

Walking Tracks

WHITE-TAILED DEER

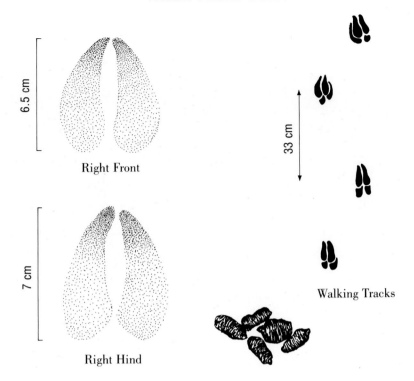

6.5 cm

Right Front

7 cm

Right Hind

33 cm

Walking Tracks

DOMESTIC DOG

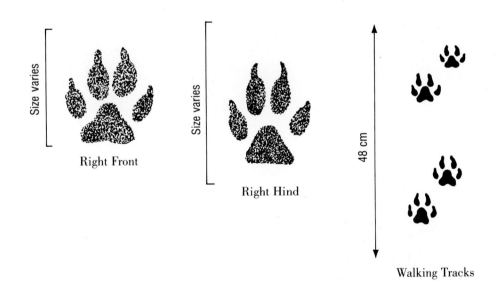

Size varies

Right Front

Size varies

Right Hind

48 cm

Walking Tracks

DOMESTIC CAT

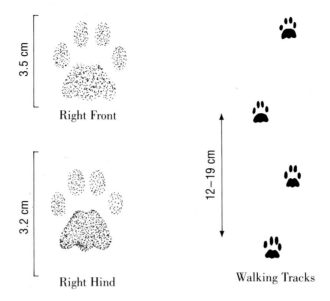

3.5 cm

Right Front

3.2 cm

Right Hind

12–19 cm

Walking Tracks

COW

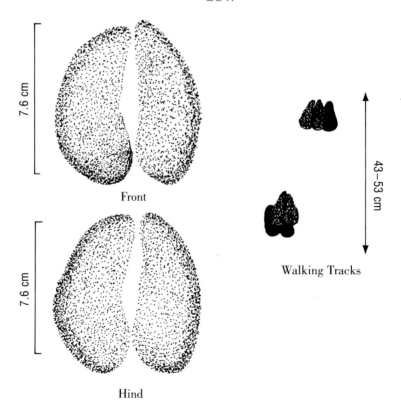

7.6 cm

Front

7.6 cm

Hind

43–53 cm

Walking Tracks

SHEEP

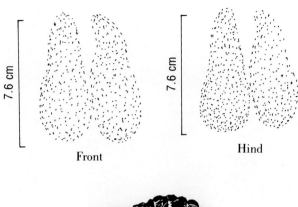

7.6 cm — Front

7.6 cm — Hind

GOAT

6.7 cm — Front

6.7 cm — Hind

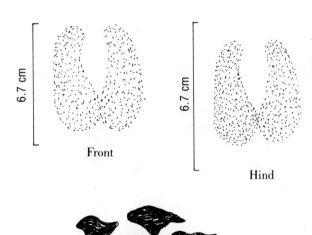

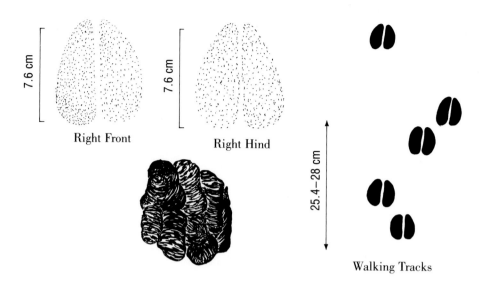

7.6 cm

Right Front

7.6 cm

Right Hind

25.4–28 cm

Walking Tracks

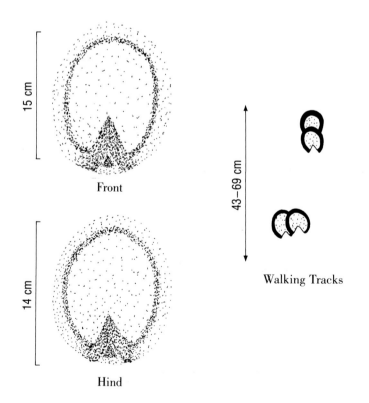

15 cm

Front

14 cm

Hind

43–69 cm

Walking Tracks

BIBLIOGRAPHY

General References

The following is a brief list of references for those who might want to do further research on mammals. This list is by no means all-inclusive, and many of the references can also be found in the Literature Cited section.

Booth, E. S.
  1982. How to know the mammals (4th ed.). Wm. C. Brown Co., Publs., Dubuque, Iowa. 198 pp.

Burt, W. H. and R. P. Grossenheider
  1976. A field guide to the mammals (3rd. ed.). Houghton Mifflin Co., Boston. 289 pp.

Chapman, J. A. and G. A. Feldhamer
  1982. Wild mammals of North America. The Johns Hopkins University Press, Baltimore. 1147 pp.

Hall, E. R.
  1981. The mammals of North America (2nd ed.). 2 vols. John Wiley and Sons, New York. 1181 pp.

Hamilton, W. J., Jr. and J. O. Whitaker, Jr.
  1979. Mammals of the eastern United States (2nd. ed.). Comstock Publishing Assoc., Ithaca. 346 pp.

Murie, O. J.
  1974. A field guide to animal tracks (2nd. ed.). Houghton Mifflin Co., Boston. 375 pp.

Novak, M., J. A. Baker, M. E. Obbard, and B. Malloch
  1987. Wild furbearer management and conservation in North America. Ministry of Natural Resources, Ontario, Canada. 1150 pp.

Nowak, R. M. and J. L. Paradiso
  1983. Walker's mammals of the world (4th ed.). 2 vols. The Johns Hopkins University Press, Baltimore. 1362 pp.

Tumlison, R.
  1983. An annotated key to the dorsal guard hairs of Arkansas game mammals and furbearers. Southwestern Nat. 28:315–323.

Vaughan, T. A.
  1986. Mammalogy (3rd. ed.). Saunders College Publishing, Philadelphia. 576 pp.

Whitaker, J. O., Jr.
  1980. The Audubon Society field guide to North American mammals. Alfred A. Knopf, New York. 745 pp.

Literature Cited

Ables, S. H.
  1975. Ecology of the red fox in North America. Pp. 148–163. *In* M. W. Fox (ed.). The wild canids. Van Nostrand Reinhold Co., New York. 508 pp.

Allen, D. L. and W. W. Shapton
  1942. An ecological study of winter dens, with special reference to the eastern skunk. Ecology 23:59–68.

Allred, B. W. and H. C. Mitchell
  1955. Major plant types of Arkansas, Louisiana, Oklahoma and Texas and their relation to climate and soils. Texas J. Sci. 7:7–19.

Anderson, R. M.
  1948. Methods of collecting and preserving vertebrate animals. Nat. Mus. Canada, Bull. 69:1–161.

Anderson, S.
  1972. Mammals of Chihuahua: Taxonomy and distribution. Bull. Amer. Mus. Nat. Hist. 148–410.

Anonymous
  1973. Threatened wildlife of the United States, U.S. Dept. Interior, Washington, D.C., Resource Publ. 113, 280 pp.

  1974. Arkansas natural area plan. Arkansas Dept. Planning (C. T. Crow, Director), Little Rock, Arkansas. 248 pp.

Antevs, E.
  1955. Geologic-climatic dating in the West. Amer. Antiquity 20:317–355.

Anthony, M.
  1962. Activity and behavior of the woodchuck in southern Illinois. Occ. Papers C. C. Adams Center 6:1–24.

Arlton, A. V.
  1936. An ecological study of the mole. J. Mammal. 17:349–371.

Armstrong, D. M. and J. K. Jones, Jr.
  1972. *Notiosorex crawfordi*. Mammalian Species 17:1–5. Amer. Soc. Mammalogists.

Asdell, S. A.
  1964. Patterns of mammalian reproduction (2nd ed.). Cornell Univ. Press, Ithaca, N.Y. 670 pp.

Audubon, J. J. and J. Bachman
  1854. Quadrupeds of North America, III. V. G. Audubon, New York. 223 pp.

Baer, G. M.
  1975. Rabies in nonhematophagous bats. Pp. 79–97. *In* G. M. Baer (ed.). The natural history of rabies, Vol. II. Academic Press, New York.

Bailey, J. W. and G. A. Heidt
  1978. Range and status of the nutria, *Myocastor coypus*, in Arkansas. Proc. Ark. Acad. Sci. 32:25–27.

Bailey, V.
  1926. A biological survey of North Dakota. The mammals. N. Amer. Fauna 49:1–226.

Baker, R. J. and C. M. Ward
  1967. Distribution of bats in southeastern Arkansas. J. Mammal. 48:130–132.

Barbour, R. W. and W. H. Davis
  1969. Bats of America. Univ. Press Kentucky, Lexington. 286 pp.

Barnes, V. G., Jr.
  1973. Pocket gophers and reforestation in the Pacific northwest: a problem analysis. U.S. Fish and Wildlife Ser. Sci. Pep. Wildl. 155. 18 pp.

Barrett, G. W.
  1969. Bioenergetics of a captive least shrew, *Cryptotis parva*. J. Mammal. 50:629–630.

Beckman, M. A.
  1969. Middle archaic complex of Northwest Arkansas. Proc. Ark. Acad. Sci. 23:197–208.

Bekoff, M.
  1977. *Canis latrans*. Mammalian Species 79:1–9, Amer. Soc. Mammalogists.

  1982. Coyote (*Canis latrans*). Pp. 447–459. *In* J. A. Chapman and G. A. Feldhamer (eds.). Wild mammals of North America. The Johns Hopkins University Press, Baltimore. 1147 pp.

Black, J. D.

1935. A new race of *Peromyscus manicula-tus* from Arkansas. J. Mammal. 16: 144–145.

1936. Mammals of northwestern Arkansas. J. Mammal. 17:29–35.

1937. Mammals of Kansas. 30th Biennial Rept. Kansas State Board Agric. 35: 116–217.

Blair, W. F.

1939. Faunal relationships and geographic distribution of mammals in Oklahoma. Am. Midl. Nat. 22:85–133.

1941. Some data on the home ranges and general life history of the short-tailed shrew, red-backed vole, and woodland jumping mouse in northern Michigan. Am. Midl. Nat. 25:681–685.

Blair, W. F., A. P. Blair, P. Brodkorb, F. R. Cagle, and G. A. Moore.

1968. Vertebrates of the United States (2nd ed.): Part 6, Mammals, pp. 454–562, McGraw-Hill Book Co., New York.

Bogan, M. A.

1972. Observations on parturition and development in the hoary bat, *Lasiurus cinereus*. J. Mammal. 53:611–614.

Booth, E. S.

1982. How to know the mammals (4th ed.). Wm. C. Brown Co., Publs., Dubuque, Iowa.

Boutin, S. and D. E. Birkenholz

1987. Muskrat and round-tailed muskrat. Pp. 314–325. *In* M. Novak, J. A. Baker, M. E. Obbard, and B. Malloch (eds.). Wild furbearer management and conservation in North America. Ministry of Natural Resources, Ontario, Canada. 1150 pp.

Brack, V., Jr. and R. K. Laval

1985. Food habits of the Indiana bat in Missouri. J. Mammal. 66:308–315.

Bradshaw, W. M.

1965. Species discrimination in the *Peromyscus leucopus* group of mice. Texas J. Sci. 17:278–293.

Bradt, G. W.

1939. Breeding habits of beaver. J. Mammal. 20:486–489.

Branner, G. C.

1942. Mineral resources of Arkansas. Ark. Geol. Surv. Bull. 6:1–101.

Brown, B.

1908. The Conard Fissure, a pleistocene bone deposit in northern Arkansas: With descriptions of two new genera and twenty new species of mammals. Amer. Mus. Nat. Hist. Memoir 9:157–208.

Brown, L. N.

1961. *Sorex longirostris* in southwestern Missouri. J. Mammal. 42:527.

1964. Ecology of three species of *Peromyscus* from southern Missouri. J. Mammal. 45:189–202.

Buchanan, G. D. and R. V. Talmage

1954. The geographical distribution of the armadillo in the United States. Texas J. Sci. 6:142–150.

Buckner, C. H.

1964. Metabolism, food capacity, and feeding behavior in four species of shrews. Can. J. Zool. 41:259–279.

Burt, W. H.

1976. A field guide to the mammals (2nd ed.). Houghton Mifflin Co., Boston. 284 pp.

Cahalane, V. H.

1950. Badger-coyote "partnerships." J. Mammal. 31:345–355.

Calhoun, J. E.

1962. The ecology and sociology of the Norway rat. U.S. Dept. Health, Education and Welfare. Publ. Health Ser. 288 pp.

Capp, J. C.

1976. Increasing pocket gopher problems in reforestation. Pp. 221–228. *In* Proc. 7th Vertebr. Pest Conf., Univ. California, Davis.

Carley, C. J., E. D. Fleharty, and M. A. Mares

1970. Occurrence and activity of *Reithrodontomys megalotis*, *Microtus ochrogaster*, and *Peromyscus maniculatus* as recorded by a photographic device. Southwestern Nat. 15:209–216.

Cartwright, M. E.
1975. An ecological study of white-tailed deer in northwestern Arkansas: Home range, activity and habitat utilization. Unpubl. M.S. thesis, University of Arkansas, Fayetteville. 147 pp.

Catlett, R. H. and H. S. Shellhammer.
1962. A comparison of behavioral and biological characteristics of house mice and harvest mice. J. Mammal. 43:133–144.

Chapman, J. A., J. G. Hockman, and W. R. Edwards
1982. Cottontails (*Sylvilagus floridanus* and allies). Pp. 83–123. *In* J. A. Chapman and G. A. Feldhamer (eds.). Wild mammals of North America. The Johns Hopkins University Press, Baltimore. 1147 pp.

Chase, J. D., W. E. Howard, and J. T. Roseberry.
1982. Pocket gophers (Geomyidae). Pp. 239–255. *In* J. A. Chapman and G. A. Feldhamer (eds.). Wild mammals of North America. The Johns Hopkins University Press, Baltimore. 1147 pp.

Clark, J. D.
1985. Range extension of the porcupine (*Erethizon dorsatum*) into southwest Arkansas. Proc. Ark. Acad. Sci. 39:121.

Clark, J. D., G. A. Heidt, T. Sheldon, and J. H. Peck.
1985. Analysis of Arkansas fur harvest records—1942–1984: III. Harvest-price relationships. Proc. Ark. Acad. Sci. 39:89–91.

Clark, W. K.
1951. Ecological life history of the armadillo in the eastern Edwards Plateau region. Am. Midl. Nat. 46:337–358.
1953. Gray Shrew, *Notiosorex*, from eastern Oklahoma. J. Mammal. 34:117–118.

Cleland, C. E.
1965. Faunal remains from bluff shelters in northwest Arkansas. Bull. Ark. Arch. Soc. 6:39–63.

Cleveland, A. G.
1970. The current geographic distribution of the armadillo in the United States. Texas J. Sci. 22:87–92.

Cockrum, E. L.
1952. Longevity in the pipistrelle, *Pipistrellus subflavus subflavus*. J. Mammal. 33:491–492.
1955. Reproduction in North American bats. Trans. Kansas Acad. Sci. 58:487–511.

Conaway, C. H.
1958. Maintenance, reproduction and growth of the least shrew in captivity. J. Mammal. 39:507–512.
1959. The reproductive cycle of the eastern mole. J. Mammal. 40:180–194.

Conley, B. W.
1977. Black bear status report of Arkansas. Workshop on the management biology of North American black bear, Kalispell, Montana. Mimeo 7 pp.

Connolly, R. A. and R. E. Lanstrom.
1969. Gopher damage to buried electric cable materials. Am. Soc. for Testing and Materials. Materials Res. and Stands. 9:13–18.

Connor, P. F.
1959. The bog lemming *Synaptomys cooperi* in southern New Jersey. Publs. Museum Michigan State Univ., Biol. Series. 1:161–248.

Constantine, D. G.
1967. Activity patterns of the Mexican free-tailed bat. Univ. New Mexico Publ. Biol. 7:1–79.

Cordes, C. L. and F. S. Barkalow, Jr.
1973. Home ranges and dispersal in a North Carolina gray squirrel population. Proc. Annu. Conf. S.E. Assoc. Game and Fish Comm. 26:124–135.

Coulombe, H. N. and B. H. Banta
1964. The distribution and ecology of the Crawford desert shrew, *Notiosorex crawfordi*, in Saline Valley, Inyo County, California. Wasmann J. Biol. 22:277–297.

Crabb, W. D.
1944. Growth, development and seasonal

weights of spotted skunks. J. Mammal. 25:213–221.

1948. The ecology and management of the prairie spotted skunk in Iowa. Ecol. Monogr. 18:201–232.

Croneis, C.
1930. Physiography of the Paleozoic area of Arkansas. Ark. Geol. Surv. Bull. 3:7–19.

Crowe, D. M.
1975. Aspects of aging, growth, and reproduction of bobcats from Wyoming. J. Mammal. 56:177–198.

Dahlem, E. A.
1975. A comparison of two techniques for aging white-tailed deer, (*Odocoileus virginianus*) in Arkansas. Unpubl. M.S. thesis, University of Arkansas, Fayetteville. 77 pp.

Dalquest, W. W.
1953. Mammals of the Mexican State of San Luis Potosi. Louisiana State Univ. Studies, Biol. Ser. 1:1–229.

Davies, R. B. and C. P. Hibler
1979. Animal reservoirs and cross-species transmission of *Giardia*. Pp. 104–126. *In* W. Jakubowski and J. C. Hoff (eds.). Waterborne transmission of giardiasis. U.S. Environmental Protection Agency, Cincinnatti. EPA-600/9-79-001.

Davis, D. E.
1953. The characteristics of rat populations. Quart. Rev. Biol. 28:373–401.

1967. The role of environmental factors in hibernation of woodchucks. Ecology 48:683–689.

Davis, L. C.
1969. The biostratigraphy of Peccary cave, Newton County, Arkansas. Proc. Ark. Acad. Sci. 23:192–196.

Davis, W. B.
1940. Distribution and variation of pocket gophers (genus *Geomys*) in the southwestern United States. Texas Agr. Exp. Sta. Bull. 590:1–38.

1974. The mammals of Texas (rev. ed.). Texas Parks and Wildlife Dept. Bull. 41:1–294.

Davis, W. H., W. Z. Lidicker, and J. A. Sealander
1955. *Myotis austroriparius* in Arkansas. J. Mammal. 36:288

de Almeida, M. H.
1987. Nuisance furbearer damage control in urban and suburban areas. Pp. 996–1006. *In* M. Novak, J. A. Baker, M. E. Obard, and B. Malloch (eds.). Wild furbearer management and conservation in North America. Ministry of Natural Resources, Ontario, Canada. 1150 pp.

DeBlase, A. F. and R. E. Martin
1974. A manual of mammalogy. Wm. C. Brown Co. Publs., Dubuque, Iowa. 329 pp.

Dellinger, S. C. and J. D. Black
1940. Notes on Arkansas mammals. J. Mammal. 21:187–191.

DeLong, K. T.
1967. Population ecology of feral house mice. Ecology 48:611–634.

Dice, L. R.
1932. The prairie deer mouse. Cranbrook Inst. Sci., Bloomfield Hills, Michigan, Bull. 2:1–8.

DiSalvo, A. F., J. Palmer, and L. Ajello
1969. Multiple pregnancy in *Tadarida brasiliensis cynocephala*. J. Mammal. 50:152.

Dodge, W. E.
1982. Porcupine (*Erethizon dorsatum*). Pp. 355–366. *In* J. A. Chapman and G. A. Feldhamer (eds.). Wild mammals of North America. The Johns Hopkins University Press, Baltimore. 1147 pp.

Dolan, P. G. and D. C. Carter
1977. *Glaucomys volans*. Mammalian Species 78:1–6. Amer. Soc. Mammalogists.

Donaldson, D., C. Hunter, and T. H. Holder
1951. Arkansas' deer herd. Federal Aid Publ., Projects 17–D and 20–R, Arkansas Game and Fish Comm. Little Rock, Arkansas. 72 pp.

Dowling, H. G.
1956. Geographic relations of Ozarkian amphibians and reptiles. Southwestern Nat. 1:174–189.

Downhower, J. F. and E. R. Hall
1966. The pocket gopher in Kansas. Univ. Kans. Mus. Nat. Hist. Misc. Publ. 44:1–32.

Dueser, R. D. and J. H. Porter
1986. Habitat use by insular small mammals: Relative effects of competition and habitat structure. Ecology 67:195–201.

Dunaway, P. B.
1968. Life history and populational aspects of the eastern harvest mouse. Am. Midl. Nat. 79:48–67.

Dunn, J. P., J. A. Chapman, and R. E. Marsh
1982. Jackrabbits (*Lepus californicus* and allies). Pp. 124–145. *In* J. A. Chapman and G. A. Feldhamer (eds.). Wild mammals of North America. The Johns Hopkins University Press, Baltimore. 1147 pp.

Dusi, J. L.
1959. *Sorex longirostris* in eastern Alabama. J. Mammal. 40:438–439.

Eagle, T. C. and J. S. Whitman
1987. Mink. Pp. 615–624. *In* M. Novak, J. A. Baker, M. E. Obbard, and B. Malloch (eds.). Wild furbearer management and conservation in North America. Ministry of Natural Resources, Ontario, Canada. 1150 pp.

Easterla, D. A.
1968a. Parturition of Keen's myotis in southwestern Missouri. J. Mammal. 49:770.

1968b. First records of *Blarina brevicauda minima* in Missouri and Arkansas. Southwestern Nat. 13:448–449.

Eaton, R. L. (ed.)
1976. The world's cats. Vol. III, No. 2. Proc. 3rd Internat. Symp. on the World's Cats, April 26–28, 1974. Univ. Washington, Seattle. 179 pp.

Ellerman, J. R.
1940–1949. The families and genera of living rodents. London, British Museum of Natural History, Vol. 1 (1940) 689 pp, vol. 2 (1941) 690 pp, vol. 3 (1949) 210 pp.

Enders, A. C.
1966. The reproductive cycle of the nine-banded armadillo (*Dasypus novemcinctus*). *In* Comparative biology of reproduction in mammals. Zool. Soc. Symp. 15:295–310.

Enders, R. K.
1952. Reproduction in the mink (*Mustela vison*). Proc. Amer. Phil. Soc. 96:691–755.

Erickson, A. W., J. Nellor, and G. A. Petrides
1964. The black bear in Michigan. Mich. State Univ. Agr. Exp. Sta. Bull. 4:1–102.

Errington, P. L.
1939. Observations on young muskrats in Iowa. J. Mammal. 20:465–478.

Evans, J.
1970. About nutria and their control. Resource Publ. 86, Bur. Sports Fish and Wildl., Denver, Colorado. 65 pp.

Ewer, R. F.
1973. The carnivores. Cornell Univ. Press, Ithaca, New York. 494 pp.

Fay, G. E.
1959. A mastodon find from southwestern Arkansas. Proc. Ark. Acad. Sci. 13:103–105.

Featherstonhaugh, G. W.
1835. Geological report of an examination made in 1834, of the elevated country between the Missouri and Red Rivers. Washington, D. C. 97 pp.

1844. Excursion through the slave states. Harper and Brothers, New York.

Ferguson, D. V. and G. A. Heidt
1980. Profile of human-rabid skunk contacts in Arkansas: 1977–1979. Proc. Ark. Acad. Sci. 34:112–113.

Fiennes, R.
1976. The order of wolves. Bobbs-Merrill Co., Inc., Indianapolis/New York. 206 pp.

Findley, J. S. and C. Jones
1964. Seasonal distribution of the hoary bat. J. Mammal. 45:461–470.

Fitch, H. S.

1957. Aspects of reproduction and development in the prairie vole (*Microtus ochrogaster*). Univ. Kans. Publ. Mus. Nat. Hist. 10:129–161.

Fitch, H. S., P. Goodrum, and C. Newman

1952. The armadillo in the southeastern United States. J. Mammal. 33:21–37.

Fitch, H. S. and L. L. Sandidge

1953. Ecology of the opossum on a natural area in northeastern Kans. Univ. Kansas Publ. Mus. Nat. Hist. 7:305–338.

Flint, R. F.

1971. Glacial and quaternary geology. John Wiley and Sons, Inc., New York. 892 pp.

Flyger, V.

1960. Movements and home range of the gray squirrel, *Sciurus carolinensis*, in two Maryland woodlots. Ecology 41:365–369.

Flyger, V. and J. E. Gates

1982. Fox and gray squirrels (*Sciurus niger, S. carolinensis*, and allies). Pp. 209–229. *In* J. A Chapman and G. A. Feldhamer (eds.). Wild mammals of North America. The Johns Hopkins University Press, Baltimore. 1147 pp.

Folk, G. E., Jr., A. Larson, and M. A. Folk

1976. Physiology of hibernating bears. Intl. Conf. Bear Res. and Manage. 3:373–380.

Forsyth, B. J.

1963. Squirrel (*Sciurus* Linnaeus) populations in northwestern Arkansas. Unpubl. M.S. thesis, University of Arkansas, Fayetteville. 43 pp.

Foti, T. L.

1974. Natural divisions of Arkansas. Pp. 11–34. *In* Arkansas Natural Area Plan, Ark. Dept. Planning, Little Rock, Arkansas.

Fritts, S. H. and J. A. Sealander

1978a. Diets of bobcats in Arkansas with special reference to age and sex. J. Wildl. Manage. 42:533–539.

1978b. Reproductive biology and population characteristics of bobcats in Arkansas. J. Mammal. 59:347–353.

Fritzell, E. K.

1987. Gray fox and island gray fox. Pp. 408–421. *In* M. Novak, J. A. Baker, M. E. Obbard, and B. Malloch (eds.). Wild furbearer management and conservation in North America. Ministry of Natural Resources, Ontario, Canada. 1150 pp.

Galbreath, G. J.

1982. Armadillo (*Dasypus novemcinctus*). Pp. 71–79. *In* J. A. Chapman and G. A. Feldhamer (eds.). Wild mammals of North America. The Johns Hopkins University Press, Baltimore. 1147 pp.

Gardner, A. L.

1973. The systematics of the genus *Didelphis* (Marsupialia: Didelphidae) in North and Middle America. The Museum, Texas Tech University, Special Publ. 4.1–81.

1982. Virginia opossum (*Didelphis virginiana*). Pp. 3–36. *In* J. A. Chapman and G. A. Feldhamer (eds.). Wild mammals of North America. The Johns Hopkins University Press, Baltimore. 1147 pp.

Gardner, J. E. and V. R. McDaniel

1978. Distribution of bats in the Delta Region of northeastern Arkansas. Proc. Ark. Acad. Sci. 32:46–48.

Garland, D. and G. A. Heidt.

1989. Distribution and status of shrews in Arkansas. Proc. Ark. Acad. Sci. 43:(in press).

Gashwiler, J. S., W. L. Robinette, and O. W. Morris

1961. Breeding habits of bobcats in Utah. J. Mammal. 42:76–84.

Genoways, H. H. and J. R. Choate.

1972. A multivariate analysis of systematic relationships among populations of the short-tailed shrew (genus *Blarina*) in Nebraska. Syst. Zool. 21:106–116.

George, S. B., J. R. Choate, and H. H. Genoways

1981. Distribution and taxonomic status of *Blarina hylophaga* Elliot (Insectivora: Soricidae). Annals of Carnegie Museum 50:493–513.

George, S. B., H. H. Genoways, J. R. Choate, and R. J. Baker

1982. Karyotypic relationships within short-tailed shrews, genus *Blarina*. J. Mammal. 63:639–645.

Gerell, R.
1970. Home ranges and movements of the mink *Mustela vison* Schreber in southern Sweden. Oikos 21:160–173.

Gerstaecker, F.
1856. Wild sports in the far west (translated from the German). B. Routledge & Co., London. 314 pp.

Getz, L. L., F. R. Cole, and D. L. Gates
1978. Use of interstate roadsides as dispersal routes by *Microtus pennsylvanicus*. J. Mammal. 50:208–212.

Getz, L. L. and J. E. Hofmann
1986. Social organization in free-living prairie voles, *Microtus ochrogaster*. Behav. Ecol. Sociobiol. 18:275–282.

Gier, H. T.
1968. Coyotes in Kansas (revised). Kansas State Univ. Agr. Exp. Sta. Bull. 393: 1–118.

Gipson, P. S.
1974. Food habits of coyotes in Arkansas. J. Wildl. Manage. 38:848–853.

1976. Melanistic *Canis* in Arkansas. Southwestern Nat. 21:124–126.

Gipson, P. S. and J. A. Sealander
1972. Home range and activity of the coyote (*Canis latrans frustror*) in Arkansas. Proc. 26th Annu. Conf. S.E. Assoc. Game and Fish Comm. Pp. 82–95.

1976. Changing food habits of wild *Canis* in Arkansas with emphasis on coyote hybrids and feral dogs. Am. Midl. Nat. 95:249–253.

Gipson, P. S., I. K. Gipson, and J. A. Sealander
1975. Reproductive biology of wild *Canis* (Canidae) in Arkansas. Syst. Zool. 23:1–11.

Gipson, P. S., J. A. Sealander, and J. E. Dunn
1974. The taxonomic status of wild *Canis* in Arkansas. Syst. Zool. 23:1–11.

Godin, A. J.
1982. Striped and hooded skunks (*Mephitis mephitis* and allies). Pp. 674–687. *In* J. A. Chapman and G. A. Feldhamer (eds.). Wild mammals of North America. The Johns Hopkins University Press, Baltimore. 1147 pp.

Goertz, J. W.
1963. Some biological notes on the plains harvest mouse. Proc. Okla. Acad. Sci. 43: 123–125.

1965. Late summer breeding of flying squirrels. J. Mammal. 46:510.

1971. An ecological study of *Microtus pinetorum* in Oklahoma. Am. Midl. Nat. 86:1–12.

Goodpaster, W. W. and D. F. Hoffmeister
1954. Life history of the golden mouse, *Peromyscus nuttalli*, in Kentucky. J. Mammal. 35:16–27.

Graham, G. L.
1976. A western extension of the southeastern shrew, *Sorex longirostris* (Soricidae). Southwestern Nat. 21:105.

Graham, R. W. and H. A. Semken
1976. Paleoecological significance of the short-tailed shrew (*Blarina*) with a systematic discussion of *Blarina ozarkensis*. J. Mammal. 57:433–449.

Griffin, D. R. and H. B. Hitchcock
1965. Probable 24-year longevity record for *Myotis lucifugus*. J. Mammal. 56:332.

Grizzel, R. A.
1955. A study of the southern woodchuck *Marmota monax monax*. Am. Midl. Nat. 53:257–293.

Guggisberg, C. A. W.
1975. Wildcats of the world. Taplinger Publ. Co., Inc., New York. 328 pp.

Guilday, J. E. and P. W. Parmalee
1971. Thirteen-lined ground squirrel, prairie chicken and other vertebrates from an archaeological site in northeastern Arkansas. Am. Midl. Nat. 86:227–229.

Hall, E. R.
1951a. A synopsis of the North American lagomorpha. Univ. Kans. Publ. Mus. Nat. Hist. 5:119–202.

1951b. American weasels. Univ. Kans. Publ. Mus. Nat. Hist. 4:1–466.

1962. Collecting and preparing study specimens of vertebrates. Univ. Kans. Mus. Nat. Hist. Misc. Publ. 30:1–46.

1981. The mammals of North America, 2nd ed. 2 vols. John Wiley and Sons, New York, N.Y. 1181 pp.

Hall, J. S.
1962. A life history and taxonomic study of the Indiana bat, *Myotis sodalis*. Reading Public Museum and Art Gallery, Sci. Publ. 12:1–68.

Hall, J. S., R. J. Cloutier, and D. R. Griffin
1957. Longevity records and notes on tooth wear of bats. J. Mammal. 38:407–409.

Hall, J. S. and N. Wilson
1966. Seasonal populations and movements of the gray bat in the Kentucky area. Am. Midl. Nat. 75:317–324.

Hallberg, G. R., H. A. Semken, and L. C. Davis
1974. Quaternary records of *Microtus xanthognathus* (Leach), the yellow-cheeked vole, from northwestern Arkansas and southwestern Iowa. J. Mammal. 55:640–645.

Hamilton, D. A.
1982. Ecology of the bobcat in Missouri. Unpubl. M.S. thesis, University of Missouri, Columbia. 132 pp.

Hamilton, W. J., Jr.
1931. Habits of the short-tailed shrew, *Blarina brevicauda* (Say). The Ohio J. Sci. 31:97–106.

1933. The weasels of New York, their natural history and economic status. Am. Midl. Nat. 14:289–344.

1934. The life history of the rufescent woodchuck *Marmota monax rufescens* Howell. Ann. Carnegie Mus. 23:85–178.

1940. Summer food habits of minks and raccoons on the Montezuma marsh, New York. J. Wildl. Manage. 4:80–84.

1943. The mammals of eastern United States. Comstock Publ. Co., Ithaca, New York. 432 pp.

1944. The biology of the little short-tailed shrew, *Cryptotis parva*, J. Mammal. 25:1–7.

1946. Habits of the swamp rice rat, *Oryzomys palustris palustris* (Harlan). Am. Midl. Nat. 36:730–736.

1953. Reproduction and young of the Florida woodrat, *Neotoma f. floridana* (Ord). J. Mammal. 34:180–189.

Handley, C. O., Jr.
1959. A revision of the American bats of the genera *Euderma* and *Plecotus*. Proc. U.S. Natl. Mus. 110:95–246.

Hartley, C. B.
1859. Hunting sports in the West. Comprising adventures of the most celebrated hunters and trappers. J. W. Bradley, Philadelphia. 320 pp.

Hartman, C. G.
1952. Possums. Univ. Texas Press, Austin. 174 pp.

Harvey, M. J.
1976a. Endangered chiroptera of the southeastern United States. Proc. 29th Annu. Conf. S.E. Assoc. Game and Fish Comm. Pp. 429–433.

1976b. Ozark big-eared bat. *In* H. O. Hillestad (ed.). Endangered and threatened vertebrates of the southeast. Tall Timbers Res. Sta. Bull.

1984. Protection of endangered gray bat (*Myotis grisescens*) colonies in Arkansas. Proc. Ark. Acad. Sci. 38:90–91.

1986. Arkansas bats: A valuable resource. Fed. Aid. Publ. Proj. E-1 (K. Sutton, ed.), Arkansas Game and Fish Commission, Little Rock, Arkansas. 16 pp.

Harvey, M. J. and V. R. McDaniel
1983. Status of the bat *Myotis keeni* in the Arkansas Ozarks. Proc. Ark. Acad. Sci. 36:89.

Harvey, M. J., M. L. Kennedy, and V. R. McDaniel
1978. Status of the endangered Ozark big-eared bat (*Plecotus townsendii ingens*) in Arkansas. Proc. Ark. Acad. Sci. 32:89–90.

Haskell, H. S. and H. G. Reynolds
    1947.   Growth, developmental food require-
          ments and breeding activity of the Cali-
          fornia jack rabbit. J. Mammal. 28:129–
          136.

Hay, O. P.
    1924.   The pleistocene of the middle region of
          North America and its vertebrate ani-
          mals. Carnegie Inst. Washington 385 pp.

Hayes, S. R.
    1976.   Daily activity and body temperature of
          the southern woodchuck, *Marmota mo-*
          nax monax, in northwestern Arkansas.
          J. Mammal. 57:291–299.

    1977.   Home range of *Marmota monax* (Sciu-
          ridae) in Arkansas. Southwestern Nat.
          22:547–550.

Heaney, L. R. and R. M. Timm
    1983.   Relationships of pocket gophers of the ge-
          nus *Geomys* from the central and north-
          ern Great Plains. Univ. Kans. Mus. Nat.
          Hist. Misc. Publ. 74:1–59.

Heath, D. R., G. A. Heidt, D. A. Saugey, and
  V. R. McDaniel
    1983.   Arkansas range extensions of the Semi-
          nole bat (*Lasiurus seminolis*) and eastern
          big-eared bat (*Plecotus rafinesquii*) and
          additional county records for the hoary
          bat (*Lasiurus cinereus*), silver-haired bat
          (*Lasionycteris noctivagans*), and evening
          bat (*Nycticeius humeralis*). Proc. Ark.
          Acad. Sci. 37:90–91.

Heath, D. R., D. A. Saugey, and G. A. Heidt
    1986.   Abandoned mine fauna of the Ouachita
          Mountains, Arkansas: Vertebrate taxa.
          Proc. Ark. Acad. Sci. 40:33–36.

Heidt, G. A.
    1977.   Utilization of nest boxes by the southern
          flying squirrel, *Glaucomys volans*, in
          central Arkansas. Proc. Ark. Acad. Sci.
          31:55–57.

    1982.   Reported animal rabies in Arkansas:
          1950–1981. Proc. Ark. Acad. Sci.
          36:34–37.

Heidt, G. A., D. V. Ferguson, and J. Lammers
    1982.   A profile of reported skunk rabies in
          Arkansas. J. Wildl. Dis. 18:269–277.

Heidt, G. A., C. Harger, H. Harger, and T. C.
  McChesney
    1985a. Serological study of selected disease an-
          tibodies in Arkansas furtrappers—A
          high risk group. J. Ark. Med. Soc. 82:
          265–269.

Heidt, G. A., A. H. Nichols, and J. J. Daly
    1985b. Incidence of *Giardia* in Arkansas bea-
          vers. Proc. Ark. Acad. Sci. 39:137.

Heidt, G. A., J. H. Peck, and L. Johnston
    1984.   An analysis of gray fox (*Urocyon cin-*
          ereoargenteus) fur harvests in Arkansas.
          Proc. Ark. Acad. Sci. 38:49–52.

Heidt, G. A., D. A. Saugey, and S. Bradford-Luck
    1987.   Reported bat rabies in Arkansas. Proc.
          Ark. Acad. Sci. 41:105–106.

Hesselton, W. T. and R. M. Hesselton
    1982.   White-tailed deer (*Odocoileus virgini-*
          anus). Pp. 878–901. *In* J. A. Chap-
          man and G. A. Feldhamer (eds.). Wild
          mammals of North America. The Johns
          Hopkins University Press, Baltimore.
          1147 pp.

Hibbard, C. W. and D. W. Taylor
    1960.   Two late pleistocene faunas from south-
          western Kansas. Contrib. Mus. Paleon-
          tol. Univ. Michigan 16:1–223.

Hickie, P.
    1940.   Cottontails in Michigan. Game Division,
          Mich. Dept. Cons. 109 pp.

Hill, E. P. III
    1967.   Notes on the life history of the swamp
          rabbit in Alabama. Proc. 21st Annu.
          Conf. S.E. Assoc. Game and Fish
          Comm. Pp. 117–123.

    1972.   The cottontail rabbit in Alabama. Au-
          burn University, Agr. Exp. Sta. Bull.
          440:1–103.

    1982.   Beaver (*Castor canadensis*). Pp. 256–
          281. *In* J. A. Chapman and G. A. Feld-
          hamer (eds.). Wild mammals of North
          America. The Johns Hopkins University
          Press, Baltimore. 1147 pp.

Hoffman, R. S. and J. K. Jones, Jr.
    1970.   Influence of late-glacial and post-glacial
          events on the distribution of recent mam-

mals on the northern great plains. *In* Pleistocene and recent environments of the central great plains. Dept. Geology, Univ. Kansas, Special Publ. 3: 355–394.

Hoffmeister, D. F. and W. W. Goodpaster
1962. Life history of the desert shrew, *Notiosorex crawfordi*. Southwestern Nat. 7: 236–252.

Holder, T. H.
1951. A survey of Arkansas game. Federal Aid Publ., Project 11-R. Arkansas Game and Fish Comm., Little Rock, Arkansas. 155 pp.

1970. Disappearing wetlands in eastern Arkansas. Arkansas Planning Comm., Little Rock, Arkansas. 72 pp.

Hooper, E. T.
1943. Geographic variation in harvest mice of the species *Reithrodontomys humulis*. Mus. Zool. Univ. Michigan, Occ. Paper No. 477. pp. 1–19.

1952. A systematic review of the harvest mice (genus *Reithrodontomys*) of Latin America. Mus. Zool. Univ. Michigan, Misc. Publ. 77:1–255.

1968. Classification. Pp. 27–74. *In* J. A. King (ed.). Biology of *Peromyscus* (Rodentia). Amer. Soc. Mammalogists, Special Publ. No. 2. 593 pp.

Hooper, E. T. and G. G. Musser
1964. The glans penis in neotropical cricetines (family Muridae) with comments on classification of muroid rodents. Mus. Zool. Univ. Michigan, Misc. Publ. 123:1–57.

Hornaday, W. T.
1889. The extermination of the American bison, with a sketch of its discovery and life history. Smithsonian Rept. 1887: 367–548.

Hornocker, M. G.
1969. Winter territoriality in mountain lions J. Wildl. Manage. 33:457–464.

1970. An analysis of mountain lion predation upon mule deer and elk in the Idaho primitive area. Wildl. Monogr. No. 21, 39 pp.

Hougart, B.
1975. Activity patterns of radio-tracked gray squirrels. Unpubl. M.S. thesis, Univ. of Maryland, College Park. 37 pp.

Hubbs, E. L.
1951. Food habits of feral house cats in the Sacramento Valley. Calif. Fish and Game 37:177–189.

Humphrey, S. R.
1974. Zoogeography of the nine-banded armadillo (*Dasypus novemcinctus*) in the United States. Bioscience 24:457–462.

Humphrey, S. R., A. R Richter, and J. B. Cope
1977. Summer habitat and ecology of the endangered Indiana bat, *Myotis sodalis*. J. Mammal. 58:334–346.

Irving, T.
1857. The conquest of Florida by Hernando De Soto. G. P. Putnam and Co., New York. 457 pp.

Jackson, H. H. T.
1915. A review of the American moles. N. Amer. Fauna No. 38, Washington. 100 pp.

1928. A taxonomic review of the American long-tailed shrews (genera *Sorex* and *Microsorex*). N. Amer. Fauna No. 51, Washington. 238 pp.

Jester, D. B.
1957. Reproduction in the fox and gray squirrels in northwestern Arkansas. Unpubl. M.S. thesis, Univ. of Arkansas, Fayetteville. 24 pp.

Johansen, K.
1961. Temperature regulation in the nine-banded armadillo (*Dasypus novemcinctus mexicanus*). Physiol. Zool. 34:126–144.

Johns, P. E., R. Baccus, M. N. Manlove, J. E. Pinder III, and M. H. Smith
1977. Reproductive patterns, productivity, and genetic variability in adjacent white-tailed deer populations. Proc. Annu. Conf. S.E. Game and Fish Comm. 31: 167–172.

Johnson, A. S.
1970. Biology of the raccoon (*Procyon lotor varius*) Nelson and Goldman in Ala-

bama. Auburn University, Agr. Exp. Sta. Bull. 401:1–148.

Johnson, M. C. and S. Johnson
1982. Voles (*Microtus* species). Pp. 326–354. *In* J. A. Chapman and G. A. Feldhamer (eds.). Wild mammals of North America. The Johns Hopkins University Press, Baltimore. 1147 pp.

Johnson, M. L. and L. K. Couch
1954. Determination of the abundance of cougars. J. Mammal. 35:255–256.

Jones, C.
1967. Growth, development and wing loading in the evening bat, *Nycticeius humeralis* (Rafinesque). J. Mammal. 48:1–19.

1977. *Plecotus rafinesquii*. Mammalian Species 69:1–4, Amer. Soc. Mammalogists.

Jones, C. and R. D. Suttkus
1971. Wing loading in *Plecotus rafinesquii*. J. Mammal. 52:458–460.

Jones, J. K., Jr. and S. Anderson
1959. The eastern harvest mouse, *Reithrodontomys humulis*, in Oklahoma. Southwestern Nat. 4:153–154.

Jones, J. K., Jr. and E. C. Birney
1988. Handbook of mammals of the North-central states. Univ. of Minnesota Press, Minneapolis. 346 pp.

Jones, J. K., Jr. and B. P. Glass
1960. The short-tailed shrew, *Blarina brevicauda*, in Oklahoma. Southwestern Nat. 5:136–142.

Jones, J. K., Jr., D. C. Carter, H. H. Genoways, R. S. Hoffman, D. W. Rice, and C. Jones
1986. Revised checklist of North American mammals north of Mexico. Occ. papers, The Museum, Texas Tech Univ. 107:1–22.

Kaffka, J.
1969. Our diminishing forests. Arkansas Game and Fish 2:2–3.

Kalmbach, E. R.
1944. The armadillo: Its relation to agriculture and game. Game, Fish and Oyster Comm., Austin, Texas. 60 pp.

Karlin, A., G. A. Heidt, and D. W. Sugg
1989. Genetic variation and heterozygosity in white-tailed deer in southern Arkansas. Am. Midl. Nat. 121:273–84.

Karnes, M. R. and R. Tumlison
1984. The river otter in Arkansas. III. Characteristics of otter latrines and their distribution along beaver inhabited watercourses in southwest Arkansas. Proc. Ark. Acad. Sci. 38:56–59.

Kaufmann, J. H.
1982. Raccoon and allies (*Procyon lotor* and allies). Pp. 567–585. *In* J. A. Chapman and G. A. Feldhamer (eds.). Wild mammals of North America. The Johns Hopkins University Press, Baltimore. 1147 pp.

1987. Ringtail cat and coati. Pp. 500–509. *In* M. Novak, J. A. Baker, M. E. Obbard, and B. Malloch (eds.). Wild furbearer management and conservation in North America. Ministry of Natural Resources, Ontario, Canada. 1150 pp.

Kaye, S. V.
1961. Laboratory life history of the eastern harvest mouse. Am. Midl. Nat. 66:439–451.

Kee, D. T. and M. J. Enright
1970. Southern records of *Microtus ochrogaster* in Arkansas. Southwestern Nat. 14:358.

Kelker, G. H.
1937. Insect food of skunks. J. Mammal. 18:164–170.

Kennedy, M. L., K. N. Randolph, and T. L. Best
1974. A review of Mississippi mammals. Studies in Natural Sciences, The Nat. Sci. Res. Inst., Eastern New Mexico Univ., vol. 2, pp. 1–36.

Kilgore, D. L., Jr.
1970. The effects of northward dispersal on growth rate of young, size of young at birth, and litter size in *Sigmodon hispidus*. Am. Midl. Nat. 84:510–520.

Kinler, N. W., G. Linscombe, and P. R. Ramsey
1987. Nutria. Pp. 326–343. *In* M. Novak, J. A. Baker, M. E. Obbard, and B. Mal-

loch (eds.). Wild furbearer management and conservation in North America. Ministry of Natural Resources, Ontario, Canada. 1150 pp.

Korschgen, L. J.
1957a. Food habits of coyotes, foxes, house cats and bobcats in Missouri. Missouri Cons. Comm., Fish and Game Div., Pittman-Robertson Series No. 15, 64 pp.

1957b. December food habits of mink in Missouri. J. Mammal. 39:521–527.

1959. Food habits of the red fox in Missouri. J. Wildl. Manage. 23:168–176.

Krulin, G. S. and J. A. Sealander
1972. Annual lipid cycle of the gray bat, *Myotis grisescens*. Comp. Biochem. Physiol. 42A:537–549.

Kunz, T. H.
1971. Reproduction of some vespertilionid bats in central Iowa. Am. Midl. Nat. 86:477–486.

1973. Resource utilization: Temporal and spatial components of bat activity in central Iowa. J. Mammal. 54:14–32.

1974. Reproduction, growth and mortality of the vespertilionid bat, *Eptesicus fuscus*, in Kansas. J. Mammal. 55:1–13.

Lagler, K. F. and B. T. Ostenson
1942. Early spring food of the otter in Michigan. J. Wildl. Manage. 6:244–254.

Lange, R. and H. Staaland
1970. Adaptations of the caecum-colon structure of rodents. Comp. Biochem. Physiol. 35:905–919.

Lauhachinda, V.
1978. Life history of the river otter in Alabama with emphasis on food habits. Unpubl. Ph.D. dissertation, Auburn Univ., Auburn. 169 pp.

LaVal, R. K.
1970. Intraspecific relationships of bats of the species *Myotis austroriparius*. J. Mammal. 51:542–552.

1973. Observations on the biology of *Tadarida brasiliensis cynocephala* in southeastern Louisiana. Am. Midl. Nat. 89:112–120.

Lawrence, B. and W. H. Bossert
1967. Multiple character analysis of *Canis lupus altrans* and *familiaris*, with a discussion of the relationships of *Canis niger*. Amer. Zool. 7:223–232.

Layne, J. N.
1955. Seminole bat, *Lasiurus seminolus*, in central New York. J. Mammal. 36:453.

1958. Reproductive characteristics of the gray fox in southern Illinois. J. Wildl. Manage. 22:157–163.

1959. Growth and development of the eastern harvest mouse, *Reithrodontomys humulis*. Florida State Museum. Bull. 4:61–82.

Layne, J. N. and W. H. McKeon
1956. Some aspects of red fox and gray fox reproduction in New York. New York Fish and Game Jour. 3:44–74.

Lechleitner, R. R.
1959. Sex ratio, age classes and reproduction of the black-tailed jack rabbit. J. Mammal. 40:63–81.

Lee, D. S. and J. B. Funderburg
1982. Marmots (*Marmota monax* and allies). Pp. 176–191. *In* J. A. Chapman and G. A. Feldhamer (eds.). Wild mammals of North America. The Johns Hopkins University Press, Baltimore. 1147 pp.

Lee, M. R., D. J. Schmidly, and C. C. Huheey
1972. Chromosomal variation in certain populations of *Peromyscus boylii* and its systematic implications. J. Mammal. 53:697–707.

Lewis, J. C.
1969. Evidence of mountain lions in the Ozarks and adjacent areas, 1948–1968. J. Mammal. 50:371–372.

1970. Evidence of mountain lions in the Ozark, Boston and Ouachita Mountains. Proc. Okla. Acad. Sci. for 1968, pp. 182–184.

Liers, E. E.
1951. Notes on the river otter (*Lutra canadensis*). J. Mammal. 32:1–9.

Linscombe, G., N. Kinler, and R. J. Aulerich
1982. Mink (*Mustela vison*). Pp. 629–643. *In*

J. A. Chapman and G. A. Feldhamer (eds.). Wild mammals of North America. The Johns Hopkins University Press, Baltimore. 1147 pp.

Linzey, D. W. and A. V. Linzey
1967. Growth and development of the golden mouse, *Ochrotomys nuttalli nuttalli*. J. Mammal. 48:445–458.

Linzey, D. W. and R. L. Packard
1977. *Ochrotomys nuttalli*. Mammalian Species 75:1–6. Amer. Soc. Mammalogists.

Llewellyn, L. M. and C. G. Webster
1960. Raccoon predation on waterfowl. Trans. N. Am. Wildl. and Nat. Resource Conf. 25:180–185.

Long, C. A.
1961a. *Reithrodontomys montanus griseus* in Missouri. J. Mammal. 42:417–418.

1961b. Natural history of the brush mouse (*Peromyscus boylii*) in Kansas with a description of a new subspecies. Univ. Kans. Publ. Mus. Nat. Hist. 14:99–110.

1973. *Taxidea taxus*. Mammalian Species 26:1–4. Amer. Soc. Mammalogists.

Lord, R. D., Jr.
1963. The cottontail rabbit in Illinois. Illinois Dept. Cons., Tech. Bull. No. 3. 96 pp.

Lowery, G. H., Jr.
1974. The mammals of Louisiana and its adjacent waters. Louisiana State Univ. Press, Baton Rouge. 565 pp.

Lowery, G. H., Jr. and W. B. Davis
1942. A revision of the fox squirrels of the lower Mississippi Valley and Texas. Occ. Papers Mus. Zool. Louisiana State Univ. 9:153–172.

Macdonald, D. W.
1981. Resource dispersion and the social organization of the red fox (*Vulpes vulpes*). Pp. 918–949. *In* J. A. Chapman and D. Pursely (eds.). Proc. Worldwide Furbearer Conf., Frostburg, Md. 3 Vol. 2056 pp.

McCarley, W. H.
1954. Natural hybridization in the *Peromyscus leucopus* species group of mice. Evolution 8:314–323.

1959. An unusually large nest of *Cryptotis parva*. J. Mammal. 40:243.

McCord, C. M. and J. E. Cardoza
1982. Bobcat and lynx (*Felis rufus* and *F. lynx*). Pp. 728–766. *In* J. A. Chapman and G. A. Feldhamer (eds.). Wild mammals of North America. The Johns Hopkins University Press, Baltimore. 1147 pp.

McDaniel, J. C.
1963. Otter population study. Proc. Annu. Conf. S.E. Assoc. Game and Fish Comm. 17:163–168.

McDaniel, V. R., M. J. Harvey, R. Tumlison, and K. Paige
1982. Status of the small-footed bat, *Myotis leibii*, in the southern Ozarks. Proc. Ark. Acad. Sci. 36:92–94.

McDaniel, V. R., J. C. Huggins, J. A. Huggins, and M. W. Hinson
1978. A summary of the status of harvest mice, Cricetidae: *Reithrodontomys*, in Arkansas. Proc. Ark. Acad. Sci. 32:63–64.

McKinley, D.
1962. The history of the black bear in Missouri. The Bluebird (Audubon Society of Missouri), 29:1–16.

McManus, J. J.
1974. *Didelphis virginiana*. Mammalian Species 40:1–6, Amer. Soc. Mammalogists.

McMurry, F. B. and C. C. Sperry
1941. Food of feral house cats in Oklahoma, a progress report. J. Mammal. 22:185–190.

Manaro, A. J.
1961. Observations on the behavior of the spotted skunk in Florida. Quart. J. Fla. Acad. Sci. 24:59–63.

Marshall, A. D. and J. H. Jenkins
1966. Movements and home ranges of bobcats as determined by radiotracking in upper coastal plain of west-central South Carolina. Proc. 29th Annu. Conf. S.E. Assoc. Game and Fish Comm. Pp. 206–214.

Marshall, W. H.
  1936.   A study of winter activities of the mink. J. Mammal. 17:382–392.

Martinsen, D. L.
  1969.   Energetics and activity patterns of short-tailed shrews (*Blarina*) on restricted diets. Ecology 50:505–510.

Mead, R. A.
  1968a.   Reproduction in eastern forms of the spotted skunk (genus *Spilogale*). J. Zool. Lond. 156:119–136.
  1968b.   Reproduction in western forms of the spotted skunk (genus *Spilogale*). J. Mammal. 49:373–390.

Melquist, W. E. and A. E. Dronkert
  1987.   River otter. Pp. 627–641. *In* M. Novak, J. A. Baker, M. E. Obbard, and B. Malloch (eds.). Wild furbearer management and conservation in North America. Ministry of Natural Resources, Ontario, Canada. 1150 pp.

Melquist, W. E. and M. G. Hornocker
  1983.   Ecology of river otters in west-central Idaho. Wildl. Monogr. 83. 60 pp.

Merriam, C. H.
  1895.   Revision of the shrews of the American genera *Blarina* and *Notiosorex*. N. Amer. Fauna No. 10, Washington. 34 pp.

Meyer, B. J. and R. K. Meyer
  1944.   Growth and reproduction of the cotton rat, *Sigmodon hispidus hispidus*, under laboratory conditions. J. Mammal. 25:107–129.

Miller, R. S.
  1964.   Ecology and distribution of pocket gophers (Geomyidae) in Colorado. Ecology 45:256–272.

Mivart, St. G.
  1890.   Dogs, jackals, wolves and foxes: A monograph of the canidae. London. 216 pp.

Mock, O. B.
  1982.   The least shrew, *Cryptotis parva*, as a laboratory animal. Lab. An. Sci. 32:177–179.

Money, P. A.
  1977.   Food utilization by the beaver (*Castor canadensis*) in river systems of northwestern Arkansas. Unpubl. M.S. thesis, Univ. of Arkansas, Fayetteville. 57 pp.

Montgomery, J. B.
  1974.   Forest habitats of the golden mouse (Genus *Ochrotomys*) and white-footed mice (Genus *Peromyscus*) along the Cossatot River in southwestern Arkansas. Unpubl. M.S. thesis, Univ. of Arkansas, Fayetteville. 60 pp.

Moore, D. W. and G. A. Heidt
  1981.   Distribution of the prairie vole, *Microtus ochrogaster* (Rodentia), in Arkansas. Southwestern Nat. 26:208–210.

Moore, G. C. and E. C. Martin
  1949.   Status of the beaver in Alabama. Alabama Cons. Dept., Birmingham. 30 pp.

Moore, J. C.
  1944.   A contribution to the natural history of the Florida short-tailed shrew. Proc. Fla. Acad. Sci. 6:155–166.
  1947   Nests of the Florida flying squirrel. Am. Midl. Nat. 38:248–253.
  1957   The natural history of the fox squirrel, *Sciurus niger shermani*. Bull. Amer. Mus. Nat. Hist. 113:1–71.

Morrison, J. D.
  1970.   The Eddy bluff shelter of Beaver Reservoir of Northwest Arkansas. Proc. Ark. Acad. Sci. 24:85–91.

Mumford, R. E.
  1973.   Natural history of the red bat (*Lasiurus borealis*) in Indiana. Period. Biol. 75:155–168.

Murie, O. J.
  1974.   A field guide to animal tracks (2nd ed.). Houghton Mifflin Co., Boston. 375 pp.

Musser, G. G.
  1969.   Notes on *Peromyscus* (Muridae) of Mexico and Central America. Amer. Mus. Novit. No. 2357, pp. 1–23.

Negus, N. C., E. Gould, and R. K. Chipman
  1961.   Ecology of the rice rat, *Oryzomys palustris* (Harlan) on Breton Island, Gulf of Mexico, with a critique of the social stress theory. Tulane Studies in Zoology 8:98–123.

Newson, R. M.
1966. Reproduction in the feral coypu (*Myocastor coypus*). Zool. Soc. Lond. Symp. 15:323–344.

Nicholson, A. J.
1941. The homes and social habits of the wood mouse (*Peromyscus leucopus noveboracensis*) in southern Michigan. Am. Midl. Nat. 25:196–223.

Noble, R. E.
1971. A recent record of the puma (*Felis concolor*) in Arkansas. Southwestern Nat. 16:209.

Novak, M.
1987. Beaver. Pp. 282–313. *In* M. Novak, J. A. Baker, M. E. Obbard, and B. Malloch (eds.). Wild furbearer management and conservation in North America. Ministry of Natural Resources, Ontario, Canada. 1150 pp.

Novak, M., J. A. Baker, M. E. Obbard, and B. Malloch (eds.)
1987. Wild furbearer management and conservation in North America. Ministry of Natural Resources, Ontario, Canada. 1150 pp.

Nowak, R. M.
1970. Report on the red wolf. Defenders Wildl. News 45:82–94.

Olsen, S. J. and J. W. Olsen
1977. The Chinese wolf, ancestor of new world dogs. Science 197:533–535.

Packard, R. L.
1968. An ecological study of the fulvous harvest mouse in eastern Texas. Am. Midl. Nat. 79:68–88.

1969. Taxonomic review of the golden mouse, *Ochrotomys nuttalli*. Univ. Kans. Mus. Nat. Hist. Misc. Publ. 51:373–406.

Pagels, J. F.
1975. Temperature regulation, body weight and changes in total body fat of the free-tailed bat, *Tadarida brasiliensis cynocephala* (LeConte). Comp. Bioch. Physiol. 50A:237–246.

Pagels, J. F. and C. Jones
1974. Growth and development of the free-tailed bat, *Tadarida brasiliensis cynocephala* (LeConte). Southwestern Nat. 19:267–276.

Paradiso, J. L.
1969. Mammals of Maryland. N. Amer. Fauna No. 66, Washington, D.C. 193 pp.

Paradiso, J. L. and R. M. Nowak
1971. A report on the taxonomic status and distribution of the red wolf. U.S. Bureau Sport Fish and Wildl., Special Sci. Rept.—Wildl. No. 145. 36 pp.

1972. *Canis rufus*. Mammalian Species 22:1–4, Amer. Soc. Mammalogists.

Park, E.
1971. The world of the otter. J. B. Lippincott Co., Philadelphia. 159 pp.

Paul, J. R.
1970. Observations on the ecology, populations and reproductive biology of the pine vole, *Microtus pinetorum*, in North Carolina. Illinois State Museum, Repts. Investigations 20:1–28.

Pearson, O. P., M. R. Koford, and A. K. Pearson
1952. Reproduction of the lump-nosed bat (*Corynorhinus rafinesquei*) in California. J. Mammal. 33:273–320.

Peck, J. H., J. D. Clark, T. Sheldon, and G. A. Heidt
1985. Analysis of Arkansas fur harvest records—1942–184: II. Species accounts. Proc. Ark. Acad. Sci. 39:84–88.

Pelton, M. R.
1982. Black bear (*Ursus americanus*). Pp. 504–514. *In* J. A. Chapman and G. A. Feldhamer (eds.). Wild mammals of North America. The Johns Hopkins University Press, Baltimore. 1147 pp.

Peterson, R. L. and S. C. Downing
1952. Notes on the bobcats (*Lynx rufus*) of eastern North America with the description of a new race. Contrib. Roy. Ontario Mus. Zool. and Paleont. No. 23. 23 pp.

Phillips, G. L.
    1966.   Ecology of the big brown bat (Chiroptera: Vespertilionidae) in northeastern Kansas. Am. Midl. Nat. 75:168–198.

Pivorun, E. B.
    1976.   A biotelemetry study of the thermoregulatory patterns of *Tamias striatus* and *Eutamius minimus* during hibernation. Comp. Bioch. Physiol. 53A:265–271.

Pledger, J. M.
    1975.   Activity, home range and habitat utilization of white-tailed deer (*Odocoileus virginianus*) in southeastern Arkansas. Unpubl. M.S. thesis, Univ. of Arkansas, Fayetteville. 75 pp.

Polderboer, E. B., L. W. Kuhn, and G. O. Hendrickson
    1941.   Winter and spring habits of weasels in central Iowa. J. Wildl. Manage. 5:115–119.

Polechla, P. J., Jr.
    1987.   Status of the river otter (*Lutra canadensis*) population in Arkansas with special reference to reproductive biology. Unpubl. Ph.D. dissertation, Univ. of Arkansas, Fayetteville. 383 pp.

Pournelle, G. H.
    1952.   Reproduction and early post-natal development of the cotton mouse, *Peromyscus gossypinus gossypinus*. J. Mammal. 33:1–20.

Preston, J. R. and J. A. Sealander
    1969.   Unusual second record of *Notiosorex* from Arkansas. J. Mammal. 50:641–642.

Puckette, W. L.
    1975a.   An occurrence of the puma, *Felis concolor*, from Svendsen cave, Marion County, Arkansas. Proc. Ark. Acad. Sci. 29:52–53.
    1975b.   The Hazen mammoth (*Mammuthus columbi*), Prairie County, Arkansas. Proc. Ark. Acad. Sci. 28:53–56.

Quinn, J. H.
    1957.   Paired river terraces and Pleistocene glaciation. J. Geol. 65:149–165.

    1958a.   Plateau surfaces of the Ozarks. Proc. Ark. Acad. Sci. 11:36–42.
    1958b.   Arkansas deserts. (Abst.) Geol. Soc. Amer. Bull. 69:1932.
    1961.   Prairie mounds of Arkansas. Newsletter Ark. Arch. Soc. Vol. 11, No. 6 (June).
    1970a.   Occurrence of *Sus* in North America. Geol. Soc. Amer., South Central Section, Annual Meeting; Abstracts, p. 298.
    1970b.   Note on *Sus* in North America. Soc. Vert. Paleont. Bull. 88:33.
    1972.   Extinct mammals in Arkansas and related C^{14} dates *circa* 3000 years ago. 24th Intl. Geol. Congress, Section 12:89-96.

Rainey, D. G.
    1956.   Eastern woodrat, *Neotoma floridana*: Life history and ecology. Univ. Kans. Publ. Mus. Nat. Hist. 8:535–646.

Raynor, G. S.
    1960.   Three litters in a pine mouse nest. J. Mammal. 41:275.

Reinhold, R. O.
    1969.   Climates of the states: Arkansas. Climatography of the United States No. 60–3, U.S. Dept. Commerce, ESSA, Environmental Data Service, Washington, D.C. 18 pp.

Rice, D. W.
    1957.   Life history and ecology of *Myotis austroriparius* in Florida. J. Mammal. 38:15–32.

Richens, G. H., H. D. Smith, and C. D. Jorgensen
    1974.   Growth and development of the western harvest mouse, *Reithrodontomys megalotis megalotis*. Great Basin Nat. 34:105–120.

Rintamaa, D. L., P. A. Mazur, and S. H. Vessy
    1976.   Reproduction during two annual cycles in a population of *Peromyscus leucopus noveboracensis*. J. Mammal. 57:593–595.

Robbins, L. W., M. D. Engstrom, R. B. Wilhelm, and J. R. Choate
    1977.   Ecogeographic status of *Myotis leibii* in Kansas. Mammalia 41:365–367.

Roe, F. G.
1951. The North American buffalo: A critical study of the species in its wild state. Univ. Toronto Press. 957 pp.

Rogers, L. L.
1977. Movements and social relationships of black bears in northeastern Minnesota. Unpubl. Ph.D. dissertation, Univ. of Minnesota, St. Paul. 194 pp.

Rolley, R. E.
1985. Dynamics of a harvested bobcat population in Oklahoma. J. Wildl. Manage. 49:283–292.

Rollings, C. T.
1945. Habits, foods and parasites of the bobcat in Minnesota. J. Wildl. Manage. 9:131–145.

Rood, J. P.
1958. Habits of the short-tailed shrew in captivity. J. Mammal. 39:499–507.

Rowan, W.
1945. Numbers of young in the common black and grizzly bears in western Canada. J. Mammal. 26:197–199.

Rucker, R. A., M. L. Kennedy, and G. A. Heidt
1989. Population density, movements, and habitat use of bobcats in Arkansas. Southwestern Nat. 34:101–108.

Rucker, R. A., R. Tumlison, G. A. Heidt, M. J. Harvey, V. R. McDaniel, and M. L. Kennedy
1985. Natural history and management of the bobcat in Arkansas. Pp. 1–177. In R. A. Rucker and R. Tumlison (eds.). Biology of the bobcat in Arkansas. Unpubl. Tech. Rept., Arkansas Game and Fish Comm., Little Rock, Ark. 225 pp.

Ryder, R. A.
1955. Fish predation by the otter in Michigan. J. Wildl. Manage. 19:497–498.

Rysgaard, G. N.
1942. A study of the cave bats of Minnesota with especial reference to the large brown bat, *Eptesicus fuscus fuscus* (Beauvois). Am. Midl. Nat. 28:245–267.

Samuel, D. E. and B. B. Nelson
1982. Foxes (*Vulpes vulpes* and allies). Pp. 475–490. In J. A. Chapman and G. A. Feldhamer (eds.). Wild mammals of North America. The Johns Hopkins University Press, Baltimore. 1147 pp.

Sanderson, G. C.
1987. Raccoon. Pp. 486–499. In M. Novak, J. A. Baker, M. E. Obbard, and B. Malloch (eds.). Wild furbearer management and conservation in North America. Ministry of Natural Resources, Ontario, Canada. 1150 pp.

Sargeant, A. B.
1982. A case history of a dynamic resource—the red fox. Pp. 122–137. In G. C. Sanderson (ed.). Midwest furbearer management. Proc. Symp. 43rd. Midw. Fish and Wildl. Conf., Wichita, Kansas.

Sargeant, A. B., S. H. Allen, and J. O. Hastings
1987. Spatial relations between sympatric coyotes and red foxes in North Dakota. J. Wildl. Manage. 51:285–293.

Saugey, D. A.
1978. Reproductive biology of the gray bat, *Myotis grisescens*, in northcentral Arkansas. Unpubl. M.S. thesis. Arkansas State University. 93 pp.

Saugey, D. A., R. H. Baber, and V. R. McDaniel
1978. An unusual accumulation of bat remains from an Ozark cave. Proc. Ark. Acad. Sci. 32:92–93.

Saugey, D. A., D. R. Heath, C. Efaw, G. A. Heidt, and T. E. Beggs
1983. First report of Brazilian free-tailed bat maternity colonies in Arkansas. Proc. Ark. Acad. Sci. 36:98–99.

Saugey, D. A., G. A. Heidt, D. R. Heath, T. W. Steward, D. R. England, and V. R. McDaniel
1988a. Distribution and status of the Brazilian free-tailed bat (*Tadarida brasiliensis*) in Arkansas. Proc. Ark. Acad. Sci. 42: 79–80.

Saugey, D. A., D. G. Saugey, G. A. Heidt, and D. R. Heath

1988b. The bats of Hot Springs National Park, Arkansas. Proc. Ark. Acad. Sci. 42: 81–83.

Saugey, D. A., D. R. Heath, and G. A. Heidt
1989. Bats of the Ouachita Mountains. Proc. Ark. Acad. Sci. 43:(in press).

Schoolcraft, H. R.
1821. Journal of a tour into the interior of Missouri and Arkansas. Sir Richard Phillips and Co., London.

Schmidly, D. J.
1973. Geographic variation and taxonomy of *Peromyscus boylii* from Mexico and the southern United States. J. Mammal. 54: 111–130.

Schwartz, C. W. and E. R. Schwartz
1981. The wild mammals of Missouri, rev. ed. Univ. of Missouri Press, Columbia. 353 pp.

Scott, T. G.
1943. Some food coactions of the northern plains red fox. Ecol. Monogr. 13:427–479.

Sealander, J. A.
1943. Winter food habits of mink in southern Michigan. J. Wildl. Manage. 7: 411–417.

1951a. Lump-nosed bat in Arkansas. J. Mammal. 32:465.

1951b. Mountain lion in Arkansas. J. Mammal. 32:364.

1952. *Notiosorex* in Arkansas. J. Mammal. 33:105–106.

1954. New mammal records for Arkansas. J. Mammal. 35:430.

1956. A provisional checklist and key to the mammals of Arkansas (with annotations). Am. Midl. Nat. 56:257–296.

1960. Some noteworthy records of Arkansas mammals. J. Mammal. 41:525–526.

1967. First record of small-footed myotis in Arkansas. J. Mammal. 48:666.

1977. New marginal records for the eastern harvest mouse and southeastern shrew in Arkansas. Southwestern Nat. 22: 148–149.

1981. Albino least shrews (*Cryptotis parva*) and a new locality record for the southeastern shrew (*Sorex longirostris*) from Arkansas. Southwestern Nat. 26:70.

Sealander, J. A. and B. J. Forsyth
1966. Occurrence of the badger in Arkansas. Southwestern Nat. 11:134.

Sealander, J. A. and P. S. Gipson
1973. Status of the mountain lion in Arkansas. Proc. Ark. Acad. Sci. 27:38–41.

1974. Threatened native mammals of Arkansas. Pp. 123–127, 247–248. *In* Arkansas Natural Area Plan, Ark. Dept. Planning, Little Rock, Arkansas.

Sealander, J. A., P. S. Gipson, and J. M. Hite Manley
1975. The distribution of the prairie vole (*Microtus ochrogaster*) and the southern bog lemming (*Synapatomys cooperi*) in Arkansas. Texas J. Sci. 26:421–430.

Sealander, J. A. and A. J. Hoiberg
1954. Occurrence of the seminole bat in Arkansas. J. Mammal. 35:584.

Sealander, J. A. and J. F. Price
1964. Free-tailed bat in Arkansas. J. Mammal. 45:152.

Sealander, J. A. and B. Q. Walker
1955. A study of the cotton rat in northwestern Arkansas. Proc. Ark. Acad. Sci. 8:153–162.

Sealander, J. A. and H. Young
1955. Preliminary observations on the cave bats of Arkansas. Proc. Ark. Acad. Sci. 7:21–31.

Seton, E. T.
1929. Lives of game animals. Vols. 1–4. Doubleday, Doran and Co., Inc., Garden City, New York.

Severinghaus, W. D. and L. E. Beasely
1973. A survey of the microtine and zapodid rodents of West Tennessee. J. Tenn. Acad. Sci. 48:129–132.

Shepherd, B.
1984. Arkansas's natural heritage. August House, Little Rock, Ark. 116 pp.

Sherman, H. B.

1937. Breeding habits of the free-tailed bats. J. Mammal. 18:176–187.

1939. Notes on the food of some Florida bats. J. Mammal. 20:103–104.

Simpson, G. G.

1941. Large Pleistocene felines of North America. Am. Mus. Novit. 1136:1–27.

1945. The principles of classification and a classification of mammals. Bull. Amer. Mus. Nat. Hist. 85:1–350.

Smith, D. A. and L. C. Smith

1975. Oestrus, copulation, and related aspects of reproduction in female eastern chipmunks, *Tamias striatus* (Rodentia: Sciuridae). Can. J. Zool. 53:756–767.

Smith, E. B.

1988. An atlas and annotated list of the vascular plants of Arkansas, 2nd. ed. 489 pp.

Smith, F. R.

1938. Muskrat investigations in Dorchester County, Md. 1930–34. U.S. Dept. Agr., Circular 474:1–24.

Smith, J. D.

1964. Second record of the eastern harvest mouse from Oklahoma. Trans. Kans. Acad. Sci. 67:204–205.

Smith, M. C.

1972. Seasonal variation in home ranges of woodchucks. Unpubl. M.S. thesis, Univ. Guelph, Ontario. 67 pp.

Smith, M. H., R. K. Chesser, F. G. Cothrum, and P. E. Johns

1982. Genetic variability and antler growth in a natural population of white-tailed deer. Pp. 365–387. *In* R. D. Brown (ed.). Antler development in Cervidae. Kleburg Wildl. Res. Inst., Kingsville, Texas.

Smith, W. W.

1954. Reproduction in the house mouse, *Mus musculus* L. in Mississippi. J. Mammal. 35:509–515.

Spenrath, C. A. and R. K. LaVal

1974. An ecological study of a resident population of *Tadarida brasiliensis* in eastern

Texas. Occ. Papers, The Museum, Texas Tech University 21:1–14.

St. Romain, P. A.

1976. Variation in the cotton mouse (*Peromyscus gossypinus*) in Louisiana. Southwestern Nat. 21:79–88.

Stanley, W. C.

1963. Habits of the red fox in northeastern Kansas. Univ. Kans. Mus. Nat. Hist. Misc. Publ. 34:1–31.

Stenlund, M. H.

1953. Report of a Minnesota beaver die-off. J. Wildl. Manage. 17:376–377.

Steward, T. W., J. D. Wilhide, V. R. McDaniel, and D. R. England

1988. Mammalian species removed from a study of barn owl (*Tyto alba*) pellets from southwestern Arkansas. Proc. Ark. Acad. Sci. 42:72–73.

Stuewer, F. W.

1943. Reproduction of raccoons in Michigan. J. Wildl. Manage. 7:60–73.

Sugg, D. W.

1988. Morphologic and genetic assessments of *Peromyscus attwateri* in Arkansas: I. Morphologic variation in the Texas mouse, *Peromyscus attwateri*; II. Genetic variation in the Texas mouse, *Peromyscus attwateri*. Unpubl. M.S. thesis, Memphis State Univ., Memphis. 136 pp.

Svendsen, G. E.

1970. Notes on the ecology of the harvest mouse, *Reithrodontomys megalotis*, in southeastern Wisconsin. Wisc. Acad. Sci. Arts and Letters 58:163–166.

Talmage, R. V. and G. D. Buchanan

1954. The armadillo (*Dasypus novemcinctus*). A review of its natural history, ecology, anatomy and reproductive physiology. Rice Inst. Pamphlet 41:1–135.

Tamarin, R. H. (ed.)

1985. Biology of New World *Microtus*. Sp. Publ. No. 8, American Society of Mammalogists. 893 pp.

Taylor, C. L. and R. F. Wilkinson, Jr.
1988. First record of *Sorex longirostris* (Soricidae) in Oklahoma. Southwestern Nat. 33:248.

Taylor, W. P.
1954. Food habits and notes on life history of the ringtailed cat in Texas. J. Mammal. 35:55–63.

Terrel, T. L.
1972. The swamp rabbit (*Sylvilagus aquaticus*) in Indiana. Am. Midl. Nat. 87: 283–295.

Tumlison, R.
1983. Harvest trends, dietary ecology, reproduction, and population demographics of the bobcat (*Felis rufus*) in Arkansas. Unpubl. M.S. thesis, Arkansas State University, State University. 158 pp.

Tumlison, R. and M. Karnes
1987. Seasonal changes in food habits of river otters in southwestern Arkansas beaver swamps. Mammalia 51:225–231.

Tumlison, R., M. Karnes, and A. W. King
1982. The river otter in Arkansas. II. Indications of a beaver facilitated commensal relationship. Proc. Ark. Acad. Sci. 36: 73–75.

Tumlison, R., V. R. McDaniel, and D. England
1988. Eastern harvest mouse, *Reithrodontomys humulis*, in Arkansas. Southwestern Naturalist 33:105–106.

Tuttle, M. D.
1964. Additional record of *Sorex longirostris* in Tennessee. J. Mammal. 45:146–147.

1975. Population ecology of the gray bat (*Myotis grisescens*): Factors influencing early growth and development. Occ. Paper No. 36, Mus. Nat. Hist. Univ. Kans. 24 pp.

1976. Population ecology of the gray bat (*Myotis grisescens*): Factors influencing growth and survival of newly volant young. Ecology 57:587–595.

Tuttle, M. D. and L. R. Heaney
1974. Maternity habits of *Myotis leibii* in South

Dakota. Bull. Southern Calif. Acad. Sci. 73:80–83.

Uhlig, H. C.
1956. The gray squirrel in West Virginia. Cons. Comm. West Virginia, Div. Game Management, Bull. 3:1–83.

Van Gelder, R. G.
1953. The egg-opening technique of a spotted skunk. J. Mammal. 34:255–256.

1959. A taxonomic revision of the spotted skunks (Genus *Spilogale*). Bull. Amer. Mus. Nat. Hist. 117:223–392.

1978. A review of canid classification. Am. Mus. Novit. No. 2646:1–10.

van Zyll de Jong, C. G.
1972. A systematic review of the Nearctic and Neotropical river otter (genus *Lutra*, Mustelidae, Carnivora). Life Sci. Contrib. Roy. Ontario Mus. 80:1–104.

Vaughan, T. A.
1962. Reproduction in the plains pocket gopher in Colorado. J. Mammal. 43:1–13.

Verts, B. J.
1967. The biology of the striped skunk. Univ. Illinois Press, Urbana. 218 pp.

Voigt, D. R.
1987. Red fox. Pp. 379–392. *In* M. Novak, J. A. Baker, M. E. Obbard, and B. Malloch (eds.). Wild furbearer management and conservation in North America. Ministry of Natural Resources, Ontario, Canada. 1150 pp.

Voigt, D. R. and B. D. Earle
1983. Avoidance of coyotes by red fox families. J. Wildl. Manage. 47:852–857.

Walker, E. P., F. Warnick, S. E. Hamlet, K. K. Lange, M. A. Davis, H. E. Uible, and P. F. Wright
1968. Mammals of the world. Second edition, with revisions by J. L. Paradiso, Johns Hopkins Press, Baltimore. 2 vols. 1500 pp.

Warkentin, M. J.
1968. Observations on the behavior and ecol-

ogy of the nutria in Louisiana. Tulane Studies in Zoology and Botany 15: 10–17.

Watkins, L. C.
1969. Observations on the distribution and natural history of the evening bat (*Nycticeius humeralis*) in northwestern Missouri and adjacent Iowa. Trans. Kansas Acad. Sci. 72:230–236.

1971. A technique for monitoring the nocturnal activity of bats with comments on activity patterns of the evening bat, *Nycticeius humeralis*. Trans. Kansas Acad. Sci. 74:261–268.

1972. *Nycticeius humeralis*. Mammalian Species 23:1–4, Amer. Soc. Mammalogists.

Whitaker, J. O., Jr.
1974. *Cryptotis parva*. Mammalian Species 43: 1–8, Amer. Soc. Mammalogists.

Wilks, B. J.
1963. Some aspects of the ecology and population dynamics of the pocket gopher (*Geomys bursarius*) in southern Texas. Texas J. Sci. 15:241–283.

Wilson, K. A.
1959. The otter in North Carolina. Proc. 13th Annu. Conf. S.E. Assoc. Game and Fish Comm. Pp. 167–177.

Wilson, S. and P. Gipson
1975. Status of black bear in the western Ozarks. Arkansas Game and Fish 8:10–11.

Wilson, S. N. and J. A. Sealander
1971. Some characteristics of white-tailed deer reproduction in Arkansas. Proc. 25th Annu. Conf. S.E. Assoc. Game and Fish Comm. Pp. 53–65.

Wimsatt, W. A.
1963. Delayed implantation in the ursidae, with particular reference to the black bear. Pp. 49–76. *In* A. C. Enders (ed.). Delayed implantation. Univ. Chicago Press, Chicago. 316 pp.

Winge, H.
1941. The interrelationships of the mammalian genera. Vol. II. Rodentia, carnivora, primates. Kobenhavn, C. A. Reitzels Forlag. 376 pp.

Wolfe, J. L. and A. V. Linzey
1977. *Peromyscus gossypinus*. Mammalian Species 70:1–5, Amer. Soc. Mammalogists.

Worth, C. B.
1950. Field and laboratory observations on roof rats, *Rattus rattus* (Linnaeus), in Florida. J. Mammal. 31:293–304.

Wright, P. L.
1948. Breeding habits of captive long-tailed weasels (*Mustela frenata*). Am. Midl. Nat. 39:338–344.

1966. Observations on the reproductive cycle of the American badger (*Taxidea taxus*). Zool. Soc. Lond. Symp. 15:27–45.

Yates, T. L. and R. J. Pedersen
1982. Moles (Talpidae). Pp. 37–51. *In* J. A. Chapman and G. A. Feldhamer (eds.). Wild mammals of North America. The Johns Hopkins University Press, Baltimore. 1147 pp.

Yates, T. L. and D. J. Schmidly
1975. Karyotype of the eastern mole (*Scalopus aquaticus*), with comment on the karyology of the family Talpidae. J. Mammal. 56:902–905.

Yerger, R. W.
1955. Life history notes on the eastern chipmunk, *Tamias striatus lysteri* (Richardson) in central New York. Am. Midl. Nat. 53:312–323.

Young, S. P.
1958. The bobcat of North America. Its history, life habits, economic status and control, with list of currently recognized subspecies. Stackpole Co., Harrisburg, Pa. and Wildlife Manage. Inst., Washington, D.C. 193 pp.

Young, S. P. and E. A. Goldman
1946. The puma, mysterious American cat. Part I, by Young. History, life habits, economic status and control. Part II, by Goldman. Classification of the races of the puma. Amer. Wildl. Inst., Washington, D.C. 411 pp.

INDEX TO SCIENTIFIC
AND COMMON NAMES